HILTON'S
Collecting Confederate Currency:
Hobby and ~~or~~ Investment?

Volume One: Criswell Types 1-4
"The Magnificent Montgomerys"

J. Wayne Hilton

Prologue by Chester L. Krause

Reminiscences by Clarence L. Criswell

Statistical Analysis by Steven A. Feller, Ph.D.

Dedication

This book is dedicated to my father, **Jerry Reuben Hilton** (1919-1987), and my mother, **Thelma Garvin Hilton** (born 1925). Daddy's sense of duty and accountability was instilled by his grandfather, **Thomas Elsberry Hilton** (a private in Company H of the 63rd Regiment, Georgia Infantry, Confederate States Army, who lost part of his hand at the Battle of Atlanta on July 22, 1864), while Mama's sense of decency and perseverance was infused by the family of her great-great uncle, **Charles W. Bell** (a private in the 2nd Palmetto Regiment of the South Carolina Infantry, Confederate States Army, who died July 14, 1863 from wounds suffered at the Battle of Gettysburg on July 2, 1863).

HILTON'S
Collecting Confederate Currency:
Hobby *and* Investment?

Volume One of a Planned Series of Books

Copyright © 2012 by J. Wayne Hilton

Additional Copies May Be Obtained From These Distributors:
(Enclose $49.95 plus $5.00 shipping and handling)

J. Wayne Hilton
Post Office Box 1
Graniteville, S.C. 29829
Email: JerryWayne1@Comcast.net

Heritage Auctions
3500 Maple Avenue, 17th Floor
Dallas, Tex. 75219
Phone: 1-800-872-6467
Website: www.ha.com

Published by J. Wayne Hilton

ISBN Number 978-0-9717991-1-0

Printed in the United States of America.

Table of Contents

Acknowledgments

I recall my amusement at watching the Academy Awards show from Hollywood's Kodak Theatre each winter, when some gorgeous but air-headed movie idol would win an important award and then bore me to tears trying to acknowledge a long list of supporters. My book is unworthy of any Oscar, nor hopefully am I quite so air-headed, but let me nevertheless try to mention those who made a prominent contribution to the eventual publication of this book.

First, I was encouraged most by Confederate currency dealers Hugh Shull, Randy Shipley and particularly Crutchfield Williams. "Crutch" spent literally years working with me – first to develop a gigantic database of over 60,000 Confederate notes sold at auction over the past 150 years, and then to acquire and edit hundreds of scans of Montgomery notes. He is not only a dealer of impeccable integrity and exceptional technical expertise, but even more importantly, a true and valued friend. Crutch, along with Hugh and Randy, gave me support when I thought this book would never be finished (it took 14 years even with their support).

Second, my brother Charles Alan Hilton got me started in collecting Confederate currency and then nagged me incessantly until I finally finished this book. Charles is a lot smarter than I am and probably would have finished the book in half the time.

Third, many authors of numismatic books have made significant contributions to this publication: the eminent and renowned Eric P. Newman, Trustee Emeritus and benefactor of the American Numismatic Society, who reaches age 100 next month; Clarence Criswell, the younger half of the legendary Criswell Brothers, who wrote his own *Reminiscences* of the early days of collecting Confederate currency; the brainy Steven Feller, Ph.D., who provided all the statistical analysis and wrote an explanatory chapter easily understood by even the layman, and Wendell Wolka, like me (in part) a Purdue Boilermaker, who had the unenviable task of compiling the *Bibliography*.

Fourth, award-winning author and columnist Fred Reed, who unselfishly shared page after page of unpublished data on historical figures and publications in the field of collecting Confederate currency, was a valued source of information for this work. If the reader finds some statement in this book missing an attribution, chances are that the omitted credit should have properly gone to Fred. (He has just discovered a previously unknown specimen of Raphael Thian's 1880 *Register of the Confederate Debt* located at the Virginia Historical Society. His discovery brings the known total to six copies.)

Fifth, since this endeavor is largely about other publications (namely, auction catalogs), it should come as no surprise that numismatic literature dealers and bibliophiles played a critical role in this book's eventual publication. Distinguished and erudite dealer George F. Kolbe provided encouragement and many hard-to-find prices realized from historic auctions like the 1908 Henry Chapman sale of the Harmon Chambers' Confederate collection. The wise Karl Moulton not only provided rare prices realized of obscure auctions like the 1914 Edward Michael sale of the Ben Green estate, but also painstakingly searched his library for biographical details of over 50 numismatic luminaries who collected Confederate currency. Most of these biographies will be used in upcoming volumes of this series. Bibliophile Dan Hamelberg provided numerous prices realized from arcane auctions, particularly those conducted by Thomas Elder, M. H. Bolender and Charles Steigerwalt, from his own private numismatic library, among the largest in the world. Venture capitalist John W. Adams wrote the indispensable two-

George F. Kolbe, Dean of Numismatic Bibliophiles

volume series entitled *United States Numismatic Literature*, without which I simply would not have attempted to write this book. Not only did I use John's summary of thousands of historical auctions to isolate those with Confederate content, but John also graciously allowed me to excerpt from biographical details of the auction houses themselves, and to portray the early auctioneers like Edward Cogan and John Haseltine through life-like drawings sketched by Alan Dietz, his talented and versatile artist.

Sixth, my frequent week-long visits to the ANS Library in New York were made far more productive with the capable assistance of long-time and recently retired Head Librarian Frank Campbell. Since his retirement, current Librarian Elizabeth Hahn has continued to provide knowledgeable advice and helpful suggestions. While I did not personally visit the ANA Library in Colorado Springs, due to its distance from South Carolina, Colorado Springs resident Joe Bradley personally researched the ANA Library on my behalf, professionally assisted by now-retired Librarian Nancy Green and current Assistant Librarian Amanda Harvey.

Seventh, this book measures 9 in. by 12 in. and contains 304 pages filled with color illustrations. It was expensive to produce, yet it was made more affordable to the reader due to the revenue generated from about a dozen personally chosen Advertisers (see Chapter 9), who were willing to take a chance on both the book's concept and on me personally. Without exception, I have used the goods and services of each of these Advertisers to my great benefit. I suggest that my readers take advantage of their expertise and integrity, and I am confident that they will not be disappointed.

Eighth, over 300 different Montgomery notes are pictured in this book. Their images were provided courtesy of all the major auction houses, numerous dealers and many private collectors who happily obliged my request to picture their own Montgomerys. I particularly thank the Honorable William ("Bill") H. Kelly, who provided images of his own eight complete sets of Montgomerys (that's right – 32 different notes) prior to their going under the auction hammer at Heritage's FUN sale in January 2012.

Ninth, this book was thoughtfully laid out and beautifully designed by Balboni Associates, Inc. (www.balboniassociates.com), a talented advertising agency I have consistently used for 20 years in preference to their stodgy Madison Avenue rivals. Although President Lucy Peterson and Art Director John Murphy are located in Springfield, Mass., John, when challenged about his allegiances during the "War of Northern Aggression," quickly insisted that "we are not Yankees. We are Red Sox fans."

Tenth, the least understood job in releasing a quality book is the task of editing and proof-reading. Few professionals are competent to challenge assertions, re-draft unwieldy sentences and correct typos. Bruce D. Miller, a co-worker at Procter & Gamble in the 1970s before co-founding the elite Suissa Miller Advertising in 1992, did these chores admirably and quickly. I offer my gratitude for a job well done and the chance to re-connect after 30 years.

Finally, I cannot forget Ann (Mrs. G.E.) Casey of Aiken, S.C., my tenth-grade advisor and an all-time-favorite high school English teacher. Indeed it was Mrs. Casey, an active and charming octogenarian now, who reassured me that the plural of "Montgomery note" is "Montgomerys," contrary to the many authors and writers not fortunate enough to have been taught by Mrs. Casey and who mistakenly spell the plural "Montgomeries."

How sad.

J. Wayne Hilton
April 5, 2011

Prologue

By Chester L. Krause

Chester L. ("Chet") Krause, Founder of Krause Publications.

When Wayne Hilton called me to ask if I would write the *Prologue* to his new book on Confederate currency, I was in the middle of completing my own book on Wisconsin canals. I've known Wayne for a number of years, and I quickly protested that I did not know enough about Confederate currency to contribute to his book in any meaningful way. But Wayne would not take "no" for an answer. He said that he wanted me to write the *Prologue* because I "transcend numismatics." I have no idea what "transcend numismatics" means, but it must have been a good answer, as here I am writing the *Prologue* to a book written by the man who helped me complete my "type set" of Confederate currency.

I first met Wayne at a FUN Show in Orlando, Florida back in the mid 1990s. Several dealers in attendance, including both Grover Criswell and Hugh Shull, told me that Wayne was trying to assemble a Confederate type set with each of the 72 notes in "Uncirculated" condition. While I don't profess to be an expert in Confederate currency, I was well aware that a number of the types -- notably the "Indian Princess" -- had never been seen in "Uncirculated" condition, so I thought that Wayne had his work cut out for him.

I continued to run into Wayne at various shows all over the country. I already owned the biggest part of a complete type set myself, so I thought I would ask Wayne to help me complete my own collection. He and I finally got together at the Memphis Show in June 2000. He quickly took care of my smaller requirements, actually going to the bourse floor and purchasing several notes for which he had no duplicates to sell. When I asked how much I owed him, he gave me copies of the invoices and I reimbursed him just for his out-of-pocket cost with no mark-up -- he was not a dealer, Wayne explained.

We completed my Confederate type set that day in Memphis, except for the exceptionally rare -- and expensive -- $500 Montgomery note. As I have now read Wayne's excellent book, I see that the $500 Montgomery is the rarest type note in the entire Confederate series, so I guess I'm not surprised that it was the last note I needed to finish my own collection.

Wayne let me choose between two $500 Montgomery notes to complete my set. I wanted to assemble a nicely balanced set worthy of any collector, but I didn't need a census-condition note. I asked Wayne which note he thought would be best for my collection, suspecting that Wayne stood to clear a higher profit on the better note of the two he offered me. But he suggested that I go with the cheaper note, because it was a better fit with the rest of my collection. I have never forgotten the integrity Wayne showed on that occasion.

After finishing my Confederate type set in 2000 -- and having so many other collecting interests besides Rebel notes -- I discovered what so many other collectors have learned over the years: "Half the fun is in the chase." So, with my Confederate type set finally complete, in September 2003 I decided to liquidate it through the firm R. M. Smythe.

While I no longer actively collect Rebel notes, I am not familiar with anyone like Wayne who has attempted to calculate a rate of return -- over 150 years, no less -- for any area of numismatics, let alone calculate a rate of return and then compare it to the rate of return of investments people usually make, like stocks, precious metals or even crude oil. But Wayne has accomplished it (with the help and expertise of Steven Feller, Ph.D.), and he has included easy-to-understand graphs in the book to show his key findings.

This volume is devoted to the Montgomery notes, and it is easy to see that these beautiful notes are Wayne's favorites in the Confederate series. I was glad to see color photos of the four Montgomerys I sold in 2003, and even now, I learned something. My $1,000 Montgomery note bearing serial number 38 was previously owned by T. Harrison Garrett, once president of the B&O Railroad and one of the greatest coin collectors of all time.

Wayne's book is not just about the quantitative side of collecting Confederate currency. One of my favorite chapters was his "Illustrated Time Line of Collecting Confederate Currency." In about 80 pages, he covered 150 years of Rebel note collecting, from Ed Cogan's auction even before the Civil War ended to Hugh Shull's new book not yet released. I also enjoyed some anecdotes Wayne gleaned from his review of Grover Criswell's files. I had vaguely heard about a Confederate book authored by Sydney Kerksis written back in the early 1950s when I was just starting Krause Publications. I knew it was never released, but I did not understand why. Wayne provided the inside story, including the influence of John Ford, Jr.

Reading about Wayne's passion for collecting Confederate currency reminded me how I first became interested in numismatics. I was born in 1923 on a farm about six miles east of Iola, a small village of around 1,300 in east-central Wisconsin. By the mid 1930s, my close friend Hank Fritz and I had started a little business fixing old clocks. But it was Hank's dad Godfrey who gave me my start as a coin collector. A veteran of the Spanish-American War, Godfrey had a bag of coins he collected as a boy. His coins included half cents, large cents, two-cent pieces, silver three-cent pieces, nickels, half dimes, dimes, quarters and half dollars.

One day Godfrey gave me a large cent. If ever a collecting seed got planted, it was right then and there. Later, an aunt of mine gave me a Whitman penny board, and I started collecting Lincoln cents from circulation. I filled many holes in the board by frequently pestering my dad to go through his pocket change. I would ask, "Dad, got any pennies in your pocket?" One day he pulled out the lone penny in his pocket, the elusive 1931-S.

At about this same time I also got the bug to collect stamps, mostly used examples that came free on envelopes and post cards sent to us. All I had to do was steam them off the paper. I put together a collection going back to about 1920 and acquired an inexpensive album with stamp hinges. I soon found ads for stamps in *Popular Mechanics*, so I learned how to use the mail to get things that weren't available in the small country stores in Iola. While my collecting means and resulting collections were modest, my collecting interest was strong. This fascination from early life portended what the future would hold.

My passion for collecting -- indeed, all of life as I had known it -- was put on hold in February 1943 when I was drafted into the Army during World War II. As the youngest of three sons, I suspect it was very hard for Mother to see her youngest son go off to war. But we all returned home with nary a scratch, with me returning in January 1946. Dad had built a backlog of carpentry jobs during the war. I wanted to get started, but little of this work could be completed, as many building materials were still being rationed.

By 1950 Dad's health had begun to deteriorate, and I set out on my own in the construction business. I was successful as a home builder, completing 23 houses while in the business, but just as I was hitting my stride as a builder, another profession beckoned. Even while I was hammering nails for a living, the coin-collecting seed planted earlier came into full bloom. In October 1952, still working as a carpenter by day, I began publishing *Numismatic News* by night, the first issue a single page printed by the publisher of the local *Iola Herald*.

By January 1954 *Numismatic News* had grown to 12 pages and had worn out its welcome at the kitchen table in the family home. An insurance agent in town and I agreed to share an office on Main Street in Iola. The business continued to grow, so by late 1956 I made the decision to give up the construction business altogether. By 1958 I laid down my hammer for the final time to become a full-time publisher. I had to choose between the two professions, and I made a good choice.

In 1959 I bought a new magazine and soon re-named it *Coins*. Now owning two titles, I began using the business name Krause Publications to identify our overall operations, while continuing to use the individual magazine names for matters pertaining directly to them.

After surviving a slowdown in the 1960s when the numismatic hobby suffered a major decline, Cliff Mishler, my closest confidant who held the company's no. 2 position, and I decided we needed to diversify. In 1971 we started *Old Cars*, our first non-numismatic magazine. Later we began publishing the *Standard Catalog of World Coins*, a highly successful publication which finally solved the company's financial distress.

The company continued to grow. We opened a new 20,000 sq. ft. building in 1976, launched a new periodical called *World Coin News*, an offshoot of the popular *Standard Catalog of World Coins*, and we purchased *Bank Note Reporter* for our paper-money collectors like Wayne, who owns a complete set of all issues dating back to the first edition in Jan. 1973.

In ensuing years, the company continued to diversify into many other hobby areas, and our 1976 building was expanded several times. My involvement with the company began to phase out with the establishment of an Employee Stock Ownership Plan in 1988. In 2002, the Krause Publications board of directors and ESOP trustees decided to sell the company to F+W Media, based in Cincinnati, Ohio.

Completely retired today, I now devote my time to travel, philanthropic interests including numerous community projects and, of course, to collecting and historical topics. I pursue these interests from my office on Main Street in Iola with the help of my valued assistant, Chris Williams. These days I mostly collect Wisconsin paper money and scrip, but I still have a few pieces of Confederate currency lying around -- although certainly not the Gem Uncirculated "Indian Princess" Wayne has his sights on.

I tried to explain what makes a person so passionate about collecting when I wrote my autobiography in 2007, ably assisted by Arlyn Sieber. While hard to put into words, the act of assembling a collection gives the collector a sense of anticipation, and completing it offers a sense of accomplishment. If the reader is anything like me, acquiring a long-sought piece of currency makes me feel like a kid with a new toy on a cold Wisconsin Christmas morning.

Chester L. ("Chet") Krause
March 30, 2012

Clarence Criswell Reminisces:

From Candy to Confederate Currency

Clarence Who?

You don't know me. I am Clarence L. Criswell and for many years my brother Grover C. Criswell, Jr. and I were in business together. Grover and I started to collect coins and stamps in the late 1940s, and by 1950 we had decided that we wanted to become dealers as well as collectors. By then we had decided to quit stamps, and we started to have an interest in old Confederate and obsolete currency. In 1957 we co-authored the first book in the very popular Criswell currency series titled, *Confederate and Southern State Currency.*

Grover (seated) and Clarence in 1957, surrounded by Confederate currency and bonds. This photo appeared on the dust jacket of their 1957 book.

Wayne Hilton asked me a number of years ago to give him some insights into our early years of collecting and dealing in Confederate currency. I really did not see the need to do this as "others" could do it as well. But Wayne did not assemble his incredible Confederate currency collection without endless persistence, and that same doggedness finally paid off with me. By April 2010 I could really see Wayne's point of view. The "others" that I thought could do a better job for Wayne were almost all dead, including Grover, who died in 1999. Being 75, I had better get going or it might not get done. I will be giving some reflections on our collecting and dealing of some 60 years ago. I may ramble a bit but at 75 that's okay too.

The Criswell family left that part of South Carolina just south of Charlotte, N.C. in the late 1700s and moved to Wilson County, Tennessee. Our dad Grover, Sr. was born in 1887 and had only one sister. Dad went through the sixth grade, and in about 1902 he went to work in a candy factory in Nashville. The master candy maker took Dad under his wing and for a number of years trained him to be a master candy maker. In 1908 Dad left and went to work in Jacksonville, Fla. By 1909 he was in Yuma, Ariz., and by 1910 in southern California. Dad traveled the country a good bit and as he told us, he made about every kind of candy there was.

By 1917 Dad was in Chicago, Ill. In 1919 he was made superintendent of a large Chicago candy factory. In 1921 he married Mom, the office manager of the factory, and they set out together. They formed the Criswell Candy Co. in 1922 and ran it until selling out in 1941.

Grover, Jr. was born in 1933 and I was born in 1935 in Oak Park, Ill. In 1939 we moved to Barrington, Ill. and grew up on a farm. Dad said we should *not* look to be in the candy business!

By 1946 Dad had to move to a warmer climate so we headed off to St. Petersburg, Fla. On trips back to Chicago starting in 1949, Grover and I began trading with our first big-time coin dealer, Ben Dreiske of Ben's Stamp & Coin Company on 31 N. Clark Street. By 1950 stamps no longer held any interest for us, as coins and paper money had become our focus. Being

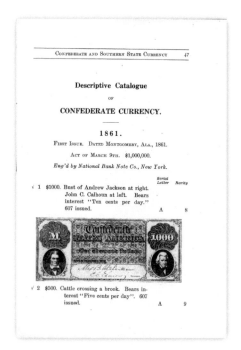

A typescript version of page 47 from Bradbeer's 1915 book, copied by Martin H. Burge around the 1930s (courtesy of the Pink Palace Museum, Memphis, Tenn.).

The same page 47 from Bradbeer's actual 1915 book.

teenagers and not having a whole lot of money to work with, we found that Confederate currency and other paper money was an opportunity. We still bought and sold coins along with the paper money.

Flying Blind

In 1950 the major Confederate currency book was still William Bradbeer's *Confederate and Southern State Currency*, printed back in 1915. By 1950 it was very hard to find an original copy, and it cost as much as what a rare note would sell for. *[Author's Note: In 1941 a Bradbeer was so rare that many Confederate collectors who wanted a copy actually borrowed an original from a library and typed by hand the entire book. There were no scanners or copy machines in 1941! Thank you to Tamara Braithwaite, Registrar, The Pink Palace Museum in Memphis, for providing a copy of the typescript version of Bradbeer she has in her library. This typescript copy came from the Confederate collection of Dr. Martin H. Burge of San Marino, Calif., who assembled his collection by 1941 and donated it to the Pink Palace Museum in 1971.]*

It was good for Grover and me that there were not too many of the Bradbeer books around, as it allowed us to have superior knowledge about which notes were rare. At that time coin dealers might have some Confederate notes but our main source was antique dealers, book dealers and other collectors. We ran ads to buy currency and asked dealers to look out for notes for us.

We started to buy lots and lots of notes and folks today ask what they cost. We purchased stacks of Confederate notes at 10 to 20 cents each! I can even remember some uncirculated notes in packs of 100 with a strip of paper around them with a rusty pin holding the strip. People today cannot believe they were so cheap. But let me point out that during this time Grover and I also purchased U.S. Gold Dollars in VF-UNC condition for $5.00 to $6.00 each. We sold a batch of 800 pieces to dealer Max Kaplan for $8.00 each.

In those days Grover and I would talk about the Montgomery series of Confederate currency, the focus of Wayne's first volume, and joke about them some day being worth face value! *[Author's Note: John N. Rowe of Southwest Numismatic Corporation, Dallas, Texas, relates that the Philpott-Schermerhorn set of Montgomerys was the first set to sell for face value – $1,650 – in 1958.]*

In 1951 Grover headed off to college at The Citadel, The Military College of South Carolina in Charleston, a nice town for a collector to be in. Confederate printers Evans & Cogswell were in Charleston and state capital Columbia had been home to Keatinge & Ball, B. Duncan and J.T. Paterson. Grover made it a point to be in contact with every antique dealer in the Charleston area and would visit their shops on the weekends. His travel back and forth to Pass-a-Grille Beach, Fla., and my visits to see him allowed us many opportunities to find notes and bonds.

In 1953 I started college at The Citadel. With both of us being in Charleston and both having cars we were able to do much looking, buying and dealing in Florida, Georgia, South and North Carolina, Virginia and Tennessee. One of our very good contacts was Herman Schindler in Charleston. He was a long-time antique

10

dealer there and sold us thousands of notes over the years.

We had dealings with lots of the dealers at that time such as Aubrey Bebee, Charlie Green, John Ford, Michael Kolman, Bob Medlar and Leonard Stark.

Contact with collectors gave us much knowledge about notes, values and rarities. Grover and I had decided that we not only wanted to be dealers but also we wanted to put together a great collection. So the best that came our way went into the collection.

I have warm memories of Howard Spain from Waverly, Va., during the 1950s. Howard was one of the premier Confederate currency and bond collectors of his day. Wayne owns a lengthy series of letters between Howard and John Ford that dates back to the mid 1950s. Around 1955 Grover and I were at Howard's home talking about notes, dealing, and many other Confederate topics. Howard and his wife had invited us to dinner and then we started talking. The conversation went on and on and on... *all* night... so Howard's wife gave us breakfast and we left the next morning. Collectors in that day took time to enjoy their collections and trade information. All of us knew that the 100th Anniversary of the Civil War was not far off and the centennial was pushing up interest and prices.

Grover's 1951 ANA Life Membership card.

Grover and I soon became Life Members of the American Numismatic Association, Grover as LM #268 in 1951 and I as LM #278 in 1954. It was important to have a good national association, and we were both able to attend national conventions while we were very young. Grover later became president of the ANA in 1977.

Clarence's 1954 ANA Life Membership card.

Between 1951 and 1955 we greatly increased our inventory of Confederate and Southern States currency and broken bank notes by purchasing from antique shops, collectors and

dealers at conventions, by mail and by personal visits. It was during this period of time that we started to see the need for us to do a reference work on Confederate and Southern States currency. Bradbeer's 1915 work was still the only reference guide, as Philip Chase unsuccessfully attempted to develop a new numbering system in a book he published in 1947 with limited acceptance. Claud Fuller of Chattanooga, Tenn., had published a pictorial guide to Confederate currency in 1949, but it was aimed at the general reader, not the specialist collector of Confederate currency.

Publishing our first book was a huge gamble. While we were becoming well known to many in the Confederate currency field, we were still "kids" with little experience. We thought that publishing our own book would effectively establish a preeminent position for us in the Confederate currency field, as well as allow us more opportunities to build our own collection. The die was cast but it would not be easy.

Clarence in his dorm room at The Citadel in 1957, reading his just-released new book.

Grover graduated from The Citadel in 1955 and entered the Air Force with his commission. I still had two more years to go. Early on we decided that our book would retain the Bradbeer numbering system that remains the standard to this day. High-quality books as the one we envisioned were printed by letterpress in the 1950s. This type of printing meant that the type

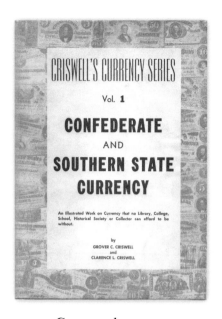

was hot set and pages were pasted together by hand. The illustrations were all zinc cuts mounted on wood blocks. Grover was having the type set in Texas, the zinc cuts mounted in St. Petersburg, the proofreading done by me at college in Charleston and the final printing done in Jacksonville, Florida!

The next question – a huge one – was how many books to print. We talked with many dealers, most of whom thought that the print run should be 750 to 1,000 copies. But we were well aware of the economies of scale. Most of the money was expended on the first copy printed to set the type, set up the presses, and the like, but after the first copy, subsequent copies were mainly just the cost of the paper. We decided that we had to make a statement and create a market for Confederate currency.

We boldly decided to print 5,000 copies. Such a large print run meant that we could sell them much cheaper, at only $6.00 each, and get much wider distribution. It was a decision that would ultimately stake our position as the leading Confederate currency dealers in the entire marketplace.

A Trunk Full of Confederate Currency

Every old-line Southern family has a story about trunks filled to overflowing with Confederate currency. From the time we started collecting and for many years after we heard similar stories from old time antique dealers who "used to have a trunk full." I cannot tell you how many times we chased after one only to find it did not exist! In 1956 Fran and I were engaged. In visiting Montreat College near Asheville, N.C., I met one of Fran's teachers who lived in Florence, S.C. In talking with her she advised that she and her sister had a trunk full of Confederate currency. Soon after Fran and I called Ms Anderson and made an appointment to see her and her trunk full of Confederate currency. We had a nice drive of two-and-a-half hours to Florence and met her and her sister at the large old family home.

Eureka! There really was a trunk full of Confederate currency! To this day it is the only one I have ever seen! There was just one small problem. I never asked what size the trunk was. There it was on a desk, a perfect-sized steamer trunk about 10 inches long, 5 inches wide and 5 inches high. But indeed it was filled with Confederate currency. The one sister kept her half and I purchased the other half from Fran's teacher.

Grover married Dolly in 1955 and I married Fran in 1957 after I graduated from The Citadel. By then Grover was out of the Air Force and both families were living in Pass-a-Grille Beach, Fla. Our first book, *Confederate and Southern State Currency*, was released in early 1957, just after Aubrey Bebee reprinted Bradbeer's book in 1956. We had remodeled the family three-car garage into offices and built a walk-in vault. Grover and Dolly were living on the south side of the offices, while Fran and I lived on the north side.

Storm Clouds Brewing

Our currency business was growing and the book was selling well, but I had begun to detect a change in the relationship between Grover and me. It was deteriorating from a partnership of equals to a "big wheel" with an unimportant younger brother. The relationship became increasingly strained, and in early 1958 Grover and I parted company. I was leaving for the Army anyway with my commission and would be stationed at Ft. Bliss, Tex., for some months before returning home to become a builder and land developer. Over the next few years I worked with Grover to help him with the second volume in the Criswell Currency Series,

Confederate and Southern State Bonds, but I insisted on working as an hourly employee.

In 1961 the ANA held its national convention in Atlanta, and Grover created a massive display of Confederate and Southern States currency. He covered 4 ft. by 8 ft. sheets of plywood with felt, placed the notes in holders that were stapled to the boards and then encased the entire display with clear plastic. It took a fair-sized trailer to haul it all and Grover pulled it behind his car. Ever the promoter, Grover erected a huge sign on the back of the trailer proclaiming that, "This trailer is carrying $1,000,000.00!" Grover's display made a really big splash with collectors, dealers and the townspeople in Atlanta. It was covered both in the newspapers and on television.

Meanwhile the printer had finished the first batch of the Confederate bond books and they were ready for pick-up in Jacksonville, just in time for the ANA Convention. Grover asked Fran and me to go to Jacksonville, get a trailer and haul hundreds of them to Atlanta. Fran and I stayed in a motel in Macon, Ga., on the trip to Atlanta. When we checked in, the motel owner looked at my name and advised that he had a copy of our first book and wished to know when the next book would be released. I always found it amusing that I – despite being "only" an hourly employee – made the first sale of the bond book to this motel owner in Macon, Ga.

Fran and Clarence Criswell in August 2010, taken on their 53rd wedding anniversary, both 75 years old.

Grover later opened a very nice Confederate Museum in the center of St. Petersburg Beach, Fla. He converted an old bank building located on a corner and did it first class… perhaps too first class, as it cost far too much to get it opened. A noted gold coin collector put a great collection on display in the museum, yet despite a high-priced alarm system the gold coins were stolen. All these costs and problems took a toll on both Grover and the museum. In 1963 Grover was forced to close it.

A Downward Spiral

After Grover was forced to close his museum, it seemed that as his fame and stature as an authority on Confederate currency increased, his ability to manage his finances diminished. Whether his financial shortcomings were self-induced or outside his control, I will never know with certainty. But it continued to create a strain on our relationship that was never resolved.

Over the years many collectors have asked me why I chose to bow out of my partnership with Grover. I thank Wayne for providing a forum to explain exactly what happened. I do not waste my time today worrying about what might have happened had we stayed in business together. Instead, I am grateful that I played a role – a significant one, Wayne tells me – in the early collecting of Confederate currency. I wish all you Confederate enthusiasts continued success as you grow your collections, and for Wayne, I hope you finally acquire your elusive Gem Uncirculated "Indian Princess."

Clarence L. Criswell, Sr.
April 5, 2011

Preface

In 1987 the Honorable William H. Kelly, then mayor of Asharoken, N.Y. and already an accomplished Confederate currency collector, wished to borrow a modest amount of money to complete his new waterfront home on Long Island Sound. Not wanting to place even a small mortgage on his new residence, Bill sought alternative ways to borrow the needed money. So he visited his friendly local banker with an album under his arm containing what he was confident would be irresistible collateral for his loan: a breathtaking Confederate currency collection.

William H. Kelly, former mayor of Asharoken, N.Y. and an advanced collector of Confederate currency.

Bill's collection was no ordinary ensemble. Originally compiled by Confederate author and historian Brent Hughes in the 1940s and 1950s, the collection was a complete "type set" of Confederate currency, containing one specimen of each of the designs or "types" issued by the Confederacy between 1861 and 1865 during its brief existence as a sovereign nation. The first four notes in the collection, called *the Magnificent Montgomerys* because they were issued in Montgomery, Ala. before the Confederate capital was moved to Richmond, Va., were pedigreed to associates of Raphael Thian, one of the earliest Confederate researchers and dealers. Pristine, nearly uncirculated and stunning in every way, the four Montgomerys were a mere prelude to the spectacular notes comprising the balance of Bill's collection.

Bill returned to his bank a few days later expecting to pick up his check. Instead, his banker asked him to take a seat in his office. With nervousness, even embarrassment in his voice, Bill's banker declined to provide the loan, explaining that while he could easily loan against Bill's new home, using a large database of similar home sales to establish fair value, Bill had provided no comparable sales data for Confederate currency to establish the value of his collection. In fact, Bill was unaware if historical records on price trends in Confederate currency even existed, despite it being sold at public auction since 1865 when the Civil War ended. Bill left the bank frustrated and bewildered: a collection he had purchased in 1985 for $45,000 (and would sell in 1989 for $125,000) was not sufficient to collateralize a $25,000 loan.

Bill was still irritated when he related this story to me in 1997. I could easily empathize with him. I also owned impressive Confederate currency, and I also knew nothing (at the time) about Confederate currency price trends. I became obsessed with finding out whether my investing in Confederate currency over time had been a sound financial decision, particularly when I had other investment options such as precious metals, crude oil or common stocks.

When I started to answer this question in 1997, I did not realize how arduous and lengthy the search would become. Early in my efforts I discovered that the first Confederate $1,000 bill (experts would later classify it as a Criswell Type-1 "$1,000 Montgomery") was sold at public auction in New York in 1865. I even learned who purchased the note: Mr. John F. McCoy. Since neither Bill Kelly nor I knew anything about Confederate currency price trends in 1997, I can only imagine how uninformed John McCoy must have felt when making his purchase in 1865, only eight months after the Civil War ended.

I suspect that John arrived a little early for the auction that day in 1865. Surely it was cold and dreary as he entered the offices of E. Cooley at 498 Broadway in New York City at about 4:00 p.m. on December 19. He was there to review the lots to be offered that evening at a public auction conducted by W. Elliot Woodward of Roxbury, Mass. John was already a skilled numismatist, having sold the bulk of his personal coin collection at public auction just a year earlier. But he never lost the collecting bug, so here he was at a rather ordinary Woodward auction to which he had consigned some material, just days before Christmas.

The auction started promptly at 6:00 p.m. with John following closely, pleased with the price realized for some of the lots he had consigned, less satisfied with others. He bought several lots, including some low-priced tin medals, a few inexpensive Washington pieces, even a cheap 1790 Massachusetts lottery ticket. A very rare 1795 Gold Half Eagle with the large eagle reverse of 1798 also caught his eye, and he was elated when auctioneer George A. Leavitt hammered the lot to him for a surprisingly high $20. With that sale, the auction recessed until the next day.

The following evening the lengthy auction was nearing its end, yet John stayed patiently in his seat. Earlier the previous afternoon he had closely examined a truly unusual lot buried at the back of the catalog. Listed as Lot 2670 of the 2678 lots in the auction, it was described with concise elegance as, "$1,000 Note of the Confederate States of America; genuine, very fine and rare." John knew

PRICED CATALOGUE

OF

AMERICAN COINS,

MEDALS, &c.,

Selected from the Cabinets of MESSRS. BACH, BERTSCH, COLBURN, EMERY, FINOTTI, ILSLEY, LEVICK, LILLIENDAHL, LIGHTBODY, McCOY, SEMPLE, SHURTLEFF, *and other collections, purchased at various times by*

W. ELLIOT WOODWARD,

OF ROXBURY, MASS.

ALSO,

A few fine Foreign Coins and Medals,

TO BE SOLD AT AUCTION,

IN NEW YORK CITY,

On Tuesday, Dec. 19th, 1865, and following days, at the Book Trade-Sale Rooms of E. COOLEY, *498 Broadway.*

GEORGE A. LEAVITT, AUCTIONEER.

· 109

2670 $1,000 Note of the Confederate States of America; genuine, very fine and rare.
2671 $500 Note, Confederate States ; genuine, fine, scarce.
2672 $50 Note, Confederate States ; genuine, fine, scarce.
2673 $20 Note, Confederate States ; genuine, fine.
2674 $10 Note, Confederate States ; genuine, fine.
2675 $5 Note, Confederate States ; genuine, fine.
1865.

The title page of W. Elliot Woodward's auction catalog dated December 19, 1865. Inset shows descriptions of Lots 2670 - 2675, including the first $1,000 Montgomery note offered at auction.

nothing about Confederate currency, but sound business judgment may have led him to suspect that a $1,000 bill was indeed rare, as few $1,000 bills had been printed by the U.S. government and John could see no reason why the Confederate government would print many either. In fact, John thought the Confederate $1,000 note might be the most unique lot in the entire auction.

Now came the dilemma – he had no idea what to bid. Was it worth the $20 he had paid for the 1795 Gold Half Eagle, or closer to the pennies he had paid for some cheap Washington pieces? Could even pennies be better invested elsewhere? John knew he had alternatives to buying "worthless Rebel money," as his Northern friends derisively called it. He already owned silver bullion as a hedge against the severe inflation seen during the Civil War, some friends were speculating in "black gold" recently found near Titusville, Pa., and he knew that stocks of clipper-ship companies on the New York Stock Exchange had been rapidly rising as the country became increasingly mobile.

Finally, the Confederate $1,000 note was announced as the next lot up for sale. John was excited but nervous. Bidding was spirited, particularly for a lot at the extreme end of the auction. John was relieved when the lot was hammered to him at a price of $4.75.

As he left the auction, John felt good about his purchase of the 1795 Gold Half Eagle. He knew it was an extremely rare piece that he had acquired at a fair price. But he felt far less comfortable about the $4.75 he had paid for the Confederate $1,000 bill. No doubt he sighed a little to himself as he thought, only time will tell.

Time indeed does tell. A sesquicentennial of history has transpired since the Confederate government began issuing its own currency. This book looks at those 150 years and finally answers John McCoy's question: *Is Confederate currency a worthwhile investment compared to alternatives like precious metals, crude oil or common stocks?*

Lead editorial from the March 2005 issue of Bank Note Reporter.

My brief glimpse at John McCoy, a New Yorker who was a celebrated coin collector of the mid-nineteenth century, suggests an inquisitive man who would have been keenly interested in the investment potential of the $1,000 Confederate Montgomery note he purchased in 1865. But many of today's prominent numismatists would prefer that the word "investment" never be used with a collectible like Confederate currency. Indeed the lead editorial in the March 2005 issue of *Bank Note Reporter* urged that collectors "Banish the word 'investment' from [the] hobby." The editor cautioned that, "selling a property that is worth owning in its own right for its aesthetic qualities and the pure joy of owning something so beautiful and desirable is a far better path to trod than talking about rates of return."

I understand the concern of those who embrace this point of view. The editor of the article quoted here was referring to the heady times in the coin business during the 1980s, but could just as easily have been referring to the tulip mania of the 1630s or the tech stock bubble of the 1990s. But all of these "sure" investments, including coins in the 1980s, suffer from extremely short time horizons. This book looks at price trends in Confederate currency for nearly 150 years, from 1865 to 2010 – from before the first transcontinental railroad was completed in 1869 to today's routine rocket travel into space. Surely those who would caution against using the word "investment" with collectibles would feel more comfortable when the data spanned a period of such length and included such depth.

I am not a securities dealer. I am not an investment counselor. I am not espousing that any investor convert his current portfolio of stocks into a collection of Confederate currency. Even I began collecting Confederate currency for all the "right" reasons as advocated by the editor of *Bank Note Reporter*: its innate beauty and historical significance.

There is no denying, though, that this book focuses on the quantitative aspects of Confederate currency like its investment potential since 1865. To evaluate its price movements, I have recorded virtually all sales of Confederate currency at public auction since the Civil War ended. Those notes have a provenance or pedigree (from their serial numbers) which serve only to increase their desirability.

But this book also pays homage to the qualitative side of collecting, where quantitative attributes do not even exist. Many notes – fully equal in splendor and desirability to their pedigreed brethren – have never passed through public auction but have nonetheless been sold via private treaty. These mongrels of the collecting universe appeared from nowhere, devoid of impressive provenances, but fully imbued with the same beauty and rarity as those specimens which passed through public auction. These non-pedigreed notes are also chronicled in this book, with breathtaking images arranged in a most attractive collage -- certainly a different way to portray Confederate currency.

Most readers of this book already invest with their minds but collect with their hearts. Such investors know that the prudent purchase of either a traditional investment like stocks or a collectible like Confederate currency requires full knowledge of all available facts. Traditional investment opportunities like stocks are already supported by armies of financial analysts and legions of economists. This book aims to level the playing field by adding a plethora of facts to the art of collecting Confederate currency.

If a future collector buys a rare piece of Confederate currency with more conviction and peace of mind because of the information contained in these pages, then I will consider my book a success.

J. Wayne Hilton, Author
April 5, 2011

Introduction

Writing has always been an integral part of my life. I wrote TV ads, edited catalog copy and simplified complicated business strategies for presentation to executives. With this background, I foolishly thought that writing a book about my personal passion would be easily done in a matter of months. Now, 14 years after starting, I must humbly agree with sportswriter Red Smith who wryly observed that, "There is nothing to writing. All you do is sit down at the typewriter and open a vein."

The five-dollar Columbian of 1893, the stamp that ended my philatelic career. (Photo courtesy Shreves Galleries)

My passion is Confederate currency. I want to know its history as a collectible. I want to embrace the intrinsic beauty and historical significance of the hobby it built. But I also want to understand its potential as a financial investment, compared to other alternatives such as precious metals, crude oil or common stocks. I want to see how the price of Confederate currency has changed since the Civil War began 150 years ago.

The history of Confederate currency is an indelible part of my own heritage. My family made enormous sacrifices for the Southern cause. My father's grandfather lost part of his hand at the Battle of Atlanta on July 22, 1864. My mother's great-great uncle died from wounds suffered at the Battle of Gettysburg on July 2, 1863. My old-line Carolina family regaled me with anecdotes about "The War of Northern Aggression," as they called it, during my childhood. Confederate currency was plentiful, and most families, including my own, had a few pieces of "worthless Rebel money" as relics of a bygone era and as links to our families' forebears.

Part I: My Start as a Confederate Currency Collector

Growing up, I knew no one who collected Confederate currency. As a child I collected U.S. regular-issue postage stamps, but my philatelic curiosity waned when I discovered that I could never afford the five-dollar Columbian of 1893 (Scott #245) on my twenty-five cents weekly allowance. My interest in Confederate currency did not surface until I began working for Procter & Gamble in Cincinnati, Ohio in 1972, after finishing graduate school. While at P&G, the world's largest advertiser, I developed a fascination with mail-order advertising and decided to start a sideline mail-order business of my own. I needed a product to sell. My childhood memories of Confederate currency made the decision easy.

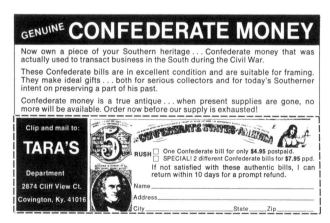

My "Tara's" ad of 1976 which started a successful mail-order career.

In 1976 I launched Tara's, a mail-order business offering "genuine Confederate money" for $4.95 a piece through advertisements in southern magazines such as *Southern Living* and *Progressive Farmer*. The business was, at best, modestly profitable, but it rekindled an interest in a part of my past not experienced for nearly 10 years. Despite limited financial achievements, Tara's was important because it introduced me to someone who would forever shape my view of collecting Confederate currency. This bridge to my future was my dealer, a larger-than-life figure who previously served as mayor of St. Petersburg Beach, Fla. at the tender age of 25, and who was as passionate about making a quick buck as I was about Confederate currency.

Of course I had discovered Grover Criswell. Outlandish and brazen, yet charming, Grover was undoubtedly the greatest promoter of Confederate currency to ever live. All I ordered from him were common, well-circulated, cheap pieces of currency that I could re-sell in my mail-order business. But Grover never shipped just what I ordered. Each delivery was accompanied by beautiful and rare Confederate treasury notes, colorful Confederate bonds, unusual treasury warrants – all on approval and all exorbitantly priced.

While a single shipment might be offered to me at a cost of hundreds or even thousands of dollars, I could never figure out why the shipments were rarely insured and certainly never registered. I was particularly amused by Grover's devil-may-care attitude as I impatiently waited in line at the Cincinnati post office while on my lunch hour to return those approvals via expensive registered mail. I always wondered how the unabashed Grover could afford to ship such "valuable" merchandise without the benefit of insurance. Was he important enough to negotiate special deals with the U.S. Postal Service? Or was the "valuable" merchandise not so valuable after all?

I never bought a single piece of expensive Confederate currency from Grover. It was just too hard to sort through all his hyperbole. But he introduced me to his critically acclaimed series of books on the subject, and he imbued me with his own passion for the hobby. For these things I will always be grateful.

My interest in Confederate currency was no secret in my family, and my brother Charles encouraged me to build my own Confederate "type set": a collection of all 70 or so different currency designs or "types" issued by the Confederate government between 1861 and 1865. Charles is a collector extraordinaire. He collects everything: stamps, postcards, "Santa" notes, milk parlor equipment, slide rules, old tractors (not replicas, the real, full-size ones – at last count, his wife tells me he has 27), and of course, Confederate currency. His own Confederate type set measures up to anyone's and includes, among other rarities, a Criswell Type-35 "$5 Indian Princess" bearing serial number 1, a Criswell Type-2 "$500 Montgomery" in the condition census Top Ten, and a Criswell Type-47 "$20 Essay" with the nearly unique checkered shield.

Criswell Type-35 "$5 Indian Princess" with serial number 1. (Photo courtesy Charles A. Hilton)

While helping Charles complete his own type set I met his dealer, Hugh Shull[1], who was then living in Leesville, S.C. Mentored by Grover Criswell, Hugh was an up-and-coming Confederate dealer – aggressive, entrepreneurial and a workaholic. In 1979, he was already well on his way to supplanting Grover as the hobby's most influential dealer. Today I count Hugh and Crutchfield "Crutch" Williams[2] as the two dealers who provided me with the most advice and encouragement in writing this book. Hugh is hard at work on his latest book, *A Guide Book of Confederate Currency*, to be released in the not-too-distant future by Whitman Publishing. This book will picture my very best Confederate type set.

My goal has long been to amass the finest Confederate type set ever assembled. But I quickly learned that even the experts frequently differ on what constitutes the finest example of a

---

[1] Hugh Shull, PO Box 2522, Lexington, SC 29071.

[2] Crutchfield Williams, PO Box 3221, Quinlan, TX 75474.

particular design or type. I recall Hugh and my close friend and mentor Doug Ball, founder of the NASCA auction firm (now Spink Smythe), declaring a $500 Montgomery note I had been offered by fellow collector Paul Gibson to be the finest known specimen; at the same time, Crutch Williams made the same pronouncement about a $500 Montgomery note I had earlier been offered from a collection assembled by Confederate researcher, author and historian Brent Hughes.

Not knowing whom to believe, I did what any zealot would do: I bought both. Then, not being content with the two exquisite $500 Montgomery notes from these magnificent collections, I bought both entire type sets. Then a third … a fifth … a tenth … I was out of control. After acquiring my twelfth complete type set, Charles sat me down one evening and admonished me – in a kind of "Confederate intervention" – that without some focus and discipline, I would soon be broke.

I thus re-directed my attention from the purchase of complete type sets to the purchase of single notes that were among the Top Ten of the condition census for that particular type. This collecting logic was far more fun. I still remember when Crutch Williams, working with Texas dealer Don Higgins, called to offer me the finest known Criswell Type-1 "$1,000 Montgomery," earlier owned by Texas obsolete-note specialist Bob Medlar. Later, Hugh offered me what he described as the finest known "Indian Princess" from the collection then

The imposing American Numismatic Society Building on Audubon Terrace in New York City.

owned by Neil Chiappa, since purchased by me and pictured in Criswell's last book published in 1996. By 2005 I had whittled down my collection to "only" ten complete type sets, where it remains today, but each note within the collection is among the finest known specimens anywhere.

Having followed an "upgrade and discard" strategy for a number of years now, new additions to my collection are increasingly difficult to find, but are as welcome as ever as I constantly attempt to trade up lesser pieces for better specimens. Just three years ago, Hugh offered me a seemingly common Criswell Type-64 "$500 Stonewall Jackson" but with impeccable image sharpness and the most beautiful, strikingly deep red color I had ever seen. Of course I bought it. In 2007 Allen Mincho, Len Glazer and I marveled at a simply stunning "$500 Montgomery" offered by Heritage Auctions at the FUN Show in Orlando. I also acquired this note, which I consider to be the third-finest known. Great census-condition notes are still out there, although becoming increasingly hard to find. Many readers may own exceptional notes that I would enjoy seeing or even purchasing, and for this reason I have included my personal contact information at the end of this introduction.

Having sunk considerable sums of money into my Confederate collection over the years, it was essential that I evaluate whether my expenditure had been a thoughtful investment or a capricious spending spree in support of a self-indulgent hobby. But finding data to support either conclusion was impossible, as it simply did not exist. Confederate currency has been sold – particularly at public auctions – since the Civil War ended in 1865. But no attempt had ever been made to catalog all public auctions conducted between 1865 and the present as a way of documenting appreciation or depreciation in the currency's value over an extended time. It struck me as a fascinating – and daunting – challenge to undertake.

Part II: My Search for Confederate Sales Data

In 1997 I began to analyze auction results on Confederate currency. This data was primarily found at the libraries of the American Numismatic Society (ANS) on Audubon Terrace in New York City and the American Numismatic Association (ANA) in Colorado Springs, Colo. Such numismatic bibliophiles as John W. Adams of Boston and Dan Hamelberg of Champaign, Ill. also granted me access to their private libraries. I thank them for their generosity, which made my analysis far more complete.

I remain unaware of any attempt to track comprehensive sales data over such an extended time period – almost 150 years – for any other area of numismatics. Since my effort with Confederate currency would be the first, it was imperative that it be complete, accurate and verifiable, so that it might provide the template for others. For the curious, I will *briefly* describe how the data was collected and examined.

Sales data was obtained almost exclusively from public auction records housed within the reference library of the ANS in New York City, but importantly supplemented by additional auction records found at the ANA Library in Colorado Springs. I received immense help from Francis (Frank) Campbell, who ably and conscientiously served as the ANS Head Librarian from 1975 until his retirement in 2008. Frank offered considerable insights and saved me valuable time, as he would pull the auction records from the shelves and organize them for review prior to my arrival for week-long visits. Frank's successor, the talented Elizabeth Hahn, continued to help as the book reached completion. ANA librarian Nancy Green, as well as personal friend and Colorado Springs resident Joe Bradley, provided similar help within the ANA Library.

Frank Campbell, distinguished Head Librarian of the ANS from 1975 to 2008.

While not quite the enormous government warehouse depicted in *Raiders of the Lost Ark*, the ANS Library nevertheless contains over 30,000 historical numismatic auction catalogs. Happily, John W. Adams eliminated the need for me to pore through all 30,000 just to find those auctions which contained sales of Confederate currency. John, an erudite investment banker from Boston with a penchant for Indian peace medals, is a past trustee of the ANS. He reviewed the Library's overwhelming inventory of catalogs, deleted those issued by minor auction houses as being largely forgettable, and exhaustively analyzed the remainder. It was an immense undertaking, beginning with the catalogs of Edward Cogan (America's first coin dealer) in the 1850s and ending with auction houses operating in 1950, including Max Mehl, Barney Bluestone, Stack's and New Netherlands. His work was published in 1982 and 1990 in a two-volume series entitled *United States Numismatic Literature*.

John graded these catalogs for content using 25 categories such as Confederate, Large Cents, Tokens and Fractional Currency, and noted the consignor of the material if shown. His trailblazing efforts made my task much easier, allowing me to skip over catalogs where he had found no Confederate content. My lower back – and my eyesight – offer thanks.

I only wish that John Adams had extended his grading system to those auction houses formed after 1950. Some of the greatest auction houses specializing in Confederate currency, like Doug Ball's NASCA auction firm, were not created until well after that date. I was left to my own devices to research those records. Not surprisingly, it took far more time to analyze the post-1950 auction houses than it took to review all the auctions from 1865 to 1950, and it is fair to say that I would never have attempted this book without John's ground-breaking effort. I am deeply appreciative.

Using John's two volumes to isolate applicable auctions through 1950, coupled with my own creative and dogged efforts to locate relevant auctions after 1950, I was able to whittle down the 30,000 auction catalogs contained within the numismatic libraries of the ANS and ANA to only 6,000 with possible Confederate content. But the project was far from finished.

I soon learned that locating 6,000 auction catalogs with possible Confederate content was the easy part of the challenge. Finding the price realized for each auction lot was even more difficult than finding the catalogs themselves, as the auction catalogs in both the ANS and ANA Libraries were often missing price data. Today we take it for granted that auction results are available online within hours of an auction's conclusion. But early auction houses did not even issue prices realized. They simply hand-priced a spare auction catalog (usually in red ink) and sold it to interested bidders for a dollar or two – a rather princely sum in those days. Since my project focused on Confederate price trends over time, a catalog with significant Confederate content, but without prices realized, was virtually worthless.

For data on prices realized, I turned to a different group of experts: collectors and dealers of numismatic literature. Collectors Dan Hamelberg of Champaign, Ill., Dave Bowers of Wolfeboro, N.H. and John Adams of Boston provided hundreds of prices realized from their own private libraries. I also extend my gratitude to Karl Moulton of Congress, Ariz. and David Fanning of Columbus, Ohio, two prominent dealers in numismatic literature who shared auction data from their own sources.

One dealer deserves special recognition. I remember studying Henry Chapman's 1908 auction of the Confederate collection of Harmon Chambers of Philadelphia. Few people know of Chambers' collection today, but it was one of the greatest assemblages of all time, as it included nearly all of the 70 or so types as well as most of the important variations or "varieties." I suspect that Chambers' collection is not better known because its monumental auction results have been lost to history. Yet George Kolbe, a distinguished dealer in numismatic literature who lives in the spectacular mountaintop village of Crestline, Calif., advised me in 2004 that he had found a priced copy of this catalog. I am much indebted to him for sharing all 26 pages of this essential price data.

Somehow I unearthed pricing data for virtually all those auction catalogs that John Adams and I had isolated, using data at the ANS and ANA Libraries, supplemented by assistance from the numismatic literature community. The sole exception is a one-page listing of 36 auctions with price data still missing.

With the raw results now collected, I needed to organize the data into a form that was both accurate and easy to "slice and dice" analytically. My loyal friend and PCDA dealer Crutch Williams worked tirelessly to transform my reams of raw data into an accessible database that did just that.

While public auction records are the only sales data used in my project, I also received access to all private sales records of famed Confederate dealer Grover Criswell, from his start in business in 1955 until his death in 1999. Contained in 26 three-foot file boxes, Grover's records offer a glimpse of the ongoing development of collecting Confederate currency over nearly half a century.

Ultimately, though, I decided not to include Grover's private records in my analysis, as I felt it might potentially skew the data. Frequently I found records of Grover purchasing a note at public auction and then selling that same note, with appropriate markup, via private treaty just days later. Since I had already recorded the public auction sale, including his private-treaty sale in essentially the same timeframe would add duplication and unfairly inflate the price realized at the auction itself. The statistician for this book concurs with this decision.

While Grover's records are not part of the quantitative analysis leading to the calculation of a rate-of-return on investment, it is hard to overstate their importance to the excitement and delight in the hobby of collecting Confederate currency itself. The editor of *Bank Note Reporter* who wanted to banish the word "investment" from the hobby (see page 16) might view me as a heretic, but in Grover the editor would find a true disciple. Grover was enamored with the hobby and his files prove that adoration. They are filled with sales of extreme Confederate rarities, many including 1970s-era glossy black and white photographs. I was fascinated by letters between Grover and the astute John Ford dating to the 1950s discussing the ultra-rare Criswell Type-27 "$10 Shield & Eagle" notes with plate numbers A_9 through A_{16} (Criswell Varieties 222-229) and guessing how many specimens survive today. I found paid membership cards to numismatic societies all over the country, knowing full well he would never have had time to visit the bulk of them. I found his election as President of the ANA in 1977, a tumultuous time for both Grover and the hobby he cared about so much.

Grover's devotion to the hobby was sometimes eclipsed by his legendary antics and exaggerations. But if my emphasis on investment potential fails to fully appreciate the hobby aspects of collecting Confederate currency, then Grover's symbolic presence is still there to serve as my alter-ego, with his pure and even child-like joy in the hobby he arguably created.

Part III: My Quest to Find Accurate Answers

Steven Feller, Ph.D. and daughter Ray, who co-authored Silent Witnesses: Civilian Camp Money of World War II.

By 2007, more than half-way through my 14-year journey, I had successfully completed my research into the valuation of Confederate currency from the end of the Civil War. Now it was time to turn my attention to the meat of the endeavor: the statistical analysis. I was ready to crunch the data to answer in a rigorous way the questions that had inspired this book: What has been the price trend of Confederate currency since the Civil War ended? How does an investment in Confederate currency compare to alternatives such as silver, crude oil or the stock market over this same timeframe?

Answering these questions was the crux of the entire project. Knowing that the statistical accuracy of those answers must be able to withstand the scrutiny of the most skeptical reader, numismatic and non-numismatic pundits alike, I enlisted Steven A. Feller, Ph.D., Professor of Physics at Coe College in Cedar Rapids, Iowa. Steve was the obvious choice, as he possesses a truly unique pair of attributes: he is both a mathematical whiz *and* a collector of Confederate currency. I provided him with the date of each auction, the Criswell type number of the note sold, the note's grade or condition as described in the auction catalog, the serial number if known, and the price realized (including the buyer's premium). For comparative purposes I also gave Steve pricing data on silver, crude oil and the stock market since 1865, as generated by the U.S. Bureau of the Census: *Statistical Abstract of the United States*.

One of Steve's most difficult tasks was to adjust the data for differences in grade or condition as found in the auction catalog's description. Compared to the nuances of Confederate currency, the alternative investments were easy to evaluate. An ounce of silver sold in 1865 is identical to an ounce of silver sold in 2010. But a $1,000 Montgomery note that was graded

Extremely Fine in a 1950 auction cannot be compared to a $1,000 Montgomery note that graded Very Good in that same auction without making appropriate adjustments. Imagine the even greater difficulty Steve had to overcome in comparing these exact same notes when they did not sell in the same auction but rather sold 100 years apart, adding the new complication of elapsed time. Nevertheless, Steve was able to solve this conundrum and simplify his results into a series of graphs and charts that anyone can easily understand.

Steve's methodology – nothing short of brilliant – is described in his own words in Chapter Four of this book. I know he enjoyed the challenge, and I am not exaggerating to say that without his expertise, this project would not have been feasible.

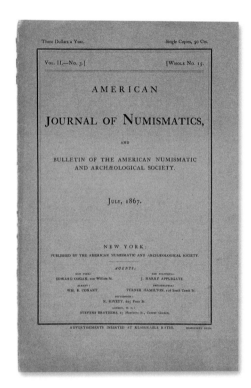

The July 1867 issue of American Journal of Numismatics, which contained one of the Thomas Emmet charts on Confederate currency.

With the statistical analysis complete, my fundamental questions have now been answered. At last I know exactly how much Confederate currency – specifically, the four Montgomery notes – has appreciated in value from 1865 through 2010. I have compared that appreciation to other investment options such as silver, crude oil and stocks. And I found something unexpected. I assumed that all four Montgomerys would appreciate at nearly the identical rate over time. Surprisingly, they did not – and the rarest Montgomerys did not necessarily appreciate as fast as their more common counterparts. My 14-year odyssey is finally complete, making it possible to share these findings with the reader.

This book, which is confined to Criswell Types 1 through 4, the *Magnificent Montgomerys*, is the first of what is intended to become a series of publications to include an analysis of all Criswell Type numbers through Criswell Type-38, the end of the Confederate issue of 1861. I will also include the mysterious and enigmatic "Essay Notes" of 1862. The second volume will pick up with Criswell Types 5 and 6, the "First Richmond" issues, and subsequent volumes will provide data through Criswell Type-38 and Types 47 and 48, the "Essays."

Beginning with the fifth Treasury issue of October 13, 1862, corresponding with Criswell Type-49, the Confederacy emitted huge quantities of notes, many of which survive to this day. Although I have collected the sales data, I do not intend to analyze any notes after Criswell Type-48, due to their abundance and my need to begin sharing what I have already learned. Perhaps some collector younger than my 62 years will be inspired to carry forward and finish the higher Criswell numbers. If so, the GPS coordinates for the ANS Library in New York City are 40.723301, -74.006241. Happy hunting!

Part IV: My Respect for the Purely Aesthetic Side of Collecting

While I wrote this book primarily to determine whether my own expenditure in Confederate currency had been a responsible investment, I also relish the purely aesthetic aspects of the hobby and wish to highlight some new insights I gleaned as I plodded through thousands of auction catalogs.

I have long yearned to read a complete history of the hobby of collecting Confederate currency. In his monthly "Shades of the Blue and Grey" column in *Bank Note Reporter*, author Fred Reed started a fascinating series on the early days of the hobby in fall 2004, but Fred digressed into collateral areas soon thereafter. He intends to return to his original focus on Confederate currency in the near future, but until that happens, I have prepared my own

150-Year Illustrated Timeline featuring the dealers, the collectors and the publications that are part of the fabric of the impressive history of collecting Confederate currency.

My time line starts even before the Thomas Addis Emmet charts which appeared in the 1867 issues of *American Journal of Numismatics* and concludes with Hugh Shull's new *A Guide Book of Confederate Currency* yet to be published. This time line is accompanied by many full-color images of the rarest publications, and places the key events in their proper historical perspective.

I also decided to tackle one of the hobby's most debated questions: Which Confederate type note is the rarest in the entire series? Nineteenth and early twentieth century dealers were virtually unanimous in labeling the Criswell Type-35 "$5 Indian Princess" the rarest, but this conclusion was challenged in 1976 when Doug Ball formed the NASCA auction house. Doug postulated that the Criswell Type-27 "$10 Shield & Eagle" was even rarer than the "Indian Princess" based on limited research of contemporary auctions.

So which side is right? Is the rarest note the "Indian Princess" or the "Shield & Eagle"? *Neither*, as the reader will soon discover!

Any discussion of the hobby of collecting Confederate currency has to include its printers. Much fact – and fiction – has been written about the printing of the Montgomerys. I include some startling new findings about the printing of these famous notes and provide a thesis that a set of very early Confederate notes, even earlier than the "First Richmond" issues, was printed in the spring of 1861 but has been lost to history.

I conclude with a full chapter consisting of two sections for each of the four "Magnificent Montgomerys." The first section features the investment potential of the note. Every auction sale since 1865 is reported in chronological order, including full-color photographs of each note for which I was able to obtain an image. Survival counts have been updated and include several new serial numbers never before reported to the collecting fraternity. Finally, the first section ends with a detailed graph showing the price trends for that particular Montgomery since 1865 and comparing it to the historical price trends of silver, crude oil and the S&P 500 Composite Index of stocks.

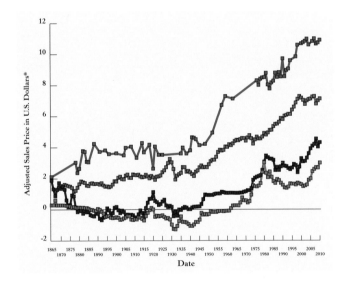

Graph comparing the $1,000 Montgomery note against the performance of crude oil, silver and the S&P 500 Index.

The second section of each chapter features an abridged look at the purely hobbyist side of collecting. Many pristine Montgomerys left no record of passing through public auction and thus do not appear in the first section of each chapter where pedigreed notes appear. I am confident, though, that many of these non-pedigreed notes have indeed passed through public auction but were not identified, as serial numbers were not routinely included as part of the auction catalog description until about 1950.

Lacking an auction pedigree in no way diminishes a Montgomery's beauty or appeal. Every Montgomery note for which no provenance could be found is pictured in the two-page second section, as part of an artfully designed collage created by John Murphy of the advertising agency Balboni Associates. These images were provided by dealers and collectors alike who appreciate Montgomery notes simply for their intrinsic allure and stunning aesthetics – with utterly no thought of their investment potential or rate of return.

The reader now knows what this book contains, and why I wrote it. Indeed, while the graphs in the first section of each chapter show the price trends of Confederate currency over time, they also serve a far more useful purpose. The collectors who read this book are now armed with sufficient ammunition to answer even the most persistent spouse's eternal complaint, "Honey, did you really have to buy more of that 'worthless Rebel money'? What makes you think that stuff will ever be worth what you paid for it?"

After waiting years for this moment, you grab this book, turn to the graphs, point to their upward trends and smugly exclaim, "Look! We're making money! Just like I always promised we would!"

Better yet, maybe you should just buy your better half a copy, too.

J. Wayne Hilton
Post Office Box 1
Graniteville, S.C. 29829-0001
JerryWayne1@comcast.net

Written April 5, 2011, on the 150th Anniversary
of the Issuance of the First Montgomery Note.

Chapter 1:

An Illustrated Timeline:
150 Years of Collecting Confederate Currency

This book focuses on the price appreciation of Confederate currency over time. But such escalation might not have occurred without a series of noteworthy events and larger-than-life collectors and dealers who provided a catalyst to stimulate interest and enthusiasm. This chapter looks at those individuals and events and evaluates their impact on collecting Confederate currency.

Collecting Confederate currency is not new. Edward Cogan of Philadelphia, America's first coin dealer, was offering Confederate currency in public auctions as early as June 1864, a full year before hostilities ended between the North and South. From this largely forgettable start, the Confederate branch of American numismatics has grown and matured over the past 150 years to assume significant proportions. This chapter is a timeline of many of the decisive events and individuals in the history of collecting Confederate currency.

June 29, 1864. First Known Public Sale of a Confederate Note.

Edward Cogan holds the honor of selling the first Confederate note at public auction. Sold on June 29, 1864 as part of an 844-lot offering at the offices of Bangs, Merwin & Co. in New York, it is obvious that cataloger Cogan did not know where to place his single lot of Confederate currency. He ultimately decided to list it within a section entitled, "Autographs To Be Sold for the Benefit of the Sanitary Commission." There, among letters from Jefferson Davis and Daniel Webster and a check from George Washington, appears lot "341. Confederate Bank Note Twenty Dollars." *(Illus. 1)* The lot was sold for an impressive twenty cents, the same price as realized by a letter from President Millard Fillmore.

Illus. 1

June 23, 1865. Last Confederate General Surrenders to End Civil War.

"Popular belief" is often wrong. For example, most Civil War buffs date the Civil War from the shelling of Ft. Sumter in Charleston Harbor on April 12, 1861. In reality, though, the first shots were fired upon the Union ship *Star of the West* on January 9, 1861, as it attempted to deliver supplies to Ft. Sumter.

Illus. 2 and 3

Conventional wisdom likewise holds that the Civil War ended with the surrender of Confederate General Robert E. Lee to Union General Ulysses S. Grant at Appomattox Court House, Va., on April 9, 1865 *(Illus. 2)*. But Lee surrendered only the Army of Northern Virginia. Other Confederate generals ceded their armies over the next three months to bring the war to its ultimate conclusion. Confederate General Kirby Smith surrendered his Trans Mississippi forces at New Orleans on May 26, 1865. Finally, on June 23, 1865, **Brigadier General Stand Watie**, a Cherokee Indian chief *(Illus. 3, prior page)*, became the last Confederate General to surrender his command – the First Indian Brigade of the Army of the Trans Mississippi – to Union Lt. Col. Asa C. Matthews at Doaksville, Indian Territory (now Okla.). The war was finally over. Collecting relics of that war – including Confederate currency – had begun even before the guns stopped firing.

December 19, 1865. First Known Public Sale of an Identifiable Criswell Type Note to Possibly the First Collector of Confederate Currency.

The importance of **W. Elliot Woodward's** public auction of a Criswell Type-1 "$1,000 Montgomery" note in December 1865 is *not* that it was the first recorded sale of a Montgomery; rather, its significance rests in its being the first sale of a Criswell type note that can be precisely classified. Luckily for us collectors, the first sale of a specific Criswell type happened to be a $1,000 Montgomery, the second-rarest in the entire series. This $1,000 Montgomery sold for $4.75 *(Illus. 4)* at a time when silver was selling for $1.34 an ounce and gold for $18.93 a troy ounce, a regulated price set by the government. For more details on this auction, see pages 14-16.

This $1,000 Montgomery was sold to John F. McCoy, a renowned coin collector of his day who sold his own extensive coin collection at a Woodward auction in May 1864. Does McCoy's purchase of the first identifiable Confederate note in December 1865 thus make him the first collector of Confederate currency?

Giving the important title of "first Confederate currency collector" to John McCoy rests the crown on the head of a known numismatist about whom Dave Bowers has written extensively. But is McCoy really the first? What about Thomas Addis Emmet, who assembled a collection of over 300 varieties of Confederate currency as early as March 1867? He did not build such an assortment overnight. Surely he too was collecting as early as the Woodward sale to McCoy in December 1865.

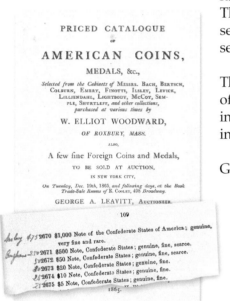

Illus. 4

A great author publishes a provocative statement and awaits a barrage of comments, some in agreement, many not. Good friend and prize-winning author Fred Reed, who writes a lively column entitled "Shades of the Blue and Grey" for the monthly publication *Bank Note Reporter*, did just that in his October 2004 column when he nominated Robert Alonzo Brock (1839-1914) as the first Confederate currency collector. Brock's contributions to Confederate currency collecting were important – as early as April 1866 he gave a collection of Confederate currency and stamps to the Boston Numismatic Society. He made a similar gift to the predecessor of today's ANS in New York in December 1867. But are two such gifts of unknown substance enough to elevate Brock to the position of our first Confederate currency collector? I think Fred answered his own question when he quipped that asking who was the first Confederate currency collector is "like asking who was the first man to write on cave walls in France."

Neither the Boston Numismatic Society (BNS) nor the ANS has any details on Brock's gifts. According to William Harkins, secretary of the BNS, in 1898 the BNS donated its cabinet, including all its coins, medals and currency, to the Boston Museum of Fine Arts, which advised through spokesperson Catherine O'Reilly that it owns no Confederate currency gifted by Brock. The ANS has the original letter from Brock accompanying its gift, and has retained a rubbing of a rare coin Brock also enclosed – but no Confederate currency. The Huntington Library in San Marino, Calif., which purchased Brock's extensive ephemera in 1922, has a record only of "a $5 and $10 Confederate note," but the Library is not certain that they are from any Brock collection. The Library of Virginia has digitized Brock's collection of ephemera – but found no Confederate currency.

Likewise, Brock does not appear to have published anything on Confederate currency, despite numerous articles on Continental and Colonial currency. There is no record of any Confederate currency collection owned by Brock being bequeathed or sold at public auction.

Fred might be correct that Brock was the first Confederate currency collector. But I am unwilling to make such a judgment, when relics of the Civil War, including its currency, were being collected by historians on both sides of the conflict even before hostilities ended. I simply cannot suggest *any* candidate on which to confer the grandiose title of "first Confederate currency collector."

And as for Robert Alonzo Brock, I am still trying to determine if he possessed *any* Confederate currency collection... at all.

December 10, 1866. First Public Sale of the Seal of the Confederate Treasury Department.

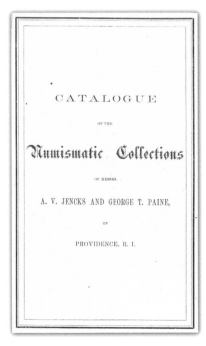

After the war ended in 1865, collecting anything Confederate became increasingly popular. Even before the Woodward sale of the $1,000 Montgomery in December 1865, Edward Cogan sold what were presumably the first "dealer lots" of Confederate currency on October 16 of that year: 23 pieces of $100 Confederate notes and 136 pieces of $20 Confederate notes. Even the venerable Seal of the Confederate Treasury Department *(Illus. 5)* was offered at a **W. Elliot Woodward** auction on December 10, 1866. From Woodward's catalog introduction, we know with certainty that the consignor was one of two gentlemen from Providence, R.I. – either George T. Paine or A. V. Jencks (*Illus. 6*, most likely Paine for reasons soon to become evident). Interestingly, the lot, estimated at an exorbitant $50, was withdrawn prior to its sale.

Illus. 5

According to a letter provided by the consignor and included in Woodward's lot description:

> The seal "was obtained from the custom house in Richmond, which was used by the rebel government for the accommodation of the Treasury Department, State Department, and for a private office for Jefferson Davis. It was obtained on the third day after the capture of Richmond by the United States forces, while the flames were still raging, and the streets were still filled with the scattered archives of the dead Confederacy. It was used to authenticate the official documents, bonds, etc., etc., that issued from the Treasury Department; its value and historic interest, therefore, will at once be seen."

Illus. 6

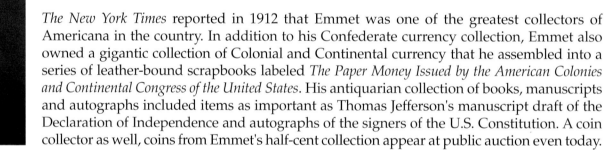

May- July- August, 1867. First Published Tabular Listing of Confederate Currency.

On March 14, 1867, the editor of the *American Journal of Numismatics*, the house organ of the American Numismatic Society in New York *(Illus. 7)*, received a request from J. T. Bowne of Long Island, N.Y. for the number, date and denominations of the different issues of Confederate currency. Editor Charles E. Anthon, a professor at the College of the City of New York, turned to **Dr. Thomas Addis Emmet** for the answer, as the editor described Emmet's Confederate currency collection as "more extensive probably than any other in existence."

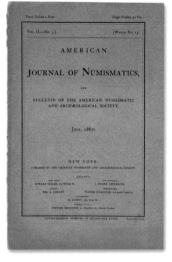

Thomas Addis Emmet *(Illus. 8)* was the perfect mouthpiece to disseminate the first hard facts about Confederate currency. Truly a "renaissance man," Emmet was the great-nephew of Irish nationalist Robert Emmet and was himself a tireless political activist for Irish home rule. Emmet was born in 1828 in Charlottesville, Va., where his father served as Professor of Chemistry and Pharmacology at the University of Virginia. In 1850 Emmet received his M.D. degree at Jefferson Medical College in Philadelphia. He left for New York City in 1855, becoming a surgeon at the Woman's Hospital and later surgeon-in-chief until 1872. In addition to his passions for medicine and collecting, he also found time to author the highly regarded *The Principles and Practice of Gynaecology*.

Illus. 7

According to Fred Reed, the Emmet family was aristocratic and blue-blooded. A later historian would describe the family as having "the status of 'Irish Royalty' in much the same way as The Kennedys have since the 1960s."

The New York Times reported in 1912 that Emmet was one of the greatest collectors of Americana in the country. In addition to his Confederate currency collection, Emmet also owned a gigantic collection of Colonial and Continental currency that he assembled into a series of leather-bound scrapbooks labeled *The Paper Money Issued by the American Colonies and Continental Congress of the United States*. His antiquarian collection of books, manuscripts and autographs included items as important as Thomas Jefferson's manuscript draft of the Declaration of Independence and autographs of the signers of the U.S. Constitution. A coin collector as well, coins from Emmet's half-cent collection appear at public auction even today.

Illus. 8 (courtesy Fred Reed)

Emmet also fancied himself as a builder. In 1912 at the age of 84, Emmet started construction on what *The New York Times* called "the most unusual, and in some cases the most interesting, home in the city... it will be on the top floor of the new sixteen-story building he is now erecting for business purposes on the southeast corner of Madison Avenue and Twenty-ninth Street... The architects state that this is the first time in the history of city architecture that provision for such an elaborate home has been made on top of a purely business building."

In essence, Emmet invented the New York penthouse. The Emmet Building at 95 Madison Avenue remains a Manhattan fixture to this day.

Emmet responded to the editor of the *American Journal of Numismatics* by assisting in the preparation of three charts tabulating Confederate currency that appeared in the May, July and August, 1867 issues of the *American Journal of Numismatics* (only the last chart is reproduced here, *Illus. 9, facing page*). His collection, consisting of 335 distinct varieties, is remarkable considering hostilities had ended less than two years earlier. He started the first chart with the 50-cent notes of 1863 and 1864 and ascended in denomination to conclude the third chart with the $1,000 Montgomery of 1861. Interestingly, though, Emmet was not aware of four of the rarest Confederate type notes when he completed his tables in 1867: Criswell Type-2 and Type-3 (the $500 and $100 Montgomerys), and Criswell Type-27 and Type-35 (the $10 "Shield and Eagle" and $5 "Indian Princess") had yet to be discovered.

Numismatic response to Emmet's publications was immediate and positive. At a meeting of the Rhode Island Numismatic Society on May 20, 1867, Emmet's first chart was brought to the attention of the entire membership and was praised for "the valuable matter contained in the published list of Confederate Currency." The member effusing such admiration was George T. Paine, the same gentleman who presumably consigned the Confederate Treasury Seal to an Elliot Woodward auction just five months earlier.

44 AMERICAN JOURNAL OF NUMISMATICS. [AUGUST, 1867.]

TABLE OF CONFEDERATE CURRENCY,

No. 3.

Denomination.	Date of Issue.	Title.	Color.	Design.	Specimens in Dr. Emmet's Collection, Denoted by Sub-Series.	Remarks.
$50.00	May 16, '61,		White; band of small 50s in green,	Group of negroes in cotton-field, in centre.	A.*	* Issued at Montgomery; interest-bearing.
"	Sep. 2, '61,	Series A,	White, with green on face,	Davis in centre.	X.†	† This, and the following ones, with exceptions noticed, issued at Richmond.
"	"	"	All white, plain back,	Female with money-chest in centre; two sailors in lower left corner.	D.‡	‡ Counterfeited from three different plates.
"	"	2d ser's A,	White, with green on face,	Davis in centre.	X.	
"	Dec. 2, '62,	3d " "	"	" "	W.	
"	Ap. 6, '63,	1st " "	"	" "	W, X.	
"	Feb. 17, '64,	Series A,	Red wavy face, blue back	" "	W, X, Y, Z.	
"	"	1st ser's A	"	" "	W, X, Y², Z.	
"	"	2d " "	"	" "	W, X, Y, Z.	
"	"	3d " "	"	" "	W, X, Y.	
"	"	4th " "	"	" "	X².	
100.00	Aug. 28, '61,		White; with C, and HUNDRED, in green on face,	Train of cars in centre; Minerva to right; female to left.	B.§	§ Printed at N. Orleans; interest-bearing, as are the ten following. Counterfeit, dated Sept. 2, '61, has negroes and cotton-wagon in centre, and sailor in left lower corner.
"	May 7, '62,	Series A,	All white,	Train of cars in centre; milkmaid in left lower corner.	b.	
"	June 16, '62,	"	"	" "	h.	
"	" 26, '62,	"	"	" "	d.	
"	July 14, '62,	"	"	" "	e.	
"	" 22, '62,	"	"	" "	c.	
"	Sep. 11, '62,	"	"	" "	a.	
"	" 18, '62,		White, with red on face,	Calhoun to left; negroes in cotton-field, in centre; female figure to right.	X.	
"	Nov. 3, '62,		"	" "	Z.	
"	Nov. 27, '62,		"	" "	W.	
"	Feb. 17, '64,		Pink face, & blue back,	Mrs. Davis in centre; Randolph in right lower corner; two soldiers to left.	A, B, C, D.	
"	"	1st series,	"	" "	A, B, C.	
"	"	2d "	"	" "	C, D.	
500.00	Feb. 17, '64.		Pink face, white back,	Stonewall Jackson to right; to left, the intended seal of the Confederate States, and the Confederate flag.	A, B, C, D.	
1000.00	June 24, '61,	Series A,	Green face, white back,	Calhoun to left; Andrew Jackson to right.‖		‖ Issued at Montgomery; interest-bearing. Extremely scarce. Engraved by the National Bank Note Company of New York.

In concluding our Tabulation of Confederate Money, it is needless to insist on its importance. The three Tables which we have furnished contain the frame-work, and much of the material, of a whole Treatise on the subject.

Illus. 9

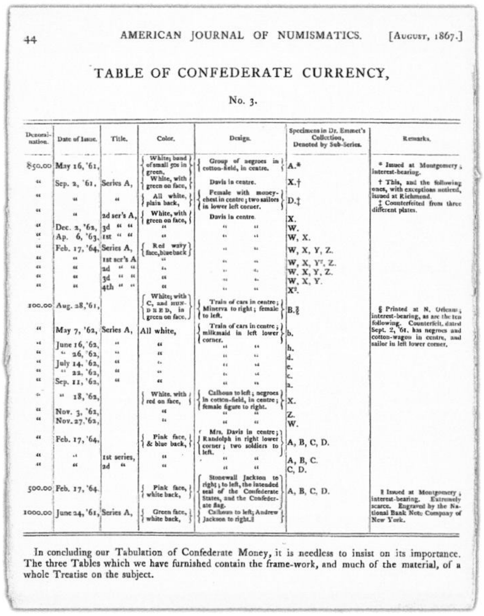

Happily, although we have no record of Emmet updating or expanding his tables in later issues of numismatic publications, his Confederate currency collection remains intact in the Rare Books section of the New York Public Library. Three leather-bound scrapbooks titled *The Paper Money and Bonds Issued by the Confederate States of America*, as well as his Colonial and Continental Currency collections and 10,800 historical manuscripts, were purchased in 1896 by John Stewart Kennedy and presented to the library. Mark Rabinowitz, who wrote extensively about Emmet in the November 2002 issue of *The Numismatist*, personally examined the collection and called it "something special. Over 150 pages, averaging four notes per page, are provided simply to cover the notes of 1861." And yes, Mark confirms that Emmet's collection by 1896 did indeed include all four of the Montgomerys.

Emmet's autobiography, *Incidents of My Life: Professional – Literary – Social, with Service in the Cause of Ireland*, was published in 1911. He died March 1, 1919, in his penthouse in New York at age 90, leaving a fortune then estimated at around a million dollars, according to the August 2 issue of *The British Medical Journal* that same year.

September 17, 1868. Discovery of S. Straker and Sons' "Chemicographic Backs."

Confederate Treasury agents traveled to Europe throughout the war to procure supplies and to look for alternatives that would save time and deter counterfeits. A considered scheme was to print each series of notes with standard backs of a European style. In 1863 Agent Joseph Walker contracted with the London firm of S. Straker and Sons to create electrotype plates using the novel and economical process called chemicography. Walker brought several of those plates with him on his return voyage home in October 1863.

Illus. 10

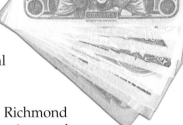

Memminger had those plates (likely the $5, $10, $20 and $50 denominations) in Richmond by January 1864. Full sets of plates, with the addition of $100 and $500 denominations and likely duplicates, were shipped on blockade runners from November 1863 through February 1864. It is unknown if any of those later shipments successfully made it through the Union blockade.

Prominent Boston numismatist **Charles Chaplin** apparently gained access to some of these plates. On September 17, 1868 he displayed a set of proofs of the Chemicographic backs, in denominations of $5, $10, $20 and $50, to the New England Numismatic and Archaeological Society (*Illus. 10*). His presentation of proofs in 1868 pre-dates by nearly nine years the generally accepted first report of the existence of these plates in the April 1877 issue of the *American Journal of Numismatics*, where he again provided illustrations of the S. Straker and Sons' designs.

1875. Publication of First Comprehensive Booklet about Confederate Currency.

William Lee, M.D. (born 1841, died March 2, 1893) was both a professor and physician practicing in Washington, D.C. Single, he lived with his parents at the time he published his booklet in 1875. Undoubtedly his interest in Confederate currency was fanned by his French-born father, who served as a clerk in the U.S. War Department.

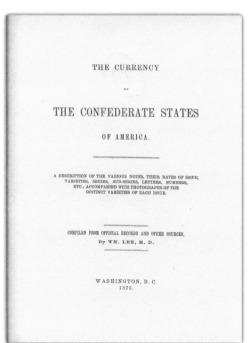

Dr. Lee applied the first systematic approach to cataloging Confederate currency when he assembled his booklet *(Illus. 11)* with a most imposing title: *The Currency of the Confederate States of America: a description of the various notes, their dates of issue, varieties, series, sub-series, letters, numbers, etc.; accompanied with photographs of the distinct varieties of each issue.* The booklet contained 27 pages, with some copies supplemented with 10 photographic plates at the back. The 10 plates depicted all the basic design "types" (except for the two "Essay Notes") that the Criswells created in their landmark 1957 edition discussed on page 82. In essence, as early as 1875 William Lee had described and photographed both the fronts and backs of 70 of Criswell's 72 modern "types."

Illus. 11

This softbound booklet is incredibly rare; in fact, numismatic literature dealer George Kolbe considers it second in rarity only to Raphael Thian's 1880 publication *Register of Issues of Confederate States Treasury Notes...*, of which a paltry half-dozen copies exist. According to Edouard Frossard, who auctioned Lee's Confederate currency collection in 1885, Lee's entire press run was limited to only 30 copies, probably reflecting the relatively small size of the collector base only 10 years after the war, with possibly 25 to 30 serious collectors and another peripheral group of 100 or so casual collectors. Perhaps half these copies contained photographic plates. Separate stand-alone plates, larger than those included in the booklet *(Illus. 12, facing page)*, were also printed and assembled in a handsome carrying case. Only two sets of these stand-alone plates are known to exist. These plates are as important as the booklet itself, as they represent the first photographs of a virtually complete "type set" of Confederate currency.

While perhaps modest by today's standards, Lee's publication was well received by periodicals such as the *American Journal of Numismatics* and the *Southern Historical Society Papers*. Dr. Lee's research was extensive, including a significant amount of correspondence with Samuel C. Upham, the famous Confederate and Southern States' counterfeiter. Despite Lee's intention to produce a second edition, regrettably he never did.

Lee might not have approved of my attempt to ascribe rates of return to Confederate currency. In a letter to his friend H. R. Storer just 10 days before his death, Lee admonished the "younger men... to collect what time makes more valuable, among the rare, the curious, the beautiful and the historic" (from the April 1893 issue of *The Numismatist*).

PLATE I.

[Entered according to Act of Congress, in the year 1875, by Wm. Lee, M. D., in the Office of the Librarian of Congress, at Washington, D. C.]

Illus. 12

December 1875. Only Appearance of John Gill, Possible Builder of "Greatest" Confederate Currency Collection.

Virtually all collectors, regardless of their area of specialization, invariably anoint some prominent enthusiast as "the greatest ever" or "the father of collecting this or that." Collectors of Confederate currency are no exception, with the title of "greatest collector ever" usually bestowed upon John C. Browne of Philadelphia, whose collection was dispersed through a number of donations, with the residue sold at a public auction conducted by Stan Henkels in 1922.

At first, my research convinced me that John Browne did indeed deserve his designation as "greatest ever," and my mentor and friend, the late Douglas B. Ball, who assembled one of the greatest Confederate collections himself, concurred. But I still wondered: who does the "greatest collector ever" turn to when even he wishes to embellish his already "greatest ever" collection?

The mysterious and elusive **John Gill** might be the answer. David Bowers reports that Gill made a single fleeting appearance at the Henry Whitmore auction conducted by Bangs, Merwin & Co. in 1859, but obviously no Confederate currency was offered at this auction as the Civil War was still two years away. Clearly, though, Gill had begun to assemble a gigantic collection of Confederate currency shortly after the war ended, as John W. Scott's monthly publication *Coin Collectors Journal* noted in its December 1875 issue the following excerpt from an article appearing in the *Nashville Banner*:

"John Gill of San Francisco, yesterday purchased from Mr. W.M. Duncan, of this city [Nashville], $750,000 in Confederate money, $50,000 worth of Confederate bonds, paying $50 in gold for them. The money and bonds were purchased by Wm. Duncan at the sale of the assetts (sic) of the Tennessee Bank, lately. Mr. Gill has five thousand specimens of Confederate issues and scrip. He left last night for Atlanta, where he will doubtless find millions more of the same sort."

By 1894, Gill's Confederate currency collection had gained a national reputation. Luther B. Tuthill of South Creek, N.C., a dealer and collector of Confederate currency who issued 25 to 30 fixed-price lists and regularly advertised in *The Numismatist* in the 1890s and 1900s, presented a paper entitled "Confederate Treasury Notes" at the ANA Convention in Detroit in August 1894. Tuthill's paper concluded with the statement that, "Mr. Gill has probably the finest collection as well as the largest in the country, closely followed by Mr. Thian, Mr. Phelps, Mr. Titcomb and others."

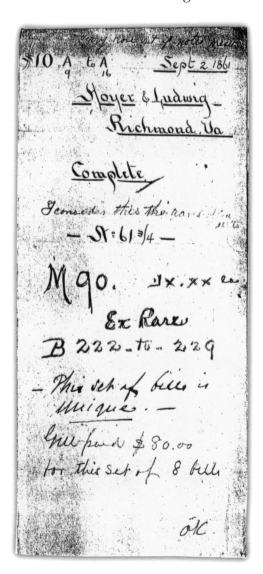

Illus. 13

Clearly Gill's collection was well known by 1894, yet he was never mentioned after the legendary collector John C. Browne claimed center stage by the early 1900s. Browne and Gill knew each other; in fact, John Browne purchased ultra-rare Confederate currency from John Gill. These rarities, listed as Criswell Varieties 222-229 in Criswell's final edition in 1996, were the $A_9 - A_{16}$ plen of the Type-27 "$10 Shield & Eagle" and were described as "extremely rare." They enjoy Criswell's highest rarity rating of 11 (meaning only one to four pieces exist). By the early 1900s Gill had sold this entire series of notes to Browne, who later donated them to the Historical Society of Pennsylvania. In turn the Society de-accessioned them and sold them to John J. Ford in 1963.

The envelope in which these notes were housed amazingly still exists and is shown at the left (the poor copy quality reflects the printer's best attempt to show all the hand-written comments). Two different handwriting styles are evident: a bold, heavy handwriting style with a slightly left tilt, and a lighter, more cursive style.

Careful study of this envelope and the notes inside is convincing evidence that they were once owned by both John Gill *and* John C. Browne. Looking at the front of the envelope *(Illus. 13)*, it appears that Gill first labeled the envelope as:

$10 A_9 to A_{16} Sept 2 1861
Hoyer & Ludwig _
Richmond, Va
Complete
I consider this the rarest of entire series.
– No 61 3/4 –
M90.   TX.XX ea.
Ex Rare
B222_ to _ 229
_ This set of bills is unique._

Further, looking at the back of the envelope *(Illus. 14)*, Gill apparently further wrote:

<u>M90</u>
These are exceedingly
Rare notes cost $80.
<u>low numbers. 1. 16. etc.</u>
A_9 – to – A_{16}

No W.M.
B_222_to_229 inc
Rarity. 8_

But there is a distinctly different handwriting on this envelope as well. And there is no question that it is the hand of John C. Browne, as he initialed his comments "JCB." Apparently Browne wrote on the front of the envelope (*Illus. 13 on facing page*):

Gill paid $80.00
for this set of 8 bills.
OK

And on the back Browne wrote:

(2) – 14
Gill considered these
the rarest notes of the
Confederate issues. He
paid $80. for set.
Have never seen other
notes of this series.
JCB

Bought one of these bills A_{14}
at Chapmans sale of
Chambers Collection
June 19, 1908.
JCB

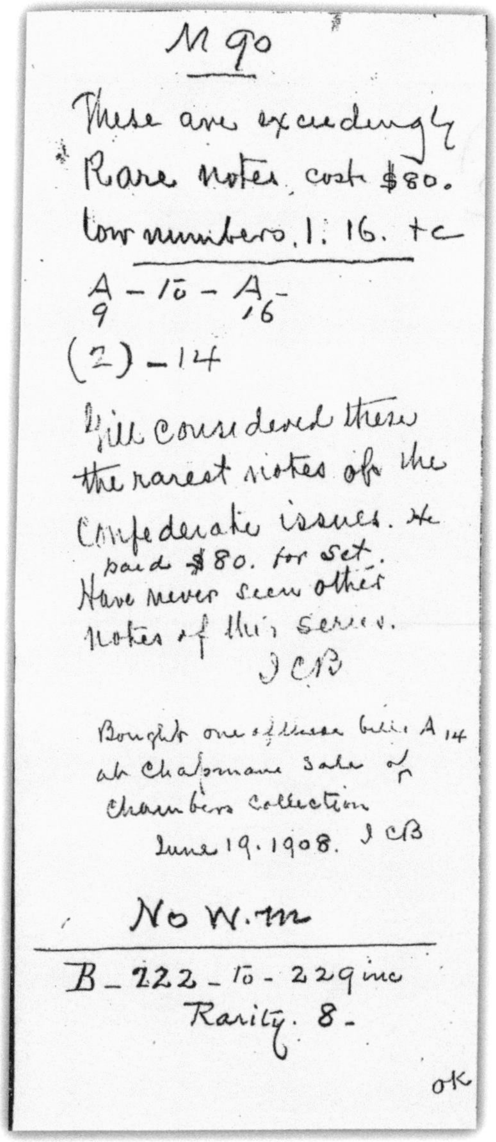
M 90
These are exceedingly
Rare notes. cost $80.
low numbers. 1. 16. tc
A_9 – to – A_{16}
(2) – 14
Gill considered these
the rarest notes of the
Confederate issues. He
paid $80. for set.
Have never seen other
notes of this series.
JCB
Bought one of these bills A_{14}
at Chapmans sale of
Chambers collection
June 19. 1908. JCB
No W.M
B_222_to_229 inc
Rarity. 8.
ok

Illus. 14

John Gill originally bought a complete set of all eight of these notes and paid $80 for the set. This fact is unassailable. But there were nine notes in the envelope – including an extra plen A_{14}. The fact that Browne bought the extra A_{14} at Henry Chapman's sale of the Harmon Chambers' collection in 1908 is equally unassailable, as Browne initialed this comment "JCB."

This envelope is remarkable. It ties together three of the greatest Confederate currency collectors ever: John Gill of San Francisco, John C. Browne of Philadelphia and Harmon Chambers of Philadelphia. It also raises a provocative question: did Browne purchase Gill's *entire* collection of Confederate currency between 1894, when Tuthill called Gill's collection "the largest in the country," and 1918 when Browne died? We *know* Browne purchased Gill's exceptionally rare set of Criswell Type-27s. There is nothing to suggest that Browne did not purchase the entire Gill collection, of which only a few envelopes used to house the collection have survived. Such a purchase would explain why Gill disappeared completely from numismatic records just after the turn of the century.

If Browne did indeed purchase the Gill collection, then I offer that Gill, and not Browne, more properly deserves the title of "greatest Confederate currency collector of all time." Or, for all the skeptics and cynics of this hypothesis, I suggest that the unknown person who sold the entire eight-note set of Criswell Type-27s to Gill in the first place is the *real* "greatest collector of all time."

1876. Assignment of First Catalog Numbers to Confederate Currency.

William Lee's 1875 booklet maintained the objectivity and teaching style expected from an author who was both a professor and a physician. But **John W. Haseltine** had a profit motive in his dual roles as both a dealer and promoter. He aggressively marketed his vast Confederate inventory in his 1876 catalog *Descriptive Catalog of Confederate Notes and Bonds for Sale (Illus. 15).* Haseltine's major contribution to the collecting of Confederate currency was the assignment of catalog numbers (he called them "H" numbers) to each of 137 variations – or "varieties" as Bradbeer and Criswell would later call them. His numbers were the first to be used as standard reference numbers by other dealers to follow. His tireless promotion popularized and created a market for Confederate currency.

Captain Haseltine (born 1838; died 1925) was a Philadelphia-born miner, artist, shoe salesman and legitimate Civil War hero, serving with great valor at both Bull Run and Gettysburg. However, he spent most of his adult life immersed in the coin business. Haseltine bridged the gap between the earliest dealers like Edward Cogan and Ebenezer Mason, with whom he worked, and the early twentieth century dealers like the Chapman brothers, whom he hired in the mid 1870s. Haseltine developed a complex and poorly understood relationship with various officials at the Philadelphia Mint, becoming a middleman between serious numismatists and the mint itself. It is generally acknowledged that John Haseltine was the leading authority in his day on four branches of numismatics, including Confederate currency.

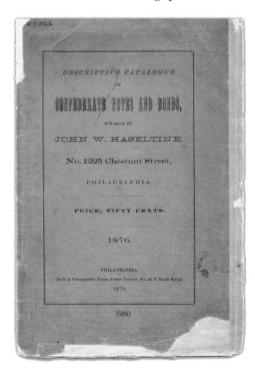

Illus. 15

Marrying well, Haseltine struck out on his own with the financial backing of his father-in-law, prominent numismatist William Idler, whose Colonial and Continental paper money collection Haseltine sold in 1870. Never shy and always unabashed (Fred Reed goes further and calls him "a showman and a slight-of-hand artist, whose life was filled with shenanigans, hyperbole, sub-rosa transactions and immaculate conceptions"), Haseltine first published a catalog of Colonial notes in 1872 before venturing into the field of Confederate currency.

Thomas Addis Emmet and William Lee both wrote publications designed to educate. But Haseltine's 1876 Confederate currency catalog was different: he offered Confederate currency *for sale.* Haseltine was a dealer in Confederate currency, maintained large inventories to satisfy demand and shamelessly prospered financially from his business acumen. How can you not be amused by such an individual, even if, as Fred suggests, he was also a con artist!

Haseltine's catalog was based on his own inventory, William Lee's 1875 booklet and the remarkable collection then being assembled by legendary and influential Confederate collector John C. Browne. The catalog contained 36 pages and is particularly rare: George Kolbe ranks it third in rarity behind only Thian's 1880 book and Lee's 1875 booklet. A reprint of Haseltine's 1876 catalog was distributed many years ago. It is frequently confused with the original, as it is not marked "Reprint" or dated in any way. The two can be easily distinguished from each other, however, by looking at the binding. The original is sewn together with thread; the reprint is bound with staples.

Of even greater rarity is a special, large-size version *(Illus. 16)* of Haseltine's catalog, "a few" of which were "printed on extra large and fine paper at one dollar per copy," according to Haseltine in the introduction to this catalog. George Kolbe has seen but two of these large-size versions in his 40-year career, the most recent selling for $7,500 in Kolbe's January 2009 public auction.

Fred Reed describes Haseltine as "the Grover Criswell of the 19th century." Both were the greatest experts of their time in the field of Confederate currency. Grover maintains his lofty position as a Confederate currency expert nonpareil to this day despite his death back in 1999. Sadly, though, numismatic bibliophile John Adams writes that Haseltine has "attracted little attention, even from advanced students."

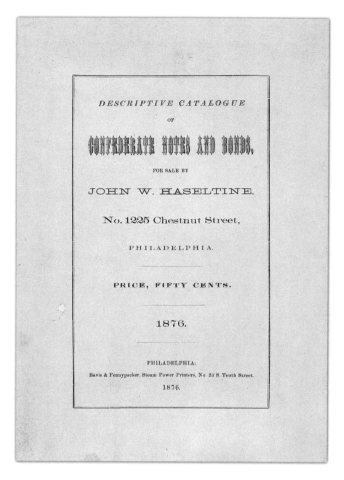

Illus. 16

![icon] **1876. Publication of First Album Designed for Confederate Currency.**

Raphael Thian, a little-known bureaucrat during his lifetime who has become one of the most important figures in the history of collecting Confederate currency over the past 50 years, produced a small supply of retail albums – perhaps 25 to 30 copies – designed to protect and display Confederate currency in an attractive manner. Thian's retail album, titled *Confederate Note Album for a Complete Collection (with Descriptive Letter-Press) of the various Designs for Face and Back selected by the Confederate Treasury Authorities for the Currency of the Confederate States of America. 1861-1865*, does not appear to have been advertised or promoted as a commercial venture, and might have been intended merely as a gift for friends who collected Confederate currency.

Douglas Ball, in his *Foreword* to the Quarterman reprint of Thian's *Register of the Confederate Debt* in 1972, advises that Thian, in his official capacity as the Chief Clerk of the Adjutant General's Office, prepared large gift scrapbooks filled with choice Confederate currency, bonds and even correspondence for presentation to several Civil War generals, including William T. Sherman. Confederate author and friend George Tremmel estimates that perhaps 13 to 14 of these large presentation albums were prepared as gifts. These albums were about four times the size of the small retail albums, having bigger dimensions as well as larger page counts – from 126 to 170 pages with notes mounted on both sides. They had room for both "types" of notes and the major "varieties" of that type. Perhaps the finest of these presentation albums was previously owned by Dave Bowers, who sold his specimen at a Stack's auction in Philadelphia in September 2010 for $126,500. This album, the crème de la crème, consisted of 418 pages containing 306 Confederate notes.

It would not take a great leap to think that Thian might have transferred some of the skills he developed in creating these large official presentation scrapbooks for Union generals and retiring politicians to the creation of smaller, privately produced retail versions to be gifted to his own friends and associates.

The possibility that Thian's 1876 retail albums were mainly designed as gifts is supported by their lack of uniformity. The small retail albums were covered in materials as diverse as inexpensive plain card stock *(Illus. 17)* to elaborate, full morocco leather. The covers were red, brown or green, some imprinted "C.S.A." in gold gilt, some bearing no imprint at all. Pages were of white, blue or purple stock.

Until recently, I believed that all of Thian's small retail albums had standard page counts: 45 pages of introductory explanatory text followed by 44 pages printed front and back with a frame or border onto which 88 Confederate notes could be attached. In January 2010, however, dealer George Kolbe sold a small Thian retail album pedigreed to the Stack Family Library with the same 45-page introductory text, but followed by 127 pages printed on one side only with a frame designed to contain 127 notes. This 127-page display section of Thian's retail album

Illus. 17 appears unique to the collecting fraternity and proves that there was some variability in the content as well as the style of his retail albums.

While Thian's small retail album might not have met, or even been designed to attract, commercial success, it is important because it showed that a need was growing among collectors to find a better way to display their Confederate currency. Thian was the first to try to satisfy that need. More biographical data on Thian will appear with his 1880 *Register of the Confederate Debt* beginning on page 41.

1877. Publication of First Commercial Album for Confederate Currency.

C.H. Bechtel was an obscure New York coin dealer who probably would have remained in numismatic anonymity if not for two noteworthy achievements: an auction catalog he prepared for the sale of J. E. Barratt's Confederate currency collection containing all four Montgomerys on March 25, 1879, and his creation of the Bechtel Confederate currency album.

It is conceivable that J. E. Barratt kept his own Confederate currency collection in a Bechtel currency album, which led him to request Bechtel to catalog his collection. More likely, though, Bechtel became involved only after Barratt consigned his collection to New York auction house Bangs, Merwin & Co. This auction house was a major presence in the sale of paintings and furniture, but played only a modest role in the field of numismatics. Bangs, knowing of Bechtel's expertise in the field of Confederate currency, probably hired Bechtel to catalog Barratt's consignment.

C. H. Bechtel is most important, though, for publishing the first commercially successful Confederate currency album. Published only a year after Thian's small-scale retail album was released with almost no advertising or publicity, it is unclear if Bechtel was even aware of Thian's effort. In the introduction to his album with title page *Album for Confederate Currency, containing numbered spaces for the insertion of a specimen of each type of the notes issued by authority of the Confederate government, together with a descriptive index*, Bechtel acknowledges contributions from William Lee and John Haseltine, but not Thian, who would not publish his own influential book until 1880.

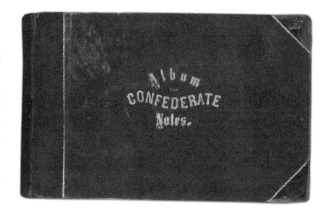

Illus. 18

Bechtel produced an elaborate, 90-page album *(Illus. 18)* designed to protect and display Confederate currency, with printed descriptions of the different types on each page. Nicely bound and professional-looking, Bechtel's album would not appear out of place in the finest libraries. I am proud of my own Bechtel album; indeed the fabled John C. Browne, a leading candidate for the title of Confederate currency's greatest collector of all time, housed his best notes in a Bechtel album, as described in the sale of his estate in 1922 by dealer Stan Henkels. Browne laid his notes loosely in his Bechtel album, as there was no easy way to mount them.

Bechtel originally sold his album for $3.50 to $5.00, an exorbitant price in line with the price of a mid-grade $100 or $50 Montgomery note at the time. Bechtel promoted his album by giving samples to prominent New York area collectors and by issuing "advertising notes" – genuine 1864 $5 Confederate Treasury Notes with a detailed advertising message printed on their backs *(Illus. 19)*. By 1877, collectors of Confederate currency had found a professional album to protect and house their Confederate collections.

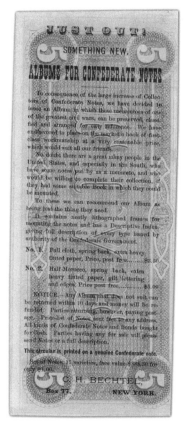

May 1879. First Effort to Define "Entirety" of a Confederate Currency collection.

Writer Fred Reed considers **John Walter Scott** "an overarching presence" in the collecting of Confederate currency. Certainly he made important contributions in at least three areas: the publication of a catalog in 1879 that included Confederate currency; an effort to define the entirety of a Confederate currency type collection at only 74 pieces, and the creation of the Confederate half-dollar restrikes.

Born in England in 1845, J. W. Scott *(Illus. 20, next page)* emigrated to New York City in 1863 and immediately attempted to start his first stamp dealership, a throwback to his stamp dealings in London begun at age 15. When his business failed, Scott left for the western gold mines but returned to New York in 1867 to try the stamp business again, this time with more success. Scott's stamp catalogs have been published continuously ever since. Besides his fixed-price lists, Scott conducted America's first public stamp auction in 1870, followed by England's first stamp auction in 1872. A whirlwind of energy, Scott justifiably has earned his title as "The Father of American Philately."

Illus. 19

Scott's accomplishments in numismatics, although exceptional in the field of Confederate currency, pale in comparison to what he did in philately. We are indebted to him, however, for first publishing *The Coin Collectors' Journal Illustrated* in 1875 and continuing it for 12 more years. It was here, in December 1875, that editor Edouard Frossard first made mention of Confederate currency collector extraordinaire John Gill (see the John Gill discussion, page 33).

In May of 1879, J.W. Scott's Scott & Company created a 40-page red-and-black catalog titled *Colonial, Continental, Confederate Currency: their present market value; to which is added a complete price list of U.S. fractional currency (Illus. 21).* Unfortunately his significant contribution to the collecting of Confederate currency was diminished by his decision to bury the Confederate section of this catalog behind the Colonial and Continental sections. Sold for a rather expensive 50 cents, this pamphlet opened with 31 pages on Colonial and Continental currency, embellished with 15 illustrations. Confederate currency, on the other hand, was relegated to pages 32 and 33 with no illustrations, followed by fractional currency on pages 34 and 35, also not illustrated.

Illus. 20 (courtesy Fred Reed)

While Scott's catalog failed to correct some of the errors that plagued the publications of William Lee and John Haseltine (like inclusion of the bogus "Female Riding Deer" note of 1861 and the $100 "Bogus Backs" of 1862), he nevertheless compartmentalized a complete Confederate currency collection into only 74 "types" neatly contained in one and a half pages. Ever the salesman, he then offered for immediate sale the more common material in a choice of grades, either Fine or Good.

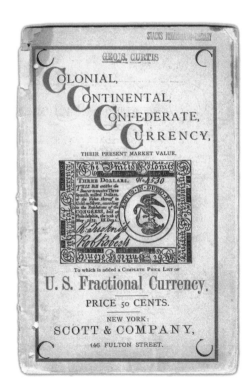

Illus. 21

Unlike the system developed by Grover and Clarence Criswell in 1957, Scott numbered his types from the lowest denominations to the highest within each of the seven authorized issues of Confederate currency; nevertheless, his system is so simple that even a casual collector of Confederate currency today could cross-reference, in a matter of minutes, the Scott type numbers to the Criswell type numbers we now rely on.

Fred Reed reports that Scott's 1879 catalog is remarkably rare – so rare, in fact, that no copies exist in collections of any of the cooperating institutions of WorldCat OCLC (a clearing house of over 10,000 libraries around the world containing over one and a half billion publications). I sheepishly must admit that the catalog shown here was part of an auction lot I purchased from numismatic literature dealer David Fanning in June 2010. Pedigreed to the Stack Family library, I bought the lot because it contained Scott's rare 4th Edition of 1894; the far rarer Scott 1879 first edition was included in the lot as literally "pure gravy."

John W. Scott gets credit for defining a complete Confederate currency collection at fewer than 100 pieces. In his 1879 catalog, he showed that he was the first dealer astute enough to recognize that collectors needed a sense of completeness and finality to their collections. In the face of an ever-increasing number of Confederate currency varieties – culminating in a savage rebuke titled "Collecting Run Mad" in the January 1877 issue of the *American Journal of Numismatics* – Scott calmly and thoughtfully went the other way and reduced the number of "types" of Confederate currency required to complete a Confederate currency collection to only 74; this number is remarkably close to the 72 or so types we use today. Collectors of Confederate currency now had a specific and realistic target to achieve a complete collection, as 74 pieces, while still not an easy task, was far less daunting than, for example, the 137 pieces listed by John Haseltine just three years earlier.

John Scott has suffered some ridicule over the years due to his propensity to mass produce and cheapen that which is rare and valuable. While perhaps a valid commentary on his own veracity, it unfairly detracts from the significant impact he had on collecting Confederate currency. It is unfortunate that Scott is primarily known in Confederate numismatics not for his currency catalogs or even for defining the entirety of a Confederate currency collection at a reasonable number of pieces, but rather for his coinage, the Scott half-dollar restrikes *(Illus. 22)*. While not on point within a book about Confederate currency price appreciation, and despite my longstanding uneasiness with these restrikes (I consider them nothing more than heavily promoted forgeries), their story deserves to be summarized here.

After obtaining from fellow dealer Ebenezer L. Mason the genuine reverse die used to strike the four authentic Confederate half-dollars, as well as one of the actual half-dollar coins, Scott located 500 regular-issue 1861 U.S. half dollars, planed off their reverses and then re-struck these regular issues with his Confederate reverse die. Despite being a slow seller at first, over time these restrikes have sold for considerable prices – a Brilliant Uncirculated specimen sold for $4,600 in Stack's 65th Anniversary Sale in October 2000.

Illus. 22 (courtesy Stack's Rare Coins)

Fred Reed calls John Walter Scott "*The* towering figure in the history of 19th century Confederate currency collecting." Not able to find an actual copy of Scott's 1879 catalog to review, Fred nonetheless reached the right conclusion but perhaps for the wrong reason. What Scott gave us Confederate currency collectors was simplification: in a period of "Confederate currency variety collecting gone wild," Scott understated with concise elegance the 74 "types" needed to achieve a complete Confederate currency collection. Who knows how many of us would have collected Confederate currency at all had this number been set much higher?

1880. Only Tabulation Covering All Details of Issuing Confederate Currency.

Raphael Prosper Thian has at times been described as a soldier, a bureaucrat, a Confederate historian, an author, a paper money dealer, an opportunist and a thief. At various points in his 60-year government career, he might have worn all these hats; but whether calculating or lucky, saint or sinner, Thian's 1880 *Register of the Confederate Debt* remains a pivotal work among all collectors of Confederate currency.

Thian would probably have remained an obscure government employee had it not been for Douglas Ball, who elevated Thian to Confederate superstar status with his excellent *Foreword* to the reprint of Thian's *Register*, published by Quarterman Publications in Boston in 1972. Only a half-dozen copies exist of Thian's original work published in 1880, making Doug instrumental in ensuring that Thian's *Register* was made broadly available to all Confederate enthusiasts through the 1972 reprint.

While Doug properly deserves credit for making Thian a household name among Confederate currency collectors, it was columnist Fred Reed who amplified Doug's writings, challenged his assertions, corrected his errors -- and discovered the existence of a hitherto unknown sixth copy of Thian's original 1880 publication right under Doug's nose at the Virginia Historical Society in Richmond. Fred's columns on Thian began appearing in the July 2011 issue of *Bank Note Reporter*, and I heartily commend the entire series to the reader.

Doug's *Foreword* provides what we know about Thian's upbringing. He was born in France in 1830, the son of a retired soldier who had served under Napoleon. At age 18, with France experiencing political unrest and high unemployment, Thian sailed to North America, arriving in French-speaking Quebec to compensate for his poor command of English. Only two years later, in November 1850, armed with new confidence in the English language, Thian followed in his father's footsteps when he enlisted in the U.S. Army, first assigned to Buffalo, N.Y.

According to Ball, by 1853 Thian had landed a desk job at the Headquarters of the Army in New York. His exemplary work was noticed by General Winfield Scott, who persuaded him to resign his active duty career and instead take a position with the civilian staff. Thian was appointed Clerk second class and remained with Scott until he retired in November 1861.

With his mentor now retired, Thian was forced to rely on his well-honed skills and a bit of good luck to get ahead. He found a new position in the Adjutant General's Office (AGO) where he advanced rapidly to Clerk fourth class by April 1864, becoming Chief Clerk of the AGO on July 1, 1871, and holding that position for the next 40 years. On December 19, 1911, Thian died at age 81, having served the government for 61 years. He left behind a wife, children and the letdown that only a crumb of his life's work would ever be published.

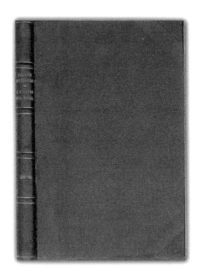

Illus. 23

After researching the War Department's Rebel Archives from 1867 to 1886, Thian originally intended to produce a ten-volume series titled *The Treasury of the Confederate States*. Five of these volumes have not been seen, even as manuscripts. A single copy of Volume I was printed, titled *Extracts from the Journals of the Provisional Congress and of the First and Second Congresses of the Confederate States of America on Legislation affecting Finance, Revenue, and Commerce*, but it has been missing from the National Archives for over 40 years. Tiny numbers of Vols. III, IV and V were printed that now reside in various institutions.

Thian's seminal volume was his Volume II, *Register of Issues of Confederate States Treasury Notes Together With Tabular Exhibits of the Debt, Funded and Unfunded of the Confederate States of America 1861-1865* – usually shortened to the *Register of the Confederate Debt*. George Kolbe states that Thian's *Register* is unquestionably the rarest publication in the Confederate currency series. In fact, in private correspondence with collector Armand Champa in 1983, John Ford went a step further and wrote that, "This is easily the rarest book in American numismatics."

For years only five copies were known to exist. According to George Kolbe, "three are now in institutional hands, namely the Library of Congress, Duke University Library, and the American Numismatic Society Library." The fourth copy "resides in a private library." The fifth copy is shown as Illus. 23 and was purchased by John Ford in 1960 for $110. It was sold to a private collector at George Kolbe's 2004 public auction of Ford's private library as Lot 896 for $35,650, a 324-fold increase over 44 years. Apparently the price appreciation enjoyed by Confederate publications rivals even that of Confederate currency! Fred Reed recently reported his discovery of the sixth copy at the Virginia Historical Society in Richmond in the October 2011 issue of *Bank Note Reporter*.

Thian's *Register of the Confederate Debt* was initially intended to be the *Appendix, The Treasury Note Bureau*. As Thian planned it, this supplementary volume was to include correspondence with Treasury note engravers and printers and similar matters about the production of Confederate securities. In addition to this correspondence, there was also to be a "full register of issues of Confederate notes, tabular exhibits of the funded and unfunded debt...", along with descriptions of the several designs used for the notes.

According to Ball, the correspondence with engravers and printers was made part of Thian's Volumes IV and V and was never printed separately. The descriptions of the designs used for the Treasury notes were left in one of four scrapbooks in Thian's personal possession which were sold by Thian's son to the Duke University Library in 1944. Thus Thian's original grand scheme for Volume II was reduced to a "full register of issues of Confederate notes, tabular exhibits of the funded and unfunded debt…" that was actually printed.

Thian's *Register* is a compilation from the official Confederate Treasury records of the precise denominations printed of each series, their plate letters, their serial numbers, their signers, their dates of issuance if the notes were interest-bearing and the total quantity of each design issued. In essence, Thian summarized virtually each individual piece of Confederate currency of the millions issued by the Confederate Treasury in a small book containing only 190 pages. Whether compiled during his "leisure time" or while on the government payroll is irrelevant – his *Register* remains a cornerstone of Confederate numismatics.

Although Thian is best known for compiling his *Register*, his role as a Confederate currency collector and dealer should at least be mentioned. He published a comprehensive catalog titled *The Currency of the Confederate States, Arranged by Issues, Denominations, and Series* in Washington, D.C., with a printed date of 1884 (but changed to "1885" in brown ink in all copies I have seen). Thian's catalog *(Illus. 23-A)* contained 19 pages and listed 275 varieties, twice the 137 varieties listed in Haseltine's catalog just nine years earlier. Like his *Register*, Thian's catalog is also very rare, suggesting a small print run. Not offering currency for sale, it thus seems designed to educate like William Lee's 1875 effort rather than to sell like Haseltine's and Scott's catalogs.

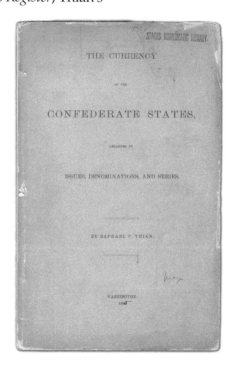

I personally believe that Thian's role as a dealer is overstated, as I suspect he managed, at most, a minor sideline dealer business. Thian has been portrayed as a prominent Confederate currency dealer, with the evidence of his dealer activities being the remarkable Confederate currency collection he sold at a David Proskey auction in 1885. But I view this sale as proof of his consummate collector passions, not his dealer inventory. In 1894 Luther Tuthill called John Gill's collection (page 34) "the finest…as well as the largest in the country, closely followed by Mr. Thian…" Tuthill's statement convinces me of Thian's abiding interest in Confederate currency as a collector, like Gill or Browne, more so than a dealer like Haseltine or Scott.

I find it unfortunate that Raphael Thian has long been subjected to much insinuation, speculation, innuendo – even outright charges – that he was a thief: allegedly researching his personal passion for Confederate currency while on government time and taking those specimens he wished to keep or sell. I am not ready to indict so quickly for three reasons.

First, Thian's research was specifically requested by his former supervisor. In a letter dated January 7, 1887 to the retired Adjutant General E. D. Townsend, Thian writes:

Illus. 23-A

> "It is now nearly twelve years since you suggested to me that my leisure hours [*'leisure hours' will be defined by the author later*] be given to preparing a history of the several issues of paper money emitted from the Treasury of the Confederate States, and that, for this purpose, you afforded me special facilities for examining the many books and papers which the War Department, in accordance with your singularly far-sighted suggestion, caused to be carefully collected and preserved from possible destruction."

This letter is clear evidence that preparing a history of the Confederate Treasury was the brainchild of General Townsend, not Chief Clerk Thian. Nothing whatsoever suggests that Thian had a pre-existing interest in Confederate currency; in fact, he possibly viewed it as nothing more than more work. The charge that Thian placed his personal interest in Confederate currency above his administrative responsibilities simply does not hold water.

Second, Thian performed his research on "leisure time," not "spare time." In Doug Ball's *Foreword* to the Quarterman reprint, he suggested that Thian performed his research "in his spare time." But in the letter dated January 7, 1887, and quoted earlier, Thian used the term "leisure" time. "Spare time," as used by Ball, and "leisure time," as used by Thian, have different meanings. "Spare time" is defined in the Free Online Dictionary by Farlex as "time available for hobbies and other activities you enjoy." But the same dictionary defines "leisure time" as "time that is free from time-consuming duties, responsibilities or activities." Leisure time can be time on the job when one's normal work duties are all caught up.

Even in an office as busy and electric as Thian's AGO, surely there were periods of time when assigned responsibilities were caught up. Today's employees use this "leisure time" to surf the Web or to participate in the office football pool. Thian, on the other hand, used his "leisure time" – at the specific request of his supervisor when official duties were finished – to research the history of the Confederate Treasury. I see absolutely nothing inappropriate about Thian's activities, despite his drawing a government paycheck.

My third reason for cutting Thian some slack reflects the fact that Confederate currency was seemingly available for the asking from Federal officials in the late 1800s. Brent Hughes, Confederate author and historian, appraised a huge hoard of 15,000 Confederate notes in 1952 in Washington, D.C. Hughes recounted this story in the May-June 1994 issue of *Paper Money*, the official publication of the Society of Paper Money Collectors. Hughes told how he, accompanied by the president of the Washington Numismatic Society, arrived at a home in suburban Washington and was met by a gracious 75-year-old lady standing next to two open suitcases filled with Confederate currency. The lady's father had gone to work at the U.S. Treasury Building in 1875. At that time, rebel paper money had little or no value and Treasury employees who expressed interest were told to take some home if they wished.

According to this lady, her "father was called into his supervisor's office around 1894 and was told that the Treasury Department was cleaning house to gain office space… so the 'rebel junk' had to go. My father was told that if he wanted the notes, he could have them, but he had to get them out that day or they would be burned. Daddy went to a nearby livery stable and rented a horse and buggy, backed it up to a door on Fifteenth Street and loaded these suitcases and several small boxes into it. He then drove the buggy home, put the items in his study and returned the rig to the stable. I inherited all his possessions when he died in 1932."

This lady's father worked at Treasury while the Rebel Archives were housed in various locations of the War Department. Nevertheless, Doug Ball's *Foreword* states that some of the Rebel Archives "were transferred to other departments." Certainly one of these departments would have been the Treasury Department, as one of Thian's responsibilities as Chief Clerk of the AGO was to answer "a growing volume of inquiries from the Treasury."

If an employee of Treasury was given 15,000 pieces of Confederate currency at no cost, then surely Thian had the same right to obtain what Confederate currency he wanted – also at no cost – from the War Department. Admittedly, Thian's extensive research gave him a huge advantage in knowing what was rare and valuable and thus exactly what to take.

But superior knowledge is no crime. Knowing that Confederate currency was being given away for free in other Federal departments like the Treasury, as this lady's anecdote attests, convinces me that if Thian also helped himself to Confederate currency – and I am confident that he did – then he did nothing inappropriate, and certainly nothing illegal.

I have long felt that Raphael Thian's significant contributions to the hobby of collecting Confederate currency have been tainted by suggestions of impropriety in how he obtained the official data and how he acquired Confederate notes at no cost. But I have never seen any proof that his actions were dishonest, or for that matter, any different from the actions of others who also had access to the Rebel Archives. Perhaps it is time to recognize his 20 years of research and place Thian on a rostrum reserved only for giants in collecting Confederate currency.

Circa 1882. First Confederate Currency Publication to Issue a Second Edition.

In many ways we measure a book's success by the number of editions or revisions it publishes. Confederate author Grover Criswell published five editions between 1957 and 1996; his friendly competitor Arlie Slabaugh published ten editions between 1958 and 2000.

But early Confederate authors were of the "one and done" genre. Thomas Addis Emmet, William Lee, even John Haseltine – none of them saw the continuing goodwill or, in Haseltine's case, the repeat business prospects that successive editions might bring. Not surprisingly, it took a dealer with vast experience in successive stamp catalogs – **John Walter Scott** – to bring a second edition to collectors of Confederate currency.

Scott's first edition was published in May 1879 and contained 40 pages (see page 39). His second edition was expanded slightly to include 44 pages, although the Confederate currency offering remained at a modest two pages. The front cover was given an entirely new look, presumably to align with the stamp and coin catalogs – a critical part of Scott's stable of products. The second edition *(Illus. 24)*, titled *Scott's Standard Catalogues. No. 2. Paper Money. Second Edition.*, was published around 1882, as estimated by *Bank Note Reporter* columnist Fred Reed, although the precise date is not known. Presumably the catalog was sub-titled *No. 2. Paper Money* to distinguish it from the more famous and far more established *No. 1. Standard Stamp Catalogue.*

The Confederate section of Scott's second edition was little changed from the first: only two pages with no illustrations. Even the errors found in the first edition, like the bogus "Female Riding Deer" note of 1861, were carried over into the second edition. The catalog price, however, was reduced to 25 cents, half the price of the first edition, presumably to be consistent with the price of Scott's other catalogs and to broaden consumer trial and awareness. Importantly, Scott maintained the concise 74 "types" required to complete a Confederate currency collection, the simplification that is Scott's most important contribution to the collection of Confederate currency.

Illus. 24

Fred Reed reports that Scott's 1882 second edition is even more rare than his first edition, of which only six copies (four in institutions) are known. Like the rare first edition, my personal copy of the second edition was a part of a much larger auction lot of 10 to 12 catalogs found

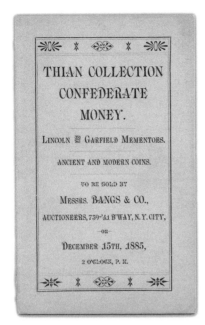

Illus. 25

in a sale conducted by the eminent George Kolbe, who later professed that John W. Scott was not well understood by dealers in numismatic literature.

Scott published two more catalogs with Confederate content in 1889 and 1894. By then he had sold his company and left the responsibility of the Confederate currency section to the new owners. The numbering system they adopted was a throwback to John Haseltine, as will soon be seen.

December 1885. Sale at Public Auction of Two Famous Confederate Collections.

This book is about the price appreciation of Confederate currency over time, with price data extracted from thousands of public auction records since 1865. It is reassuring to note that two of the three earliest giants in collecting Confederate currency – **Raphael Thian** and **William Lee** – both chose to liquidate their own collections via the public auction (the collection of the third, Thomas Addis Emmet, is part of the Rare Books section of the New York Public Library). Coincidentally, both collectors chose different auction houses for their sales held just one week apart in December 1885.

Thian's collection was sold on December 15, 1885, at the offices of Bangs & Co., New York *(Illus. 25)*. The collection, catalogued by David Proskey of Patterson, N.J., contained thousands of pieces of Confederate currency: Lot 193 alone contained 853 pieces and sold for $21.33.

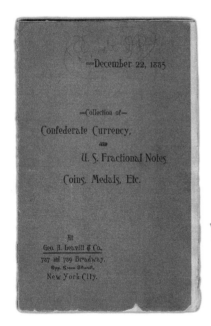

Illus. 26

A week later on December 22, 1885, Lee's collection was sold at the offices of George A. Leavitt & Co., New York *(Illus. 26)*. Lee's collection, catalogued by Edouard Frossard, contained 1,435 notes and a very rare copy of the Bechtel Confederate Currency Album (see page 38). Interestingly, the album sold for only 93 cents, the value of the 37 pieces of common currency it contained. On the other hand, a copy of Lee's own ultra-rare pamphlet published in 1875 sold for $13.25, nearly as much as the $15.00 realized by the Criswell Type-1 "$1,000 Montgomery"!

1889. Publication of a Simplified and Corrected Version of Previous Catalogs.

George W. Massamore was a refreshing alter-ego to the shenanigans-and-antics style of Confederate currency promoter and dealer John Haseltine a decade earlier. Humble and self-effacing, Massamore came along at a time when collecting Confederate currency was becoming overheated. His low-key and understated approach helped to rein in the excesses Haseltine started, putting collecting Confederate currency on a sustainable growth curve that we continue to enjoy today.

As different in style as were Massamore and Haseltine, their backgrounds were quite similar. Maryland born in 1845, a 16-year-old Massamore enlisted in the army – on the Confederate side, unlike Haseltine – at the beginning of hostilities in 1861 and served until the war's conclusion. While Union Captain Haseltine became an artist after the war, Confederate veteran Massamore became a dentist, receiving his D.D.S. degree in 1868. John Adams writes in his *United States Numismatic Literature* that Massamore also "found time to participate in a variety of civic responsibilities and was one of the area's first conservationists."

The trigger for Massamore's interest in numismatics is unclear, although it might have been the myriad of pieces of Confederate currency he exchanged during the war itself. Regardless, we know that he became a founding member of the Baltimore Numismatic Society in 1876. Four years later, in 1880, he became its secretary and concurrently formed a coin and stamp dealership named Massamore and Co.

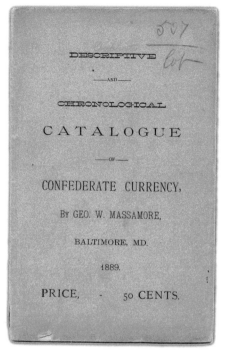

It would be four more years before Massamore broadened his product line to include Confederate currency. But his membership in the Confederate Hall of Fame stems from his Confederate currency catalog issued in 1889 titled *Descriptive and Chronological Catalogue of Confederate Currency*. Published in a soft orange cover and containing 24 pages, Massamore's catalog *(Illus. 27)* was seemingly designed to simplify and correct some of the mistakes found in Haseltine's and Scott's previous works. Being a dealer, Massamore had inventory on hand to back up his realistic pricing. He thus became the third dealer after Haseltine and Scott to market-price his Confederate currency for immediate sale.

Bank Note Reporter columnist Fred Reed considers Massamore's catalog extremely rare – more rare even than Haseltine's 1876 effort. Surely Massamore's pamphlet is hard to find, but I am confident that it does not approach the rarity of the Haseltine booklet, and I doubt that Massamore's effort is even as rare as the first two editions of Scott's catalogs in 1879 and 1882. Not being an expert on rarity of various numismatic publications, though, I consulted the venerable George Kolbe who considers Thian's 1880 book to be the rarest of all Confederate publications, followed by William Lee's 1875 booklet as the second rarest, and Haseltine's 1876 pamphlet as third.

Illus. 27

Fred expresses great admiration for Massamore's catalog in his June 2005 column in *Bank Note Reporter*, calling Massamore's effort "a monumental contribution to the evolution of [the Confederate] note collecting hobby." Fred issues his kudos based on a comparison of Haseltine's effort in 1876 with Massamore's work product in 1889. Massamore's presentation – just Date, Issuer and Denomination – was indeed much cleaner and simpler than Haseltine's rather haphazard organization. In addition, Massamore corrected most of the errors found in earlier works, and in his humble style, even excused his predecessors for making the mistakes in the first place. Massamore took a more didactic approach to the bogus "$20 Female Riding Deer" note of 1861, simply stating that:

> "I have always regarded this note...a fraud. The one in my collection, and all others that have come under my observation are undoubtedly frauds; [I] will not call them counterfeits, as I have no knowledge of there ever having been a genuine note of this type issued."

Massamore's 1889 Confederate currency catalog came at an important point in the chronology of collecting Confederate currency: about 15 years after the initial efforts of Lee, Haseltine and Scott, and about 25 years before Bradbeer's historic work in 1915 that would serve as the template for Grover and Clarence Criswell's 1957 landmark publication. His importance as a cataloger will always be recognized, but in my opinion, he will forever rest a step below the field's true giants for at least two reasons.

First, I believe Massamore failed to give proper credit for major discoveries made by his competitors. For example, his discussion about the nature of the bogus "Female Riding Deer" note in his 1889 catalog quoted on the previous page was at best disingenuous and at worst downright deceitful. Massamore knew, or should have known, that the spurious character of this note had been questioned at least as early as 1875, almost 15 years previously. William Lee's 1875 pamphlet noted that his photograph of the "note is taken from a fac-simile." Eminent dealer Edouard Frossard had written in a December 1883 auction that the "Female Riding Deer" note was a "fac-simile." Leading dealer Lyman Low was more blunt; in cataloging an auction in March 1885, Low headlined his Confederate Currency section by flatly stating that the "Female Riding Deer" note "does not exist. It was a fraud copied from a design used in 1863 on Monroe County, Tenn. notes." The July 1886 issue of *The Stamp and Coin Gazette* further debunked the "Female Riding Deer" note. Yet Massamore, when announcing in his catalog that these notes "are undoubtedly frauds," failed to mention that similar comments dating back to 1875 had been first trumpeted by his competitors. Massamore simply appropriated for his own use what other dealers had already discovered.

Second, I am even more disappointed in Massamore for further variety proliferation. He failed to build on what John W. Scott had already started with his first two catalog editions in 1879 and 1882. At a time when the proliferation of Confederate currency varieties had "gone mad," John Scott, as described earlier, took the courageous and astute action of reducing the number of "types" required to complete an entire Confederate currency collection to 74. Massamore increased that total to a whopping 314, more than double the count of Haseltine's 137 varieties.

Massamore missed the significance of Scott's 74 "types." Had he taken Scott's 74 "types" and further differentiated them into his 314 "varieties," he would have accomplished what the Criswells did in 1957 – and Massamore would have initiated the modern phase of the collecting of Confederate currency nearly 75 years earlier. While Massamore failed to capitalize on his opportunity, he nevertheless *almost* got it right.

Massamore died on April 7, 1898. His large collection was liquidated via public auction, like Thian's and Lee's before him, but this time by the Chapman Brothers on April 11-12, 1899. While extensive, the collection was missing many rarities, including all four Montgomerys.

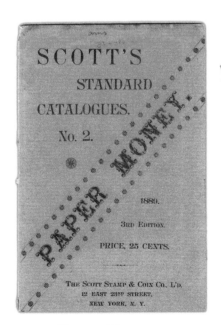

Illus. 28 (Courtesy Eric Newman)

1889 & 1894. The Start of Repetitive Editions of Confederate Currency Catalogs.

John Walter Scott brought back a measure of sanity to the collecting of Confederate currency with his first two paper money catalogs issued in 1879 and around 1882. We will never know what Scott's ultimate impact on Confederate currency might have been, however, because in 1885 he sold all his business interests, including the company name (Scott Stamp and Coin Co., Ltd.), his catalogs and his copyrights.

The purchasers of Scott's assets were **Henry Collin** and **Henry L. Calman**, younger brother of Gustavus B. Calman who operated the largest stamp wholesale business in the country at the time. Four years later, in 1889, the company issued the third edition of its paper money catalog, titled *Scott's Standard Catalogues. No. 2. Paper Money. 1889. 3rd Edition (Illus. 28)*. This third edition was advertised as being enlarged to 52 pages with 23 new illustrations, but the Confederate currency section remained a paltry two pages, the same size as the first two editions when J.W. Scott still owned the company.

Fred Reed reports that Scott's third edition is rare, although not quite as rare as the first two editions. Fred is aware of at least three copies, with two of them archived in institutions.

Five years later, in 1894, the company issued its fourth and final edition, titled *Scott's Standard Catalogues. No. 2. Paper Money. 1894. 4th Edition (Illus. 29)*. This release is the most common of the four Scott paper money catalogs – although by no means easy to find. It contained 144 pages, a sharp increase in page count from the previous three editions, and was perfect bound. The Confederate currency section was also enlarged from only two pages in the first three editions to five pages in the fourth edition. The extra pages were used to provide more complete descriptions of each of the varieties listed. For example, the dates of the acts authorizing each issue were shown, printers and their locations were listed and serial-letter combinations were provided. Prices were reduced from the third edition, either in an attempt to grow the market, or to reflect a return to more sustainable times after the heady days of the 1880s – or simply to reduce inventory, as Collin and Calman wished to concentrate their interests on the philatelic side of the business.

Comparing Scott's third and fourth editions to its first two editions is meaningless, since the first two editions were published when Scott still owned the firm, while the final two editions were published under the Collin/Calman brothers' ownership. Unfortunately, in my opinion, under the new ownership, the company reverted to the seemingly mindless proliferation of the number of varieties in both the third and fourth editions. For example, in the *Introduction* to the Confederate currency section of the fourth edition, the editor wrote:

> "The varieties of the several series enumerated are too numerous for description here... The prices here affixed are for the most common notes. When particular serial letters or varieties are wanted, we are prepared to quote prices on same when in stock."

Scott's third and fourth editions were arranged using John Haseltine's numbering system found in his 1876 Confederate currency fixed-price list, although this fact was not disclosed to the reader. Haseltine's numbering system (using "H-numbers") ranged from 1 to 137; Scott chose to list only about 70 of the most common of Haseltine's 137 varieties. The confused reader would thus find consecutive listings numbered as 92, 98, 104, 109, 112 – with no explanation whatsoever for the missing numbers. Perhaps the company assumed the reader understood that the missing numbers were rare varieties, although failure to describe the numbering system seems inconsistent with the firm's presumed desire to appeal to a new and broader group of hobbyists.

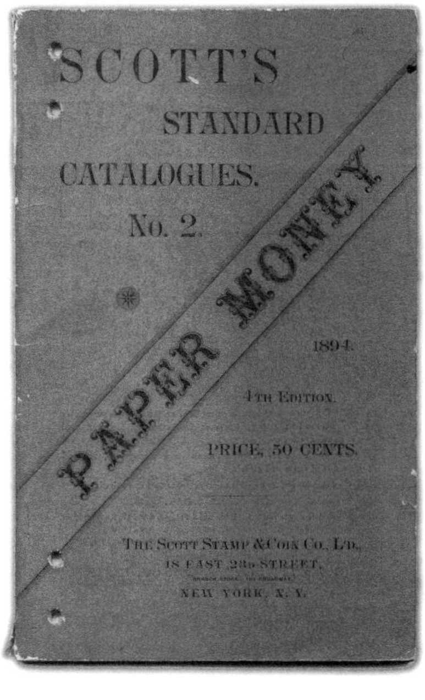

While the company reverted to the Haseltine numbering system for its third and fourth editions, at least it chose to list only about 70 varieties (72 in the third edition and 70 in the fourth). Unwittingly, perhaps, Scott reinforced the "70-something" major designs listed in the company's first two editions and the similar number introduced by Grover and Clarence Criswell in 1957 as the 72 "types" we use today.

While Scott's old company continued to thrive, John Scott himself suffered seller's remorse. In 1889 he organized a new company called J.W. Scott & Co., Ltd., and after

Illus. 29

a protracted legal battle was able to resume his role as a leading philatelic and numismatic dealer. Scott joined the ANA in 1903 and the ANS three years later. He sold his second company in 1917 to J.E. Handshaw. Scott died on January 4, 1919, when he was president of the American Philatelic Society. To this day, John Scott remains the only individual elected to both the American Philatelic Society Hall of Fame *and* the American Numismatic Association Hall of Fame. Truly he was, as labeled by Fred Reed, the "outstanding presence in the [Confederate currency] field in the half century following Appomattox."

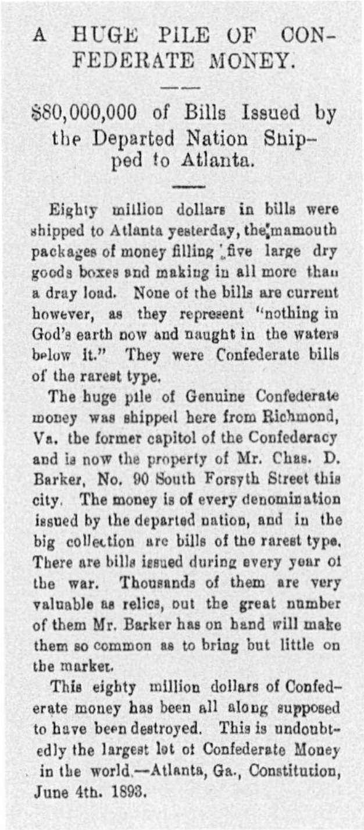

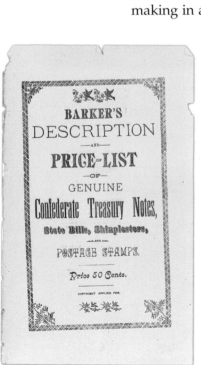

A HUGE PILE OF CONFEDERATE MONEY.

$80,000,000 of Bills Issued by the Departed Nation Shipped to Atlanta.

Eighty million dollars in bills were shipped to Atlanta yesterday, the mammoth packages of money filling five large dry goods boxes and making in all more than a dray load. None of the bills are current however, as they represent "nothing in God's earth now and naught in the waters below it." They were Confederate bills of the rarest type.

The huge pile of Genuine Confederate money was shipped here from Richmond, Va. the former capitol of the Confederacy and is now the property of Mr. Chas. D. Barker, No. 90 South Forsyth Street this city. The money is of every denomination issued by the departed nation, and in the big collection are bills of the rarest type. There are bills issued during every year of the war. Thousands of them are very valuable as relics, out the great number of them Mr. Barker has on hand will make them so common as to bring but little on the market.

This eighty million dollars of Confederate money has been all along supposed to have been destroyed. This is undoubtedly the largest lot of Confederate Money in the world.—Atlanta, Ga., Constitution, June 4th. 1893.

Illus. 30

1893. Largest-Ever Hoard of Confederate Currency Is Sold to an Atlanta Dealer.

Hidden treasure. The words evoke dreams of discovering a huge cache of something valuable, like gold coins from an old shipwreck or Impressionist paintings in a cluttered attic. Even steamer trunks filled with Confederate currency.

In his *Reminiscences* on page 12, Clarence Criswell recounted that he and brother Grover never found a huge hoard of Confederate currency, despite being on the lookout starting in the 1940s. The great early Confederate currency collector John Gill found a large hoard of $750,000 of Confederate currency in Nashville, Tenn., in 1875, which was previously the property of the Tennessee Bank. Brent Hughes, Confederate historian and author, found two suitcases filled with 15,000 pieces of Confederate currency in suburban Washington, D.C. in 1952, the property of the daughter of a former Treasury Department employee during the 1880s.

But all these discoveries pale by comparison to the hoard found in Richmond, Va., in 1893. According to an article that appeared in *The Atlanta Constitution* on June 4 of that year *(Illus. 30)*, a cache of 80 million Confederate dollars was found in Richmond, the capital of the Confederate government. Scheduled for destruction that never happened, the hoard was shipped to its new owner in Atlanta, with that same article describing "the mammoth packages of money filling five large dry goods boxes and making in all more than a dray load… The money is of every denomination issued by the departed nation, and in the big collection are bills of the rarest type. There are bills issued during every year of the war… This is undoubtedly the largest lot of Confederate Money in the world."

Charles D. Barker, a little-known Atlanta dealer filled with big dreams that quickly evaporated, was the purchaser of this huge hoard of Confederate currency. He opened a storefront at 90 South Forsyth Street in downtown Atlanta in the 1890s and was unique for two reasons. First, he was a Southern numismatist at a time when virtually all numismatics was conducted on the East Coast in the big cities of New York, Philadelphia and Boston. Even the Midwestern dealers like Ben Green of Chicago were at least 10 years away from opening their doors. Second, at a time when most dealers specialized in coins and carried paper money almost as an afterthought, Barker was strictly a dealer in paper currency, explaining in one of his catalogs that, "I do not deal in old coins, and can give no information regarding their value."

Barker issued periodic catalogs *(Illus. 31)* offering Confederate currency, Southern State currency, shinplasters, Confederate and Southern State bonds and Confederate postage stamps. He claimed an inventory of 100 million

Illus. 31

Confederate dollars; indeed, if he bought 80 million dollars' worth in this one purchase, he might have been correct. Atlanta city directories show him only as a "flash in the pan," as he was in business only for 1893 and 1894.

June 1908. First Perfect-Bound Auction Sale to Feature Exclusively Paper Money.

What a pity that so little is known about one of the biggest paper money collectors of all time. **Harmon Augustus Chambers** was born in Fairfield County, Conn., on June 25, 1822, before moving to Philadelphia by 1870. He built a highly successful insurance brokerage business while in Philadelphia, but his life's work was spent in amassing a magnificent collection of paper money. At the time of his death on January 16, 1905, his cataloger Henry Chapman called it the largest paper money collection ever formed.

Chambers' specialty was Continental and Colonial notes, although he also had a massive assortment of obsolete bank notes and Confederate bonds. His collection of Confederate currency alone certainly rivaled even the great Confederate collections of later years.

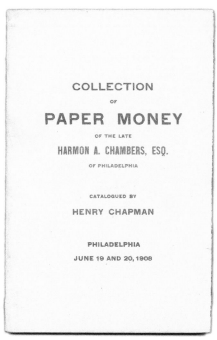

Illus. 32

After Chambers died, his paper money collection was sold at public auction on June 19-20, 1908, by the highly respected and conservative Henry Chapman. The catalog *(Illus. 32)*, the earliest perfect-bound catalog of a single collection I have come across, befitted the collection it contained. The cover was printed on heavy white cover stock and lettered in gold gilt. Within its 1,003 lots was Chambers' entire collection of nearly 6,900 Confederate notes, as well as what Chapman called the largest Colonial collection assembled to that time.

The breadth of his Confederate currency collection was striking, as Chambers owned multiple specimens of virtually all of today's "types," as well as nearly all of the major "varieties." Even John Browne – arguably the greatest Confederate currency collector ever – attended this auction and purchased the ultra-rare Criswell Type-27 "$10 Shield & Eagle" Variety 227 with plate letter A_{14}, one of only four known to this day.

While the breadth of Chambers' collection was remarkable, I am even more impressed by its quality – particularly his Montgomery notes. Chapman had the foresight to include serial numbers for all of the Montgomerys, even as early as this 1908 auction, so we have been able to track the notes' whereabouts. Chambers' $500 Montgomery remains the finest known to this day; his $1,000 and $100 are also among the Condition Census Top Ten.

As magnificent as was Chambers' collection, its prices realized had been lost to history until 2004, when numismatic literature dealer George Kolbe found a priced catalog. Upon inspection, the Montgomerys were found to have sold for the highest prices then achieved by Confederate currency. For example, Chambers' $500 Montgomery sold for $50, over 40% more than any $500 Montgomery to date – a sales price that would not be eclipsed until 1921. Truly Chambers was a man who not only appreciated the quantity of his collection with its myriad types and varieties, but also valued its quality, as he clearly had an eye for exceptional beauty and visual appeal.

Harmon Chambers cannot be discussed without wondering about the relationships among the "Confederate Triumvirate": Harmon Chambers, John Gill and John Browne. We know that Gill and Browne traded with each other, and we also know that Browne purchased at least a few notes from Chambers' estate sale. I suspect that all three were friendly rivals. I would be fascinated to learn the full contribution of each of these numismatic giants to the advancement of our hobby. I look forward to future columns by Fred Reed in *Bank Note Reporter* to broaden our understanding of these prominent collectors.

May 1914. First Midwestern Sale of a Complete Set of Confederate Montgomery Notes.

John Adams tells us that numismatics, even the collecting of Confederate currency, was essentially an East Coast hobby for the latter part of the nineteenth century and the early part of the twentieth. Even the Deep South failed to develop any prominent numismatic dealers during this time period despite being surrounded by hoards of the currency itself.

Ben G. Green was an anomaly. Born in Ohio, and later moving to Illinois, Green was a Midwesterner through and through. Although a coin collector as a child, Green had no local dealers to emulate and probably never considered numismatics as a profession. Instead, he tried his hand at teaching, writing, bookkeeping and even traveling sales. Later he moved to Chicago in 1890 and became a salesman for a distributor of orthopedic supplies.

But Green's childhood interest in numismatics never left him. While still selling orthopedic supplies, he opened a sideline numismatics business from his home. He distributed his first mail-bid auction catalogs in February 1902, and later that year left his employer to begin selling orthopedic supplies on his own. Both operations grew so large that he soon needed to rent outside office space. The businesses continued to prosper and Green moved to even larger quarters. Still managing both ventures, Green had backed his way into becoming the first Midwestern numismatics dealer.

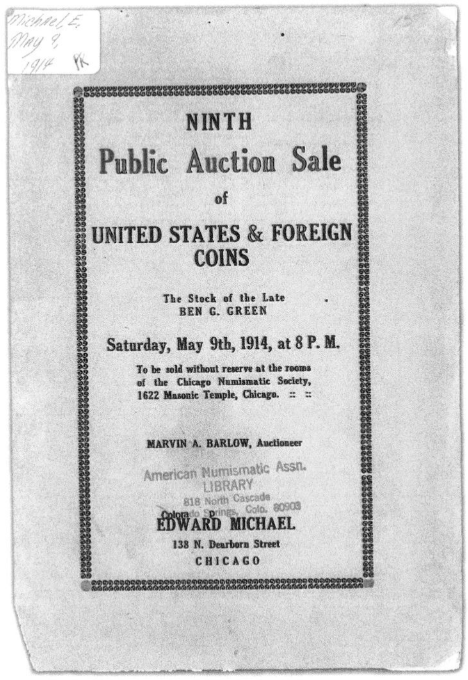

While continuing to pursue both businesses, Green began to give back to the hobby he loved. He was one of the founders of the Chicago Numismatic Society in 1904 and served as its secretary for the remainder of his life.

Green handled his first auction of Confederate currency in January 1908, although the material was far from noteworthy. Still, he built on this modest start and in June 1910 was consigned Confederate material by William West Bradbeer, who wrote the landmark *Confederate and Southern State Currency* just five years later.

In his March 1913 auction of the collection of Charles Morris VI, Green had the pleasure of offering for sale his first Montgomery notes, both the $100 and $50, but not the rarer and more valuable $1,000 and $500.

At the height of his personal success, Ben Green died unexpectedly in January 1914 at only 53 years of age. The entire numismatics community was shocked, as Green had built his own business – and the Chicago Numismatic Society – to national prominence.

NINTH
Public Auction Sale
of
UNITED STATES & FOREIGN
COINS

The Stock of the Late
BEN G. GREEN

Saturday, May 9th, 1914, at 8 P. M.

To be sold without reserve at the rooms
of the Chicago Numismatic Society,
1622 Masonic Temple, Chicago. :: ::

MARVIN A. BARLOW, Auctioneer

EDWARD MICHAEL
138 N. Dearborn Street
CHICAGO

Illus. 33

Four months later, on May 9, 1914, the first Midwestern sale at public auction of a complete set of all four Montgomery notes took place in Chicago *(Illus. 33, facing page)*. The sale was conducted by Edward Michael, a minor dealer on the Chicago numismatics scene.

The irony was that the set of Montgomery notes was owned by the estate of Ben G. Green. What he had been unable to accomplish in life – sell a complete set of Montgomerys – he was finally able to do in death.

1915. First Hardbound Book Describing all Aspects of Confederate Currency.

Timing is everything. Perhaps no one in numismatics benefited more from this old axiom than did **William West Bradbeer**, who issued his book titled *Confederate and Southern State Currency* – the first hardbound book about Confederate currency – in 1915 from his home in Mt. Vernon, N.Y., in Westchester County just outside of Manhattan. While Bradbeer's book was certainly an improvement over John Haseltine's 1876 publication, George Massamore's 1889 work and John W. Scott's four editions between 1879 and 1894, Bradbeer timed his book to fill a 21-year void in publications about Confederate currency. In an unpublished manuscript kindly loaned by author and friend Fred Reed, Fred writes that Frank Duffield, then editor of *The Numismatist*, flatly stated that the book not only filled a time gap, but its incremental improvement over previous efforts also met a huge need, since the last Scott catalog issued in 1894 was "the only guide collectors of paper money have generally had."

Bradbeer was not unknown to numismatics when he released his book in 1915. He had been an employee of dealer Rud Kohler in Manhattan for years. Many experts have assumed that Bradbeer used Kohler's extensive inventory as source material for his book. However, Bradbeer himself gives no such credit to Kohler; rather, he acknowledges "Mr. John C. Browne for placing his splendid collection at my service" (that Browne guy again), and also credits "Mr. Luther B. Tuthill and F.A. Sondley, LL.D. for valued aid."

Like any good author, Bradbeer wished to hype the release of his upcoming book. He leaked its development to George H. Blake as early as 1911. Blake was an officer of the National Association of Leather Belting Manufacturers, a collector of paper money and author of *Paper Money of the United States*. Fred tells of Bradbeer further publicizing his publication by presenting a lecture about Confederate currency to the New York Numismatic Club in February 1914. This lecture, just a year prior to the book's release, was underwritten by prominent dealer Lyman H. Low, who served as Bradbeer's mentor and was acknowledged in the publication "for the inspiration to collect Southern currency."

Bradbeer's book is vitally important today, not only because it filled a 21-year void in Confederate currency publications, but also because of what it failed to do: lead to a plethora of other books on the subject. With the exception of Philip Chase's hardbound publication in 1947 proposing a classification system radically different from what Bradbeer had published, the next major hardbound opus on Confederate currency did not appear until 1957. In that year the Criswell Brothers released their identically titled *Confederate and Southern State Currency* and unabashedly explained that the "numbering system set down by Mr. Bradbeer still remains the standard, and it is significant that it should be used as the basis of the new Criswell Numbering System." Net, Bradbeer's 1915 book was the only accepted publication about Confederate currency between Scott's 1894 Fourth Edition and the Criswells' 1957 First Edition – a 63-year period when Bradbeer enjoyed a virtual monopoly.

We do not know the size of Bradbeer's print run, but it must have been limited, perhaps a few hundred copies. Demand was high and copies were scarce. Since photocopy machines were not yet around, obtaining a duplicate required sitting down and typing a copy by hand (see page 10 for an illustration of a page typed by California collector Martin H. Burge, whose entire typescript is owned by the Pink Palace Museum in Memphis, Tenn.). To fill the need for more copies, both Charles E. Green in 1945 and Aubrey E. Bebee in 1956 offered reprints of the original 1915 Bradbeer publication, as the copyright had earlier expired.

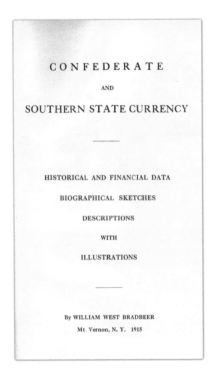

Illus. 34

Bradbeer's hard binding gave his book a permanence and importance lacking in any of the earlier Confederate currency publications *(Title Page, Illus. 34)*. He further improved what had been previously published by summarizing the acts of the Confederate Congress and the amount of money authorized, by providing a degree of rarity (although the source was Bradbeer's own observations) and by illustrating a limited number of notes themselves (e.g., only five notes were pictured of the 38 types issued in 1861). The book contained 162 pages and expanded the already inflated variety count of 314 found in Massamore's 1889 work to a new eye-popping total of 579. Nevertheless, the feeling continued to be "more is better" and the book was generally well received, with venerable Philadelphia dealer Henry Chapman calling it "splendid," according to Fred Reed.

But "generally well received" does not mean "universally well received," and Bradbeer had at least two noted detractors. The first was the eminent John J. Ford, who confided in a 1957 letter to Clarence Criswell that he did "not care for the Bradbeer numbers in any way, shape or form." Since Ford was advising Sydney Kerksis on a competing Confederate currency book at the time, his comments probably lack objectivity. However, the second naysayer – armed with the numismatic credentials of one Herbert A. Brand of Cincinnati, Ohio – provided criticism that I felt merited inclusion in my book.

Herbert A. Brand – who Dave Bowers tells me is not related to the legendary paper money collector Virgil M. Brand (I still have suspicions) – was a founding member of the Cincinnati Numismatic Association in 1930. He served as the Association's first chairman and was instrumental in landing the 1931 ANA National Convention for Cincinnati. In 1931, the Association limited its charter members to 35, with Brand as official charter member number 1. Seventeen of the members were wealthy collectors from Cincinnati, with the balance mainly coming from the Northeast and including some of the greatest numismatists of the time.

Herbert A. Brand was a specialist in medals and obsolete bank notes, whose vocation was a sales engineer and general manager for a New York firm. Of more recent vintage, Brand was also the primary instigator in the founding of the Florida United Numismatists (FUN) in 1955, along with Bob Hendershott, Doug Brown, Jack Sweetman and Grover Criswell. It was Brand, a well-known dealer and collector then living in Miami Shores, Fla., who suggested that Florida organize a state numismatic association and hold its annual meeting in the winter to entice Northern dealers and collectors to attend to escape their harsh weather. To this day the FUN Show takes place in the winter.

Brand's credentials with the founding of both the Cincinnati Numismatic Association and the Florida United Numismatists were enough to cause me to pause at his comments about Bradbeer's book, but I was most surprised with his own Confederate currency inventory over the years. In my personal library, I own Brand's annotated copy of Bradbeer, complete with his personal identifying name plate (as is seen in books previously owned by John Ford or

Harry Bass). By far, this book is the most annotated I have come across in any discipline. For example, on one of the back flyleaves, Brand penned the following in blue ink *(Illus. 35)*:

> "I have owned this book for more than thirty years. Every CSA note and Southern State note I have handled has been checked with this book. I have had thousands of them. The great stock of Luther B. Tuthill of South Creek N.C., which I bought. The large Mams collection of Denver Colorado, which I bought, the great Waldo C. Moore Collection of Lewisburg Ohio, the large Charles Theel collection of Cincinnati, many items bought for stock and now the large Krueger hoard of Seattle, Washington.
>
> – H. A. Brand.   5/30/55"

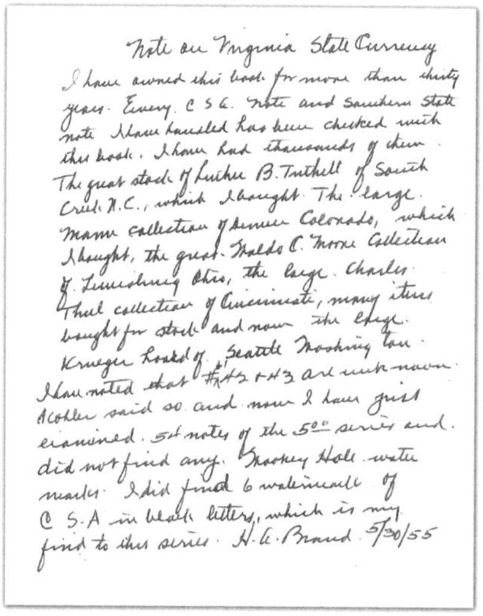

Brand owned some of the great variety collections of all time, including those of Luther Tuthill (who personally knew John Gill and Raphael Thian) and Waldo Moore. His criticisms of Bradbeer's book come from knowledge and experience; they deserve our consideration. In a "Note for paper money collectors" penned on the front flyleaf *(Illus. 36)*, Brand writes:

Illus. 35

> "Note for paper money collectors. Five very large collections and stocks have passed through my hands and I have checked every CSA and Southern State note with this book. The book is filled with errors; silly stupid errors, many omissions and I have added many notes not listed. It is still the best work on the subject although several attempts have been made to classify on a different method. *[Author's Note: Here he is referring to the Chase book of 1947.]* Some day, one of you collectors will write a new book employing all the old Bradbeer numbers known to be in existence and adding those that have been found since publishing this book. Paper money collecting is growing in popularity and this study does need a good text book. Good luck to the new author.
>
> H. A. Brand
> Miami Shores Fla.
> Memorial Day
> 1955"

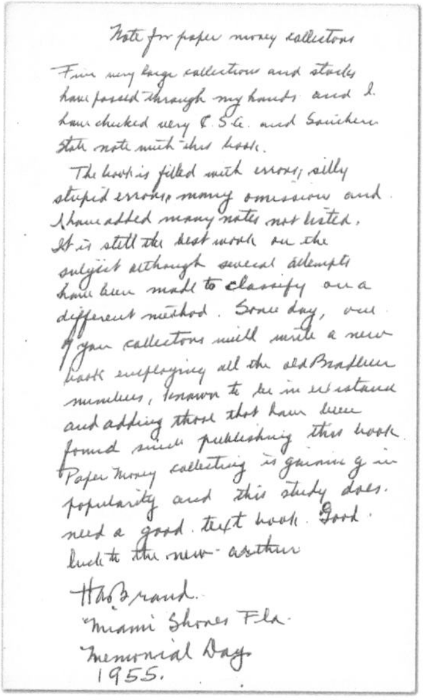

Perhaps Brand's use of adjectives like "silly" or "stupid" may not be politically correct today, but he wrote what he felt and I cannot fault his honesty. His criticisms were valid – indeed there are numerous typographical errors in Bradbeer's book – and Criswell included in his 1957 book many of Bradbeer's earlier omissions. While stinging, Brand's comments were nevertheless on point.

Illus. 36

Brand's final impressions were penned in 1960, three years after the Criswells released their first book. Brand appears to have mellowed somewhat, but still references Bradbeer's numerous typographical errors. He penned his comments on April 12, 1960, the 99th anniversary of the bombardment of Ft. Sumter *(Illus. 37, next page)*:

> "April 12 - 1960. In his day Mr. Rud Kohler was the Criswell. While Kohler did sell coins he specialized in paper and did have large stocks on hand. Mr. Bradbeer was employed by Rud Kohler for years and to the greatest extent it was the stock of Mr. Kohler that gave Mr. Bradbeer his information. *[Author's*

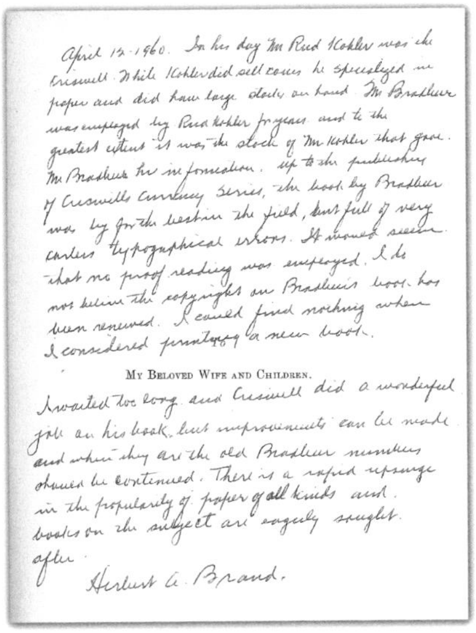

MY BELOVED WIFE AND CHILDREN.

Illus. 37

Note: Bradbeer contradicts this statement in his Acknowledgments.] Up to the publishing of Criswells Currency Series, the book by Bradbeer was by far the best in the field, but full of very careless typographical errors. It would seem that no proof reading was employed. I do not believe the copyright on Bradbeer's book has been renewed. I could find nothing when I considered printing a new book.

I waited too long and Criswell did a wonderful job on his book, but improvements can be made and when they are the old Bradbeer numbers should be continued. There is a rapid upsurge in the popularity of paper of all kinds and books on the subject are eagerly sought after.

– Herbert A. Brand."

Despite severe criticism from the highly respected numismatists John Ford and Herbert Brand, William Bradbeer's 1915 book remains one of the most important in the history of collecting Confederate currency. He performed copious research; he was the first to produce a hardbound book; he was the first to try to quantify rarity in an understandable way, and he was the first to use illustrations (William Lee illustrated his 1875 pamphlet, but printed only 30 copies). With so many firsts, it was inevitable that some errors – even silly mistakes as Brand charged — would crop up.

The Criswells got it right in 1957: they retained the strength of Bradbeer's numbering system while correcting most of the mistakes. Most importantly, they consolidated Bradbeer's unwieldy 579 varieties under an exquisitely simple umbrella of only 72 major design "types." The greatest monument to Bradbeer's success is his numbering system, which the Criswells did not change and which remains the standard to this day, as Hugh Shull's contemporary book now in development also uses Bradbeer's numbers.

June 1917-February 1919. First Descriptions of Confederate Notes in Serialized Format.

I wish **H. D. Allen** had collected all the articles he contributed to the ANA's *The Numismatist* between 1917 and 1919 and compiled them into a hardbound book. Such a publication would have met with immediate success among serious numismatists of the day. But individual issues of 21 different magazine articles spread over three years are easy to lose. Further, they lacked the permanence of William West Bradbeer's hardbound book issued just two years before the start of Allen's articles. H. D. Allen seems to have been one of the keenest researchers in the Confederate currency field. It is my belief that he has never received the recognition he deserved, and only because he chose an extended, serialized format in which to publish his findings.

H. D. Allen of Boston burst onto the numismatics scene in 1916 when he waged a one-man campaign to ascertain the identity of the person who appears in the lower left vignette on the $10 Confederate note of September 2, 1861, which we call today the Criswell Type-23. For years the portrait had been called that of Oldham and later of Elmore, but by 1916 Allen had conclusively shown that it was neither of these men.

How Allen became interested in such a mystery makes a good story in itself. According to *The Numismatist* of February 1917, Allen was born in Chicopee, Mass., in 1858. He later moved to Boston and lived there until 1878, when the lure of the Wild West became irresistible to a 20-year-old. After working on a cattle ranch in Colorado for a year, he moved to Topeka, Kan., to take a job in the accounting department of the Atchison, Topeka and Santa Fe Railroad. He worked there for nearly 14 years until his father died in Boston in 1892. Allen immediately returned home to run the family business, an occupation that he continued while he was researching and writing articles about Confederate currency from 1917 to 1919.

Illus. 38, Courtesy
The Numismatist

H. D. Allen *(Illus. 38)* was an antiquarian in the sense of both the trailblazing Thomas Addis Emmet and next-to-be-showcased John C. Browne. Although he professed to have never seen a piece of Confederate currency until 1914, he had already developed a keen interest "in coins, [other forms of] paper money, stamps, curios, antiques, relics, or anything belonging to the past that is historically worth collecting" (*The Numismatist*, February 1917 issue).

Allen was first exposed to Confederate currency when he read an article by the Associated Press on August 13, 1912, stating that the Federal Government had on hand a large quantity of Confederate paper money. The space it took up was needed for other purposes, so rather than destroying it, a selection of this currency would be sent to any public library agreeing to preserve and display it as an historical exhibit.

At the time Allen's niece was a librarian in Shirley, Mass., and he sent her the newspaper clipping with the suggestion that she apply for some of the currency. In due course the currency arrived, but the library's trustees did not know how to best display it. After two years, the trustees sent the currency – 14 pieces in all – to Allen with a request that he get them framed. Ragged and soiled when they arrived in 1914, these were the first pieces of Confederate currency Allen had ever seen. Despite their condition, Allen became extremely interested and decided to assemble a complete set of notes to donate to the public library in Brookline, Mass., where he then lived. He placed the notes in glass-topped frames 3 ft. square and put a typewritten historical summary under each bill. He also arranged for a smaller exhibit at his niece's library in Shirley.

The August 1916 issue of *The Numismatist (Illus. 39)* reports that Allen recognized that many minor varieties existed, but "for the purpose of a public display, one note of each 'kind' *(author's quotes)* would be sufficient, without going into minor varieties." Allen's collection contained a total of 84 notes. If Allen had replaced his word "kind" with "type," he would have gained a 40-year head start on the Criswells, who finally had the foresight to take Bradbeer's 579 varieties and classify them all under 72 "types" in 1957.

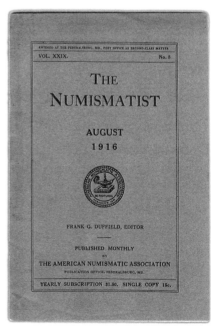

Allen was introduced to the readers of *The Numismatist* in its June 1916 issue, when his search to determine the identity of the man on the Type-23 was announced. He was again mentioned in August 1916, when an updated report on the identity was published. Then in February 1917 Allen had the pleasure of announcing that the vignette was that of John E. Ward, a former mayor of Savannah, Ga.

His series on Confederate currency debuted in June 1917. Titled "The Paper Money of the Confederate States, with Historical Data," the editor was quick

Illus. 39

to point out that the installments were a history of Confederate currency and not a catalog. The editor complained that with all catalogs previously published, including even Bradbeer's,

> "the collector has felt that there was something still lacking to give him a real and friendly familiarity with the series. He takes up a list... and identifies his notes by such designations as these: '$100 Cars at Depot, Montgomery, 1861'... '$5 Five Females, Statute of Washington at Right, Sept. 2, 1861,' and so on throughout the series. But if someone should casually ask him certain direct questions about the allegorical or historical designs or portraits on some of the notes… or any of the numerous questions that might reasonably be asked about the actual history connected with the notes, his answer would probably be: 'I don't know: the catalogue doesn't say.' "

Allen succeeded in emphatically answering this complaint: he illustrated all 84 of his "kinds" of notes, becoming only the second publisher to do so (following William Lee). Allen devoted at least several paragraphs to a description of each note, with multiple pages reserved for certain critical pieces in the series. He provided the actual quantity of each "kind" printed to aid the reader in determining rarity. He showed the serial number of each note pictured – even the common varieties of 1864 – as he recognized that the serial numbers found on Confederate currency provided a unique identifying feature not found on coins or stamps.

To my knowledge, Allen was also the first to illustrate and analyze in detail the $10 Essay Note, Criswell Type-48, the unquestioned rarest note in the Confederate series. Allen described the note as "neither genuine, bogus, nor counterfeit, but is stated to be an 'essay note' submitted to the Treasury Department of the Confederate States and refused, but the reason for such refusal is shrouded in mystery." The note pictured was owned by Mr. W. A. Clark of Columbia, S.C. Allen placed the census at that time at only six pieces.

H. D. Allen is proof that even a novice can quickly have an impact on collecting Confederate currency. In only five years he made available to the entire readership of the ANA a thorough education in the art and intricacies of collecting Confederate currency. And he "almost" invented the "type" numbering system made so popular by the Criswells nearly a half-century later. Quite a resume! His own collection was sold at auction by William Hesslein in 1929.

Illus. 40 (courtesy Fred Reed)

July 1922. Public Auction Sale of the "Greatest Confederate Collector Ever."

With both respectful awe and sheer amazement, **John C. Browne** *(Illus. 40)* has been bestowed the title of "greatest Confederate collector ever" by those of us who are passionate about Confederate currency. For years no one has known the full extent of Browne's collection at its pinnacle before being sold, donated or auctioned. With new details emerging, though, it might be that his collection was even *greater* than once thought.

I only wish my mentor Douglas Ball was still around to see these findings. On August 24, 2001, Doug and I had dinner at the Barbaresco Restaurant on Lexington Avenue in New York, just around the corner from Doug's co-op. I asked Doug many questions that evening, including, "Who was the greatest Confederate collector of all time?" Doug answered firmly and without hesitation, "John Browne." Coming from the man who might well be number two or number three, Doug's forceful assertion seals the case for me.

Fred Reed did a masterful job of humanizing this iconic figure in his superb article that appeared in the April 2005 issue of *Bank Note Reporter*. I commend this entire article to the reader, and I will not repeat details of Browne's non-numismatic interests to save space.

John Coates Browne was born in Philadelphia on February 18, 1838, to a family of wealth and privilege. His grandfather graduated from the University of Pennsylvania in 1793 and was a member of the First Troop Philadelphia City Calvary -- the first volunteer calvary troop organized during the American Revolution. His mother, Ann Taylor Strawbridge, descended from the family that founded the Strawbridge & Clothier department store chain.

I have long been fascinated by John C. Browne's Confederate collection. To determine both the condition of its types and the breadth of its varieties, I will divide his collection into three parts: that part now at Lincoln Memorial University's Abraham Lincoln Library and Museum, that part sold at public auction in July 1922, and that part once at the Historical Society of Pa.

Much of Browne's Civil War ephemera is now housed at the Abraham Lincoln Library and Museum in Harrogate, Tenn., where it is mounted in six huge, leather-bound scrapbooks that ended up in the possession of Raymond Sanger Wilkins, a noted jurist from Boston who served as Chief Justice of the Massachusetts Supreme Court from 1956 to 1970. Wilkins' gift to the library was made in early 1944, as confirmed in a short article in the February 1944 issue of the *Lincoln Herald*, a publication issued to promote research in the field of Lincolniana.

I have made three visits to the library to inspect these scrapbooks and remain overwhelmed by their content. In the first scrapbook I reviewed, mixed in with broadsides and patriotic covers, I was amazed to find two Montgomery notes, each one unknown to the Montgomery census. While scattering Montgomery notes within scrapbooks of Civil War ephemera provides little help in establishing the scope or magnitude of Browne's Confederate currency collection, it offers an enticing prelude to what the balance of his collection might contain.

The second part of Browne's collection, mainly Americana, was sold at auction on July 22, 1922 after Browne's death on June 20, 1918 by a minor Philadelphia auction firm owned by Stan V. Henkels. The collection contained a several-hundred-piece lot of 1862 and 1863 issues and a 114-piece lot of Confederate counterfeits -- as well as one other lot that I consider for advanced type collectors the single most significant lot ever offered by an auction house since 1865:

> "217 **Bechtel's Album** for Confederate Currency. Containing specimens of each type of the notes, issued by the authority of the Confederate Government, embracing 90 notes, *all uncirculated*, and laid loosely in the Album. Sold as a lot. This is almost a unique collection. It embraces the $1000, $500, $100 and $50, Montgomery, 1861; the $100 and $50, Richmond, 1861, all with written date; the $100, $50, $20, both varieties; $10 and $5, both varieties of the issue of July 25, 1861; the $100, $50, the three varieties, $20, five varieties, $10, ten varieties, $5, six varieties, and $2, issue of Sept. 7, 1861; interest notes of the 1862 issue, viz., $100, five varieties, $2, two varieties, and $1, two varieties, etc., embracing the whole series noticed by Bechtel in compiling his book. *All uncirculated*."

Grover Criswell defined the modern Confederate type set at 72 different designs. The Bechtel album John Browne used to house his collection included all 72 of these types except for the $10 Essay note, which was not yet discovered. Browne's type set -- each note "Uncirculated" -- is unique. To this day, a number of the 72 designs have not been seen since in "Uncirculated" condition, e.g., the Criswell Type-11 "$5 Liberty & Eagle", the Type-27 "$10 Shield & Eagle" or the Type-35 "$5 Indian Princess." *I am simply astounded.*

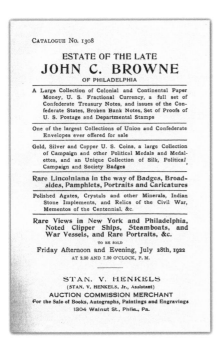

Illus. 41

This second part of Browne's collection disposed of at auction in 1922 (*Illus. 41*), adds about 500 more pieces to his known holdings ("several hundred pieces" of 1862 and 1863 material, 114 counterfeits and the 90-piece "Uncirculated" type set). But this part of the collection is not about "piece count" but rather about "preservation" --the only set of Confederate "type notes" ever to be labeled "Uncirculated." Thus the assemblage of Confederate "types" reached its pinnacle in 1922 with the auction of Browne's "Uncirculated" type set. The compilation of Confederate "varieties" would not reach its zenith until the gift of Browne's "variety collection" to the Historical Society of Pennsylvania (hereafter "the Society"), as will next be examined.

In the "Index to Board Minutes" dated May 18, 1959, I found this comment:

> "Confederate Money
> H.S.P [*the Society*] owns relatively large collection. Suggestion of Director to sell some of collection and use money so derived for purposes more in keeping with usual objectives of the Society.
> C.M.M.   May 18, 1959"

Six months later I found a second card with this remarkable comment:

> "Confederate Money
> At the June Meeting, the Director was instructed to investigate whether it would be feasible to dispose of a collection of Confederate currency which had *no provenance* (my italics)…
> The matter was referred back to the Director for further study.
> Council Meeting, 11/16/59"

John Browne (or his estate) bequeathed his Confederate currency collection to the Society no later than 1920, when a plaque was unveiled in Browne's honor. Yet less than 40 years later in 1959, the Society's Director reported that the collection "had no provenance"!

Moving at a most leisurely pace, the Society met again on June 19, 1961 when I excerpted this resolution from a meeting of the Executive Committee:

```
    The matter of disposing of our large collection of Con-
federate bank notes was considered at length.  Many sugges-
tions were made.  After discussion, it was moved, seconded,
and carried that a representative of the New Netherlands
Coin Co., Inc. of New York be asked to send a representative
here to examine the collection and advise us on the best
method of disposing of it.
```

Four months later, at another Committee meeting on October 16, 1961, this action was taken:

> " In regards to our collection of Confederate notes, we received a long letter from the New Netherlands Coin Co., Inc. suggesting we turn over the collection to them to sell over a period of time for a commission of 20%. It was moved, seconded, and carried to leave the matter in the hands of the Director with power."

The Society accepted the proposal from New Netherlands, and on May 8, 1962 the Director wrote New Netherlands to warn that the Society "would like to advise you that my Board finally decided to keep one of each denomination in our collections. These will not be sold." Later that month the *duplicates only* from the collection were delivered to New Netherlands.

Upon John Ford receiving the duplicates, accompanied by a detailed inventory listing, he saw that the Society had not kept one of each *denomination* as had been advised in their May 8 letter, but rather one of each *variety* -- and the Browne collection had the mind-numbing total of 3,500 different varieties -- not including the 6,002 duplicates already delivered.

Ford wrote on September 12, 1962 to define "denominations" and "varieties," as shown below:

> "What your letter says, and the list says, are two entirely different things. What you have left with us, are duplicates by varieties. There are 70 different "types" of CSA notes, 10 different "denominations" and about 3500 different varieties. Your board has decided to keep one of each <u>variety</u>, and thus we do not have anything resembling a collection here. It was my thought, that the Society could retain one of each of the 70 types, in the finest possible preservation but what they have done is attempted to keep the entire Browne Collection as intact and complete as possible..."

I thought Ford's mention of Browne's "varieties" totaling 3,500 had to be in error -- after all, Bradbeer recorded only 579 varieties in his 1915 book, and Bradbeer thanked "Mr. John C. Browne for placing his splendid collection at my service." When I reviewed the detailed listing of duplicates, though, I saw for myself how John Browne amassed a variety collection totaling 3,500 notes. Browne merely used Bradbeer's 579 varieties as a starting point before suffixing them with " /1, /2, /3,.../11" to indicate sub-varieties. Grover Criswell followed Browne's numbering scheme in his first edition in 1957 to delineate sub-varieties of the basic variety itself. It is easy to see how Bradbeer's 579 varieties morphed into Browne's 3,500 sub-varieties.

Ford's letter of September 12, 1962 to the Society had its desired effect. In the Minutes of a Meeting on September 17, 1962, the Board relented and agreed not to retain the variety collection but to also "forward it to the New Netherlands Coin Co., Inc. for sale with the rest." While the Minutes suggest that the entirety of the retained variety collection was shipped to New Netherlands, we know from later records that a portion was kept at the Society.

New Netherlands received the second shipment, the variety collection, in early October 1962, when it had in its possession the John Browne duplicates totaling 6,002 pieces and the bulk of the 3,500-piece variety collection. Assuming the Society retained about 500 notes, New Netherlands had about 9,000 Confederate notes from John Browne's collection in its possession -- 6,002 duplicates and 3,000 or so (out of a total of 3,500) of Browne's basic variety collection.

On October 17, 1962, President Charles Wormser sent the first payment to the Society. The firm continued to send regular monthly payments to the Society through April 1963. But this normal routine came to an abrupt halt with the transaction shown below dated May 1, 1963:

```
                                        MAY  1  1963

9-2-61  $10.   Chase 126 B Plews A9-A16- some damage.
                           VG-VF plus.  8 for $1200.00  20%
```

These notes are Browne's extraordinary set of all eight Criswell Type-27s "$10 Shield & Eagles" with plate letters A_9 - A_{16} (Criswell varieties 222-229), originally pedigreed to John Gill (pages 34-35). These notes were not "sold" by New Netherlands at all. Ford bought them for his own account, finally disposing of them via private treaty in 1999. Yet, in a covering letter accompanying the payment, Wormser wrote that "we have now been paid by one of the individuals from whom monies were coming on account, and enclose our check."

Wormser's statement is not true, only leading to suspicions regarding *all* the reputed sales. Was New Netherlands simply purchasing notes for inventory and paying as it saw fit? The answer to this question came with this transaction dated May 29, 1963. These items include three more Type-27s including the ultra-rare A_{14} plen from Harmon Chambers in 1908, and perhaps the rarest varieties in the Confederate series, the Type-16 "$50 Jefferson Davis" with plens A_1 - A_4 (Criswell varieties 95-98):

9/2/61	$5.	C-278 Uncut,closely trimmed sheet. VF;Imp.	8 for			$40.00
9/2/61	$10.	Lib. Shield eagle. G-VG.				75.00
9/2/61	$10.	Similar; "short note".				85.00
9/2/61	$10.	Similar; A-1⁴. F-VF;Imp.				150.00
9/2/61	$50.	1A; 3A. VG-F.		2 for		125.00

All five of these Type-27s and Type-16s with remarkably rare plate letters were part of Ford's private-treaty sale in 1999. Within seven months of receipt, Ford had removed many of the rarest and most valuable Confederate variety notes in the entire collection. We will never know how many notes were removed for Ford's account and how many were legitimate sales.

New Netherlands slowly made "sales" for nearly five years before the Society abruptly recalled the entire collection of unsold notes in early April 1967. The reason is unclear. In a file memorandum dated March 22, 1967, the Society stated that John Ford had called the previous day, advising that he and Wormser felt "that some misunderstanding has arisen between the Coin Co. and the Society in regard to the firm's handling of the sale of the Confederate bills."

The Society advised Ford that the Director was new in his position and that they "felt the whole situation should be reviewed and that probably the best way of doing this was to recall the collection now." In a final attempt to reverse the decision to recall the collection, "Mr. Ford stressed the fact that approximately half the collection had been disposed of for a price equal to the total estimated value of the collection under the original arrangement."

Apparently at the time of the original agreement in May 1962, New Netherlands had estimated the Society would generate $10,000 from the sale of the entire collection -- the 6,002 duplicates and the bulk of the 3,500-piece variety collection. Indeed Ford was correct that his firm had already generated about $10,000 in revenue for the Society, as I reviewed all payments received from New Netherlands between October 17, 1962 and April 6, 1967 and calculated total revenue of $9,926.32 on sales of 1,199 pieces, which aligns with the Society's Minutes of a Board Meeting on May 15, 1967 stating that the collection had been "recalled from the Company so that it might be seen by an independent, impartial expert in the matter, with a…recommendation as to future disposition. The collection is now back in the Society's custody less the approximately $10,000 worth of it which has been sold."

The Society finally asked Thomas Affleck (presumably a relative of Charles J. Affleck, who owned about 7,000 pieces from the Browne collection, as estimated by Fred Reed in *Bank Note Reporter*) to appraise the recalled notes. In a Board meeting on April 21, 1969, the Director "reported that Mr. Thomas Affleck had recently surveyed the Society's remaining Confederate notes, and had estimated their value as between twelve and fifteen thousand dollars."

Soon after the Board met again on September 15, 1969 and "approval was given the Director to accept the best bid for their purchase." The saga concluded with a final entry from the Minutes of a Board Meeting on October 20, 1969, stating that " the Director has sold the remainder of our Confederate notes to the high bidder, the New Netherlands Coin Company for $10,500."

The Society's final record of the John Browne gift was a memo from the Director advising its employee "Conrad" that Charles Wormser of New Netherlands would arrive September 18, 1969 to reclaim the Confederate notes recalled two years earlier. His final comment, "Be sure he gets only those notes which were originally in his possession -- no others" confirms that the Society had retained part of the John Browne collection, but it provides no details.

Presumably New Netherlands sold all the notes it bought from the Society by 1971 when John Ford, the Confederate expert in the company, retired. But two perplexing questions remain about the John Browne collection. First, what and when did Douglas B. Ball acquire his portion of the John C. Browne collection? And second, how did Charles Affleck acquire the roughly 7,000 Confederate notes he attributed to John Browne in the NASCA sale of his estate in 1983?

Doug Ball's Confederate notes pedigreed to John Browne have always been attributed to the Society. But there are inconsistencies in dates which make an exact determination of the provenance more difficult. In Ball's bond book published in 1998, John Ford (who wrote the *Foreword*) stated that he first met Ball "in the early spring of 1962" when "we were…helping the Historical Society of Pennsylvania liquidate the legendary John C. Browne collection." But the entire collection was not delivered until October 1962. Thus Ford could not have shown the Browne material to Ball "in the early spring of 1962" as claimed, as it was not yet in New York.

The Society's records indicate that Doug Ball actually made his first major purchase of the Browne material -- 234 pieces -- on March 30, 1964, nearly two years after Ford claimed. Over three years later Ball returned 13 of these notes for credit, as Wormser wrote the Society on April 18, 1967 that "our customer came to town today and has gone over the notes and has also returned the material that has proven, because of his studies, to be fraudulent; these were purchased by him in 1964 and the Society was paid in full."

Fred Reed's April 2005 article in *Bank Note Reporter* includes a statement from a "modern writer" that Browne's collection of about 7,000 pieces was bought in the 1960s by Douglas Ball and his father George, who had it appraised on October 15, 1969 by Stack's.

Since we know from Society records that Charles Wormser picked up the collection on September 18, 1969 that had been earlier recalled by the Society, and the Stack's appraisal is dated just a month later on October 15, 1969, I am confident in suggesting that John Ford simply sold the Browne collection intact -- less the 1,199 notes sold before the recall -- to Douglas Ball and his father between its pick-up on September 18 and its appraisal dated October 15, 1969. Presumably the rarest and most valuable pieces, like the T16s and T27s, had already been removed when New Netherlands first took possession in October 1962.

If my assumptions are valid that the entire Browne collection at the Society originally totaled about 9,500 pieces (6,002 duplicates and a 3,500-piece variety collection), then Ball acquired about 7,200 pieces of the entire collection (about 7,000 pieces appraised by Stack's in 1969 and 234 pieces acquired in 1964 before the recall). Since a total of 1,199 pieces were sold before the recall, of which Ball bought only 234, about 1,000 pieces were dispersed to collectors other than Ball (many to Ford himself). Finally, we know the Society kept some pieces. I earlier guessed about 500 pieces -- perhaps the actual number was closer to 1,200 -- but I am now satisfied that the John Browne material at the Historical Society of Pennsylvania is accounted for.

The source of Charles J. Affleck's Confederate notes attributed to John Browne is much harder to determine. The Society asked "Thomas Affleck" -- presumably a relative of Charles' -- to appraise the Browne material in 1969 after it was recalled from New Netherlands. But there is correspondence between "Charles" and the Society's Director dated July 8, 1969 advising

Charles that New Netherlands would be making an offer in August and soliciting Charles' own offer. Certainly Charles had the opportunity to buy it directly from the Society if he wished -- the appraisal was $12 to $15,000 yet New Netherlands acquired it for only $10,500 -- but I do not think Charles did so. In 1969 Charles Affleck was already 77 years old. I doubt he would have consummated such a large purchase only a few years before his death in 1974.

Perhaps Charles Affleck acquired his notes from the Society *before* New Netherlands took its first delivery in 1962, as there is no record of the Society doing anything with the collection between their decision to de-accession it in 1959 and contacting New Netherlands in 1961.

While the Society moved deliberately, there is nothing to suggest that its records are not complete, or that Affleck could have made such a purchase without it being recorded. I thus think that perhaps Affleck's 7,000 notes pedigreed to John Browne might have come from a source other than the Historical Society of Pennsylvania. John Browne's notes surfaced at the Abraham Lincoln Library and Museum, his estate sale in Philadelphia and the Historical Society of Pennsylvania. There is nothing to suggest that a fourth repository did not also exist.

Finally, it is possible that Doug Ball's NASCA sale of the Affleck material attributed to Browne in 1983 also contained some of Doug's notes he purchased from the Browne collection in 1969. It is not unusual to mix other consignments into a sales catalog purporting to be a single collection -- in this case, it might be even more likely since all the material traced back to John Browne. If the two collections were co-mingled, though, then it would be virtually impossible to sort out which notes were originally Affleck's and which were Ball's.

Much misinformation has been written about John Browne in recent years in an apparent attempt to replace him from the pinnacle of collecting Confederate currency with my mentor Doug Ball. If there were any way within the bounds of propriety and fair play to give Doug the "greatest ever" title I probably would have done so. But facts only reaffirm Browne's preeminence. For "type collectors" Browne's 90-note typeset, all notes "Uncirculated", might never be equaled again. For "variety collectors" his 3,500-piece variety collection might also be unique. Browne's collection totaled at least 10,000 notes, not including the 7,000 owned by Charles Affleck with unknown origin. He owned virtually every Bradbeer variety known today, including *all* the great rarities (except the Essays). In my opinion, John Browne has only solidified his position as the "greatest Confederate currency collector of all time."

1936 and 1947. First Effort to Re-Classify the Accepted Confederate Numbering Scheme.

Philip Hartley Chase tried to build a better mouse trap. Had he succeeded, we collectors today would probably classify our Confederate type sets by Chase numbers rather than Bradbeer/Criswell numbers. Chase's numbering system, a radical departure from what Haseltine, Massamore and Bradbeer had developed earlier, was the product of an Ivy League-educated, MIT-grounded, Philadelphia Electric Company-trained scholar and collector. But he encountered stiff resistance in garnering acceptance of his new classification system for Confederate currency, which was open-ended to allow for the addition of new discovery notes. He thus became relegated to a footnote in the collecting of Confederate currency, when his ideas should probably have propelled him to the forefront. His inability to achieve acceptance of his classification system is particularly unfortunate, because it lessens the impact of Chase the collector, and as a collector he clearly had few peers.

In an unpublished manuscript set to appear in an upcoming column in *Bank Note Reporter*, author Fred Reed has kindly allowed me to excerpt from his paper for use in this book. Fred advises that Chase was born May 18, 1888, graduated from Dartmouth in 1907, from MIT in 1909 and from Harvard in 1910. He went to work as an engineer for the Philadelphia Electric Company in 1911 and stayed there until his retirement in 1951. We do not know what led to Chase's interest in collecting Confederate currency, but by 1936 he was already both advanced and passionate.

From his home in Bala-Cynwyd, a bedroom community of Philadelphia, Chase privately issued in card covers a modest 32-page pamphlet *(Illus. 43)* titled *Confederate States of America Paper Money, 1861 – 1865: Basic Classification and Listing*. In his *Foreword* to this 1936 publication, Chase outlined the reasons he wrote it: "The writer finds the collection and study of Confederate States of America paper money so interesting, but of such breadth, that he has been impelled to develop for his own use a classification of the types and main varieties, which it is believed will be of interest to other collectors."

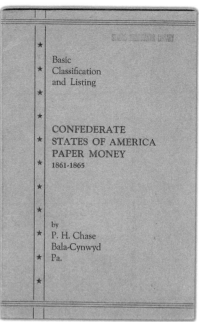

Illus. 43

Chase was one of the first, if not *the* first, to label the basic designs issued by the Confederate Treasury as "types." He then labeled minor differences in the basic designs as "varieties" and attempted to distinguish further between "major varieties" and "minor varieties." His efforts were laudable and represented the first scholarly effort to create a hierarchy of design elements, starting with the "type" at the top, followed by the "major variety" in the middle and finally the "minor variety" at the bottom. Recognizing that his system was entirely unprecedented and might be confusing, he cross-indexed his new numbers to those numbers used for the same notes by Scott, Allen and Bradbeer.

Chase's efforts were altruistic and sincere. In an unparalleled move to generate collector feedback to his new numbering system, he inserted a letter at the front of each pamphlet *(Illus. 44)* requesting comments and provided a postage-free envelope to encourage response. His letter read:

"To the Purchaser:

I hope you will find "Basic Classification and Listing – Confederate States of America Paper Money" helpful and convenient. After you have become familiar with the simple scheme of classification and listing, and have tried it out in actual use with your collection, I would appreciate your sending me your comments and suggestions. The reverse side of this sheet may be used for your comments. The enclosed envelope provides for payment of postage by me.

Very truly yours,

(signed) P. H. Chase"

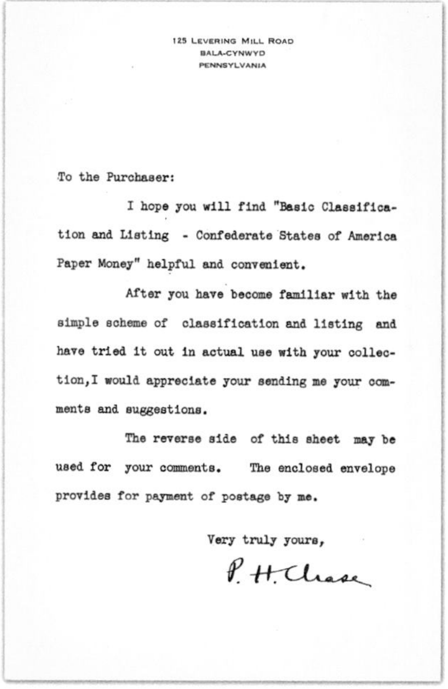

Illus. 44

After his ground-breaking 1936 pamphlet introduced his new classification system, Chase followed with a *Price List Supplement* published in 1941 *(Illus. 45, next page)*. Chase was a collector and not a dealer; he advised that his prices were developed "after consideration of dealer price lists, auction and private sale prices, degree of rarity in fine condition, nature of variety, and collector interest."

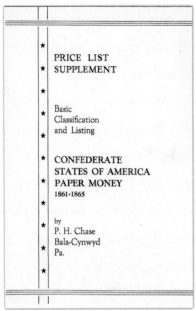

Illus. 45

Chase continued to promote his new classification system through the encouragement of *The Numismatist*, the monthly publication of the ANA. Like H. D. Allen 25 years earlier, Chase began to serialize an expanded and refined manuscript titled *Confederate States of America Paper Money: Classification and Listing* in the November 1944 issue of *The Numismatist*, where it continued to run in 20 installments through March 1947. He revised and consolidated the 20 articles into a privately printed hardbound book he published *(Illus. 46)* in Philadelphia in 1947 titled *Confederate Treasury Notes: the Paper Money of the Confederate States of America, 1861 – 1865*. Containing 148 pages and originally offered at a price of $3.50, the book was illustrated throughout and was favorably reviewed in *The Numismatist* in October 1947.

In his book, Chase amplified the reasons he felt the need to develop a new numbering system. He thought that all existing numbering schemes were inflexible or failed to distinguish between designs called "types" and their variations called "major varieties" or "minor varieties." Chase was driven to develop a system that worked equally well with the advanced type collector who cared little about varieties and the variety collector who was fascinated by different watermarks, paper types or engraver markings. Chase developed his system "to describe a flexible, comprehensive scheme of classification and its underlying principles." He borrowed heavily from the previous publications of Raphael Thian and William West Bradbeer. Chase maintained that his contribution to collecting Confederate currency was in clearly distinguishing between types and varieties, and in providing a flexible arrangement "to meet the wide range of collector needs." From the time his first pamphlet was released in 1936, Chase claimed that his new classification system "had gained considerable acceptance because of its adaptability to the needs of all classes of collectors in this field."

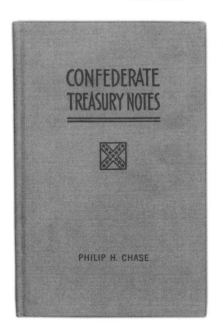

Illus. 46

Despite Chase's claims to the contrary, his numbering system never gained broad support. That said, it is clear that the Criswell Brothers were heavily influenced by Chase's work when they developed their own "Criswell Type Number" system in 1957. Chase and the Criswell Brothers both came up with about the same number of basic designs – 71 for Chase, 72 for the Criswells – although Chase seemingly complicated his numbering system by using a three-digit "type" number compared to Criswell's two-digit system.

While Chase's classification scheme never received universal acceptance, he nonetheless had some prominent supporters. The scholarly and well-read Sydney Kerksis, who reported the existence of the previously unknown $10 Manouvrier note in 1952, defended Chase's system to John Ford, perhaps America's preeminent numismatist of the twentieth century. In a letter dated February 21, 1956 that discussed Chase's classification system, Kerksis wrote:

"I grant you that it may SEEM complicated, but it really isn't and while not perfect (what is?) it at least is an intelligent listing, with flexibility, which Bradbeer's isn't and never was."

Ironically, the same William West Bradbeer whose 1915 publication influenced Chase so greatly might have unwittingly contributed to the rejection of Chase's new classification system. Chase introduced his revolutionary system in 1936, supplemented it with a price list in 1941 and released a hardbound version in 1947. While Chase's new system was trying to gain traction, Charles E. Green released a reprint of the hard-to-find Bradbeer book in 1945, leaving collectors with the choice of learning Chase's entirely new system or simply refreshing their memory of Bradbeer's system, now readily available with the release of Green's reprint. Most took the easy out: they bought the Bradbeer reprint that required no further thought.

Sydney Kerksis agreed that Green's reprint of Bradbeer undermined any chance that Chase's new system might take root. In the same letter to John Ford quoted earlier, Kerksis continued:

> "It is very unfortunate, in my opinion, that Green's re-print and Chase's book both hit the market about the same time."

Chase is best known for a new classification system for Confederate currency which failed to gain broad acceptance. But his unsuccessful classification system should take nothing away from the fact that he assembled one of the most remarkable Confederate currency collections ever, consisting of both the basic type notes – but in an extraordinary state of preservation – and the rarest of the variety notes.

Chase's variety collection was remarkable both for its breadth and its degree of rarity. Much of this collection was acquired by Doug Ball, who wrote comments like, "It took the Chase, McCoy and Browne collections to complete this set!" when he was describing the Criswell Type-16 with Whatman watermarks in his 1987 NASCA sale. The private correspondence between Sydney Kerksis and John Ford mentioned earlier reveals that Chase owned at least one of the famous Type-27 "$10 Shield & Eagle" rarities with plate number A_{10} (today's Criswell variety 223). Other correspondence between Ford and Waverly, Va., collector Howard Spain also establishes that Chase owned at least two of the Type-16s with plate numbers A_1 - A_4 (today's Criswell varieties 95-98), perhaps the rarest varieties in the entire Confederate series with only nine notes known today.

The quality of Chase's type notes was best illustrated with his Montgomerys, three of which are in the Condition Census Top Ten. His $1,000 Montgomery bore serial number 88, a note graded Extremely Fine+ (cut canceled) by the conservative Doug Ball, who acquired it for his own collection and later sold it at a NASCA auction in 1987 to Texas oil man Frederick Mayer. Chase's $500 Montgomery bore serial number 107 and is pedigreed to a Thomas Elder auction in 1924 where it was graded Uncirculated and described as "the finest known example." His $100 Montgomery bore serial number 913, was graded Uncirculated by Doug Ball in 1987 and eventually became a part of Paul Gibson's fabulous type set. The $50 Montgomery bore serial number 955 and was graded About Extremely Fine by Doug Ball in 1987. This note is not quite the quality of Chase's other Montgomerys.

While Chase was disposing of his currency collection, he continued to work tirelessly to promote his classification system. In 1962 he wrote a superb article for *The Numismatist* entitled "CSA Issues of 1861 In Panorama." This article was privately reprinted as a 24-page pamphlet *(Illus. 47)*. Ever true to his convictions, Chase discussed the 38 types that comprise the Confederate issue of 1861 using his own classification system, but, mindful of the times, he also cross-referenced his numbers to the old Bradbeer numbers – and also dutifully to two new upstarts named Grover Criswell and Arlie Slabaugh.

CSA ISSUES
of 1861
IN PANORAMA

By
PHILIP H. CHASE
ANA 4286

Reprinted From
THE NUMISMATIST
1962

Illus. 47

Philip Chase died in Wynnewood, Pa. on the outskirts of Philadelphia on July 4, 1977, at 89 years of age. With the facts provided here, I hope his huge contributions to collecting Confederate currency – particularly in defining the differences between "types" and "varieties"– will someday be more fully recognized.

1945. First Hardbound Re-Print of a Major Confederate Currency Publication.

Chicago coin dealer **Charles E. Green** would probably have remained a numismatic unknown had he not had the foresight to reprint William Bradbeer's *Confederate and Southern State Currency*, a book issued in limited quantities 30 years earlier and nearly impossible to find by 1945. Green made his decision to reprint Bradbeer's 1915 hardbound book after a fruitless search for an original copy, as recounted by Fred Reed. After being forced to pay $35 when a copy finally turned up (that same $35 would have bought a $100 Montgomery *and* a $50 Montgomery in 1945), Green decided to reprint Bradbeer's original work.

Illus. 48

Green was not the first to encounter difficulty in obtaining a copy of Bradbeer's 1915 book, nor was he the first to consider reprinting it. Clarence Criswell noted in his *Reminiscences* on page 10 how difficult it was to find an original copy in 1950. Many collectors desperate for the book actually borrowed an original from a friend or a library and typed a complete copy. One such collector was Dr. Martin H. Bunge of San Marino, Calif.; a page from his typescript version of Bradbeer's original book is pictured on page 10. We also know that Cincinnati collector Herbert A. Brand went so far as to determine that Bradbeer's copyright had expired when he considered reprinting Bradbeer's opus in the 1940s.

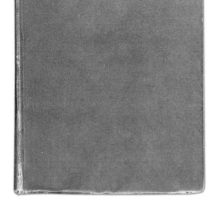

But Charles E. Green gets the credit for doing it, not talking about it. Published under the pseudonym "R. Green" (for his wife Ruth who was also active in the business), Green wished to do more than simply reprint Bradbeer's work. He received permission from the ANA to reprint the excellent series of articles about Confederate currency written by H. D. Allen and serialized in *The Numismatist* between 1917 and 1919. Recognizing that Bradbeer's book was not only about Confederate currency but Southern State currency as well, he also reprinted D. C. Wismer's work on Texas treasury notes and Rudolph Kohler's (Bradbeer's employer) data on Virginia and Louisiana notes. Illustrations of the Republic of Texas notes were provided by dealer Max Mehl of Ft. Worth, making Green's reprint a major improvement over Bradbeer's 1915 original.

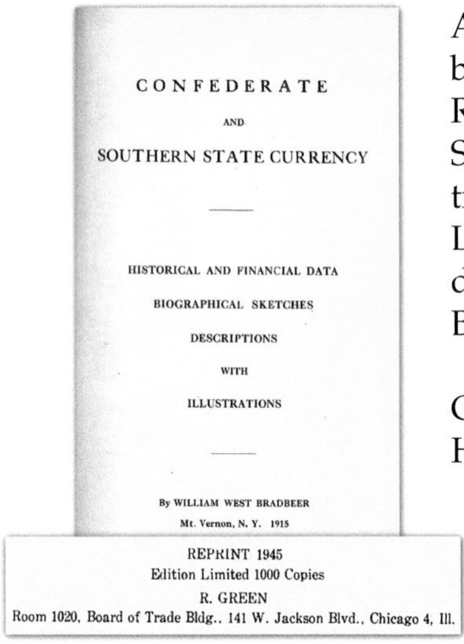
CONFEDERATE

AND

SOUTHERN STATE CURRENCY

HISTORICAL AND FINANCIAL DATA

BIOGRAPHICAL SKETCHES

DESCRIPTIONS

WITH

ILLUSTRATIONS

By WILLIAM WEST BRADBEER

Mt. Vernon, N. Y. 1915

REPRINT 1945

Edition Limited 1000 Copies

R. GREEN

Room 1020, Board of Trade Bldg., 141 W. Jackson Blvd., Chicago 4, Ill.

Illus. 49

Green printed 1,000 copies of his expanded version of Bradbeer in 1945 *(Illus. 48)*. His reprint contained 277 pages, compared to only 162 in the original. Green proclaimed that, "I feel certain the interest in this series of paper money will increase a hundredfold in the coming five years as a result of giving the collectors a standard reference book within the price range of all." Green was right. Within 10 years all 1,000 copies *(Illus. 49)* of his reprint had been sold, and Aubrey Bebee released his own Bradbeer reprint in 1956.

Green, a disabled military veteran of World War I, died in Skokie, Ill., in December 1955 at age 61. His wife Ruth continued running the business until 1959.

1949. First Coffee-Table Size Confederate Currency Book for the Casual Reader.

All publications about Confederate currency – beginning with Thomas Addis Emmet's tables in 1867 and going through Philip Chase's new classification system in 1947 –

were written for numismatists by numismatists. As time progressed, these publications became increasingly detailed and complex. There was nothing in the field for the generalist or casual reader who simply wanted an overview on the subject of Confederate currency.

The United Daughters of the Confederacy (U.D.C.) helped to fill this void. With their support, **Claud E. Fuller** released a beautiful, deluxe, oversize hardbound book titled *Confederate Currency and Stamps* in 1949 *(Illus. 50)*. Complete with a full-color dust jacket, it was certainly a worthy addition to any parlor or living room (I suspect that the fine ladies who sponsored this book might have been more concerned about its aesthetics than its content).

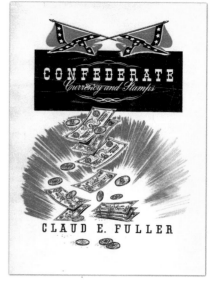

According to the *Foreword*, the book was published to meet the U.D.C.'s "paramount aims; that of preserving for future generations some of the more obscure historical facts concerning the Confederate Government. History is complete and in great detail covering the able officers and brave men of the Confederate armies, but the civil officers who started with almost nothing and were able to carry on the greatest and most costly of all conflicts up to their time, have been almost entirely neglected in the general histories of the period… The U.D.C. are confident that the present volume, *Confederate Currency and Stamps*, will be equally well received by the public." Fuller and his wife Zenada gave the manuscript to the Tennessee Division of the U.D.C., which raised funds to print 1,000 copies. The book contained 236 pages and was copiously illustrated.

Illus. 50

While the U.D.C. seems to have thought that Fuller's manuscript was written for the benefit of the casual reader, it was hardly a broad-brush look at the topic. Detailed examination reveals that Claud Fuller was a consummate numismatist and an avid collector of Confederate currency whose book was equally apropos to the passionate collector or the Southern history buff. He developed his text using the Bradbeer classification system, but borrowed from Chase to start with 68 "types" and then summarized Chase's 574 "varieties"; he discussed the organization of the Confederate government with particular emphasis on the Treasury Department; he provided biographical sketches of key Confederate officials; he illustrated each "type" with an oversize photograph and then described in words the various "varieties" of that type.

Despite being written over 60 years ago, Fuller's book might be the best starting point – even today – for the novice collector of Confederate currency. His book is well written, the illustrations are very large, the "varieties" are succinctly explained, and the underlying acts are described and quoted. In short, the book is an exceptional primer for the beginning collector, but intriguing reading even for the advanced collector.

Illus. 51, Courtesy Ron Herzfeld

One of the most interesting features of Fuller's book was his rarity scale, which ranged from 100 for the rarest notes down to 20 for the most common. Collateral reading shows just how much Fuller knew about Confederate currency. In a letter to "Herman" dated January 27, 1951 *(Illus. 51)*, Fuller wrote that, "The second series of the $50 notes signed by Ellet & Keesee… are about the scarcest of them all; I was never able to get one of them. The $10 dollar essay note of Sept. 2, 1862, is about as hard to get and are [sic] quoted at from $95 to $125 depending on condition while the $20 dollar note of the same issue is a bit easier to find."

Fuller wrote these words in 1951, well before the Criswell series started in 1957. Yet his views in 1951 still hold weight today. The two essay notes (today's Criswell Type-47 for the $20 and Type-48 for the $10) are the rarest "type" notes of all 72 types Criswell identified, based on my review of thousands of auctions between 1865 and 2010. The $50 notes to which Fuller referred are what we now call Criswell Type-16 varieties 95-98 with plate letters A_1 - A_4. Many advanced currency collectors still consider these to be the rarest varieties in the entire Confederate series.

Reading Fuller's book on Confederate currency and stamps quickly establishes that he was no first-time author. Indeed he had written three earlier books on firearms from "Fulleridge," his home on a ridge with extensive views about 10 miles from Chattanooga, Tenn. They were *The Springfield Shoulder Arms, The Breechloader in the Service* and *The Whitney Firearms.* Fuller is said to have owned the largest collection of American Military Shoulder Arms in the world. A retired mechanical engineer who did not move to the South until the early 1930s, he died in 1957 in his eightieth year. He bequeathed to the Tennessee Division of the U.D.C. his extensive collection of manuscripts, Confederate currency, Confederate bonds and Confederate stamps.

1954. The Definitive Reference Work on Confederate Currency Was… Not Published.

To create *the* authoritative reference on Confederate currency, I would anchor my foundation on William Bradbeer's widely acclaimed 1915 book, which bridged John Scott's 1894 catalog and Philip Chase's 1936 pamphlet; I would then build on Chase's revolutionary yet sensible numbering system to classify all the Bradbeer varieties under Chase's 71 types; I would accessorize the text with major new discovery notes on a par with John Browne's legendary variety collection; I would then put it under cover and proudly proclaim it as *the* ultimate Confederate currency reference work.

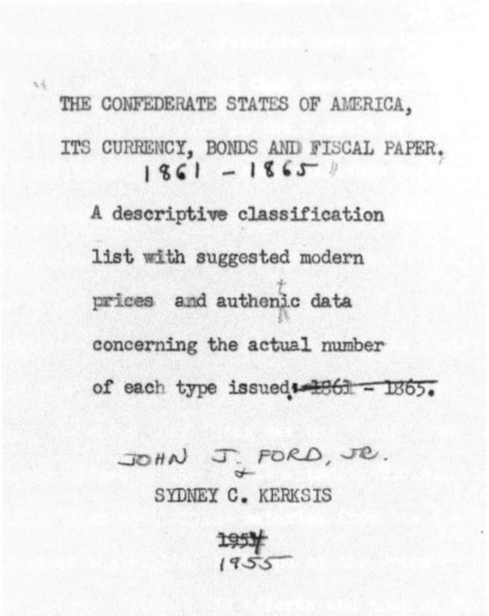
THE CONFEDERATE STATES OF AMERICA,
ITS CURRENCY, BONDS AND FISCAL PAPER,
1861 - 1865
A descriptive classification
list with suggested modern
prices and authentic data
concerning the actual number
of each type issued ~~1861 - 1865.~~
JOHN J. FORD, JR.
&
SYDNEY C. KERKSIS
~~1954~~
1955

Illus. 52

Written by **Sydney Kerksis** from 1950 to 1954 and critiqued by his financial backer **John J. Ford, Jr.** in 1956, this book actually exists. Still in manuscript form, the typescript, with copious editorial changes on top of older revisions, fills a well-worn, 1950-ish binder with 187 pages of text and no illustrations *(Illus. 52).* Yet it was never printed for bizarre, greedy and egotistical reasons. Its story deserves to finally be told in full.

Sydney Kerksis, at the center of this controversy, deserved better. He remains one of the great researchers in the field of Confederate currency, despite the fact that his crowning achievement was never published. But Kerksis had written extensively on the topic well before his book was even drafted, with his first article entitled "A Mystery of the Confederate Currency Solved" appearing in the July 1950 issue of *The Numismatist*, the monthly publication of the ANA.

Kerksis would later publish two books that reflected both his love of – and personal involvement with – military history: *Field Artillery Projectiles of the Civil War, 1861-1865* in 1968, and *Plates and Buckles of the American Military, 1795-1874* in 1974. Kerksis' fascination with this topic was shown by his 1960s purchase of 12 acres in Cobb County, Ga., where the Battle of Gilgal Church was fought in 1864. After his death in the late 1980s, this land was donated to the county for a public park. His personal involvement in the military began during World

War II as a private at Fort Benning, Ga., when he volunteered for service in the highly secretive "Test Platoon" of the 29th Infantry Regiment, which was commended "for meritorious conduct in the performance of hazardous service." As its name implies, the "Test Platoon" evaluated the feasibility of employing paratroopers in modern warfare. Successful airborne operations in all theaters throughout World War II attest to its achievement (for additional information, refer to: *www.corregidor. org/BEA503/features/test_platoon.html*).

Kerksis was one of the first authors to take a scholarly look at the so-called Essay Notes of September 2, 1862 (Criswell Type-47 "$20 Essay" and Criswell Type-48 "$10 Essay"), and wrote a major article titled "Enigmatical Confederate Currency Issues" for the March 1951 issue of *The Numismatist*. He continued to publish fascinating articles during 1951 before reaching the pinnacle: his September 1952 article in *The Numismatist* about the mysterious $10 note printed by Jules Manouvrier of New Orleans. Indeed it was Kerksis who reported the existence of the holy grail of Confederate currency, a note that was never issued because a number of pieces were pilfered en route from New Orleans to Richmond. A specimen has yet to be seen.

Private correspondence during the 1950s among Kerksis, the highly acclaimed and frequently controversial John J. Ford, and both Grover and Clarence Criswell answers why Kerksis' book was never published. Certainly the lead role was played by John Ford, who died in 2005 and is frequently labeled as the greatest American numismatist of the twentieth century. But in the early 1950s Ford was a neophyte, busy burnishing his reputation as a numismatic scholar and authority. Indeed his fellow numismatist John Kleeberg wrote that Ford once confided to an associate, "...my reputation is of paramount concern to me. I want to be remembered for the work I have done and for the esteem the numismatic world has held me in." The trouble was that Ford knew little about Confederate currency (and bonds) and relied heavily on such capable researchers and prodigious authors as Sydney Kerksis and Philip Chase for much of the information needed in cataloging the auctions for his firm, The New Netherlands Coin Company.

A series of confidential letters suggests that Kerksis, already a well-respected author and owner of a huge Confederate currency variety collection by 1950, agreed to write *the* definitive reference works on both Confederate currency and Confederate bonds in return for Ford naming him as at least one of the authors and for Ford's assurance that he would find financial backers to get the books printed reasonably quickly. Kerksis was not paid for hundreds of hours of work over several years and was reimbursed only for the expenses he incurred in writing the manuscripts. Presumably the currency book was written between 1950 and July 12, 1954, when Kerksis delivered the manuscript to Ford *(Illus. 53)*:

> "Herewith is the MS [manuscript] of the book for your perusal. It is somewhat scratched over with corrections but I think, legible... Think that you will agree that it has a tremendous amount of data never before published and which will be of interest to Confederate collectors."

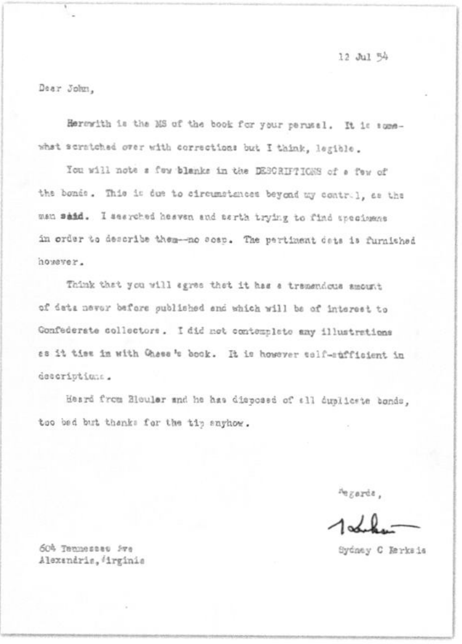

12 Jul 54

Dear John,

Herewith is the MS of the book for your perusal. It is somewhat scratched over with corrections but I think, legible.

You will note a few blanks in the DESCRIPTIONS of a few of the bonds. This is due to circumstances beyond my control, as the man said. I searched heaven and earth trying to find specimens in order to describe them--no soap. The pertinent data is furnished however.

Think that you will agree that it has a tremendous amount of data never before published and which will be of interest to Confederate collectors. I did not contemplate any illustrations as it ties in with Chase's book. It is however self-sufficient in descriptions.

Heard from Bleuler and he has disposed of all duplicate bonds, too bad but thanks for the tip anyhow.

Regards,

Sydney C Kerksis

604 Tennessee Ave
Alexandria, Virginia

Illus. 53

Ford was slow to formally respond to the receipt of Kerksis' manuscript. But it is clear that its content was on his mind and that he was contemplating major revisions. He wrote Kerksis on February 4, 1956, fully 18 months after receipt of the manuscript:

> "I have been up to my neck with the book on CSA... The book will have to be completely revised and greatly enlarged. We *[presumably his financial backers]*

have decided that it will have to be <u>the</u> book, and not just a supplement to Chase. Collectors do not want the Chase numbering system."

Kerksis responded on February 21, 1956, relieved to hear "from [Ford] again and glad to hear that the book is at least being thrashed around – it's yours and you may do as you wish with the MSS [manuscript] as long as I end up as at least one of the authors." A week later Ford replied, writing:

"It is very difficult to try and clear up a lot of points via letters. I would like very much to sit down with you, and ask a lot of questions, and get your slant on many ideas I have for the book. The problem is simple, I just can't find time. The coin business can drive you out of your mind...

I have no interest in putting out a priced book on CSA paper [*Author's note: presumably meaning a book providing estimated current retail prices for each type*] in order to try and make a fast buck. First of all, if the intention is to make money, the book wouldn't be worth a damn. Something should be done that would end all references on the subject, yet flexible to include the stray rarity that is bound to show up. The basic idea and arrangement is clear in my mind, but I would like to go over it with you, even before presenting it to the people who are putting up the big money.

It is particularly important to find out just what background data is available from sources known to you. I have been thinking of even including Thian signature data against serial numbers, in order to clearly establish forgeries of the McCoy type, and to prove rarity. I would like to get Chase to rewrite a complete record of the contemporary fakes, using many notes I have unearthed in the last two years. I have got to figure out how to illustrate bond vignettes; I have even considered full color plates for some types."

Kerksis continued the dialogue, writing Ford on March 8 that he would:

"Save the discussion re the book until I see you and we can really thrash it out. I will say now, tho, that the matter of including signature data etc has been quite thoroughly discussed between Chase and myself and I advise against it. The reason? It would just help the forgers out."

The exchange between Ford and Kerksis from transmittal of the manuscript in July 1954 through March 1956 seems typical of the correspondence between an author and his financial backer. Yet I am perplexed by an entirely separate stream of private letters between Ford and the Criswell brothers, which started only a year after Ford's receipt of the Kerksis manuscript and before Ford had provided any comments at all to Kerksis. In a letter on New Netherlands letterhead dated September 14, 1955 to the Criswell Brothers *(Illus. 54, page 73)*, Ford wrote:

"This morning I sent to you under separate cover, the original Kerksis manuscript (photostat copy) re Confederate Currency. This copy embodies all but three or four unimportant pages of Kerksis' document.

It is to be clearly understood (as discussed in Omaha), [*Author's note: the 1955 ANA National Convention took place in the summer in Omaha, Neb.*] that this photostat copy is only to be used by yourselves personally; is not to be shown or loaned to any other party or institution; and that any or all of the contents are not to be reproduced, used, or utilized in any manner or form, except as a personal means of reference. It is also to be understood, that the entire contents of this copy are the property of the undersigned, and that this copy was made for your personal use and reference only."

I am puzzled – and astonished – that Ford would provide a secret copy of Kerksis' manuscript to the Criswell Brothers, who were intent on writing their own standard reference work on Confederate currency. A race was underway for supremacy in publishing *the* standard reference work. I found it remarkable that Ford would give his competition a draft of Kerksis' manuscript without disclosing that fact to Kerksis, until I read a fascinating 1957 exchange between Ford and Clarence Criswell, just weeks before the release of Criswells' landmark book. That Kerksis was unaware of Ford's deception is proven by my review of extensive Ford files labeled "Personal Hot Correspondence" from 1954 through 1959, which I purchased from a George Kolbe auction sale in 2005. The letter quoted earlier confirms that Kerksis was not aware of the transmittal. Indeed the final paragraph of the letter from Ford to the Criswells emphasizes:

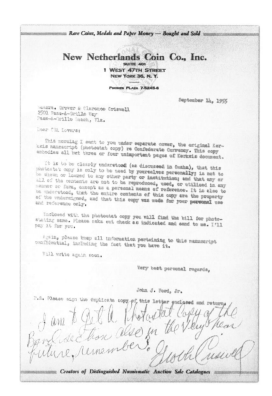

Rare Coins, Medals and Paper Money — Bought and Sold

New Netherlands Coin Co., Inc.
SUITE 401
1 WEST 47TH STREET
NEW YORK 36, N. Y.
PHONES PLAZA 7-5245-6

September 14, 1955

Messrs. Grover & Clarence Criswell
2501 Pass-A-Grille Way
Pass-A-Grille Beach, Fla.

Dear CSA Lovers:

This morning I sent to you under separate cover, the original Kerksis manuscript (photostat copy) re Confederate Currency. This copy embodies all but three or four unimportant pages of Kerksis document.

It is to be clearly understood (as discussed in Omaha), that this photostat copy is only to be used by yourselves personally; is not to be shown or loaned to any other party or institution; and that any or all of the contents are not to be reproduced, used, or utilized in any manner or form, except as a personal means of reference. It is also to be understood, that the entire contents of this copy are the property of the undersigned, and that this copy was made for your personal use and reference only.

Enclosed with the photostat copy you will find the bill for photostating same. Please make out check as indicated and send to me. I'll pay it for you.

Again, please keep all information pertaining to this manuscript confidential, including the fact that you have it.

Will write again soon.

Very best personal regards,

John J. Ford, Jr.

P.S. Please sign the duplicate copy of this letter enclosed and return.

I am to Get a Photostat Copy of the Bond section also in the very near future, remember?

Creators of Distinguished Numismatic Auction Sale Catalogues

"Again, please keep all information pertaining to this manuscript confidential, including the fact that you have it."

Illus. 54

Ford continued regular correspondence about the currency book with Kerksis throughout 1956. No further communication about the manuscript exists between Ford and the Criswells until January 3, 1957, when Ford and Clarence Criswell held a phone conversation summarized in a lengthy letter from Clarence to Ford *(Illus. 55)*. During this conversation, Ford apparently accused the Criswells of the unauthorized use of the Kerksis manuscript in Criswell's own currency book about to be released, for Clarence was quick to defend their actions thusly:

"We have been intently studying and working on Confederate and Southern State Currency for a number of years… Grover and I have been working toward the end of publishing books which would remain as the Standard References Works for many many years to come… When we purchased [*"purchased" will be discussed on page 74*] a portion of the Kerksis manuscript from you in Omaha, we had a manuscript in our room, which was superior to the one we bought. Our only purpose in purchasing it was to check ourselves and ascertain if our progress was sufficient. We were most pleased with our progress, and found that all of the information in that manuscript was contained within our own notes, and thus it was a useless purchase to some extent.

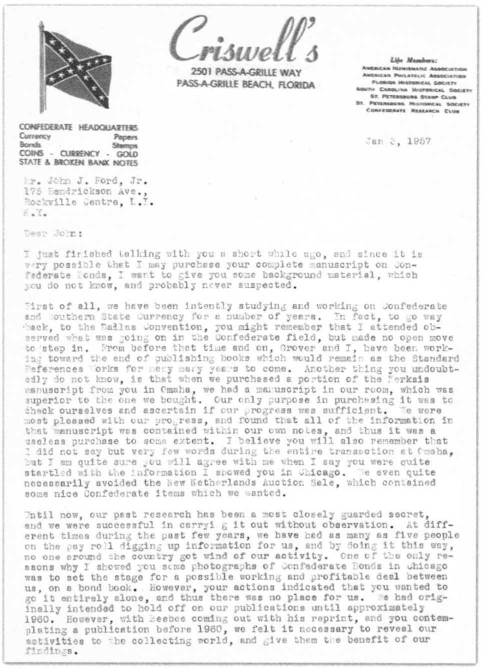

Criswell's
2501 PASS-A-GRILLE WAY
PASS-A-GRILLE BEACH, FLORIDA

Life Members:
American Numismatic Association
American Philatelic Association
Florida Historical Society
South Carolina Historical Society
St. Petersburg Stamp Club
St. Petersburg Historical Society
Confederate Research Club

CONFEDERATE HEADQUARTERS
Currency Papers
Bonds Stamps
COINS - CURRENCY - GOLD
STATE & BROKEN BANK NOTES

Jan 3, 1957

Mr. John J. Ford, Jr.
175 Hendrickson Ave.,
Rockville Centre, L.I.
N.Y.

Dear John:

I just finished talking with you a short while ago, and since it is very possible that I may purchase your complete manuscript on Confederate Bonds, I want to give you some background material, which you do not know, and probably never suspected.

First of all, we have been intently studying and working on Confederate and Southern State Currency for a number of years. In fact, to go way back, to the Dallas Convention, you might remember that I attended observed what was going on in the Confederate field, but made no open move to step in. From before that time and on, Grover and I, have been working toward the end of publishing books which would remain as the Standard References Works for many many years to come. Another thing you undoubtedly do not know, is that when we purchased a portion of the Kerksis manuscript from you in Omaha, we had a manuscript in our room, which was superior to the one we bought. Our only purpose in purchasing it was to check ourselves and ascertain if our progress was sufficient. We were most pleased with our progress, and found that all of the information in that manuscript was contained within our own notes, and thus it was a useless purchase to some extent. I believe you will also remember that I did not say but very few words during the entire transaction at Omaha, but I am quite sure you will agree with me when I say you were quite startled with the information I showed you in Chicago. We even quite necessarily avoided the New Netherlands Auction Sale, which contained some nice Confederate items which we wanted.

Until now, our past research has been a most closely guarded secret, and we were successful in carrying it out without observation. At different times during the past few years, we have had as many as five people on the pay roll digging up information for us, and by doing it this way, no one around the country got wind of our activity. One of the only reasons why I showed you some photographs of Confederate Bonds in Chicago was to set the stage for a possible working and profitable deal between us, on a bond book. However, your actions indicated that you wanted to go it entirely alone, and thus there was no place for us. We had originally intended to hold off on our publications until approximately 1960. However, with Beebee coming out with his reprint, and you contemplating a publication before 1960, we felt it necessary to reveal our activities to the collecting world, and give them the benefit of our findings.

We had originally intended to hold off on our publications until approximately 1960. However, with Bebee coming out with his reprint, and you contemplating a publication before 1960, we felt it necessary to reveal our activities to the collecting world, and give them the benefit of our findings.

Illus. 55

We did not use any material out of the Kerksis manuscript, since we already knew all of the facts that were contained therein. However, it was impossible for us to tell you that at the time, due to our operating policy. Second of all, we can both make money off of the book as long as we play our cards right. Of course, I have considered the possibility of you giving us some difficulty on it, and if this is the case, I am sorry if it would have to be that way. We have put many years of study into this, as well as a considerable amount of money, and everything we done [sic], has been on a sound legal and financial basis, and when it comes to the publication of a bond book, we will be able to put it out at even a cheaper price than the currency book, if we so desire to follow that course… I have always considered you as being a friend, even though at times, you did petty things which were quite annoying. I want to do everything I can, to work with you, or I should say have you work with us on the next couple of publications. But now I must insist that you listen to our terms, rather than attempting to establish your own. Criswell's Publications, will be publishing currency books, for a number of years to come, and in view of that fact, we wish to keep peace in the Numismatic family.

I want you to think over the things I talked to you about, and also the things contained in this letter, and I feel sure that you will agree, co-operation will benefit you a great deal. You have a great many irons in the fire, and this is one that you could pull out of the fire to your benefit. We do not object to running your name in the book, saying that you aided us to a great extent, and thus helping your popularity, and we don't object to being reasonable on any situation…

I will send you a Presentation Copy of our book, as soon as it is ready, and I am sure that once you see this fine work, you will agree, that we were the only ones in the country today, which were capable of turning out such a comprehensive publication."

This letter is remarkable for a number of reasons. First, it was written by a 21-year-old cadet at The Citadel in Charleston, S.C., who exuded a confidence and business savvy far beyond his years. Second, it explains the reason Ford permitted the Criswells access to the Kerksis manuscript in the first place: the Criswells bought, with good money, the right to review Kerksis' manuscript. Ford had no altruistic motive at all; it was purely a profitable financial proposition. Third, Clarence demanded Ford's respect at a time when Ford was already a leading numismatist of the time. Clarence's statement, "I must insist that you listen to our terms, rather than attempting to establish your own," was a direct challenge to Ford's preeminence in the hobby. I cannot imagine another numismatist issuing such a directive.

Ford responded to Clarence just five days later. While his letter was filled with threats and accusations, it seems rather restrained given the enormity of the charges leveled by Ford:

"Even if you changed the numbering system used by Kerksis (i.e. Chase), and scrambled the whole thing up, you are still wrong if you describe in any shape or fashion, notes that are not listed either in Chase or Bradbeer. I could very easily bring civil action against you for plagiarism, and could no doubt restrain the sale of your book and embarrass you no end. However, Clarence, that would do neither of us any good. You know, in your heart, if you utilized the information in the Kerksis manuscript, and both Kerksis and I will know it too. I am bound by an agreement with Kerksis to protect his work, as well as my own.

...I shall be forced to give all of your correspondence and pertinent facts of the situation to my attorney. He will then probably leave it up to you to prove where you got the information on the unpublished items contained in the Kerksis manuscript. I must do this to protect myself under the agreement I have with [Kerksis]."

Within this same letter, Ford then abruptly reversed course and offered to sell all publication rights to Kerksis' manuscripts to the Criswells – remarkably without seeking the agreement of Kerksis who wrote both the currency and bond manuscripts:

"If you have utilized the Kerksis manuscript in your forthcoming publication, I would rather sell all rights to it to you for publication. That will get me off the hook, and will get [Kerksis] off the hook. What do you want to pay me for full publication rights to the Kerksis manuscript, and what do you want to pay me for full publication rights to the bond manuscript. Let me have these figures separately. The bond manuscript is of considerable value, as ALL of its contents are unpublished. If I sell it to you, I will lose any advantage I have in collecting the series, as it tells specifically how many were issued of each and every bond. This information is almost priceless."

I am overwhelmed by Ford's unabashed audacity in offering Kerksis' manuscripts – both of them – for sale without Kerksis' approval. Still without Kerksis' concurrence, Ford wrote Clarence again just two weeks later on January 16, 1957, with concrete terms:

"I will give you the use of both publications, including everything that I have, for thirty common date, nice condition, unmutilated, double eagles. I arrived at this valuation as a small percentage of what I would lose in both information, prestige and publication profits under the terms of this proposal. I would like to reserve the right to publish any or all parts of these manuscripts myself, under a form or abridgement agreeable to you on or after July 1, 1961. This will permit me to some day use some of the information, in a different style, possibly as a tie in with one of my other publications. Naturally, I would work with and clear things through you, so that we would never be at odds.

My interest in double eagles is based upon the fact that they make excellent trade-in material on my western trips for pioneer gold items. There is no reason why I should sell for cash, when I do not need the money."

Apparently Clarence could not locate 30 double eagles quickly at a good price, leading Ford to write him again on January 27, 1957, telling him that "If you cannot supply the coins by June 1, 1957, you then can send me $38" each, which would have created a cash price of $1,140. This price of $1,140 for publication rights was outrageous, as just two weeks earlier on January 13, 1957, Michael Kolman of Federal Coin Exchange had sold the finest known $1,000 Montgomery note in Crisp Uncirculated condition for only $675 – and this $675 price itself was an all-time record for any Montgomery note at the time.

Illus. 56

While the Criswells were evaluating their options, Clarence sent Ford a Presentation copy of their monumental Confederate currency book on February 16, 1957 *(Illus. 56)*. A week after receipt, on March 2, 1957, Ford acknowledged getting it but dismissed the book as "not scientific" and offered to reduce the cost of the Kerksis bond manuscript to $950.

"About your book. I like it because it will help the hobby, and because it is out now. Also, I think it is a good deal for anybody at $6.00. However, I do not think it is anything like the last word on the subject, in fact, I feel a book twice the size could just be written on C.S.A. Also, I do not care for the Bradbeer numbers in any way, shape or form. It is intended for popular (and not scientific) appeal, and I'm sure it will sell. After all, I guess that is what you want.

I will let you have the bond manuscript and the six note Mississippi sheet (your No. 49a) for $950. I value the sheet more than you do, that is our real problem. You offer $850, I came down to $1,050, we can split the difference."

Predictably, Clarence was furious upon receipt of Ford's letter panning his new book. Clarence responded with a scathing letter, to which Ford replied on March 17, 1957 *(Illus. 57)*:

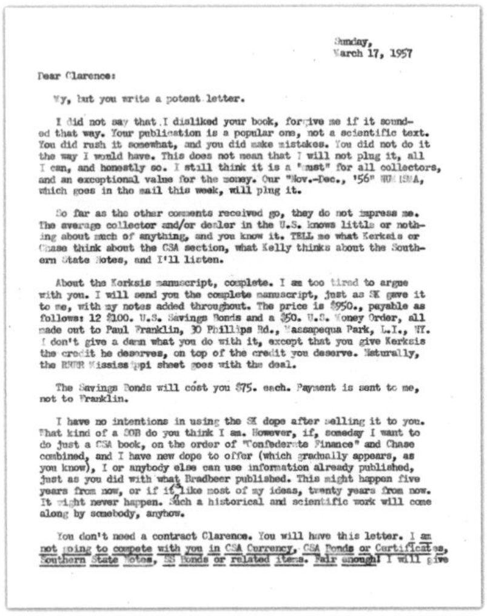

Illus. 57

"My, but you write a potent letter.

About the Kerksis [bond] manuscript, complete. I am too tired to argue with you. I will send you the complete manuscript, just as [Kerksis] gave it to me, with my notes added throughout. The price is $950, payable as follows: 12 $100 U.S. Savings Bonds and a $50 U.S. Money Order, all made out to Paul Franklin… Massapequa Park, L.I., NY. I don't give a damn what you do with it, except that you give Kerksis the credit he deserves, on top of the credit you deserve. Naturally, the RRRR Mississippi sheet goes with the deal.

The Savings Bonds will cost you $75 each. Payment is sent to me, not to Franklin…

You don't need a contract Clarence. You will have this letter. I am not going to compete with you in CSA Currency, CSA Bonds or Certificates, Southern State Notes, SS Bonds or related items. Fair enough! I will give you any help or dope that I can, in addition to the [Kerksis] manuscript, if you want it. If you had asked for it, prior to printing your book, I would have proof read that for you.

My last letter to you was stupid, and both of us know it. What I was trying to say, is that I would like to see Thian's signature tables, the Acts of the CSA Congress, the history, and a lot of what Chase tried to do in print someday. How this could hurt you, particularly when it would appear, if it ever did, long after you left the field, I do not know. Forget what I said before, I have too much to do, to worry about competing with you or Grover."

Clarence accepted Ford's counter-offer but ignored Ford's payment terms. Clarence simply submitted a check for $950 with a letter dated April 1, 1957:

"…please send the Ford-Kerksis Manuscript to us in its complete form. I would also want the letters and a copy of the contract that you had with Kerksis. As we agreed, you may retain a copy of this work, but it is to be seen by you only."

In response on April 5, 1957, Ford returned Clarence's check for $950 and reiterated the original payment terms:

"Upon the receipt of the 12 U.S. Savings Bonds and $50 payable to Franklin, I shall ship to you everything that Kerksis gave me, along with the few loose papers pertaining thereto, and Sydney's letter. I never had any kind of an agreement with [Kerksis], just a verbal understanding, in that I would give him credit when the book was published. While I did not spell the credit angle out in the agreement sent to you, it is my understanding that Sydney and I will receive full credit whenever the manuscript or parts of it is published."

Clarence accepted this method of payment and sent the savings bonds and money order to Ford on April 12, 1957, with the promise that "I will take care of Sydney in our bond book as well as you. How I will do it is not yet set. However, I will do more for you than you would have done for us if you were putting out the book…"

As the reader might expect, this story about subterfuge, deceit and greed does not end with Ford's receipt of $950 for full rights to the Kerksis manuscript. On May 2, 1957, Sydney Kerksis wrote Ford in response to a letter Ford sent on April 2 *(Illus. 58)*. The usually reserved and understated Kerksis, caught off guard when he saw the Criswell currency book for the first time, nevertheless threatened legal action, writing:

"I may say that I am somewhat unhappy with the course of action you have chosen to take with my manuscript, and in fact am seriously thinking about referring the matter to my attorney for legal action. As you know I sold it to you for the absolute cost only, and at that an underestimate, of what expenses I had incurred in writing, with no view of any profit, with the agreement that it was to be published in the reasonably near future, subsequent to the sale. Apparently it was a profitable transaction on your part."

Illus. 58

Ford immediately responded on May 7, writing Kerksis that:

"From my conversation with you of a year ago last month, and from our various letters, there should be no doubt in your mind that I ever intended to dispose of your manuscript. I bought it from you, at your price, and honestly intended to add to it, and publish, giving you full credit. As I remember, all you asked for was that it would be published, fair credit for your work, and several copies…

In the meantime, completely unknown to me, the Criswells were putting together their own book. The first volume, including Confederate currency, included just about all the unpublished material that you had so carefully unearthed. When I found out that they were going ahead with the bond book also, and that they had engaged your services, I saw the handwriting on the wall. Thus, when they asked me for the rights to your manuscript, and agreed to give you full credit, and finally told me that you were working for them, I knew I was licked. As a last resort, I put a price on the manuscript coupled with a very important paper money item, which I thought prohibitive. I did not wish to dispose of your manuscript, but could see no alternative. Prior to the Criswells entrance into the field, I had a fighting chance to break even with what I wanted to do. My backer in my various publishing ventures retreated quickly when the Criswell's program was clearly apparent. As you know, this publishing venture is all mine, and has no connection with New Netherlands…

I am more sorry than you are that things did not work out exactly the way I contemplated. I think that had you been in my shoes, you would have chosen the same way out, as I did."

Even the professional, courteous and non-confrontational Kerksis was unwilling to accept Ford's outlandish attempt to pacify him with a "sorry things did not work out" response. He wrote Ford on June 11 *(Illus. 59)* that:

"I am not questioning your original intentions at all. As you know, I let you have the [manuscript] at a somewhat ridiculous figure, based solely on what actual expenses I had incurred in writing it, and completely irrespective of the hundreds of hours of my time involved. I did this solely to get it published and with, naturally the understanding, that you would make some profit from the published work, as would be expected in any business venture. I did not contemplate, nor is it in any way implied in our agreement, that the end results would be that you would sell the [manuscript], at a considerable financial profit to yourself, AFTER the best part of my labors had appeared in print, under circumstances that precluded my being given any credit for my original discoveries and the fruits of my research.

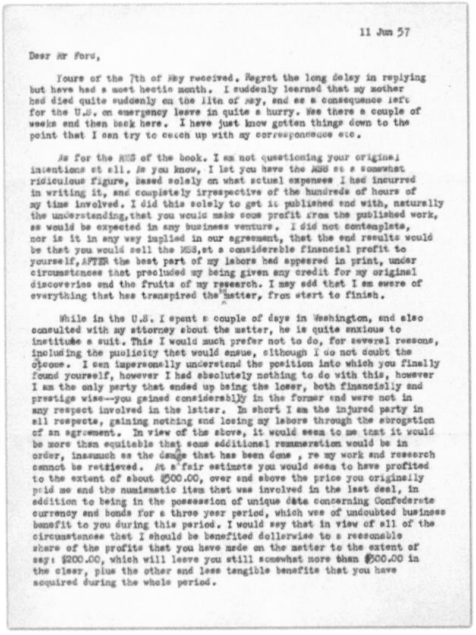

Illus. 59

While in the U.S., I spent a couple of days in Washington, and also consulted with my attorney about the matter, he is quite anxious to institute a suit. This I would much prefer not to do, for several reasons, including the publicity that would ensue, although I do not doubt the outcome. I can impersonally understand the position into which you finally found yourself, however I had absolutely nothing to do with this, however I am the only party that ended up being the loser, both financially and prestige wise – you gained considerably in the former and were not in any respect involved in the latter. In short I am the injured party in all respects, gaining nothing and losing my labors through the abrogation of an agreement. In view of the above, it would seem to me that it would be more than equitable that some additional remuneration would be in order, inasmuch as the damage that has been done, re my work and research cannot be retrieved. As a fair estimate you would seem to have profited to the extent of about $500.00, over and above the price you originally paid me and the numismatic item that was involved in the last deal, in addition to being in the possession of unique data concerning Confederate currency and bonds for a three year period, which was of undoubted business benefit to you during this period. I would say that in view of all of the circumstances that I should be benefited dollarwise to a reasonable share of the profits that you have made on the matter to the extent of say: $200.00, which will leave you still somewhat more than $300.00 in the clear, plus the other and less tangible benefits that you have acquired during the whole period.

Trust that you will acquiesce in the preceding. I have given much thought to the matter and am trying to be quite fair about it, however, as it stands, something to equalize things must be done. If during the course of the events leading up to the final, and unknown to me at the time, sale of the [manuscript], you had seen fit to consult with me on the matter, it is quite likely that we could have come to a better understanding. I am quite reasonable and can understand the various difficulties germane to business affairs and life in general. On the other hand some things cannot be borne in silence."

Upon receipt of Kerksis' letter dated June 11, Ford must have been relieved to learn that he could extricate himself from his apparent greed and duplicity for a mere $200.00. Yet Ford chose to roll the dice once more, offering Kerksis only $125.00:

"There is little in your letter that I can disagree with, as I feel that you understand to a certain extent that rather than being a complete knave, I was victimized more or less by circumstances…

I made $250.00 on the rights of the manuscript, plus enjoying its use. I am willing to pay you one half of the profit, namely $125.00. This I feel to be satisfactory. I am enclosing my check in that amount for your consideration."

Ford guessed right. In the final chapter to this saga, on July 28, 1957, Kerksis wrote Ford, "Under the circumstances, as enumerated in your letter, the check is acceptable, and we will call it quits on the manuscript deal, and consider the matter completely closed." *(Illus. 60)*

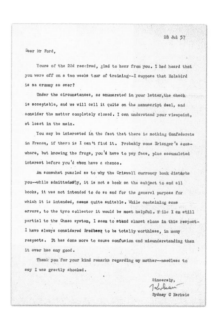

Illus. 60

Sydney Kerksis conducted himself honorably and professionally during the tumultuous time between submitting his own currency manuscript to John Ford in 1954 and reading the published Criswell manuscript three years later. Similarly, the Criswells did nothing inappropriate; they independently developed their own currency manuscript to exploit the imminent Civil War Centennial, and they dedicated their second book on Confederate bonds to Kerksis, who rightfully deserved the accolades. On the other hand, John J. Ford apparently suffered a complete shutdown of his moral compass during this episode. At the risk of understatement, the reputation he cared so much about was not polished by his conduct toward Sydney Kerksis.

It is a reasonable question to ask which document – Kerksis' unpublished manuscript completed in 1954 or the Criswell book published in 1957 – would better have served the fledging hobby as *the* standard reference work on Confederate currency. It is my personal opinion that Kerksis' unpublished draft is the better of the two. Kerksis' manuscript is more thorough and more deeply researched. After all, Kerksis had the benefit of much conversation and consultation with the cerebral Philip Chase (see page 64) while writing his manuscript. Certainly the two texts are vastly different in terms of substance: Kerksis' text is filled with fascinating information for the more advanced collector, such as types of paper used, watermarks, Trans Mississippi issues, control stamps, and a formula to price notes in various grades and with various methods of cancellation. Amazingly, some of the material in Kerksis' 1954 manuscript remains unpublished to this day.

Conversely, the Criswell publication is long on illustrations but short on explanatory text. All things considered, Criswell's 1957 publication is an updated and refined version of Bradbeer's 1915 book with far more illustrations. Indeed the longest editorial text in the entire Criswell book is the "Fundamentals" page with only 26 lines of copy. (Admittedly, though, in a masterful stroke of genius that I consider the Criswells' major contribution to the hobby, they consolidated all of Bradbeer's 579 varieties under the umbrella of only 72 types.)

The only credit that Sydney Kerksis received in Criswell's 1957 Confederate currency book was having his name listed, along with 15 other collectors, on the Acknowledgments page. I suspect this brief mention was a personal favor to John Ford (who was not acknowledged), as none of the Kerksis material found its way into the Criswell publication, exactly as Clarence Criswell had earlier advised Ford.

Happily, though, Kerksis finally received at least a portion of the credit he deserved in the second volume of Criswell's Currency Series on Confederate Bonds. In a full-page Dedication including a large photograph, the book honored Kerksis, who was working for the Criswells by the time of its publication in 1961. Kerksis continued writing and publishing despite his misfortune with John Ford. He died in the late 1980s.

1956. First Reprint of a Reprint of a Major Confederate Currency Publication.

By the mid 1950s interest in Confederate currency was peaking as the country was about to commemorate in 1961 the centennial of the start of the Civil War. As might be expected, on the eve of this milestone event, the numismatic market, once again, exhausted all available copies of William Bradbeer's original 1915 book, plus the 1,000 copies of the Bradbeer reprint released by Charles E. Green in 1945.

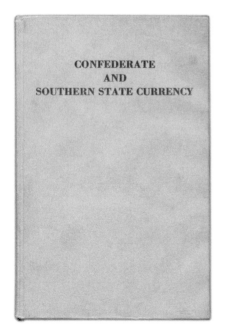

CONFEDERATE
AND
SOUTHERN STATE CURRENCY

Illus. 61

Omaha (by way of Chicago) dealer **Aubrey E. Bebee**, a friend of Charles and Ruth Green, who had published the first Bradbeer reprint in 1945, was unable to field the numerous requests for a copy of Bradbeer in his own coin shop. Knowing that the demand for Bradbeer's book would only increase as the calendar counted down to the Civil War centennial in 1961, Bebee stated in his *Foreword* that he "decided to have [Bradbeer] reprinted and made available to collectors."

Aubrey E. Bebee was my kind of "make it happen" guy. His friend Charles Green had just died in December 1955, so Bebee took the initiative and found a way to get Bradbeer's book reprinted a second time – and quickly *(Illus. 61)*. First, he was granted permission to borrow all the plates, including the illustrations, from Ruth Green, Charles' widow. Second, he was granted permission by the ANA to reprint three items: H.D. Allen's series of articles about Confederate currency published in *The Numismatist* between 1917 and 1919; D.C. Wismer's article on Texas treasury notes that appeared in the September 1927 issue of *The Numismatist*, and Rudolph Kohler's material on Virginia and Louisiana notes. Third, since dealer Max Mehl, who had supplied illustrations of Republic of Texas notes for Green's reprint had retired (and would die in 1957), Bebee was given permission to use illustrations of Republic of Texas notes from the collection of R.F. Schermerhorn as replacements. Fourth, Bebee made editorial changes to only two pages in the entire 277-page Green reprint: he removed the "Green" name and address from the bottom of the Title Page and replaced it with his own *(Illus. 62, p. 81)*, and he rewrote the one-page *Foreword*. Fifth, Bebee placed an order for books and collected his profits. Quite a simple recipe for success!

The reader might feel that the achievements of Aubrey Bebee are not on a par with those described so far. But Bebee deserves many kudos for his major contributions to numismatics. His reprint of Bradbeer provides a good excuse to review some of those accomplishments. I am indebted to Fred Reed (again) for much of the biographical data on this renowned numismatist.

Born in 1906 in Huntington, Ark., Bebee first dabbled in real estate before becoming a bookkeeper for a bank in Ft. Smith, Ark. He relocated to Chicago as a bookkeeper for a jeweler and a hotel. After a brief stint with Illinois Bell, where he met and married Adeline Dorsey in 1930, he purchased the Blackstone, a Chicago hotel that he managed and then sold at a handsome profit in 1939.

Bebee used his profits to open a coin shop in 1941 in Chicago. He relocated to Omaha, Neb. in 1952, opening another coin shop, and began buying paper money, particularly from the collections of Albert Grinnell and James Wade. He was a founding member of the Professional Numismatists Guild, boasting charter member number 1. He conducted his own auctions from 1953 to 1957, including the prestigious ANA sale in 1955.

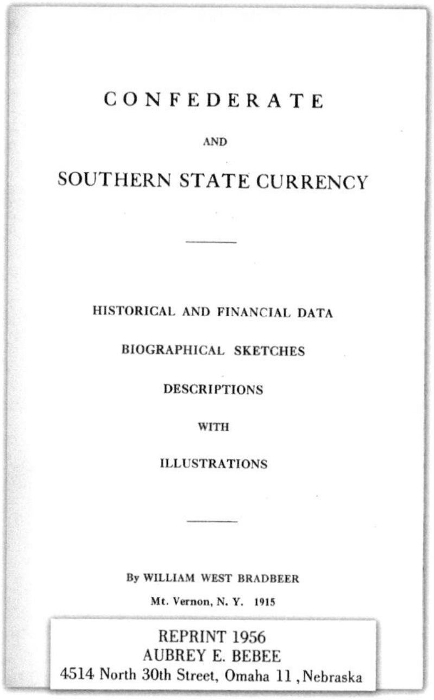

CONFEDERATE

AND

SOUTHERN STATE CURRENCY

———

HISTORICAL AND FINANCIAL DATA

BIOGRAPHICAL SKETCHES

DESCRIPTIONS

WITH

ILLUSTRATIONS

———

By WILLIAM WEST BRADBEER

Mt. Vernon, N. Y. 1915

REPRINT 1956
AUBREY E. BEBEE
4514 North 30th Street, Omaha 11, Nebraska

Illus. 62

Numismatics treated Aubrey Bebee kindly. He owned both of the arguably greatest coins in the U.S. series. In 1967 he purchased the McDermott 1913 Liberty Head nickel for $46,000, a record price for any U.S. coin at the time; in 1985 he purchased the Jerry Buss 1804 Silver Dollar. In 1988 the ANA presented him with the Farran Zerbe Memorial Award, its highest honor in recognition of numerous years of outstanding, dedicated service to numismatics. Just a year later the Bebees donated their 1913 nickel to the ANA, followed by the 1804 dollar in 1991.

Aubrey E. Bebee died in Omaha in 1992 at age 85. In 1996 he was inducted posthumously into the ANA Hall of Fame. After his death his U.S. paper money collection was also donated to the ANA, making the Bebees among the ANA's most generous benefactors.

1957. The modern notion of collecting Confederate currency "by type" is born.

From the beginning, the hobby of collecting Confederate currency has been seemingly obsessed with proliferating the number of varieties discovered – no matter how minor the variations might be. Thomas Addis Emmet identified 335 distinct varieties in his charts that appeared in the *American Journal of Numismatics* as early as 1867. Ever the salesman, John Haseltine reduced the number of varieties in his 1876 catalog down to 137 – which conveniently aligned with the 137 varieties he maintained in inventory. George Massamore sharply expanded that number to 314 varieties in his own catalog released in 1889. With a 26-year hiatus before the next major publication about Confederate currency, it seems as if the varieties multiplied on their own, as William West Bradbeer's 1915 seminal book listed the staggering total of 579 varieties. Even Philip Chase, who unsuccessfully tried to introduce a rival numbering system to Bradbeer's in his 1936 pamphlet, still maintained a huge total of 574 varieties.

It took the **Criswell Brothers** to organize and simplify this madness. Biographical details of this essential family to the collecting of Confederate currency are provided on pages 9-13.

The Criswells maintained all 579 of the varieties found in Bradbeer. They even added a few discovery notes. But the Criswells had the foresight to know that 579 of any collectible is simply too many. They combined all 579 varieties under the umbrella of only 72 major design "types" – the same 72 types that comprise a complete Confederate type set to this day.

Illus. 63, Courtesy
Fred Reed

Lest we overstate the Criswells' contribution, several much earlier dealers came close to giving us the 70 or so types we now use. To refresh the reader's memory, as early as 1879 John Walter Scott set the number of "types" to complete a Confederate type set at only 74, a dramatic decrease from the 1,500 varieties mentioned in a strongly worded reproach titled "Collecting Run Mad" in the January 1877 issue of the *American Journal of Numismatics (Illus. 63)*. H. D. Allen, in his series of articles appearing in *The Numismatist* between 1917 and 1919, discussed 84 "kinds" of notes, "without going into minor varieties." By 1936 Philip Chase was already labeling the basic designs issued by the Confederate Treasury as "types," with minor differences in the basic designs called "varieties." Chase came up with 71 types, virtually identical to the Criswells' 72. In fact, had Chase's revolutionary numbering system received broader acceptance among collectors in the 1930s and 1940s, we would probably be referring to "Chase Type Numbers" today, not "Criswell Type Numbers."

Grover Cleveland Criswell, born in 1933 two years before brother **Clarence**, was an author of five hardbound editions of his Confederate Currency Series (in addition to other books, price lists and pamphlets not relevant to this book). He was the leading dealer in Confederate currency for most of his adult life and a promoter of Confederate currency without equal. Each of his contributions will be discussed briefly.

Grover Criswell the author will undoubtedly be his most lasting legacy to the hobby. But the first currency book co-authored with Clarence in 1957 was not his initial printing venture. There were at least two editions of *Criswell's C S A Catalog* issued prior to their hardbound book in 1957. These catalogs, each with well over 100 pages and soft-covered, are exceptionally rare today. They were issued even before the Criswells coordinated designs with specific type numbers. The numerous $20 and $10 designs of the third issue dated September 2, 1861, that we now label Criswell Types-17 through 30, were numbered entirely differently when *Criswell's C S A Catalog No. 2* was published around 1954 *(Illus. 64)*.

Most importantly, though, the Criswells did not initially intend to include the two Essay notes (Criswell Types-47 and 48 today) as "types," probably because the notes were not authorized and issued by the Confederate Treasury. Thus the original complete type set consisted of only 70 types compared to the 72 types when the hardbound book was finally released in 1957.

Illus. 64, Courtesy
Charles A. Hilton

The Criswells' first hardbound edition in January 1957, titled *Criswell's Currency Series: Vol. 1. Confederate & Southern State Currency. A Descriptive Listing, Including Rarity*, benefited from timing and technical developments in the printing industry as much as anything the Criswells did in an editorial sense. The 1957 first edition was nothing more than a reprise of William Bradbeer's 1915 book with four major benefits and improvements.

First, it had been over 40 years since Bradbeer's original book in 1915, and the hobby was thirsty for something new. Chase's efforts in 1936 and 1947 did not capture the hobby's interest, and the Green and Bebee reprints of Bradbeer in 1945 and 1956, respectively, were exhausted. With the imminent centennial of the Civil War in 1961, interest was sky-high but publications were nil. The Criswells certainly benefited from this timing.

Second, the Criswells had the clear-headedness to take Bradbeer's 579 varieties and combine them under only 72 types. This creation of a manageable number of types can easily be considered the Criswells' most significant contribution to the collecting of Confederate currency.

Third, advances in printing technology allowed the Criswells to illustrate all 72 types in a 277-page hardbound book offered at only $6 retail, making the book affordable to anyone with even a casual interest. By contrast, Bradbeer provided illustrations of only six types, as more illustrations using 1915 printing techniques would have made his book cost prohibitive.

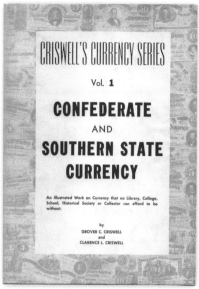

Illus. 65

Fourth, being dealers as well as authors, the Criswells knew that every collector in the field had immense interest in knowing what his Confederate notes were worth right then. Yet they also recognized that inserting current market prices into a book simply served to quickly date the book. Thus the Criswells published separate annual price lists to provide present market values, with the *1957 Price List and Supplement to Volume 1 of Criswell's Currency Series* issued concurrently with the first edition. These price lists exist at least for 1957, 1958-59, 1960, 1961 and 1962. By the 1964 second edition, prices were incorporated into the book itself.

The Criswells' first edition *(Illus. 65)*, self-published in 1957, resembled a picture album of Confederate currency rather than a thoughtful discussion of its many nuances. The truth is that the Criswells' 1957 effort contained far less text than Bradbeer's 1915 book that it replaced. But the Criswells had remarkable courage at the tender ages of 23 and 21; they boldly printed 5,000 copies and sold them at only $6 each. The exposure they gave the hobby by making their book easily available to all was nearly as important as their developing the notion of collecting by "type."

Criswell's second edition *(Illus. 66)* of the currency series was published by Krause Publications in 1964 and was more properly titled *Criswell's Currency Series: Vol. 1, 1st Revised Edition. Confederate and Southern State Currency. A Descriptive Listing, Including Rarity and Prices.* Now owned exclusively by Grover, the Confederate currency portion of the 1964 edition was virtually identical to the original 1957 edition, with one important addition: Criswell incorporated current market values for each of the varieties in both Uncirculated and Very Good condition. Criswell must have felt that publishing separate annual price lists was too time-consuming or too expensive or both, as I cannot find any separate price lists released after 1962. The 1964 edition was modestly increased from 277 pages to 291 pages, but all the extra pages were in the Southern States' portion of the book, not the Confederate currency section.

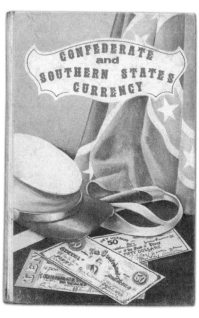

Grover's third edition of the currency series was disappointing. Self-published in 1976 under the title *Criswell's Currency Series: Vol. 1, 2nd Revised Edition. Confederate and Southern State Currency. A Descriptive Listing, Including Rarity and Prices*, the page count of the Confederate currency section was actually reduced from 104 pages in the first two editions to only 85 pages in the 1976 edition. *Illus. 66*

The book's total page count of 294 was about the same as the 291 pages in the 1964 edition, with the increase coming entirely in the Southern States section. It would appear as if the 1976 edition served only to update current market pricing, as it had been 12 years since the 1964 edition had been released. Overall, this largely forgettable edition was Grover's poorest effort.

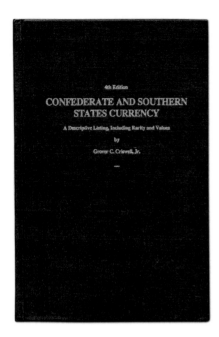

Illus. 67

Grover's fourth edition, published by Fred Schwan of BNR Press, was seriously delayed. Although promised as early as the mid 1980s (and prepaid orders, including my own, were taken), the book was not released until late 1992 – a full 16 years after the 1976 publication of the third edition. To my knowledge, though, Grover delivered all the long-overdue orders in a special presentation version with a black cover and silver lettering *(Illus. 67)*. I recall having completely forgotten about my old order, with three moves between order placement and receipt. Nevertheless, somehow Grover found my new address and shipped me the special presentation version with profuse apologies for his tardiness.

Grover's fourth edition was by far his best to date. Despite some serious and even comical typographical errors for which publisher Fred Schwan took the blame (e.g., the word "Confederate" was spelled "Confererate" on the book's spine), it was clear that Schwan understood currency and capably contributed to a much better book. The fourth edition, properly titled *Criswell's Currency Series: Vol. 1, 4th Edition. Confederate and Southern States Currency. A Descriptive Listing, Including Rarity and Values*, included a detailed section on Confederate counterfeits for the first time. Grover illustrated both the obverse and reverse sides of the issues of 1862, 1863 and 1864. Presumably at the insistence of Schwan, he included a Bibliography to add an air of authority and careful research. Grover even introduced his brand-new type note – "first major type to be discovered in 127 years," according to Grover – the dubious and clearly variant note he labeled the Type-32 1/2. The book's page count was sharply increased to 417 pages. While the presentation copies were covered in black with silver lettering, the regular run was covered in red with silver lettering.

Illus. 68

Grover's fifth and final edition *(Illus. 68)*, simply titled *Comprehensive Catalog of Confederate Paper Money*, was co-authored with Doug Ball and Hugh Shull and featured updated and enlarged illustrations from Neil Chiappa's fabulous Confederate currency collection, frequently on display at the Museum of the Confederacy in Richmond, Va. Also published by Fred Schwan of BNR Press, the fifth edition was released in 1996, only four years after the fourth edition finally showed up in 1992.

The combination of author Grover, publisher Fred Schwan and Confederate currency experts Doug Ball and Hugh Shull made the fifth edition by far the best of a series that spanned nearly four decades. Even my own friend and statistician, Steven Feller, Ph.D., made his debut in a Confederate currency book in Grover's fifth edition. With a page count of 352 pages, the total was a bit shy of the 417 pages found in the fourth edition, but for the first time ever the newest edition was devoted exclusively to Confederate currency – no Southern States currency, which Grover intended to feature in a separate book that sadly never materialized due to Grover's untimely death just three years later in 1999.

Grover's fifth edition opened with a comprehensive background discussion of the formation of the Confederate government and the seven issues of Confederate currency authorized by the Confederate Treasury. It even included a summary of the collecting of Confederate currency, from the charts prepared by Thomas Addis Emmet in 1867 to Grover's fifth edition published in 1996. It is hard to believe that this historical perspective did not appear until Grover's final edition, but it is a testimony to Hugh Shull and particularly Doug Ball (who clearly wrote it) that they were able to convince Grover of the need for such explanatory material – particularly for new collectors.

While Grover wrote only five editions of his *Criswell's Currency Series*, it would be misleading to suggest his authorship was limited to these five volumes. Sensing an unfilled need for a monthly publication featuring exclusively paper money to keep up with several publications already promoting coinage, in 1973 he launched *Bank Note Reporter* – now the leading publication in the field of paper money. He wrote two volumes about Confederate bonds and also authored a primer titled *Confederate Money is Good*. Lest the implication that Grover's numismatic acumen was limited to Confederate and Southern States currency and bonds, he also authored the important reference work titled *North American Currency* in 1969. While his passion as a promoter of the hobby and his skills as a dealer might be more greatly appreciated today, I suspect his lasting legacy will be his publications that showcased his brilliant idea of collecting by major "type" and not by minor variety.

Grover Criswell's second hat – as a dealer – began when he started selling coins by mail in 1945 at age 12. By the early 1950s he and brother Clarence were already buying and selling Confederate and Southern States currency and bonds. In 1951 Grover enrolled at The Citadel in Charleston, S.C., and spent his spare time visiting antique shops in Charleston and the surrounding areas, buying all the notes and bonds he could find for just pennies a piece. Grover joined the ANA in 1951 as Life Member #268 at only 18 years of age. By 1953 he was already exchanging correspondence with the celebrated John J. Ford, who clearly was impressed with this 20-year-old neophyte. Early letters between the two establish that they were already transacting business at the ANA Convention in Dallas in 1953.

Grover's personal files, which I inspected over several years, date back to 1954. They contain literally tens of thousands of transactions. Many are important and significant, but I wish to summarize only one to portray Grover's skills as a dealer: his purchase of seven Criswell Type-3 "$100 Montgomery" notes from a reputed descendant of the Spanish consul to the Confederate Government's New Orleans' office. This story involves charm, deceit, misrepresentation, greed and even a bit of terrorism thrown in for good measure.

The story begins routinely enough when Grover received a short letter dated April 29, 1976 from Barcelona, Spain *(Illus. 69)*. Grover was quickly impressed, though, as the author advised that he was writing in "Castilian Spanish," which like "The King's English" was primarily used by the aristocracy and other members of the upper class. The letter, translated below, included photocopies of five Confederate bills, offered to Grover at the reasonably fair price of $5,000. Confirming his lineage, the author advised that the notes came from the distribution of an estate whose ancestor served as Consul to the Confederate States in their New Orleans office:

Illus. 69

> "Sir: First of all excuse me for writing in Castilian Spanish, but if I wrote in English, this letter would have been delayed. In the catalog that you edit, I read that you are interested in buying Confederate bills and therefore I offer for sale the five bills, photocopies of which are enclosed, for a price of $5,000.

They are in a perfect state of preservation and come from the distribution of an estate, one of whose ancestors was Consul of Spain in New Orleans. Awaiting your news. Yours sincerely,

Jose-Andres Bonet B—"

Even with 25 years of dealership experience, Grover was surely impressed with the photocopies. While not in the "perfect state of preservation" claimed in the letter, Grover certainly wished to purchase five beautiful Montgomery notes as follows:

Two Criswell Type-2 "$500 Montgomerys," serial #149 in Very Fine and serial #569.
Two Criswell Type-3 "$100 Montgomerys," serial #1286 in Extra Fine and serial #859.
One Criswell Type-4 "$50 Montgomery," serial #997 in Choice Extremely Fine.

The first complication in what would ultimately become a remarkable deal cropped up shortly after Grover received the initial communication. While sent by the Spanish nobleman on April 29, 1976, the letter was mailed to Grover's St. Petersburg, Fla., address from which Grover had moved eight years earlier. It was not until May 27, 1976, that Grover received the forwarded letter and immediately responded to the nobleman, stating that he "would certainly be interested in the 5 Confederate notes of which you sent photocopies... I would pay you somewhere around $2,000."

But the Spaniard had become inpatient in the meantime. Not hearing from Grover for a month after first writing, he wrote an expert in Spanish Colonial coinage named Alcedo Almanzar in San Antonio, Texas, enclosing the actual notes and also asking for $5,000. Almanzar, knowing Grover's reputation in the field of Confederate currency, phoned Grover on June 23, 1976, described the notes in great detail and told Grover that the notes were worth more than the $2,000 Grover had offered.

Grover, feeling that his potential client was not operating in good faith, wrote him a second time on June 23 – the same day he talked to Almanzar. Indignant, Grover explained that Almanzar confirmed that the notes were not in Uncirculated condition; nevertheless, Grover would increase his offer "but not a great deal more."

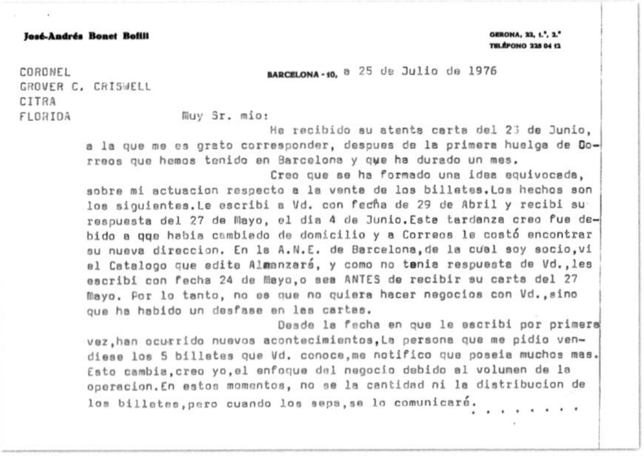
José-Andrés Bonet Bofill GERONA, 22, 1.°, 2.ª TELÉFONO 228 04 12

CORONEL
GROVER C. CRISWELL
CITRA
FLORIDA

BARCELONA - 10, a 25 de Julio de 1976

Muy Sr. mio:

He recibido su atenta carta del 23 de Junio, a la que me es grato corresponder, despues de la primera huelga de Correos que hemos tenido en Barcelona y que ha durado un mes.

Creo que se ha formado una idea equivoceda, sobre mi actuacion respecto a la venta de los billetes.Los hechos son los siguientes.Le escribi a Vd. con fecha de 29 de Abril y recibi su respuesta del 27 de Mayo, el día 4 de Junio.Esta tardanza creo fue debido a qqe habia cambiado de domicilio y a Correos le costó encontrar su nueva direccion. En la A.N.E. de Barcelona,de la cual soy socio,vi el Catalogo que edita Almanzarś, y como no tenia respuesta de Vd.,les escribi con fecha 24 de Mayo,o sea ANTES de recibir su carta del 27 Mayo. Por lo tanto, no es que no quiera hacer negocios con Vd.,sino que ha habido un desfase en las cartas.

Desde la fecha en que le escribi por primera vez,han ocurrido nuevos acontecimientos,La persona que me pidio vendiese los 5 billetes que Vd. conoce,me notifico que poseia muchos mas. Esto cambia,creo yo,el enfoque del negocio debido al volumen de la operacion.En estos momentos, no se la cantidad ni la distribucion de los billetes,pero cuando los sepa,se lo comunicaré. . . . .

Illus. 70

Grover's potential client responded on July 25 *(Illus. 70)*, again in Castilian Spanish, with the assertion that indeed he was operating in good faith and then dropping a bombshell on Grover: there were far more Confederate notes available than the five already photocopied, as his translated letter attests:

"Dear Sir: I have received your letter of June 23, which I am promptly answering after having been through the first mail strike in the history of Barcelona, and that lasted a month. I think you have an erroneous impression about my actions with respect to the sale of the bills. The facts are the following: I wrote to you on April 29, and received your answer dated May 27 on June 4. This delay was due, I believe, to your change in residence and the Post Office must have had trouble finding your new address. In the A.N.E. of Barcelona, of which I am a member, I saw the catalogue that Almanzars publishes, and since I had not received an answer from you, I wrote to them on May 24, before receiving your letter dated May 27. Therefore, it is not that I do not want to do business with you, rather that the letters crossed in the mail.

Since I initially wrote to you, new developments have occurred. The person who asked me to sell the five bills, about which you already know, notified me that he had many more. This, I believe, changes the scope of our transaction because of the volume of the operation. At this time I do not know either the quantity or the distribution of the bills. I will let you know as soon as I find out.

I am providing you with this information so that you may start thinking if you are interested in buying all the bills…

Sincerely,

Jose-Andres Bonet B——"

Predictably, Grover responded on August 17, confirming that he was "very much interested in either a quantity of Confederate notes or even just the few better ones which [he] sent photocopies of." Grover suggested that the entire collection of notes be sent to his bank for Grover's personal inspection. This means of confirmation seems perfectly reasonable today, but nevertheless met with resistance in Spain back then. Grover's client was unwilling to send the notes to Grover's bank and further required that the collection be sold as a single lot, yet he never provided Grover with a full list of what was available so an informed offer could be made.

But Grover persisted in at least acquiring the five Montgomery notes that he knew existed. His efforts were finally rewarded over a year later in December 1977 when he telegrammed his client that he would pay $6,500 for the five Montgomery notes and his offer was accepted. Grover's earlier offer showed the downside of low-balling the price: it encouraged his client to seek alternative offers, and Grover wound up paying 30% more than he would have just 18 months earlier. *(Illus. 71)*

The Spanish nobleman finally shipped the five Montgomery notes – without registration – directly to Grover in early 1978. Grover sent payment in February 1978 and seemingly the story was finished.

But upon receipt of Grover's payment in full, the Spaniard seemed more inclined to sell the remaining notes and finally, in May 1978, provided Grover with a list that allowed him to make an educated offer. While there were a few specimens of the First Richmond issues (Criswell Types-5 and 6), the bulk of the notes were common, well-circulated specimens in which Grover had only minimal interest.

Illus. 71

Yet Grover's attention increased dramatically upon receipt of another letter dated October 30, 1978 *(Illus. 72, next page)*, translated below:

"Dear Mr. Criswell:

I would like to apologize for the delay in my reply. As usual it was due to the owner who is constantly changing her mind.

The problem is that the owner wants to sell all the bills and you only want to buy some of them.

When I sent you a list of the bills I did it thinking of you as a collector and not as a businessman; therefore, I only included in that list one bill of each kind and its variants. The fact is that we have duplicate bills included in the list that I sent you. For example, we have 100 bills of number CR 5 [Criswell Type-5 "$100 First Richmond"], seventeen bills of number CR 6 [Criswell Type-6 "$50 First Richmond"], and so on. It is the same situation with almost all the other bills.

As I see it, it will be very difficult for us to come to an agreement by mail. The ideal situation would be if you could come to Barcelona in order to solve this matter while we have the bills in front of us.

Awaiting your reply. Cordially,

Jose-Andres Bonet B—-"

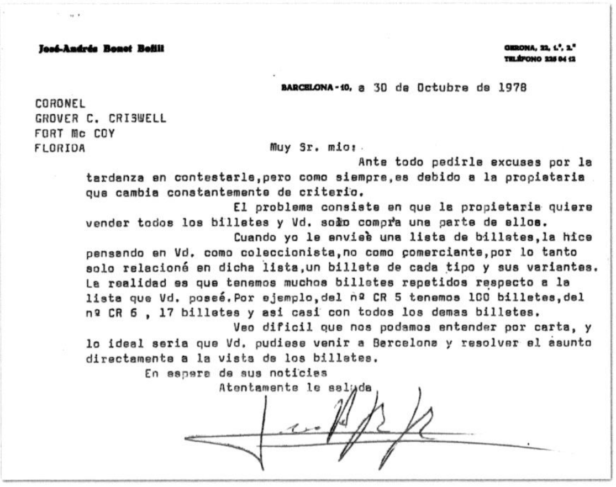
José-Andrés Bonet Bofill

GERONA, 22, 1.°, 2.ª
TELÉFONO 225 04 12

BARCELONA-10, a 30 de Octubre de 1978

CORONEL
GROVER C. CRISWELL
FORT Mc COY
FLORIDA

Muy Sr. mio:

Ante todo pedirle excuses por la tardanza en contestarle, pero como siempre, es debido a la propietaria que cambia constantemente de criterio.

El problema consiste en que la propietaria quiere vender todos los billetes y Vd. solo compra una parte de ellos.

Cuando yo le envieè una lista de billetes, la hice pensando en Vd. como coleccionista, no como comerciante, por lo tanto solo relacioné en dicha lista, un billete de cada tipo y sus variantes. La realidad es que tenemos muchos billetes repetidos respecto a la lista que Vd. poseé. Por ejemplo, del nº CR 5 tenemos 100 billetes, del nº CR 6 , 17 billetes y asi casi con todos los demas billetes.

Veo dificil que nos podamos entender por carta, y lo ideal seria que Vd. pudiese venir a Barcelona y resolver el asunto directamente a la vista de los billetes.

En espera de sus noticias
Atentamente le saluda

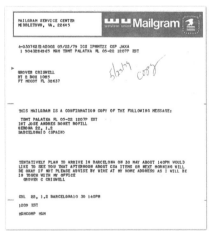

Illus. 72

Grover had considerable interest in 100 "$100 First Richmond" issues (Criswell Type-5), which Grover probably felt were consecutively numbered. The 17 specimens of Criswell Type-6 and the other varieties were pure gravy. Grover committed to go to Spain, apparently unaware that some of the $100 First Richmond bills had been misidentified.

Grover and his Spanish client, now joined by two other Spaniards presumably also with some financial interest in the estate, finally agreed to meet in Barcelona on May 30, 1979. Grover's Western Union Mailgram dated May 22 *(Illus. 73)* confirmed the details:

" Tentatively plan to arrive in Barcelona on 30 May about 1:40 PM. Would like to see you that afternoon about CSA items or next morning will be okay. If not please advise by wire at my home address as I will be in touch with my office. Grover C. Criswell"

MAILGRAM SERVICE CENTER
MIDDLETOWN, VA. 22645

western union Mailgram

4-030762E142002 05/22/79 ICS IPMMTZZ CSP JAXA
1 9043284965 MGM TDMT PALATKA FL 05-22 1207P EST

GROVER CRISWELL
RT 2 BOX 1085
FT MCCOY FL 32637

5/23/79 copy

THIS MAILGRAM IS A CONFIRMATION COPY OF THE FOLLOWING MESSAGE:

TDMT PALATKA FL 05-22 1207P EST
INT JOSE ANDRES BONET BOFILL
GERONA 22, 1.2
BARCELONA10 (SPAIN)

TENTATIVELY PLAN TO ARRIVE IN BARCELONA ON 30 MAY ABOUT 140PM WOULD LIKE TO SEE YOU THAT AFTERNOON ABOUT CSA ITEMS OR NEXT MORNING WILL BE OKAY IF NOT PLEASE ADVISE BY WIRE AT MY HOME ADDRESS AS I WILL BE IN TOUCH WITH MY OFFICE
GROVER C CRISWELL

COL 22, 1.2 BARCELONA10 30 140PM

1209 EST

MGMCOMP MGM

Grover was joined by his son Grover, Jr. on the trip to Barcelona. Collateral information establishes that Grover and his son, along with his three Spanish clients, met the afternoon of May 30, 1979. I do not know who discovered that seven of the so-called Criswell Type-5 "$100 First Richmond" issues were actually Criswell Type-3 "$100 Montgomery" issues, exceedingly rare and far more valuable. The two notes are quite similar in appearance (Type-5 shows a locomotive pointing to the left; Type-3 shows a locomotive pointing to the right), but they are not so similar that even a cursory inspection would quickly show the differences. The first Spaniard was a numismatist, a member of the Asociacion Numismatica Española, (the Spanish equivalent of our ANS), and had already sold two Type-3 Montgomerys in the earlier transaction with Grover; he should have (and might have) spotted the difference.

Illus. 73

I suspect that it was the Spaniards, not Grover, who discovered the misidentification, and that they made their discovery before Grover arrived in Spain. Their own detection of the misidentification would explain their insistence on Grover making the long and expensive voyage to Barcelona. Once Grover arrived and saw seven extremely rare Criswell Type-3 "$100 Montgomey" notes for himself, the Spaniards knew there was little likelihood that Grover would return home empty-handed. As bigger-than-life as Grover was, I believe that this time he met his match and might even have been upstaged.

Grover paid a strong price for the seven Type-3 $100 Montgomery notes (and the remaining Confederate material), contrary to the stories I had heard over the years. At the conclusion of their meeting, Grover wrote three checks: two for $5,000 each to the two new clients and the third for $6,000 to his original client. Interestingly, all three Spaniards demanded payment directly into Swiss bank accounts at the Societe de Banque Suisse. The significance of this request is not clear, although it might reflect chronic Spanish political instability. In any event, Grover completed the transaction, gathered his purchases and returned home.

Ever the promoter, and then the sitting president of the ANA, Grover sponsored all three of his new friends for membership in the ANA. In a follow-up letter dated September 24, 1979, Grover again requested that the original Spanish nobleman provide the name of the grandfather who was the Spanish Consul to the Confederate States, his appointment date, his age and any other relevant information – all the better to enhance the bills' provenance and mystique. Despite numerous requests, this information was never forthcoming. (I always found it surprising that Grover's Spanish friend chose not to reveal the notes' provenance. Was this a perilous time in Spain? Or were the notes pilfered?)

The final chapter in this remarkable tale was not written until several months after Grover returned home from Barcelona. On December 11, 1979, three months after submitting ANA membership applications for his new Spanish clients, Grover received a phone call from the sister of the original client. In a shocking climax to this story, sister Nuria Bonet B— advised Grover that her brother, as well as his two friends whom Grover also met, had all been assassinated by the Spanish terrorist organization called the ETA (translated to mean "Basque Homeland and Freedom") on December 7 while they were vacationing at the luxury Hotel Corona de Aragon in Zaragoza, Spain. Their deaths were caused by a blazing fire that killed 80 guests. Originally traced to the cafeteria and labeled accidental by the Spanish government, the Spanish equivalent of OSHA later ruled that the fire resulted from an explosion in the lobby set off by the ETA, an armed Basque nationalist and separatist organization with the goal of gaining independence for the Basque area of Spain and France. Just this year, the ETA declared a "permanent, general and verifiable" ceasefire with the expressed aim of ending its decades-long campaign.

While I chose to highlight Grover's purchase of the misidentified $100 Montgomery notes to illustrate my discussion of Grover the dealer, I had countless more choices. Over his 50-year career, Grover handled virtually all the great Confederate rarities, including the incomparable "Walton Indian Princess," the only virtually Uncirculated Criswell Type-35 "$5 Indian Princess" ever catalogued, which Grover purchased in 1963 and placed so secretively that it has not been seen since.

Grover Criswell's third and final hat – Grover the promoter – is unrivalled in the history of collecting Confederate currency. Naturally colorful, physically imposing and innately charming, Grover found it easy to promote the hobby he loved. In 1955, at age 22, he joined several far more famous and much better known numismatists in founding the Florida United Numismatists (FUN), where he was a regular exhibitor and served as the organization's president.

On June 21, 1959, Grover appeared on the popular television show "What's My Line," where he was proclaimed as the "richest man in the world – in Confederate currency," with 20 million Confederate dollars in his inventory (while immense, Grover's 20 million Confederate dollars paled in comparison to the 80 million owned by Atlanta currency dealer Charles D. Barker, according to an article in *The Atlanta Constitution* on June 4, 1893).

In 1961 Grover worked with several other numismatic giants to found the Society of Paper Money Collectors (SPMC). On March 27, 1961, the eve of the centennial of the start of the Civil War, Grover appeared on another television series, "To Tell the Truth," to promote the hobby. He also made an appearance on the widely watched "The Today Show." From 1961 to 1965, Grover served on the U.S. Civil War Centennial Advisory Council. As he completed this work in 1965, he was presented with the Society of Paper Money Collectors' Nathan Gold Memorial Lifetime Achievement Award, which is given for making a continuing contribution toward the advancement of paper money collecting over a period of years – yet Grover was only 32 years of age.

AMERICAN NUMISMATIC ASSOCIATION
Devoted to the Advancement and Study of
Numismatics Since 1891.

Grover Criswell Jr
Life Member 268
Member Since 1951

Illus. 74

Grover was ardent in his support of the ANA. After joining in 1951 at age 18 *(Illus. 74)*, he was elected to the Board of Governors in 1965 and continued to be re-elected until 1977, when he successfully ran for Vice President. Two years later in 1979 Grover was elected President of the ANA, a tenure remembered by old-timers as lively and controversial. After his presidential stint, Grover was re-elected to the Board of Governors for the period 1981 to 1983, and served again from 1991 to 1993.

Grover tirelessly promoted local numismatic clubs throughout the country. He was a life member of 20 such clubs, and a member of 40 more. He was also a founder and member of the little-known Rittenhouse Society, founded in 1960 for the sharing of information and goodwill among numismatic researchers. The other founders – David Bowers, Walter Breen, Eric Newman, Ken Bressett, Ken Rendell, Dick Johnson and George Fuld – are a veritable "Who's Who" among numismatic bibliophiles for their gigantic contributions to its scholarship.

Grover Criswell admittedly had his foibles. His personal financial reverses, regardless of the reasons, clouded his judgment as a respected dealer. Yet it is impossible to overstate his importance to the modern hobby. Grover never had the incredible variety collection of John Browne or even Doug Ball; he might not have had the breadth of numismatic knowledge of John Haseltine or Max Mehl; he lacked the research acumen of Philip Chase or Sydney Kerksis. Yet no one in history has been so exclusively and single-mindedly immersed in the hobby of collecting Confederate currency and bonds as was Grover Criswell. He gets my vote as the hobby's most important personality of all time.

1958. The hobby's longest-running series of books ever – 42 years – gets its start.

What a difference a year makes. **Arlie R. Slabaugh** authored the perfect primer for the beginning collector of Confederate currency. It was ideal for the novice, as it contained far more text and explanatory material than the first Criswell edition in 1957, with illustrations of all the types. Slabaugh then released nine more editions for a total of 10 between 1958 and 2000: a 42-year span with twice as many editions as in Criswell's Currency Series.

While popular and well known, the Slabaugh series never gained the traction enjoyed by the Criswell series, which was designed for the serious Confederate collector. I can surmise at least four reasons why. First, Grover released his first edition in January 1957 to wide acclaim and broad distribution. Slabaugh's first edition was thus relegated to a "me too" also-ran a year later in 1958, as the market simply was insufficiently mature to support two new books on Confederate currency released only a year apart. As Elle Lawliet stated, "He who moves first always wins." Second, Arlie's first edition – indeed all 10 of his editions – was in paperback form. His soft cover editions lacked the permanence and shelf presence that Grover's hardbound editions commanded.

Third, Arlie introduced a new numbering system for the various types, a hybrid of the Criswell type numbers and the Chase type numbers. Collectors had already voted "no" when Chase tried to introduce his radically different numbering system in the 1930s and 1940s. While Slabaugh's numbering system was a more modest revision, forcing the collector to choose between two different options to number the types was just not tenable, particularly when the grand total of all the types was different under each scheme (Criswell had 72 total types, Slabaugh 73). Fourth, Arlie just did not have the physically imposing, bellowing presence of Grover, who was the consummate promoter.

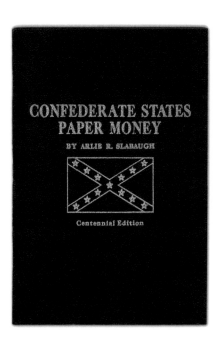

Illus. 75

Slabaugh's ten-edition series, simply titled *Confederate States Paper Money*, was intended for the generalist, not the specialist. Indeed, the *Preface* to his 9th Edition released in 1998 stated that "it should be understood that this catalog is intended primarily for the general reader and collector rather than the specialist." Dealer Crutchfield Williams always kept a good stock of Slabaugh's books on hand, as Crutch believes they are, by far, the best books available for beginning collectors of Confederate currency. Since the series was intended for the general reader, refreshingly there were no varieties listed – just the types. Slabaugh merely referenced the number of varieties of each type in a few sentences within his discussion of the types themselves.

Slabaugh explained the genesis and ongoing development of his series in the "Introduction" to his 10th edition in 2000. He wrote:

> "I began compiling a catalog in 1957 which was published the following year by the Whitman Publishing Co., Racine, Wis. Two further editions (1959 and the 1963 Centennial Edition [*Illus. 75*]) were similarly distributed by this company, well-known publishers of the *Guide Book of United States Coins….* The fourth edition appeared in 1967 and was published jointly by me and Hewitt Brothers, Chicago, as a part of its "Numismatic Information Series." The same holds true for the fifth edition in 1973 and the sixth edition in 1977. Probably not many collectors own a complete set, but each edition contains price changes or data not in others. The seventh (1991), eighth (1993), ninth (1998) and the current tenth edition have been published by Krause Publications, Iola, Wis. No other Confederate paper money catalog has gone through as many editions."

Arlie was probably correct that few collectors own a complete set of all 10 editions, particularly since his earliest editions have now been out of print for nearly 50 years. In fact, the only complete set of which I am familiar is owned by my brother Charles, who also owns the infamous 11th edition. The 11th edition was released in 2008 by F+W Media, which acquired Krause Publications in 2002 before Slabaugh's death in 2007. The effort was filled with errors and, to me at least, was an affront to the fine gentleman who personally wrote the first 10 editions.

Arlie R. Slabaugh was born in Springfield, Penn., in 1925. His obituary appeared in the December 2007 issue of *The Numismatist* and is excerpted here. Slabaugh was an antiquarian in the mold of a Thomas Addis Emmet or a John Browne, once saying that he was a "19th-century person in a 21st-century world." He found an 1864 Indian Head cent when he was seven, leading to his first currency purchase nine years later when he mailed 10 cents to a coin dealer to buy a bank note and a world coin. He joined the ANA in 1941.

That same year, Slabaugh lost his hearing after the double whammy of both mastoiditis and spinal meningitis, but it never interfered with his passion for the hobby. Slabaugh was a frequent attendee at local and national conventions in his role as a collector, exhibitor, researcher and author. Always furiously writing on a ubiquitous notepad, Slabaugh found a way to communicate to overcome his hearing loss. I have a thick file of typed correspondence with Arlie, who never failed to thoroughly research and document any question I raised.

Starting in 1941, while only 16, Slabaugh self-published his own magazine titled *The Hobby Spotlight*. By 1948 he was writing for *The Numismatist* and later for *Paper Money* and Krause Publications. In 1954 he was made associate editor of *Numismatic Scrapbook*, a position he held until 1967 when he became director of numismatic information and chief archivist for The Franklin Mint, from which he retired in 1982. He remained an active contributor to the *Token and Medal Society (TAMS) Journal* for at least 40 years.

Slabaugh's devotion to the hobby resulted in numerous awards and honors, some of which included the Numismatic Literary Guild's "Clemy" in 1981, the Numismatic News' Numismatic Ambassador in 1989, the ANA's Medal of Merit in 1991, the Glenn Smedley Memorial and Presidential Awards in 1997, and the Lifetime Achievement Award in 2004.

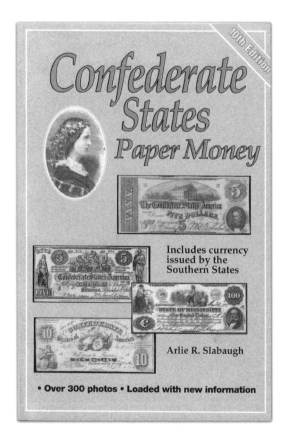

Illus. 76

In addition to his series on Confederate currency, he authored *United States Commemorative Coinage: The Drama of America as Told by Our Coins, American Centennial Tokens and Medals*, and a series of books on war money in Germany, Mexico and Japan.

Arlie was as detail-oriented and averse to typographical errors as any author I have ever met. (His awareness of the little things is what makes the mistake-filled 11th edition such a slap in his face.) His attention to detail is aptly demonstrated by our saga over a Confederate $500 Montgomery note, which began when I wrote to him in August 2002. At that time I was conducting research into Confederate pricing data found in old auction catalogs at the ANS Library in New York City. In the *Introduction* to his 10th edition released in 2000 *(Illus. 76)*, Arlie picked up a sentence which had also appeared in the 9th Edition in 1998 and was later to appear in the 11th Edition, despite the 11th Edition being published posthumously and with no regard to plagiarizing Arlie's personal first-person account:

"The purchase I remember best is that of the $500 Montgomery note (No. 3) which I obtained in XF condition at Kosoff's New York auction in 1942, at what was then said to be a record price of $88."

I was about three years into my 14-year book project when I completed my analysis of all Abe Kosoff auction sales. The trouble was, I had not located *any* Kosoff sales of a $500 Montgomery note in Extremely Fine condition in 1942; in fact, my analysis showed Kosoff did not sell *any* $500 Montgomery notes during the decade of the 1940s. I wrote Arlie that I could not find any Kosoff sale of a $500 Montgomery note in 1942, but since my analysis was far from complete at that time, I could not suggest to Arlie where he might have obtained his note. I was also afraid that I might have missed this auction catalog altogether, as my confidence in my database then was far less sanguine than it is now.

Arlie quickly responded, highly concerned that he had made a serious error in his *Introduction* for the most recent two editions and asking for my help in correcting the error. We continued writing as we attempted to find the note he had purchased in the 1940s. In a September 3, 2002 letter he wrote:

> "Hopefully, we will get to the source of the $500 Montgomery note before long. I feel very embarrassed about the statement I made in my catalog which I will now have to change in the 11th edition in some manner. It won't be the first time I've been upset but the other errors have been printer's typos. So maybe I will survive this error, too. I hope so, since the next edition is likely to be my last due to my age and health.
>
> "I've always prided myself as having a photographic memory, being able to describe a medal or whatever down to minute details long after I had originally made the examination. But apparently my memory is no longer as sharp as when I was younger."

Arlie and I continued to correspond as my research project uncovered more and more possibilities that might have been the note he purchased. Ultimately we were successful in finding where and when Arlie purchased this note: indeed it was in February 1943, just a few months later than Arlie's recollection, but from an M.H. Bolender auction, not Abe Kosoff. Arlie even went to the trouble to research his old files located in his home's basement (quite a feat itself as he had suffered a major flood in 1968) and found the note's serial number, which was not part of the auction catalog's description. His note with serial number 104 ultimately became part of Frederick Mayer's collection sold by R. M. Smythe in 2007.

By 2003 Arlie had re-drafted the *Introduction* to what would have been his final 11th edition, correcting his slightly imperfect memory. Sadly, he would not live to publish his own 11th edition, as he died September 26, 2007, at age 82. Several months later, after I heard of his death, I called the editorial staff of *Bank Note Reporter* published by Krause Publications, a division of F+W Media. Krause Publications had released Arlie's final editions and had purchased the rights to his future editions. I told the folks at *Bank Note Reporter* about Arlie's desire to correct the errors found in his 9th and 10th editions and hoped that my information would be relayed to the appropriate people in the book division.

Instead, I received a request that I re-write the *Introduction* myself, despite Arlie having done so at least five years earlier. What gall!

Perhaps things indeed do work out for the best. Arlie would have been so upset about the error-plagued 11th edition released in 2008 that he likely would not have wished his corrected *Introduction* to appear in such a sloppily prepared manuscript. I am certain that Arlie would be happy to know that the record has finally been set straight on his acquisition of a beautiful $500 Montgomery note in the 1940s, although the correction was finally made in my book, not his own.

1972. Thian's Complete Analysis of Confederate Treasury Records is Reprinted.

After earlier describing the difficulty that Confederate currency collectors encountered in finding original copies of William West Bradbeer's monumental *Confederate and Southern State Currency* published in 1915, and later reprinted in 1945 and 1956, it would be logical to assume that Raphael Thian's 1880 *Register of the Confederate Debt* was a less significant publication because it was never reprinted.

But reprinting any book requires an original to copy. Even though Bradbeer printed only a few hundred copies of his 1915 tome, it still dwarfed the mere six copies extant of Thian's 1880 compilation. After permanently impounding one of the copies in the Library of Congress and a second copy with the Thian family, only four copies were left to satisfy the demand of Confederate currency collectors nationwide. No wonder the classic 1880 Thian work was not reprinted until 1972. There were simply no originals to copy.

In 1960 John J. Ford, the celebrated American numismatist, acquired one of the original copies of Thian in private hands. Unknown to Ford, another Confederate researcher was about to acquire a photostatic copy of one of the impounded Thians. This young professor type, in his early twenties, prevailed upon his father, the powerful Undersecretary of State in the John Kennedy administration, to have a copy made of the original Thian that resided in the Library of Congress. In the spring of 1962 in New York, Ford met this unknown researcher for the first time and was astonished at both his encyclopedic knowledge and his unassailable integrity. Ford and his new business associate, my colleague and mentor **Douglas B. Ball** *(Illus. 77)*, would remain steadfast friends for the rest of their lives.

Illus. 77

While Doug Ball did not publish the Thian reprint – that honor goes to **Al Hoch** – Doug certainly provided the inspiration to Hoch and wrote a superb *Foreword* to the reprint that provided virtually all the biographical details we know about Thian himself. Doug Ball has had a huge impact on the modern-day collecting of Confederate currency, and it is time to review his resume.

Doug Ball was born in 1939 into a family of privilege. The younger of two sons of the Honorable George W. Ball, Doug spent his childhood on both sides of the Atlantic, as his famous father was a chief foreign policy advisor to several presidents, including John F. Kennedy to whom he forcefully argued against U.S. military involvement in Vietnam during the 1960s.

George W. Ball first came to Washington, D.C. in 1933 as an attorney working on Franklin D. Roosevelt's New Deal programs. He and his wife Ruth Murdoch Ball maintained a home there for most of their professional lives. With all the repositories of both military and Confederate history at his fingertips in Washington, it is no surprise that Doug developed a fascination with history, and specifically the history of the Confederate Treasury.

In 1963 George Ball sent his precocious son Doug to the Millbrook School near Poughkeepsie, N.Y. According to classmate Peter Savage, Doug thrived in this elitist prep boarding school and could hold his own as a liberal Democrat in a sea of conservative Republicans. By the time he enrolled at Millbrook, Doug had already developed an interest in Confederate currency. Peter recalls that Doug invited him to visit the Morgan Guaranty Trust in Manhattan during their junior year, where Doug proudly opened a safe deposit box and displayed the beginnings of what would become his extraordinary Confederate currency collection.

Doug was unsuccessful in gaining admission to Yale University in New Haven, Conn., upon graduation from Millbrook, even with the influence of his famous father. He instead enrolled at the College of Wooster in Ohio, a small, prestigious private liberal arts school with a consistent ranking as one of the country's premier undergraduate programs.

By his freshman year at Wooster, Doug was both a numismatist and a serious philatelist with a considerable holding of nineteenth century stamps. His primary stamp dealer was the firm of Jack O. King, whose offices were near the Ball residence in Washington. One day Ball walked to King's offices and found a shoebox filled with Confederate, Southern States and Virginia currency resting on a countertop. King, who had just paid $50 for the shoebox, offered it to Ball for $100. Doug accepted, and then found six very rare Northumberland and Lancaster County notes that he later sold to Charles Affleck. These Virginia notes were the start of Ball's career as a numismatics dealer, a calling that would continue until his death in 2003.

After completing his undergraduate degree at the College of Wooster, Doug was finally accepted at Yale University where he received his M.A. in History. While at Yale, he met John Ford for the first time. Ford described their initial meeting in the spring of 1962 in his *Foreword* to Doug's *Comprehensive Catalog and History of Confederate Bonds*, which R. M. Smythe published in 1998. Ford wrote that:

> "I was confronted by a specialist intent upon acquiring every possible variety of note of the 1861-1864 Confederate issues. It was not long before I learned that thanks to his father, George W. Ball and his influence with the Library of Congress (the senior Ball was second man in the State Department from December 1961 until September 1966), that Douglas had procured a Photostat copy of Raphael P. Thian's *Register of the Confederate Debt*. I had an original of this extremely rare publication (one of [six] known) in my library, but had never found time to peruse thoroughly its contents. On the other hand, Doug Ball had apparently put his copy of the Thian book to better purpose.
>
> On top of having the use of Thian, Douglas had also been in touch with Philip H. Chase, an authority on CSA paper, who had published a definitive work on *Confederate Treasury Notes* in 1947… Much of his knowledge had registered with Doug Ball. I found this out early on when [Ball] corrected me about the quantity emitted of a note whose issue figures were published in Thian."

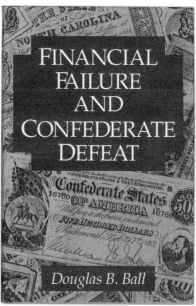

Illus. 78

Ford had considered reprinting at least parts of Thian's book back in 1954, but he had been unsuccessful in convincing his researcher Sydney Kerksis or Kerksis' influential friend Philip Chase. But in Doug Ball Ford found an enthusiastic ally who also wished to see Thian reprinted. While it would be 10 years after their first meeting in 1962 that Thian's book was finally reproduced, at least the wheels had been set in motion.

After receiving his Master's degree in history from Yale, Doug earned an M.B.A. from Columbia University in New York and then embarked on a Ph.D. in Economics from the University of London, London School of Economics. Doug completed his thesis, entitled *Confederate War Finance, 1861 - 1865: Economic Policy-Making in the South during the American Civil War*, in January 1974, and was awarded the Ph.D. later that year. In 1991 his expanded thesis, re-titled *Financial*

Failure and Confederate Defeat (Illus. 78, page 95), was published by the University of Illinois Press. But even before receiving his Ph.D., Doug had begun to write for numismatic publications, with an article appearing in *The Numismatist* as early as 1966.

With kind usage of unpublished material from Fred Reed, who has written extensively about Doug Ball's *Foreword* to the Thian reprint, it is clear that while Ball wished to see Thian's 1880 masterpiece reprinted, he was in no position to take on such a task while he was still polishing his Ph.D. thesis. But the way became easier in 1972 when Doug met Al Hoch of Lawrence, Mass. Hoch, like Philip Chase a graduate of MIT and a Colonial coin collector, had just founded a publishing company called **Quarterman Publications**, whose objective was to preserve and reprint classic early American Colonial numismatic literature long out of print.

Hoch's Quarterman Publications was a specialty reprinter of at least two dozen publications, according to Fred who personally knew him. In reprinting Thian's 1880 *Register of the Confederate Debt*, he found the perfect vehicle to exhibit his talent. He also reprinted under his own trade style for the Token and Medal Society (TAMS) and co-founded and edited the "Colonial Newsletter" for its first three years.

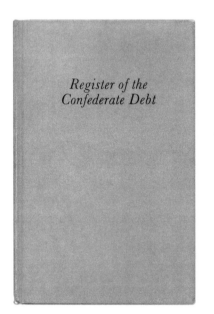

Register of the Confederate Debt

Illus. 79

Hoch's books were all of high quality and provided extra value by having updates or commentary inserted by contemporary scholars of the day, like Eric Newman and Walter Breen. Certainly Doug Ball joined this illustrious group when he wrote the *Foreword* to Quarterman Publications' reprint of Thian's *Register of the Confederate Debt* in 1972 *(Illus. 79)*.

Doug Ball recognized that virtually no Confederate currency collectors had any idea what to expect when they purchased Quarterman's reprint of Thian. With only six originals around, the book's existence was known only to a few scholars. Thus Doug wrote a *Foreword* that was extensive and comprehensive to help fill in the gaps. He divided it into five sections: first, a biography of Raphael Thian; second, a history of the Confederate archives captured by the Federal government in 1865; third, Thian's connection to and use of those archived records; fourth, Thian's actual publications drawing from those records, and finally, a primer on how to use Thian's *Register of the Confederate Debt*.

The original publication Thian printed in 1880 was designed to be the statistical portion of a 10-volume series Thian had drafted. Since it was intended to supplement copious text, Thian was intentionally brief in explaining how it was to be used. Quarterman's reprint of Thian's original 1880 compilation may be the only version of Thian actually seen by a Confederate currency collector. I am convinced that the fame of Thian's original 1880 publication owes as much to Doug Ball's brilliantly conceived *Foreword*, written almost 100 years later, as it does to the data collected by Thian himself.

According to the bibliophile Karl Moulton, the obscure Quarterman Publications went out of business around 1992 after about 20 years of reprinting quality numismatic books long out of print. Its founder Al Hoch died in November 2010 at age 75. But the stature of Doug Ball, who authored the *Foreword* to the Thian reprint, would rise and dramatically outlive Quarterman Publications.

May 1976. Creation of History's Most Prolific Auction House Ever For Confederate Currency.

Many great auction firms sold Confederate currency starting in the 1870s. Their principals – such luminaries as John Haseltine, J.W. Scott, M.H. Bolender, Edouard Frossard, Lyman Low, Thomas Elder, the Chapman Brothers, Max Mehl, Joseph and Morton Stack and Barney Bluestone, to name a few – represent a Who's Who of American Auction Dealers. Yet I included only a few of their auction firms in this Timeline, as all of these dealers treated Confederate currency as a sideline business – they were all coin dealers at heart, with a smattering of currency added to the mix.

But in 1976 a new auction firm would rock the Confederate currency universe. Its impact on both the consignment and sale of rare Confederate notes was staggering. More concrete details of its success will be left to the next chapter. But its formation deserves recognition in this Timeline.

This auction firm was the personification of **Douglas B. Ball**. After he crafted the brilliant *Foreword* to Al Hoch's reprint of Thian's *Register of the Confederate Debt* in 1972, Doug was awarded the Ph.D. in Economics in 1974 and sought a career in academia. According to John Ford in his *Foreword* to Doug's *Comprehensive Catalog and History of Confederate Bonds*:

> "[Douglas Ball's] lack of success in getting and keeping a foothold in an academic career… suggested to me the need for him to turn a part time hobby into a full time career. At my suggestion and with help from myself and my friends, Douglas opened his own company, NASCA (Numismatic and Antiquarian Service Corporation of America) at the end of May 1976. Since NASCA was located in my home town of Rockville Centre, New York, and as I had withdrawn from New Netherlands in 1971, I was able to take an active advisory role in NASCA's affairs."

While Ford might have exaggerated his contributions to the formation of NASCA, numismatics literature dealer Karl Moulton confirms in an unpublished manuscript that Ford was heavily involved with NASCA's operations. Ford consigned a large quantity of material (e.g., several Massachusetts silver pieces) to NASCA's first auction in December 1976, and he even delayed his plans to retire to Arizona, instead staying in New York for the next several years to help Doug with his start-up.

NASCA's Chairman of the Board and financier was George Ball, Doug's father. Doug served as President and hired Herbert Melnick away from F.C.I. to serve as Executive Director. Both Doug and Melnick did some cataloging, along with Carl Carlson, Martin Gengerke and Paul Bosco.

With Ford and Melnick lining up consignors, and Ball superbly performing the cataloging function, the business was off to a good start. While the first sale in December 1976 was lacking any Confederate currency, by the fifth sale in May 1977 Ball was already selling the Confederate currency collection of the Maryland Historical Society, including three Montgomerys *(Illus. 80)*.

Illus. 80

As NASCA gained momentum, Doug's reputation for both unrivalled expertise and impeccable integrity brought in more and more consignments. Between 1976 and June 1991 when NASCA was fully integrated into R.M. Smythe & Company, Inc., NASCA sold a remarkable 85 Montgomery notes. This total represents over 15% of *all* Montgomery notes sold in history and is more than the second, third and fourth most-prolific Confederate currency auctioneers *combined*.

Selling more Montgomery notes than any other auction house in history, while an impressive achievement, does not necessarily translate into running a profitable business. Regrettably, NASCA was forced into liquidation in 1982. To pay the bills, Ball was left with no alternative other than to sell his storied Confederate currency collection.

September 25-26, 1987. Most Complete Confederate Variety Collection to Sell at Auction.

While I am confident that John C. Browne created the most comprehensive Confederate variety collection ever assembled, his compilation was primarily dispersed via donations to such prestigious institutions as the Historical Society of Pennsylvania and the Abraham Lincoln Library and Museum (via a gift from Raymond Sanger Wilkins). On the other hand, the remarkable Confederate variety collection assembled by **Douglas B. Ball** was sold virtually intact at public auction on September 25-26, 1987.

Held in conjunction with the Virginia Numismatic Association Convention at the Hyatt Hotel in Richmond, Va., the sale was conducted by Doug's NASCA firm, which had since become a division of R.M. Smythe & Company, Inc., with the cerebral John Herzog at the helm. The catalog, whose title page described the offering as "the Confederate Collection of Notes, Bonds, Warrants, Depository Receipts, Plates and Stamps of Douglas B. Ball," included 2,573 lots spread over 178 pages *(Illus. 81, facing page)*. But even that gargantuan total of 2,573 lots understated the complete collection, as many of the lots contained multiple items. In the April 2005 issue of *Bank Note Reporter*, Fred Reed estimated the number of items pedigreed to John Browne's collection *alone* totalled about 7,000 notes.

Before discussing the enormity of the collection itself, the reasons for its sale merit our attention, as I have always been puzzled about why Doug sold his collection. He maintained that business losses at his NASCA auction firm forced the liquidation of its assets, and Doug was ultimately required to sell his treasured Confederate collection to pay his remaining creditors.

Doug's insistence on paying off every cent of his business debt is laudable and entirely consistent with his unimpeachable integrity. But because his losses were suffered in the course of running a corporate business, he enjoyed personal protection from his creditors. So technically, Doug could have kept his personal Confederate collection. Yet he was unwilling to walk away from his creditors who had legitimate claims against his business. He thus took the selfless act of selling his beloved collection to repay those creditors. Such an attitude is refreshing, particularly these days when so many people just walk away from lawful real estate debt when they find it inconvenient to honor their financial obligations.

Debts aside, Doug consistently (and perhaps psychologically) put the blame of NASCA's failure at the feet of Herbert Melnick, the company's Executive Manager. Indeed in his *Foreword* to Ball's bond book in 1998, John Ford alluded to "the executive manager's personality change and disastrous business decisions following a well nigh fatal heart attack in 1981 and his resignation at the end of the year."

Given my experience as a fairly successful business entrepreneur, I know the difficulty in starting a new company. For each success I have enjoyed, I have suffered at least two or three failures along the way. As a new business, the odds were stacked against NASCA from the beginning, despite Doug's father's deep pockets and the sage counsel from John Ford. Doug was a brilliant researcher, a prolific writer and a steadfast and loyal friend. But I would never have hired Doug as president of any of my businesses, as I never felt he had the management skills needed to run a profitable company. As President, Doug should have adopted Harry Truman's truism, "The buck stops here." I suspect, as Doug maintained, that Melnick shared much of the blame for NASCA's insolvency. But I have always thought that NASCA failed primarily due to Doug's own shortcomings, not because of an Executive Manager who is no longer around to defend himself.

Regardless of who was to blame for NASCA's failure, there is no denying the magnificence of Doug Ball's Confederate collection. Crafted over a 30-year period, Doug's objective, according to John Ford, was to acquire "every possible variety of note of the 1861 – 1864 Confederate issues." While I am confident that no one has succeeded in assembling all 579 varieties cataloged by William Bradbeer in 1915, Doug Ball probably came closer than anyone except the esteemed John C. Browne. Indeed I find it striking that Doug, in his own meticulous, unadorned writing style, attributed so many of his great rarities to Browne, as he frequently wrote comments like "Ex the John C. Browne Collection" or "The note comes with Browne's envelope."

Illus. 81

In addition to John C. Browne, Doug attributed his collection to Ben Douglass, Charles J. Affleck, Philip H. Chase, John J. Ford, the Criswells, Stanley Gibbons and the McCoy Collections. Most of these names are synonymous with the great Confederate collections of all time. However, I was surprised at the numerous references to Criswell and to Stanley Gibbons. Grover Criswell has already been featured in this Time Line in his roles as an author, a dealer and a promoter. But a perusal of Doug Ball's collection shows the extent to which Doug also saw Grover as a consummate collector, as Doug relied on the auction of Grover's collection by NASCA in 1982 as one of the major underpinnings of his own collection.

The well-known London stamp dealer named Stanley Gibbons, whose Confederate relics were sold at a series of NASCA auctions beginning in 1981, also provided far more material to Doug's collection than I ever imagined. Finally, I was amused that Doug attributed many significant rarities, including the so-called "Sherman Manouvriers" that I now own, to Robert McCoy, a mysterious, elusive and enigmatic collector who ostensibly lived in the late nineteenth century. Evidence is growing that Robert McCoy existed only in the tortured mind of John J. Ford, Jr.

The public auction of Doug Ball's Confederate collection in 1987 marked an end to an era of the great old-time Confederate currency compilations. Beginning with the assemblage of a remarkable set of Confederate currency by John C. Browne in the late 1800s, virtually all the fabulous old collections had been transferred via private placement. Browne donated the bulk of his material, reserving for public auction only his Bechtel album (although filled with an entire type set of uncirculated Confederate notes); Philip Chase sold his collection exclusively via private treaty; Charles Affleck disposed of his collection via both private treaty and public auction.

There were benefits to future Confederate currency collectors from the veterans choosing to dispose of their collections via private treaty, because the bulk of the material was placed with only a few institutions or individuals who maintained its intactness. These purchasers recognized the difficulty encountered by their predecessors in assembling these great collections, and they shared the passion and enjoyment of the old-timers. But when Doug Ball chose to dispose of his collection via a widely advertised public auction, his prized rarities were dispersed into collections owned by a multitude of collectors, both new and old.

I cannot fathom the difficulty a collector would have today in attempting to re-assemble Doug Ball's collection sold in 1987. Rather than musing over whether Doug Ball or John Browne created the greatest Confederate currency collection of all time, I think Doug's greatest achievement was the re-assembly of much of John Browne's fabled collection a hundred years after its initial break-up. Based on personal experience, I believe the re-assembly of something previously taken apart might be even more difficult than the effort required to put it together in the first place. Doug Ball succeeded in the re-assembly and then chose to dispose of his magnificent collection in a single, well-advertised auction sale in 1987.

Doug's decision to keep his collection intact until its complete sale in 1987 afforded all Confederate collectors – those advanced as well as those just beginning – equal opportunity to buy both type notes in a remarkable state of preservation and variety notes with extreme rarity. Doug's decision on how to dispose of his extensive collection also allowed later collectors to assemble far more comprehensive collections than would have been possible had Doug adopted some willy-nilly, haphazard approach to his collection's disposition. All of us who are passionate about collecting Confederate currency – particularly those of us who own some of Doug's notes – owe Doug our gratitude.

June 2003. Most Recent Confederate Variety Set Owned by a Living Collector and Sold at Public Auction.

Before June 2003, the public auction of Doug Ball's immense Confederate currency variety collection in 1987 had been the watershed disposition event since Max Mehl's public auction of the William Dunham collection in 1941. Advanced type collector Neil Chiappa, whose type set adorned the pages of Grover Criswell's final edition in 1996, was a major participant at Doug's auction. Advanced variety collector Arnold Cowan, whose massive variety collection was offered by R.M. Smythe at public auction in 1998, was another key player.

MEMPHIS INTERNATIONAL
PUBLIC AUCTION No.229
FRIDAY & SATURDAY, JUNE 13TH AND 14TH, 2003 • 6:00 PM

Illus. 82

But Neil Chiappa sold his exemplary Confederate type set via private treaty in 2002 as he gracefully exited the Confederate currency hobby. And Arnold Cowan's death in 1997 led to the sale of his variety collection in 1998. Fortunately, though, another key participant at Ball's 1987 auction – **Gene D. Mintz** – continues to collect, although his collection is now limited to Southern States notes. When younger, he collected both high-end Confederate type notes and the great rarities of the Confederate variety notes.

It is fitting that Gene is the latest Confederate currency collector to have the bulk of an entire auction catalog devoted to his collection, made even more personally meaningful because Gene was present at the sale and seated to my right. It is particularly appropriate since Gene was probably the last client Doug Ball visited prior to his unexpected death in March 2003. Doug spent three days with Gene in California in February 2003, literally only weeks before he died.

Gene Mintz has had an active and interesting life that deserves discussion prior to a review of his collection. Gene, still actively managing his own GSM Business Services, Inc. (an accounting and tax advisory service) at age 71, is a rare breed: a native Californian born before World War II. Born in San Luis Obispo County, Gene has spent his entire life within 15 miles of his birthplace (had I started life so close to the central California coast, I would have never moved either).

While Gene is a native Californian, his father was a self-described "Georgia Cracker" reared along the Georgia coast between Savannah and Brunswick. Gene's grandfather served in the Georgia Calvary during the Civil War, and Gene spent his boyhood listening to his father and other family members relate stories of Confederate currency and bonds stuffed into trunks and plastered on walls of their Southern homes.

Gene's father and uncle left the Georgia coast in 1925 for the big city of Atlanta where they bought a new car and headed west. In 1925 there were no interstate highways, not even paved roads; there were no roadside motels for overnight accommodations; it was even difficult to find gasoline for their new car. The trip to California took weeks, not days; each night they pulled off the main road to throw a sleeping bag on the ground and sleep beneath the stars.

When Gene's father and uncle reached west Texas and the southwestern desert, the rutted road became covered in planks, and they continued driving on this plank road across the desert. When they finally reached the central California coast – where they knew literally no one – they sold their then well-used car for more than they had paid for it as a new car back in Atlanta, as late-model cars had not yet reached the West Coast.

As a teenager, Gene began acquiring his first Confederate currency, inspired by the stories he had heard from his family and after reading everything available about the Civil War, with emphasis on articles and books about Confederate finances.

After marrying his high school sweetheart and rearing two children and now three grandchildren, Gene became increasingly active in local civic activities. Despite the time constraints of running a business, Gene, a Certified Public Accountant, has served as president of the Central Coast Chapter of the California Society of Enrolled Agents, is involved in a number of real estate development projects, and is also a Founder and Director of Coast National Bank, headquartered in San Luis Obispo.

Gene is currently Director and President of the South County Performing Arts Foundation, as well as Past President and a 42-year member of the Greater Pismo Beach Kiwanis Club and 38-year member of the Oceano/Five Cities Elks Club. He has served the City of Grover Beach for 12 years as a Planning Commissioner, and served as Chairman of the Coastal Valley Planning Council of South San Luis Obispo County for five years.

While active in professional and civic affairs, numismatics – particularly as related to the Civil War – has always been Gene's major hobby. Like most Confederate currency collectors, Gene started by acquiring anything new to his collection and then upgraded as opportunities arose. Gene's complete type set, as well as numerous rare varieties he acquired from the sale of Doug Ball's collection in 1987 and other NASCA and Smythe sales between 1980 and 1998, was auctioned as part of Smythe's 229th Public Auction at Memphis, Tenn., on June 13, 2003 *(Illus. 82, page 100)*. The title page of this auction simply read "Memphis International Paper Money Auction Featuring the Gene D. Mintz Confederate Currency Collection." Along with some Confederate bonds and stamps, Gene's collection encompassed 420 lots spread over 50 pages. The collection was well illustrated, with the rarest notes appearing in full color.

Since this book focuses on the Montgomery notes, Gene's Montgomerys deserve special mention, particularly his $1,000 Montgomery (Criswell Type-1 Variety 1), which bore serial number 61 and was graded "Extremely Fine - About Uncirculated, perhaps better." With no cut cancels of any sort, this note was part of the Sexton-Philpott-Schermerhorn collection assembled in Dallas in 1958 while a young John Rowe (now principal of Southwest Numismatic Corporation in Dallas) watched in amazement. This $1,000 Montgomery is generally considered the second finest in the condition census. Gene's $100 Montgomery (Criswell Type-3 Variety 3) and $50 Montgomery (Criswell Type-4 Variety 4) were both pedigreed to the Stack's auction of March 1984, when the important John L. Roper Collection was sold.

Gene made the decision to sell his Confederate currency collection only after agonizing over his inability to upgrade his type set or to add more varieties to his variety collection. Happily, though, Gene continues to collect Southern States notes and is more committed than ever to this area so closely aligned with Confederate currency. Indeed it was Gene Mintz's collection of Southern States notes which graced the pages of Hugh Shull's *A Guide Book of Southern States Currency*, released by Whitman Publishing in 2007.

2003. The Advent of Niche Books on Specialized Confederate Currency Topics.

Collecting Confederate currency has come a long way. In 1867 Thomas Addis Emmet provided what little was known about Confederate currency at that time – all told in only three charts that were missing a number of the major types now recognized and hundreds of the minor varieties that Bradbeer was to catalog in 1915. By contrast, 120 years later, Doug Ball sold his immense Confederate currency collection of all the major types and most of the minor varieties. His sale featured a lavishly illustrated catalog with accurate, well-documented text that not only described the minor varieties but also pictured many of them. The hobby of collecting Confederate currency was growing and maturing.

Commercial markets – and hobbies – eventually grow and expand into maturity when they can both meet an initial consumer demand and adapt as that demand changes over time. Henry Ford debuted the Model T horseless carriage in 1908 originally for $950, but a year later reduced it to only $220 "painted any colour that [the customer] wants so long as it is black" (from Ford's 1922 autobiography). Yet over the next 100 years consumer demand changed and the mature automotive market reacted by creating product niches: numerous body styles with multiple price points and varying degrees of luxury – and in any color imaginable under the sun.

It is reassuring that the hobby of collecting Confederate currency is reacting in a similar way. In 1880 Raphael Thian published only a handful of copies of his landmark *Register of Issues of Confederate States Treasury Notes Together With Tabular Exhibits of the Debt, Funded and Unfunded of the Confederate States of America 1861-1865*. This tabulation contained the names of all those persons who signed Confederate currency for the Register and the Treasurer; importantly, it also showed which specific issues they signed, including the serial number runs. Such data would have been invaluable in determining whether a dubious note was in fact counterfeit, but with only a few copies printed, the data simply could not be broadly assimilated, particularly as interest in Confederate currency continued to increase.

Al Hoch of Quarterman Publications, along with Doug Ball who provided the exceptional *Foreword*, finally reprinted Thian's 1880 opus in 1972 under the title *Register of the Confederate Debt*. As collectors began to see the magnitude of the data Thian had collected in the 1870s and 1880s, their interest in the specific signers of Confederate currency began to increase as a way to confirm that their notes were not counterfeit.

Michael McNeil of Nederland, Colo. was one of those who had a passionate interest in persons who signed Confederate currency. When Mike was 12 years old, his grandmother gave him a Confederate Treasury Note signed by Sarah Pelot, Mike's great-great grandmother. Mike's interest in the signers of Confederate currency skyrocketed, and he became obsessed with finding more notes signed by his own great-great grandmother, as well as sample signatures of other signers.

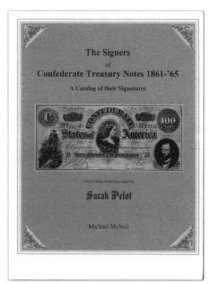

Mike soon discovered, as he wrote on page eight of his book, that 368 men and women signed Confederate currency from 1861 to 1865. In December 2003 Mike self-published *The Signers of Confederate Treasury Notes 1861-'65, a Catalog of Their Signatures (Illus. 83)*. Remarkably, this book provided color photographs of all but nine of those 368 signatures – an intensive effort that took Mike three years to complete.

Mike's book was clearly a niche publication, as he printed only 150 copies. It was exceptionally well researched and capably written, with 146 pages in an attractive hardbound binding. More importantly, it showed the evolution of collecting Confederate currency. Despite Thian providing the data in 1880, it was not readily disseminated until the Quarterman reprint in 1972. Since that date, collectors' interest in signers had grown enough to justify the release of a book dedicated solely to picturing, in full color, the signatures of virtually everyone who laboriously signed those notes between 1861 and 1865.

It takes an inquisitive man to author such a specialized book, and Mike certainly meets that requirement. A California native, he now lives in an old mining town high in the Colorado Rockies where he can exploit his undergraduate studies in geology and paleontology. While he earned his living as an engineer working on disk drives (he owns 30 patents), his real love is the design and construction of classical pipe organs. Most Confederate currency collectors visit the hallowed Duke University Library to view the Thian collections; when Mike visited, he was equally interested in the University's chapel, which houses the world-class Flentrop pipe organ.

Illus. 83

Less than 50 years ago, Confederate currency naysayers would state that a book picturing the signatures of those who signed Confederate currency had no chance at commercial viability, even among a specialized group of Confederate currency collectors. Mike McNeil proved them wrong.

The well-known **George B. Tremmel** is another author who has benefited from the growth and maturity of the Confederate currency hobby. Although the owner of a superb complete Confederate type set, George's real passion has long been the counterfeit issues that plagued the Confederate Treasury almost from the beginning. While collectors of counterfeit currency have been around for years, Grover Criswell did not choose to devote even a small chapter to this specialized area of collecting until his fourth edition in 1992.

George (and his neighbor and fellow researcher Ned Lea) was in a quandary. He wished to release a full-length, hardbound book exclusively devoted to counterfeit Confederate

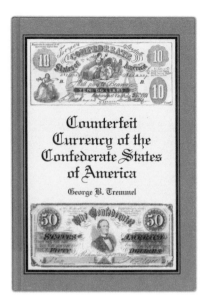

Illus. 84

currency, but he too questioned whether there was a market for such an arcane topic. George summoned the courage and released his 198-page, hardcover *Counterfeit Currency of the Confederate States of America*, published by McFarland & Company in 2003 *(Illus. 84)*. The market remains interested in this esoteric subject, with a 2007 update released by Whitman Publishing and titled *A Guide Book of Counterfeit Confederate Currency*.

A native of Atlanta, Ga., George Tremmel, as I am, is a proud "Ramblin' Wreck from Georgia Tech." He graduated from Tech in 1965 and received his M.B.A. from the University of South Carolina a decade later. Like Mike McNeil, George spent his career in technology, retiring as Information Technology Director. He has lived mostly in the Carolinas and now resides in Raleigh, N.C., with his wife and near two grown daughters. In addition to two books about counterfeit Confederate currency, George has written numerous articles for *Paper Money* magazine, the house organ of the Society of Paper Money Collectors, and has collaborated on a book cataloging Confederate interim depository receipts.

July 2007. Largest Number of Montgomery Notes Ever to Sell at a Single Auction.

Perhaps the most noteworthy aspect of the sale of 13 Confederate Montgomery notes at a single R.M. Smythe auction in 2007 was not the sheer enormity of so many expensive notes offered at one time, but rather the ease with which the market was able to assimilate all 13 of them. Earlier I suggested how much the Confederate currency market had expanded as it reached maturity. But the sale of the **Frederick R. Mayer** Collection of 13 Montgomery notes on July 6, 2007 *(Illus. 85, facing page)* definitively proved that the market was sufficiently large and developed to absorb a gigantic quantity of rare notes at one time without depressing retail prices.

Stephen L. Goldsmith, Executive Vice President and Auction Director of R. M. Smythe at the time of the Mayer sale, provided an excellent biography of Mayer in a tribute placed immediately before the descriptions of the Montgomery notes. Steve related that Frederick R. Mayer was a Texas oilman, although he was born in Ohio in 1928. He started the Exeter Drilling Company in 1953 at only 25 years of age with a single, truck-mounted, portable drilling rig. Through sheer effort, hard work and determination, he soon was able to add a second rig, then a third, and ultimately many more. By 1980 when he sold Exeter, Mayer controlled the largest privately owned drilling company in the country. In 1982 he founded the Captiva Corporation to manage his assets, particularly the proceeds from the sale of Exeter.

Mayer's business successes permitted him to indulge his passions for skiing, deep-sea diving, fine wine and collecting. He was best known as a philatelist, and his collection of Costa Rican stamps was legendary. He also owned an extraordinary collection of encased postage, which was auctioned by Heritage Auction Galleries in Long Beach, Calif., in September 2007.

But Mr. Mayer had been assembling a secret collection at his beautiful home in downtown Denver, Colo. for a number of years. It was this collection – a remarkable grouping of Confederate Montgomery notes and Confederate bonds – that led Steve Goldsmith to visit Mr. Mayer in 2006 at Mr. Mayer's personal invitation.

After a two-hour meeting, during which neither currency nor bonds was shown, the two men felt that they had gotten to know and trust each other. Based on his initial impressions, Mr. Mayer consented to consign his Montgomery notes and bonds to a future Smythe auction.

Mr. Mayer told Steve that his approach to collecting was simple. He found an expert he could completely trust, and he then relied on that expert to make purchase decisions. While he enjoyed each individual acquisition, his real goal was to create a collection that could be turned into a book or catalog and add to the knowledge and pleasure of future collectors.

Of course, Mr. Mayer's expert on his acquisition of Confederate currency and bonds was R. M. Smythe's esteemed Douglas B. Ball, who literally "wrote the book" on Confederate bonds in 1998. Indeed it was the Mayer collection that was used to provide the plate illustrations of many of the great rarities in Ball's bond book, although that fact was never disclosed. At his own request, Mayer was never mentioned in Doug's book, and Doug even went so far to protect his client's confidentiality as to simply refer to him as "Mr. Big" in the office.

Mayer's collection of Confederate Montgomery notes was eclectic and extremely impressive, but lacked the balance and consistency usually seen in large Confederate accumulations. Without doubt the star of Mayer's collection was a $1,000 Montgomery note bearing serial number 88. With a distinguished provenance to Philip Chase and then Doug Ball himself, this note is one of the most famous $1,000 Montgomerys known, graded by Doug in the 1987 sale of his own collection as "Extremely Fine, plus, cut cancelled." A second $1,000 Montgomery grading "Fine-Very Fine, cut cancelled" was also offered, as well as two $500 Montgomerys, both grading "Very Fine." The better of the two $500 Montgomerys, serial number 104, was previously owned by author Arlie Slabaugh and was discussed on p. 93.

Illus. 85

The $1,000 and $500 Montgomerys were followed by a run of five beautiful $100 Montgomery notes (Criswell Type-3 Variety 3) grading "Extremely Fine" down to "Very Fine." Sale prices were orderly and consistent with the grade for all of these $100 Montgomerys. The finest of the "Extremely Fine" notes, serial number 1492, sold for a very strong $25,300 despite immediately following four $1,000 and $500 Montgomerys which sold for even more. Even the weakest of the five $100 Montgomerys grading "Very Fine" sold for $9,775, a fair price for a note with considerable circulation. The sale of the Montgomerys ended with a four-note run of $50 Montgomery notes (Criswell Type-4 Variety 4) grading "Very Fine-Extremely Fine" down to "Fine plus." Again, pricing was fair and consistent with the grade, as the finest specimen sold for a solid $16,100. The poorest example of the $50 Montgomery – and the 13th and final Montgomery in the sale – still managed a very respectable price of $9,775, despite a grade of only "Fine plus."

While the reader might question the wisdom of releasing 13 Montgomery notes at a single sale, it is most reassuring that the Confederate currency market was able to absorb them in an orderly fashion, with superior quality generating eyebrow-raising prices and even average quality commanding solid prices. Indeed the Confederate currency market had come of age, without any semblance of the price weakness feared by many dealers and collectors alike.

Frederick R. Mayer died February 14, 2007, from complications following heart surgery. Steve Goldsmith had found him "to be one of the most pleasant, down-to-earth, and downright friendly men" he had ever met. A noted philanthropist and a world-class collector of art in addition to his other collecting interests, his death was a great loss to his family, to the City of Denver, and to the collecting fraternity worldwide.

2011. Record 36th Consecutive Annual Confederate Currency Catalog Released.

Today's leading dealer in Confederate currency and bonds, and a disciple of Grover Criswell himself, **Hugh Shull** began issuing annual and semi-annual Confederate currency catalogs in 1976; his Winter 2011/Spring 2012 Edition will mark 36 consecutive years, with no end in sight. Unlike authors who have provided updated pricing data for the various issues of Confederate currency based on historical auction results, Hugh releases softbound catalogs filled with currency from his own inventory and priced for immediate sale based on his intimate knowledge of current value and worth. As such, Hugh makes the market for Confederate currency – and has been doing so since the early 1990s, when Grover Criswell's failing health and financial difficulties led him to pass the baton. Hugh was Grover's prized pupil and, as stated in Grover's final 1996 edition, "has been like a son to me for many years."

As he recounts in the *Preface* to his 2007 book *A Guide Book of Southern States Currency*, Hugh got his start as a coin collector when he was given some old coins by his father when he was only age seven – coins previously owned by Hugh's grandfather. In addition to the coins, Hugh also received a badly torn Confederate $5 bill from the 1864 issue, all stored in an old tin pickle can. Over the years Hugh disposed of the old coins, but the Confederate $5 bill, along with the old pickle can, are still among his most treasured mementos.

In 1974 after serving a four-year stint with the U.S. Air Force, Hugh went to work for a coin dealer in Gulfport, Miss. Previously Hugh had little interest or knowledge about collecting paper money. But as part of his new job responsibilities, he was required to both buy and sell Confederate and Southern States currency that he regularly encountered at various regional shows. Hugh was immediately drawn to the beauty and history of this paper money, and a love affair with Confederate and Southern States currency was kindled.

Just 18 months later, the owner of the coin shop where Hugh worked was forced to close for health reasons. While in Gulfport, Hugh had met Graeme Ton, a leading U.S. small-size dealer who understood Hugh's predicament of losing his job and immediately befriended him. Graeme Ton, along with Grover Criswell whom Hugh had also met, began to mold him into a first-rate dealer in paper money – particularly Confederate and Southern States currency. A few months later Graeme introduced Hugh to Don Fisher of Decatur, Ill., who is a prominent dealer in U.S. obsolete currency. Don wanted to sell a collection of Confederate currency to Hugh for a great price of only $1,200, but Hugh simply did not have the money.

Without hesitation – and despite Hugh being a stranger without credit – Don consigned the collection to Hugh and allowed him to pay for it over time. This collection, along with a small group of Confederate bonds, formed the entirety of Hugh's first fixed-price list mailed in the spring of 1976. As Hugh described it, the mailing piece "was a simple hand-typed, double-spaced, one-page listing on front and back, with one-fourth of it filled with hot air!"

Two years later, in 1978, Hugh moved his business to his boyhood home of Leesville, S.C. My brother Charles was in the process of completing his own Confederate currency type set of all 72 distinct designs described in Grover Criswell's 1957 book. I met Hugh for the first time on Christmas Eve a few years later when I was looking for a Christmas present for Charles. My brother's wife had given me a list of "holes" in his album needed to finish his type set. I was living in Cincinnati at the time and had come to South Carolina to visit my parents over the Holidays. I drove the 35 miles to Leesville from my parents' home in Graniteville, S.C. to sit down with Hugh and choose a piece of Confederate currency to give my brother the following day. Hugh and I have been the best of friends ever since.

Hugh has justly earned his title as today's preeminent dealer in Confederate currency and bonds. He is a charter member of the Professional Currency Dealers Association (PCDA), serving as both their president and member of the board. He is a life member of the ANA, the Society of Paper Money Collectors (SPMC) and the South Carolina Numismatic Association (SCNA), where he has served four terms as president and as a board member for over 25 years. He also actively participates in many regional numismatic associations.

Hugh's first effort in authoring a book came with his assistance to Grover Criswell in Grover's fourth edition in 1992. Hugh next teamed up with Douglas B. Ball to co-author with Grover his fifth and final edition in 1996. He finally went solo with his well-received and critically acclaimed *A Guide Book of Southern States Currency*, released by Whitman Publishing in 2007.

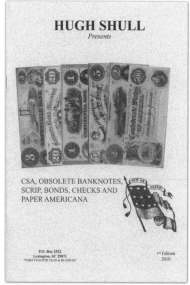

While a successful author, Hugh became the de facto market maker for Confederate currency with his annual 64-page catalogs offering Confederate currency, Southern States currency, Confederate bonds and other obsolete and miscellaneous items for immediate sale in a choice of several grades. His catalogs have become standard reference works, particularly among other dealers on the bourse floor, and document the consistent price appreciation enjoyed by Confederate currency from his first catalog in 1976 to the Winter 2011/Spring 2012 Edition soon to go to the printer *(Illus. 86 is his 2010 edition)*.

Hugh's catalogs have come a long way from the one-page, double-spaced version of 1976. Today's catalog, titled *Hugh Shull Presents CSA, Obsolete Banknotes, Scrip, Bonds, Checks and Paper Americana*, is remarkably comprehensive. The Confederate currency section, in addition to all the type notes in multiple grades and many of the rarest varieties, also includes sections on Confederate counterfeits, "Bogus Backs," Trans-Mississippi issues and complete sheets. Hugh has even added sections on U.S. Colonials to augment his Confederate specialties.

Illus. 86

The modern-day collecting of Confederate currency was chronicled in books authored by Grover Criswell and Arlie Slabaugh. Sadly, a third titan, Douglas B. Ball, worked for years on a manuscript of Confederate currency unpublished at the time of his death. Hugh Shull *(Illus. 87)* becomes the logical successor to this literary trio of Criswell, Ball and Slabaugh. Indeed, Hugh is now developing a hardbound book on Confederate currency to reinforce his widely accepted annual catalogs, as the hobby is in dire need of a new author with the wisdom of Arlie, the integrity of Douglas and the knowledge of Grover. Hugh will fill the void.

The book, already titled *A Guide Book of Confederate Currency*, will be released by Whitman Publishing in the not-too-distant future. Since Hugh purchased the future rights to the indispensable Criswell series of Confederate publications, I look forward to seeing how he melds the accumulated knowledge of Grover Criswell with his own business savvy, gleaned as he wrote his recent book on Southern States currency. Undoubtedly Hugh's new book will become the standard Confederate currency reference work for many years to come.

Illus. 87

With Hugh Shull's new book not released yet, I conclude my discussion of the major auctioneers, dealers and collectors – some saintly, some wicked, all intriguing – that provided the match to ignite the hobby of collecting Confederate currency. But rather than focus on the personalities and their egos that led to the famous and historic auctions just described, the next chapter will delve into the auction process itself and why it is a valid instrument to accomplish my goal of measuring a rate of return for Confederate currency over 150 years.

Chapter 2:

The Numismatic Auction Process:
Its History and What It Can Teach Us

Part I: The Evolution of Numismatic Auctions

The auction form of determining fair market value is old. Herodotus the Greek historian mentioned public auctions as early as 400 B.C. In 2007 over 30 million Americans attended public auctions and spent over $257 billion -- more than the Gross National Product of fast-growing Brazil[1]. Thus my decision to base the conclusions I reached in this book solely on results from numismatic auction catalogs is neither new nor precedent-setting. My contribution to numismatics rests in the thoroughness of my research and its statistical rigor.

Unfortunately we realize that public auctions are sometimes imperfect mechanisms to establish fair market value. On occasion even the snootiest of auction houses fails to play by the rules. Indeed in 2002 Alfred Taubman, head of the haughty Sotheby's auction firm, and equally prominent Christie's International were both found guilty of price fixing. Further, at auctions we sometimes see auction lots failing to reach some predetermined reserve price which should lead the auction house to report the results as "no sale." Yet actual results frequently show a price realized – presumably the reserve price – when we know no sale occurred. Sales of Confederate currency today are not immune to such misrepresentations; it is difficult to believe that similar shenanigans did not take place at auctions a century ago.

Despite their faults, though, "auctions are still the best way of determining fair market value," as observed by attorney Alexander Forger, then with Milbank, Tweed, Hadley & McCloy, the law firm that handled the estate of Jacqueline Kennedy Onassis. "There's no question of the validity and integrity of public auction," added *The New York Times* in 2001.

Such assertions by newsmakers like leading law firms and newspapers reinforce the strongly held conviction most of us share in the validity of the public auction process to establish fair market value. So let us look expressly at the history of numismatic auctions.

Edward Cogan, first professional coin dealer (drawing courtesy artist Alan Dietz).

Numismatic auctions have been around almost as long as the hobby of numismatics itself, a pastime that Webster defines as the study of coins, tokens, medals or paper money. According to David Bowers, American numismatics started in the mid 1850s when the U.S. government replaced its large copper cent with a smaller, copper-nickel version. Many citizens used this changeover to start coin collections of the various different dates then in circulation.

This growing army of new collectors needed expert advice, so professional numismatists soon began servicing them from businesses in New York, Boston and Philadelphia. John K. Curtis and Augustus B. Sage each claimed the title as the first dealer of prominence, but Edward Cogan of Philadelphia generally gets the vote as the father of U.S. coin collecting. By the early 1860s while the Civil War was raging, the collecting of rare coins had become a dynamic and serious hobby.

[1] Data provided by Walton & Associates, a Medina, Ohio-based auction firm.

The first numismatic auction catalogs followed soon after the establishment of the first dealers. John W. Adams writes that the first auction catalogs were not broadly distributed. In late 1858 Edward Cogan posted in his retail store a single copy of a list of coins for sale. His local customers were given the opportunity to review this list to search for coins needed for their collections. If found, the customer could submit his best offer in a sealed envelope, which was opened, along with all other offers, on an appointed day. By December 1859 Cogan must have viewed his in-store auctions as a success, as late that month he began printing and distributing his auction catalogs in the conventional manner we still use today.

Just a year later in 1860, Edward Cogan achieved another first: he began stocking in his retail store the first fixed-price list of American coins. Written by George Jones and titled *The Coin Collectors' Manual*, a photo of this important publication is provided to the right.

Our discussion so far has been limited to the sale of coins, which were being sold to both the walk-in trade and through public auctions by the late 1850s. However, similar interest in paper money had yet to surface. Although paper money had been issued by the various colonies even before this country was formed, Bowers writes that "In the 1860s…there was virtually no interest in collecting…paper money." With such a dearth of curiosity about paper money, I find it very curious that Confederate currency made its debut in a public auction catalog, albeit only a single lot, as early as June 1864, nearly a year before the Civil War ended.

Coin Collectors' Manual, *first fixed-price list for coins.*

It should come as no surprise that this same Edward Cogan who claimed to be America's first coin dealer also holds the distinction of offering this first lot of Confederate currency at public auction. In an 844-lot auction of coins and medals conducted on June 29-30, 1864, Cogan included a single-line mention of his only Confederate item: Lot "341. Confederate Bank Note Twenty Dollars." Cataloged with "Autographs To Be Sold For The Benefit Of The Sanitary Commission," it is clear that Cogan was unsure where such an item should be placed. It is impossible to determine which specific $20 note under Criswell's classification system was sold, as the Confederate Treasury issued numerous twenty-dollar designs. The twenty-cents sales price, however, was impressive – the same price as realized by an autographed letter from President Millard Fillmore.

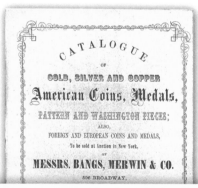

It is difficult to understand why the numismatic collecting fraternity was so indifferent to the collecting of paper money – including Confederate currency – in the latter half of the nineteenth century, despite its embrace of the collection of coins. Part of the apathy might be attributable to a lack of knowledge, as the first publication about Confederate currency – a series of charts running in three different issues of the *American Journal of Numismatics* – did not appear until 1867 and was not further amplified until 1875 when William Lee published a paltry 30 copies of his book entitled *The Currency of the Confederate States of America.*

Edward Cogan's June 1864 catalog, with first Confederate lot.

With little curiosity about Confederate currency and little education afforded to stimulate any enthusiasm, it is not surprising that the number of auctions containing Confederate currency was limited in the 1800s and much of the 1900s, before an explosion of interest occurred in the mid 1970s. Since this first volume focuses on the Montgomerys, I have shown below the number of auctions offering Montgomery notes for sale by decade, starting with the W. Elliott Woodward auction in December 1865 and ending with the Neal Auction Company sale in November 2009:

Number of Public Auctions Offering Confederate Montgomery Notes by Decade:

Decade	Number of Auctions with Montgomerys	Decade	Number of Auctions with Montgomerys	Decade	Number of Auctions with Montgomerys
1860s	1	1910s	10	1970s	8
1870s	3	1920s	9	(1970-1975)	(2)
1880s	21	1930s	12	(1976-1979)	(6)
1890s	18	1940s	16	1980s	24
1900s	8	1950s	6	1990s	23
		1960s	3	2000s	41

This chart shows that interest in Confederate currency, at least as revealed by auction exposure from the Montgomery notes, did not explode until the latter half of the 1970s. This result is surprising. I would have thought that the proliferation of publications about Confederate currency starting in the 1940s and 1950s with the Philip Chase book and the Criswell and Slabaugh series of publications, coupled with the start of the centennial anniversary of the start of the war itself in 1961, would have led to quickened interest in Confederate currency as early as the 1950s. Indeed, as will be seen in Chapter 4, Confederate Montgomery notes did begin to enjoy a much faster rate of financial appreciation starting around 1950. But the chart above is clear: Montgomery notes in quantity did not begin to be offered to the collecting fraternity until the late 1970s.

So what happened in the late 1970s to spur such interest in Confederate currency, and particularly the Montgomery notes? Remarkably the answer seems to rest on the formation of the auction firm named Numismatic and Antiquarian Service Corporation of America (usually simply called "NASCA") by my friend and mentor Douglas B. Ball in May 1976. Between 1976 and June 1991 when NASCA was fully integrated into R.M. Smythe & Co., NASCA tendered nearly 15% of all the Montgomerys offered in history to that time, far more than any other auction firm.

I find it astonishing that Doug's total of 85 Montgomerys proffered in only 15 years while he managed NASCA is more than the second, third and fourth most prolific Confederate currency auctioneers between 1865 and 1991 *combined* (i.e., Charles Steigerwalt is in second place with 30 Montgomerys offered between 1865 and 1991, M.H. Bolender is in third with 26 offered and Thomas Elder and Christie's are tied for fourth with 22 offered). I suspect that it is more than sheer coincidence that the explosion of interest in Confederate currency occurred concurrent with Doug's formation and management of NASCA in 1976. All who share my passion for Confederate currency owe Doug our gratitude.

The chart on the facing page offers a one-page summary of all 588 Montgomery notes offered for sale in history, arranged chronologically by auction house -- all 57 of them -- and detailed by the number of notes tendered of each denomination.

Snapshot of All Montgomery Notes Offered for Sale by Auction House and Denomination:

Name of Auction House	First Mont. Sale	$1,000	$500	$100	$50	Total
William Elliot Woodward	19 Dec 1865	3	2	2	2	9
John W. Haseltine	24 Apr 1878	4	1	6	5	16
Bangs & Company	16 Nov 1878	1	1	2	2	6
Sigismund K. Harzfeld	9 Apr 1880	1	1			2
John Walter Scott	20 Mar 1882	2		4	4	10
Edouard Frossard	12 Dec 1883	4	3	6	7	20
Charles Steigerwalt	19 Dec 1884	7		9	14	30
Henry G. Sampson	12 Feb 1885			1	1	2
Lyman Haines Low	26 Mar 1885	4	3	4	4	15
George W. Massamore	21 Nov 1885	1			2	3
David U. Proskey	15 Dec 1885	1	1	1	1	4
S.H. & H. Chapman	17 Oct 1888	3	3	2	3	11
Thomas Lindsay Elder	26 Feb 1908	5	5	6	6	22
Henry Chapman	19 Jun 1908	2	2	1	1	6
Edgar Holmes Adams	10 Feb 1911	1				1
Ben G. Green	28 Mar 1913			1	1	2
Edward Michael	9 May 1914	1	1	1	1	4
Samuel Hudson Chapman	27 May 1914	1	1	1	1	4
U. S. Coin Company	29 Jun 1914			1	2	3
Wayte Raymond	4 Dec 1918				1	1
B. Max Mehl	23 Nov 1920	6	5	4	4	19
Stan V. Henkels	28 Jul 1922	1	1	1	1	4
William Hesslein	20 Sep 1929	1	1	2	2	6
Barney Bluestone	26 Jan 1935	1	3	1	2	7
Milfred Henry Bolender	15 Oct 1935	6	6	8	6	26
Benjamin B. DuBose	18 Nov 1935		1			1
John Milford Henderson	4 Apr 1936	1	1	1	1	4
Stack's	3 Dec 1937	6	6	8	5	25
New Netherlands Coin Co.	5 Dec 1940	1	1	1	2	5
Abe Kosoff	25 Aug 1942	1				1
Federal Coin Exchange	10 Jan 1957	1	1	1	1	4
James, Inc.	29 Mar 1957			1	1	2
D&W Auction Sales	26 Oct 1957	2	1	1	1	5
Federal Brand Enterprises	13 Jul 1963	1	1	1	1	4
Lester Merkin	28 Mar 1969	1		1	2	4
Hans M. F. Schulman	23 Mar 1970		1		1	2
NASCA	27 May 1977	15	17	30	23	85
Kagin's	29 Sep 1978	1	2	3	2	8
Grover C. Criswell	17 Oct 1980	2	2	2	2	8
Bowers & Ruddy Galleries	25 Mar 1981	1	1	1	1	4
Christie's	17 Sep 1982	6	4	5	8	23
Coin Galleries	10 Apr 1985	2			1	3
R. M. Smythe & Company	27 Jun 1991	14	18	27	22	81
Currency Auctions of America	2 May 1997			1		1
Signature House	15 May 1997	1				1
Withington Auction	28 Aug 1998	1				1
Lyn Knight Currency Auctions	20 Oct 1999	3	5	5	4	17
Bowers & Merena Galleries	9 Aug 2000	1	1	1	1	4
Early American History Aucts.	14 Oct 2000	1			1	2
M&M America, Limited	3 Aug 2001		1			1
Heritage Auctions	21 Sep 2001	5	8	11	14	38
Centennial Auctions	24 Sep 2002			1		1
Butterfields, a Div. of eBay	16 Dec 2002	1				1
Briggs Auction	3 Dec 2004				1	1
Spink Smythe	16 Jul 2008	1	2	2	4	9
Neal Auction Company	21 Nov 2009	3	2	2	1	8
Dix Noonan Webb	30 Sep 2010	1				1
Totals:		**129**	**116**	**170**	**173**	**588**

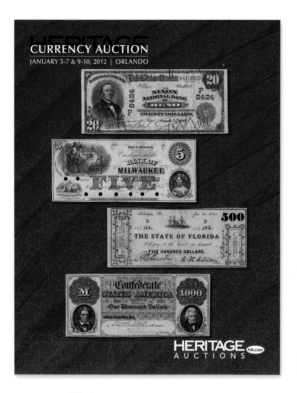

Heritage Auction's Jan. 2012 FUN Sale, featuring Bill Kelly's 32 Montgomerys.

Certainly Doug's NASCA firm, along with NASCA's acquirer R. M. Smythe & Co., have controlled the market for Confederate currency, and particularly its Montgomery notes, during the last 25 years of the twentieth century. But with Doug's untimely death in 2003, coupled with Heritage Auction Galleries' acquisition of Currency Auctions of America (CAA) in 2001, a serious new contender has emerged for supremacy in the consignment and sale of Confederate currency.

The founders of CAA, good friends Allen Mincho, Len Glazer and Kevin Foley, made a fortuitous decision in 2001 to sell out to Heritage, already a behemoth in the auction business but lacking a presence in currency as a collectible. To gauge the success of this purchase, it is necessary only to look at its recent results. From 2001 through 2010, Heritage offered 38 Montgomery notes for sale, second only to R. M. Smythe. In a sign of its ever-increasing momentum, though, Heritage announced in late 2011 the consignment of the entire Confederate collection of my good friend, the Honorable William H. Kelly, whom I discussed on page 14. This extraordinary collection, to be sold at the FUN Show in Orlando, Fla., in January 2012, contains 32 Montgomery notes alone. Upon the sale's completion, Heritage Auctions will have tendered nearly as many Montgomery notes to the collecting fraternity in only 11 years as R. M. Smythe had proffered in 20. Clearly Heritage intends to become a major player in the area of currency, and particularly in Confederate Treasury notes.

Part II: What Can Be Learned from Reviewing Auction Records

So far this chapter has discussed the evolution of the numismatic auction process, particularly its Confederate Montgomery notes, and has provided a detailed chart summarizing all the Montgomery notes offered for sale between 1865 and 2010. But the Confederate sales data I collected on numerous trips to the ANS Library in New York beginning in 1997 was not limited to just the Montgomerys. I have gathered auction results for all 38 types Grover Criswell enumerated as the issues of 1861 (i.e., Criswell Type-1 through Type-38) plus the two mysterious and poorly understood "Essay" notes of 1862 (i.e., Criswell Type-47 and 48).

With the capable and tireless assistance of Crutchfield Williams in building the database, I have now recorded the impressive total of 63,506 individual identifiable pieces of Confederate currency that have moved through auction channels between 1865 and 2010.

Grover C. Criswell, creator of modern classification system (photo from R.M. Smythe & Co.).

As large as this database might appear to be, however, I am sure that I have failed to count some pieces, and unfortunately, some of the pieces I missed (either because they appeared in minor auction houses reviewed by neither John Adams nor me, or because they were in catalogs that indeed I did review but simply missed) are probably rarities like the Montgomerys, the Shield & Eagles or the Indian Princesses. While regrettable, Dr. Steven Feller, the project's statistician, assures me that a few missing notes, even if rarities, will not change the conclusions I have drawn.

Despite such shortcomings, though, owning such a huge database makes it fairly easy to answer questions, with a very high degree of certainty, that have intrigued Confederate collectors for years. To illustrate the power of the database, I will address a century-old question: which Confederate type note is the rarest in the entire series?

Part III: Which Confederate Type Note Is the Rarest In the Entire Series?

Ever since 1879 when John Walter Scott began classifying the entirety of the Confederate currency issues under the umbrella of only 74 different designs, it was logical to wonder which of those designs -- under Criswell's classification system, those designs are called "types" -- appears least frequently, and conversely, which type appears most frequently. It thus comes as no surprise that the two earliest auctioneers of Confederate Montgomery notes, W. Elliott Woodward and John W. Haseltine, were also the first to suggest the relative rarity of various types in the entire series.

John W. Haseltine moves to center stage about this time, offering a total of 16 Montgomerys beginning in April 1878. Haseltine was born in Philadelphia in 1838 and spent a life of 86 years working as a miner, a shoe salesman, a commercial artist, a captain in the Union army and a professional numismatist.

John W. Scott (drawing courtesy artist Alan Dietz).

He married the daughter of William Idler, a noted early collector of colonial and continental currency, superb patterns and choice early silver. Around 1869 Haseltine formed a business partnership with another famous early numismatist, Ebenezer Mason, and later, in the mid 1870s he offered employment to both Chapman brothers. In 1870 Haseltine was given the opportunity to sell his father-in-law's magnificent collection, an event which put Haseltine on the numismatic map.

Haseltine built a close relationship with key officials at the Philadelphia Mint and became the middleman between the Mint and collectors of many rare pattern coins. According to John Adams, Haseltine was the leading authority of his day in at least four branches of U.S. numismatics: colonial paper, early silver varieties, mint patterns and Confederate paper. His 1876 catalog titled *Descriptive Catalog of Confederate Notes and Bonds for Sale* remains one of the rarest and most important of the early publications about Confederate currency (see page 36 for a discussion of Haseltine's Confederate catalog).

John Haseltine cataloged 87 different sales between 1870 and 1898, including his March 1883 sale of the so-called Confederate cent complete with dies. He forsook the coin business to become a stock broker in 1885 before returning to numismatics ten years later. Despite the ten-year hiatus, Haseltine had not lost his capacity to surprise. Just as he had announced the Confederate cent in his 1883 auction, in 1909 he revealed the existence of two unique double eagle patterns in gold.

In the 1870s and 1880s, when Woodward and Haseltine were at the top of their game, there was little factual data on which either could have based a conclusion about rarity. Raphael Thian's *Register of the Confederate Debt*, which would have provided vital information on the number of pieces of each design that were issued, was published during this time frame, but with only six copies known to exist, it is doubtful that any of the earliest auction houses were privy to Thian's landmark findings.

Haseltine seems to be the first to offer an opinion on rarity. In an April 1883 auction that featured Harold Newlin's Confederate Montgomery notes,

John W. Haseltine (drawing courtesy artist Alan Dietz).

Haseltine made the initial claim about rarity, flatly stating that the Criswell Type-35 "$5 Indian Princess" was the rarest in the entire Confederate series:

"… the rarest of the Confederate issue. Of greater rarity than either the $1000 or $500 of the first issue." [i.e., the Montgomery notes]

Criswell Type-35 $5 "Indian Princess" (photo courtesy Spink Smythe).

Not to be outdone by his competitor, W. Elliott Woodward, while cataloging an October 1884 auction also featuring Montgomery notes, made an identical observation about the "Indian Princess" in his catalog description: "A very satisfactory example of the rarest of all the Confederate notes."

Lyman Low, who according to John Adams might be the most cerebral of the nineteenth century auctioneers (for 18 years he co-authored the prestigious *American Journal of Numismatics*), could not resist offering his own opinion about the "Indian Princess" in a March 1885 auction:

"Very good, the rarest of the series."

Over the next 75 years, auction catalogs fall silent on the issue of rarity, or at least appear to be unwilling to make any bold statements without the benefit of careful analysis. It is not until October 1963 that the eminent John J. Ford, while cataloging the benchmark estate sale of George O. Walton for Stack's, gushed that the "Indian Princess":

"Has the distinction of being the rarest and most sought-after by all collectors of the series."

Another 30 years elapsed before Coin Galleries, a sister company of Stack's, wrote in an April 1996 auction that the "Indian Princess":

"Is arguably the rarest and most important type note in the Confederate series."

Just a few years later Lyn Knight shared his opinion, writing in a June 1999 auction catalog that the "Indian Princess" is:

"Truly the rarest type of Confederate currency and it has long been under appreciated."

After Heritage Auction Galleries acquired Currency Auctions of America in 2001, it agreed in near unanimity with other auction houses that the "Indian Princess" was the rarest note in the Confederate series, writing in a January 2004 auction catalog that the "Indian Princess" is:

"The rarest Confederate type and a note that is nearly always found in low grades…"

…and writing again in an April 2006 auction about:

"The heralded Indian Princess note, the rarest Confederate type."

There was one notable exception to the "near unanimity" of opinion expressed earlier that the "Indian Princess" was the rarest type note in the entire Confederate series. In January 1974 Douglas B. Ball completed his Ph.D. thesis entitled *Confederate War Finance, 1861-1865: Economic Policy-Making in the South during the American Civil War*, and his recollections of the extensive research he had just concluded convinced him that the Criswell Type-27 "$10 Shield & Eagle" was the rarest type note in the Confederate series, rarer even than its sheet-mate, the "$5 Indian Princess."

After creating a platform to express his views with his formation of the NASCA auction firm in 1976, Doug did not publish his conviction about the "Shield & Eagle" in the early auctions he cataloged, preferring instead to reference its "elusiveness" or the "difficulty in procuring" the "Shield & Eagle."

But in NASCA's January 1983 auction of Charles Affleck's portion of the massive John Browne collection, Ball finally memorialized his opinion when he wrote that the "Shield & Eagle" was:

> "A much scarcer type than the Indian Princess which has long overshadowed it."

Ball felt no pressure to justify his provocative opinion from other Confederate experts of the day, including Grover Criswell or Brent Hughes. Doug thus sharpened his judgment in cataloging for Smythe's November 1994 auction (Smythe completed its acquisition of NASCA in 1991), when he advanced that his belief in the "Shield & Eagle's" supreme rarity was based on "its recorded appearances." Specifically, Ball wrote of the "Shield & Eagle":

Criswell Type-27 $10 "Shield & Eagle" (photo courtesy Spink Smythe).

> "Some 7160 of this type…were printed with the Indian Princess note, which to judge by its recorded appearances is far more available."

An ever-emboldened Doug Ball, still unchallenged by his peers, next quantified just how much more plentiful the "Indian Princess" was compared to the "Shield & Eagle" in the June 1998 Smythe sale of the magnificent Arnold Cowan collection:

> "The ratio of appearance of Indian Princess $5 notes, Type 35, to Liberty, Eagle and Shield notes, Type 27, remain in the 3 to 2 ratio range."

Even on his deathbed in early 2003, cataloging for Smythe's sale of Gene Mintz's far-reaching collection in June 2003, Ball wrote that:

> "Survival rates seem to slightly favor the Indian Princess notes in a ratio of about 3 to 2."

In 1997 I began my own investigation, which I suspected would ultimately settle the argument once and for all: was the "$5 Indian Princess" or the "$10 Shield & Eagle" the rarest Confederate type note in the entire series? But even before I started my research, I never accepted the notion that either the "Indian Princess" or the "Shield & Eagle" was the rarest in the entire series. Neither argument in support of either note made any sense to me.

We know from Confederate Treasury records compiled by Raphael Thian in 1880 that over 7,000 pieces of both the "Indian Princess" and the "Shield & Eagle" were issued, compared to only 607 pieces of both the Criswell Type-1 "$1,000 Montgomery" and Criswell Type-2 "$500 Montgomery." We also know that the lower denominated $5 "Indian Princess" and $10 "Shield & Eagle" saw significantly more circulation than did the Montgomerys, as both the "Indian Princess" and "Shield & Eagle" were among the main vehicles of daily commerce. We finally know that the Montgomerys were printed on fine bank note paper far more durable than the inferior-quality paper used for the "Indian Princess" and the "Shield & Eagle."

But it is hard to ignore that over ten times as many "Shield & Eagle" and "Indian Princess" notes were issued as $1,000 and $500 Montgomerys. Despite differences in abrasion and paper quality, my sometimes-challenged common sense shouted that both the $1,000 and the $500 Montgomerys simply *had* to be rarer than the "Shield & Eagle" or the "Indian Princess."

My work is now complete. Public auction appearances between 1865 and 2010 indeed support the unassailable conclusion that the Criswell Type-2 "$500 Montgomery", with 116 appearances at public auction since 1865, is the rarest type note among those authorized and issued by the Confederate Treasury. It is closely followed by the Criswell Type-1 "$1,000 Montgomery" as the second rarest, with 129 appearances at auction since 1865.

The Type-27 "Shield and Eagle" and Type-35 "Indian Princess" are next and virtually tied in the third and fourth positions, with 147 and 150 appearances, respectively. Indeed the "Shield & Eagle" and "Indian Princess" are about halfway between the rarity of the $1,000 and $500 Montgomerys and the remaining Montgomerys: the Type-3 "$100 Montgomery," with 170 auction appearances, and the Type-4 "$50 Montgomery," with 173 appearances. And as to Doug Ball's well publicized conviction that the "Shield & Eagle" was "a much scarcer type than the 'Indian Princess,'" I can find no factual data to support its validity.

Criswell Type-48 $10 "Essay" (photo from Crutchfield Williams).

For traditionalists who consider the bogus yet enigmatic "Essay" notes (Criswell Types-47 and 48) as key components of a Confederate type set, despite neither being authorized nor issued by the Confederate Treasury, both notes are undeniably rarer than even the $500 and $1,000 Montgomerys. The $20 "Essay" note (Criswell Type-47) has made only 44 appearances at public auction since 1865, with its first appearance in a Ben Green auction in 1913. The $10 "Essay" (Criswell Type-48) is rarer still, making only 30 appearances at public auction since 1865, with its first appearance not coming until a William Hesslein auction in 1929.

There is a great sense of satisfaction -- almost relief -- when the results of 14 years of research are consistent with preconceived notions. For years collectors have agreed that the "Big Six" -- the four Montgomery notes plus the "Indian Princess" and the "Shield & Eagle" -- are the rarest types in the entire series. Collectors have disputed, however, the relative rarity ranking among the "Big Six," with most enthusiasts believing the "Indian Princess" was the rarest of all. While certainly scarce, auction records spanning nearly 150 years conclusively prove that the "Indian Princess" is *not* the rarest. The honor of rarest in the entire series goes to the $500 Montgomery, closely followed by the $1,000 Montgomery.

The relative rarity of all 38 Criswell types that comprise the authorized issues of 1861 are summarized in the chart on the next page (the two "Essay" notes, Criswell Types-47 and 48, are included as well). Four columns are used to describe each type. The first column ranks the rarity, from most rare to most common; the second column provides the note's Criswell type number; the third column offers a brief description of the note, and the fourth column provides the total number of appearances at all auctions I studied between 1865 and 2010.

Ranking of Rarity of the Confederate Currency Issues of 1861 (including the "Essays"):

Rarity Ranking	Criswell Type No.	Description of Criswell Type	No. of Auction Appearances
(n. a.)	T-48	1862 $10 Essay	30
(n. a.)	T-47	1862 $20 Essay	44
1	T- 2	1861 $500 Montgomery	116
2	T- 1	1861 $1,000 Montgomery	129
3	T-27	1861 $10 Shield & Eagle	147
4	T-35	1861 $5 Indian Princess	150
5	T- 3	1861 $100 Montgomery	170
6	T- 4	1861 $50 Montgomery	173
7	T-15	1861 $50 Locomotive & Train	214
8	T-19	1861 $20 Navigation & Blacksmith	258
9	T-12	1861 $5 Manouvrier	319
10	T-38	1861 $2 Error: South Striking Union	358
11	T-23	1861 $10 Wagon of Cotton	360
12	T- 5	1861 $100 First Richmond	372
13	T- 6	1861 $50 First Richmond	389
14	T-11	1861 $5 Liberty & Eagle	403
15	T- 7	1861 $100 Ceres & Proserpina	428
16	T-32	1861 $5 Machinist	443
17	T-17	1861 $20 Three Females	461
18	T-22	1861 $10 Indian Family	651
19	T-31	1861 $5 Five Females	744
20	T-21	1861 $20 Alexander H. Stephens	866
21	T-10	1861 $10 Liberty, Shield & Eagle	988
22	T-34	1861 $5 Memminger (Black)	1,066
23	T-29	1861 $10 Slave Picking Cotton	1,080
24	T-33	1861 $5 Memminger (Green)	1,107
25	T-25	1861 $10 Hope with Anchor	1,435
26	T-24	1861 $10 Hunter & Child	1,547
27	T- 9	1861 $20 Sailing Vessel	1,570
28	T-16	1861 $50 Jefferson Davis	1,589
29	T- 8	1861 $50 George Washington	1,849
30	T-13	1861 $100 Slaves Loading Cotton	2,146
31	T-26	1861 $10 Hope with Anchor - Red XX's	2,363
32	T-14	1861 $50 Moneta & Chest	2,599
33	T-37	1861 $5 Sailor beside Cotton Bales	3,029
34	T-30	1861 $10 Sweet Potato Dinner	3,774
35	T-20	1861 $20 Industry & Beehive	4,850
36	T-28	1861 $10 Two Women & Urn	5,154
37	T-18	1861 $20 Sailing Ship with Sailor	8,883
38	T-36	1861 $5 Commerce on Cotton Bale	11,252

Chapter 3:

A Possible Noteworthy Discovery: The Tumultuous Birth of the Confederacy's First Treasury Notes

By W. Crutchfield Williams, II and J. Wayne Hilton

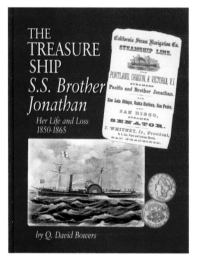

Dave Bowers' book about an 1865 ship wreck.

Few things are more captivating than the idea of lost treasure. I remember waiting in a long line at a movie theater in Montgomery, Ala. in 1981 to watch Indiana Jones in his quest for the revered Ark of the Covenant, or later when he sought the iconic Holy Grail. More recently, noted author Q. David Bowers thrilled us with his book entitled *The Treasure Ship S. S. Brother Jonathan*, with its immense cache of brilliant gold coins lost in an 1865 shipwreck.

The announcement of any new "discovery piece" in Confederate numismatic circles is met with similar exhilaration and euphoria. After all, discovery pieces come around once in a generation at best, with the most famous discovery piece of Confederate currency the fabled "$10 Manouvrier" printed in New Orleans by Jules Manouvrier during July 1861.

The $10 Manouvrier was actually first theorized by the cerebral Confederate researcher Philip H. Chase of Philadelphia around 1950, but he allowed his good friend and fellow researcher Sydney C. Kerksis to publish his findings in a September 1952 article in *The Numismatist* titled "A Newly Discovered Confederate Treasury Note: The $10 Manouvrier." As Kerksis wrote:

> "As most information concerning this note is contained in the form of letters to and from the Confederate Treasury Department, these letters will be presented in their chronological order, with comments relative to their content. This correspondence presents in a very definite fashion the fact that such a note was prepared, why it was not put into circulation and the destruction of the unused notes."

Like the $10 Manouvrier note, much has been said over the years about the possible existence of other Confederate notes and bonds that might have been printed in New York City in April 1861, but were confiscated by U.S. authorities shortly after the Civil War erupted. Unlike the $10 Manouvrier note, however, these events occurred in a foreign country (the U.S.) where the Confederate Treasury had only an agent, and the paper trail is confusing and missing important letters and telegrams between the Treasury and its agent.

After an exhaustive four-year search, though, it appears that a previously unknown group of Confederate Treasury notes was indeed printed in New York City, possibly totaling 5,000 sheets, each sheet bearing a $100 and $50 denomination, and most likely printed by the American Bank Note Company. All these impressions, along with the plates, were confiscated by U.S. marshals on April 25, 1861. Like the $10 Manouvrier note, none of these notes is known to survive.

My interest in this heretofore unknown Confederate print run was a natural outgrowth of the research I started in 1997 which led to my writing this book. Early in my research I came across a copy of the front page of the April 26, 1861 issue of the *New York Tribune*, a fervent anti-secessionist paper owned by the celebrated Horace Greeley of "Go West, young man" fame. The article proclaimed, "Seizure of Treasury Notes of the Southern States" and read:

> "United States Marshal's officers Horton and Borst yesterday seized twelve plates of Treasury notes and bonds of the "Confederate States of America," some of which were completed and others in progress. Ten of the plates were found in the establishment of the American Bank-Note Company, and two in the National Bank-Note Company. The plates were of the denomination of $1,000, $500, $100 and $50. The officers of the Bank-Note Companies stated that they had stopped printing the notes, and ceased work on the plates not yet completed, when the President's Proclamation was issued, but the Federal authorities claim to have proof that they were engaged in printing the notes as late as last Sunday."

Front page, New York Tribune, *April 26, 1861.*

Upon reading this article, I immediately thought that the seized Treasury notes must have been an additional printing of Montgomery notes, and I resolved to find out exactly what these notes were. I approached my good friend and mentor Douglas Ball, who pointed out an inconsistency in the article itself -- the headline spoke of the confiscation of "Treasury notes," but the body of the article talked about only the "seizure of plates" -- and Doug advised that no such missing notes existed, as all the Montgomery notes made it safely from New York City to Montgomery and all were accounted for.

Doug Ball was probably the leading authority on Confederate notes and bonds for most of his adult life, so I dropped any further plans to study what happened in New York in March and April 1861, particularly since I still had thousands of auction catalogs to pore through to create the database for this book.

But I could never get this article out of my mind. In July 2007 I sent columnist Fred Reed an email outlining my suspicions, and I copied dealers Hugh Shull and Crutchfield Williams. Hugh, today's leading dealer in Confederate currency, was unconvinced, and Fred professed that he had no facts to confirm or disprove my thesis.

But dealer Crutchfield Williams immediately became captive to the possibility that unknown Confederate Treasury notes had been printed even before the $10 Manouvrier note, and he began a comprehensive analysis which debunked my own theories about the origins of these notes, and instead he offered additional letters from the Confederate Treasury found in the National Archives that had not been previously reported. Crutch then consented to co-author this chapter with me, as many of the findings are the results of his efforts.

It is impossible to understand the first printing of Confederate Treasury notes in New York just after the formation of the Confederate States without also studying the first issue of Confederate bonds being prepared in New York at the same time. Similar to the way Sydney Kerksis organized his article for *The Numismatist* in 1952, I will present the correspondence among the Confederate Treasury, its New York agent and various other Confederate officials in chronological order, with comments from Crutch and me to suggest what might have been written in missing correspondence.

The paper trail starts even before the Confederate Congress authorized either bonds or currency. Jefferson Davis appointed Christopher Gustavus Memminger as Secretary of the Treasury on February 18, 1861 -- the same day Davis was inaugurated as President of the Confederate States of America. Just nine days later, on February 27, 1861, Secretary Memminger sent "Richard Jones, *Engraver*" of New Orleans the following telegram:

C. G. Memminger, Secretary of the Treasury, Confederate States of America.

"We shall want a plate and paper to strike off about twenty thousand bonds for the Confederate States loan. Paper must be watered and look like bank-note paper, and plate handsome and difficult to counterfeit. Coupons attached to bonds. Can you undertake the job, and in what time can they be furnished and at what price nearly?"

The following day, February 28, the Confederate Congress authorized its first bond issue for $15 million. According to Douglas Ball in his *Comprehensive Catalog and History of Confederate Bonds*, the issue consisted of both 8.0% coupon bonds and 8.0% registered bonds (known as "stock" at the time). Each bond was issued in denominations of $50, $100, $500 and $1,000, so the total issue consisted of eight different bonds -- four coupon bonds and four registered bonds ("stock").

March 1 was a busy day for Secretary Memminger. His February 27 telegram to "Richard Jones, *Engraver*" in New Orleans was answered and is reproduced below. Although he was not an engraver, but rather a cotton broker with the firm Battle, Noble & Co., Jones advised that he had obtained two quotes for the coupon bonds from New Orleans' suppliers. His response indicated that a quote from engraver John Douglas was attached, but if so, it has been misplaced over the years. Jones gave Douglas his highest endorsement, calling him a "Southern institution" and adding that he hoped Douglas "will get the order." Jones advised that a second quote was being separately provided by the local agent of the American Bank Note Company (ABNC). Jones explained that the ABNC quote was for comparative purposes only, as the ABNC was headquartered in New York City, and "they do no engraving on the spot of this sort." Unfortunately, Memminger had forgotten this critical fact a few weeks later.

"DEAR SIR: Your dispatch of yesterday came to hand too late to respond by the mail of yesterday, owing to its being addressed to me as the engraver. There have gone forward to you, by Adams Express, specimens of the engravings of Mr. Douglass (sic), who is a Southern institution and has a high reputation for ability and faithfulness, and executes nearly all the orders for engraving for the city of New Orleans. You will find herewith a bid from him. The other bid you receive is from the agent here of the American Bank Note Company, but their headquarters are New York, and they do no engraving on the spot of this sort. I only got the bid in order that you might have some guide as to cost. This price is evidently based on the New York execution. From inquiries made, Mr. Douglass (sic) may be relied on, and as we have him, identified with the South, on the spot, and as New Orleans deserves well of the Confederation, we hope that he will get the order. He will, I am satisfied, execute it with a feeling of patriotism, and make a good job. In case you wish to address me again, do so to the care of my firm Battle, Noble & Co., and command my services, if needed. You have the most difficult office in the Government. I wish you every success."

In a letter also dated March 1, Samuel Schmidt, manager of the New Orleans' branch of the ABNC, provided Memminger with his own detailed quote for the coupon bonds. In reading this letter reproduced below, I can easily see how Memminger might have mistakenly thought that Schmidt's quote was for work done in New Orleans, despite Jones' letter of the same date stating that the New Orleans' branch of the ABNC did "no engraving on the spot of this sort." Schmidt's letter did not indicate that the work would be done in New York, and his final sentence -- "All prices given herein are as low as Northern prices" -- certainly suggests that the work would be done in the South.

> "SIR: Your telegraphic dispatch relative to engraving and printing bonds for the Confederate States loan has been laid before me, and I find great pleasure in giving you the desired information, and remark that I would be very happy to have one more opportunity to prove that I am fully prepared to execute in the most perfect style any order intrusted (sic) to me. Prices for engraving bond plates (on steel) without coupons, from $400 to $600, depending on size of the bond and quality of work; each twenty coupons to be attached increases the price charged for the bond $100. That generally termed watered appearance of the paper is produced by printing on the paper, previous to the printing of the bonds, another plate (tint plate), made for this purpose, and in another color, to prevent counterfeiting by photography. Such plate will cost from $100 to $150. The price for printing the bond plate is $40 per thousand impressions, and every twenty coupons attached are charged $10 additional for one thousand impressions. The price for printing the tint plate will be about $25 for one thousand impressions. The paper must be and is, actually, bank-note paper, only made of larger size, and its cost is from $30 to $50 per thousand sheets, depending on size and quality. I would be able to deliver bonds in forty to fifty days after having received the order. All prices given herein are as low as Northern prices."

Memminger had succeeded in obtaining quotes as early as March 1 for the coupon bonds from two different suppliers in the South. On that same date he wrote two letters of introduction to officials in the North. First he wrote the New York company Bainbridge & Bros. to get a quote on both the coupon bonds and registered bonds ("stock"), but these bonds were to be produced in New York City. Second, he wrote Gazaway Bugg Lamar, president of the Bank of the Republic in New York City, the first of what would become many letters. Lamar, a highly successful cotton grower from Savannah, Ga. who moved to New York City about 1845 and founded the Bank of the Republic with some associates in 1851, was a known Southern sympathizer and catered to a Southern clientele at his bank. Memminger first asked Lamar for help in securing New York investors for the Confederate States' $15 million loan, but later Lamar would become Memminger's agent in New York to place orders for financial instruments needed by the Confederate States.

There is a two-week gap in the official records before they resume on March 13. Yet collateral events clearly show the Confederate Treasury was extremely busy. According to Douglas Ball's bond book released in 1998, Doug wrote that Memminger did not wish to place the order for the coupon bonds in the North, as the political climate between the two countries was becoming increasingly tense with Abraham Lincoln's inauguration on March 4. Conversely, Memminger had concerns that John Douglas' anti-counterfeiting measures were not as sophisticated as those in the North.

With two quotes already in hand for the coupon bonds from New Orleans, it appears that Memminger decided to split the order. While we do not have copies of the contracts, it is likely that Douglas was awarded a contract for the $50 and $100 coupon bonds, the two lowest denominations which would be less susceptible to counterfeiting efforts, and another contract was awarded to the New Orleans' branch of the ABNC for the $500 and $1,000 bonds -- as Memminger still thought that ABNC would be producing them in New Orleans. (It is likewise possible that an agent for Memminger, most likely Samuel Smith, negotiated a single contract with Schmidt of the ABNC in New Orleans, who in turn subcontracted part of the job to Douglas. A similar situation unfolded with the first Treasury notes as will be seen later.)

Other authors, including Douglas Ball himself, have stated that Memminger awarded all four coupon bonds to ABNC in New Orleans in March 1861, and gave the $50 and $100 denominations to John Douglas only after U.S. marshals seized the plates for the coupon bonds at ABNC -- but in New York -- on April 25, 1861. Facts prove that this scenario is impossible. According to Raphael Thian's *Register of the Confederate Debt*, and confirmed in Ball's own bond book, the $50 and $100 coupon bonds produced by Douglas were both issued beginning on April 17, 1861. After allowing about a week for transit time, the printing of these bonds would have been completed no later than about April 10. It would be impossible for *any* engraver -- Douglas or ABNC -- to complete these two coupon bonds by April 10 unless the engraver was awarded the contract in March. Samuel Schmidt, manager of ABNC in New Orleans, said as much in his March 1 letter to Memminger: "I would be able to deliver bonds in forty to fifty days after having received the order."

Ball's bond book and Thian's *Register* are a bit at odds on the precise dates of the first issuance of the coupon bonds. Thian showed a block of dates when all four coupon bonds were first issued -- "April 17-30" -- although Thian indicated that far more of the $50 and $100 bonds produced by Douglas were issued during this date range (1,847 bonds) than the $500 and $1,000 bonds produced by Schmidt at the ABNC in New Orleans (only 594 bonds). This difference in production output is reasonable if indeed Douglas had a big head-start on Schmidt as I contend. Yet Ball's book shows none of Schmidt's $500 and $1,000 bonds was issued until May 1, while Ball shows both of Douglas' $50 and $100 bonds being issued starting on April 17. It is unclear why this discrepancy exists between the official record (Thian's *Register*) and Ball's reference work.

With the coupon bonds all ordered, Memminger next turned his attention to the registered bonds, or "stock." Again we have no copy of the contract in hand, but we have later proof that Memminger appointed his New York agent, G. B. Lamar, to contract this part of the loan with ABNC in New York. Memminger was under extreme time pressure; in about a week, he had placed contracts for the two lower denominations of coupon bonds with John Douglas in New Orleans, the two higher-denominated coupon bonds with ABNC in New Orleans (mistakenly thinking they would be produced in New Orleans) and three of the four registered bonds ("stock") with ABNC in New York through his agent G. B. Lamar (the order for the $50 registered bond would follow a few days later on March 23). By spreading the $15 million loan over three different printers, Memminger must have believed that he had done all he could to expedite the printing of all eight bonds.

On March 9, 1861, the Confederate Congress authorized its first issue of 3.65% interest-bearing Treasury notes for a nominal $1 million. The bill was remarkable for its lack of detail: the only requirement was that the denominations be "not less than fifty dollars for any such note." With James Denegre now overseeing two print contractors in New Orleans, and each presumably busy with the coupon bonds, Memminger again turned to G. B. Lamar to place the order for the Treasury notes with ABNC in New York. While no copy of the contract has yet been discovered, Lamar asked Memminger some follow-up questions that are a part of the official record, signifying Lamar indeed did receive the contract. Memminger replied on March 13, 1861…

> "Notes are to be at one year at rate of one cent per day for every hundred dollars. Put the calculation on back. None to be below fifty dollars."

… and again on March 16, 1861:

> "Letter of 12th received [*Author's note: Lamar's letter not found*]. The notes are, by law, to be at twelve months at one cent per hundred dollars per day; are receivable for all debts except the export duty on cotton; are not legal tender, and should not be made fundable. We wish to use them for twelve months. Have sent you copy of act."

Gazaway Bugg Lamar, New York agent for the Confederate States (courtesy Wendell Wolka).

Lamar wrote Memminger again on March 18, apparently providing his own quote for coupon bonds to be printed in New York and requesting that Memminger prioritize the various printing jobs already underway. Memminger quickly telegraphed on March 22 (reproduced below), advising Lamar that the coupon bonds had already been ordered in New Orleans and for Lamar to remove them from his contract. Lamar was told to give the highest priority to the Treasury notes, followed by the registered bonds ("stock"). When Lamar relayed these instructions to ABNC, the printing company must have been confused: Memminger had made it clear that the Treasury notes had highest priority, followed by the registered bonds, but Memminger had failed to mention the $500 and $1,000 coupon bonds that ABNC was also executing in New York that had been ordered in New Orleans.

> "Yours of 18th received. Thanks for your attention. The bonds are already ordered at New Orleans. Leave them out of your contract and press on the notes first, then the stock."

Memminger himself must have recognized that his rapid-fire instructions to Lamar were confusing at best and perhaps creating tension at ABNC at worst. The following day, March 23, Memminger sent Lamar the following letter, first thanking him for his help, then officially adding the $50 denomination of registered bonds or "stock" to Lamar's contract and finally reiterating the order of priority of the various jobs Lamar was overseeing. Memminger also presumed that the back of the Treasury notes had "a form for entering the daily interest." We know that such a form did not appear on the back of the Montgomery notes, necessitating all styles of hand-written endorsements which only add to their charm:

> "DEAR SIR: I am much indebted to you, in common with our other Southern friends, for your many attentions. Our plans have called for plates of stock for fifty dollar subscribers, and I would be obliged to you to include that denomination in your contract. The bonds are ordered in New Orleans for all the forms of coupon bonds. May I request you to hasten the Treasury notes and have them forwarded promptly? I presume the form adopted has on the back of the notes a form for entering the daily interest. That was the course taken with the United States issue of this kind bearing interest at a

cent per cent per annum. We only issue one million, and can only reissue once; so that to fund in our loan would be extinguishing one by the other."

C.G. Memminger's herculean efforts were finally paid off on April 2, 1861, when he received 607 four-subject sheets, each with impressions of all four of the Treasury notes -- the "magnificent Montgomerys" -- as well as a proof of the $1,000 registered bond or "stock." With his Montgomery notes in hand and work progressing smoothly on the registered bonds, only the coupon bonds were at issue. Despite being ordered well before the registered bonds or the Treasury notes, Memminger professed that the coupon bonds "are greatly behind time." Memminger was still unaware that ABNC in New York, upon Memminger's instructions, had placed the registered bonds in front of the two coupon bonds it was producing for its New Orleans' branch.

Upon receipt of the Montgomery notes, Memminger realized that the print run included too many of the large denominations and too few of the smaller $50 and $100 notes. Recognizing that demand would be stronger for the smaller denominations, Memminger sent Lamar a letter on April 2 as shown below, asking if it were feasible to print just part of the plate to obtain additional small bills:

> "SIR: Your letters of the 28th and 30th ultimo have been received, also 607 impressions of treasury notes of $50, $100, $500, and $1000, amounting to $1,001,550, also a proof certificate of stock for $1,000. The execution of the whole is quite satisfactory, and I beg you to accept my thanks for your promptness and dispatch....There will arise one difficulty about the Treasury notes. There are too many of the $1,000, and to (sic) few of the $50 and $100. Our calls will be for the smaller issues. Is there any way by which impressions could be taken of part of the plate?"

With the Confederacy's first Treasury notes just arriving in Montgomery, Memminger recognized that his Southern countrymen had never seen any Confederate currency and might be hesitant to accept it in routine commerce, as it was not legal tender. With only 607 notes of each denomination received, on April 6 Memminger instructed Treasurer E. C. Elmore to place a tiny number of the Montgomery notes with the assistant treasurers in Charleston, Savannah, Mobile and New Orleans to introduce the public to the new Confederate notes.

E. C. Elmore, Treasurer of the Confederate States.

Memminger then made a puzzling comment in this letter dated April 6 and reproduced below. Recognizing that much more currency would be needed to familiarize the public with the new Confederate notes, Memminger advised Elmore that after April 17, "a larger amount can be furnished."

> "SIR: I desire to place a small amount of Treasury notes with each of the assistant treasurers at Charleston, Savannah, Mobile, and New Orleans, with a view to their paying them out and introducing to the public notice. After the 17th instant a larger amount can be furnished them.
>
> You will therefore send as soon as possible, by express, to the assistant treasurer at Charleston and to the depositary at Savannah each five thousand dollars; to the assistant treasurer at New Orleans ten thousand dollars, and to the depositary at Mobile ten thousand dollars."

But what was this "larger amount?" Just four days earlier on April 2, Memminger had inquired of Lamar whether it was even feasible to re-print a part of the Montgomery plate. Memminger's letter to Lamar was not telegraphed, so it would have taken at least a day or two just to get the inquiry to Lamar in New York. Yet on April 6, Memminger was promising Elmore a definite delivery date for more Treasury notes: "after April 17." It seems physically impossible for Memminger to have only inquired about the possibility of re-printing a part of the Montgomery plate on April 2, yet receive an answer to his request, place an additional order and be given a delivery date "after April 17" in just four days.

We will soon see that this unlikely scenario did not occur. Today, 150 years after the fact, we know that Memminger discovered that indeed he could re-print a part of the Montgomery plate, and he ordered another 1,000 half-sheets to include more $50 and $100 Montgomerys. But, as will be seen, these notes were delivered to Montgomery on or before May 3.

So which Treasury notes was Memminger promising Elmore "after April 17?" One cannot discount the tantalizing possibility that Memminger, during the two-week gap in the official records between March 1 and March 13, 1861, had instructed Lamar to revise his contract to initiate *two* orders for Treasury notes to ensure that at least one order was delivered in a timely fashion. I suggest that the notes to be delivered "after April 17" are just as likely to be a new, heretofore undiscovered Treasury-note print run, as they are the 1,000 half-sheets that we know were delivered on or before May 3. The first order -- the Montgomerys -- got through. I surmise that an additional order, expected about two weeks later, was printed but confiscated along with the plates by U.S. marshals on April 25.

Chapter co-author Crutchfield Williams advances another theory about this "larger amount" of Treasury notes Memminger promised to have available "after April 17," based on Memminger's statement to Lamar in an April 11 letter: "I had intended to order another impression of $50 and $100 Treasury notes in place of the $1000, and to suppress most of these last." Crutch notes that Memminger obviously could not suppress the $1000 Montgomery notes that had already been printed, so he must have been referring to an additional print run of Montgomery notes not yet produced.

Crutch believes that the *original* contract for the first issue of Treasury notes called for a total print run of slightly more than $2 million in face value. The Act of March 9, 1861 authorized only $1 million, but Section 10 of the Act allowed for the issue or re-issue "of such treasury notes as may have been paid and redeemed" so "that the aggregate sum outstanding under the authority of this act shall at no time exceed one million of dollars." As each note was issued and redeemed, Memminger could then re-issue the same amount, one note at a time, as long as the amount outstanding never exceeded the authorized $1 million.

When Memminger indicated an immediate need for Treasury notes, Lamar requested a hurried printing from the ABNC. Since they were still very busy printing registered bonds ("stock") and engraving coupon bonds, they sub-contracted the tint plate and printing to the National Bank Note Company. Crutch hypothesizes that the 607 four-subject impressions received April 2 was a partial delivery that covered the initial face value of the authorization and relieved Memminger's immediate needs. The second shipment of 1,000 two-subject sheets of $50 and $100 notes shipped and received a short time later would allow Memminger to suppress roughly 25% of the $1,000 notes, and the final print run to be delivered "after April 17" would be the balance of the order approximating an additional $900,000 that would cover any future re-issues authorized under the Act over the next year.

Crutch's hypothesis is reasonable and indeed might be correct. I think that Memminger's comment about suppressing the $1,000 Montgomerys, though, was achieved simply by not issuing many $1,000 Montgomerys from those notes received on April 2. As late as May 27, 1861, Thian's *Register* shows only 69 $1,000 Montgomery notes had been issued, out of 607 available for release.

War clouds hung ominously on the horizon. In a letter dated April 11, 1861 to G. B. Lamar, Memminger offered three important observations. First, he was sending payment for Lamar's invoice that day. Since only the Treasury notes had been delivered, presumably payment was made only for the currency. Second, with war inaugurated, Lamar was asked to immediately send all plates and impressions of the Treasury notes and registered bonds ("stock") to Montgomery "lest we may be embarrassed by their seizure." Third and most importantly, Memminger advised that he "had intended to order another impression of $50 and $100 Treasury notes… if the matter could be securely done and forwarded… If that cannot be done, then please forward the whole immediately by express."

This final statement helps us understand what Memminger meant by his "after April 17" date to deliver more Treasury notes to Elmore. It conclusively establishes that Memminger did not order the 1,000 additional impressions of $50 and $100 Montgomery notes until this letter written on April 11 (letter reproduced below). His earlier letter to Elmore dated April 6 referencing a "larger amount" of Treasury notes being available "after April 17" suggests an entirely different print run of Treasury notes. The original Montgomery notes had been delivered on April 2, and the additional 1,000 half-sheets of $50 and $100 notes were not even ordered until April 11. Unless Memminger was clairvoyant, he could not have known on April 6 that he would be ordering more Montgomery notes on April 11 and promising their delivery "after April 17."

"DEAR SIR; The draft, for account sent by you, is remitted to-day. It seems from your letter and our own information that war is inaugurated. Under these circumstances would it not be well to send me immediately all the impressions and plates of the Treasury notes and stock certificates, lest we may be embarrassed by their seizure or detention? I had intended to order another impression of $50 and $100 Treasury notes in place of the $1000, and to suppress most of these last. If the matter could be securely done and forwarded, I would be glad to have it done immediately and the impressions forwarded. If that cannot be done, then please forward the whole immediately by express, and I will have the work done at New Orleans."

Registered Bond ("Stock") with serial no. 185, courtesy Crutchfield Williams.

Four days later, on April 15, Memminger wrote Lamar again that he had received the first part of his order for registered bonds, or "stock." As the letter below reveals, some books of all four denominations were received, except for the $50 bonds which were ordered after the first three denominations.

"SIR: I have this day received five books of blank certificates of transferable stock described as follows: --
One book of 250 certificates for $100 each, numbered from 1 to 250.

One book of 250 certificates for $100 each, numbered from 251 to 500.
One book of 250 certificates for $500 each, numbered from 1 to 250.
One book of 250 certificates for $1000 each, numbered from 251 to 500.
One book of 250 certificates for $1000 each, numbered from 501 to 750.
The book of certificates for $1000 each, numbered from 1 to 250 inclusive,
has not been received."

In similar letters dated April 16 and April 19, Memminger confirmed that additional books of the registered bonds had been received, including most of the $50s. However, while it is clear that 1,000 of each of the registered bonds were printed, all of the bonds may not have arrived in Montgomery. Perhaps some of these books of registered bonds were part of the material confiscated by U.S. marshals on April 25. It is also possible that some of the books for which the official records contain no confirmation indeed were received, but the records confirming their receipt have been lost or were never issued in the first place.

In two letters dated April 17 and April 19, we can conclusively establish that the National Bank Note Company ("NBNC") merely acted as a sub-contractor for the ABNC; no contracts were executed between the NBNC and Lamar or the Confederate Treasury. The first letter, dated April 17 to Memminger from James Denegre, president of the Citizens Bank of Louisiana in New Orleans, was a formal letter of introduction to Mr. Lloyd Glover, a trustee of the National Bank Note Company of New York. Memminger had already received the first shipment of Montgomery notes printed by the NBNC two weeks earlier. There would have been no need to formally introduce the NBNC to Memminger had the two previously established a business relationship -- unless, of course, Denegre himself was not aware that the NBNC had printed the Montgomery notes.

The second letter dated April 19 and reproduced below was an apology from Memminger to Lamar, explaining that payment to the ABNC for the Treasury notes printed by the NBNC had been made in error in gold when it should have been made by check. Clearly ABNC was the lead contractor, as the NBNC which printed the notes was not even mentioned in the letter. Memminger also confirmed that his order for the additional $100 and $50 Montgomery notes had been placed, although they had not yet arrived.

> "SIR: Yours of the 15th is received. Ere this reaches you my letters acknowledging receipt of various parcels of certificates will have been received by you. I am sorry to find that my untrained officials increase the difficulties of doing business. After I wrote to you my letter of the 11th [*shown earlier*] the treasurer concluded to send gold to the American Bank-Note Company instead of a check, and the money was sent by Adams Express, and I presume has been received, although we have as yet no acknowledgment. I hope soon to receive the remainder of the fifty and one-hundred-dollar Treasury notes."

The date of the above letter, April 19, 1861, coincided with Abraham Lincoln's Presidential Proclamation of Blockade. While the effects of the blockade were far-reaching, an immediate impact on engravers and printers in New York City was to make commerce unlawful between the U.S. and the states in insurrection. A violation of the act could be viewed as a treasonable offense. All work completed for the Confederate Treasury by ABNC and the NBNC before April 19 was perfectly legal, although it might not have passed the "smell test" administered by many Union loyalists of the day.

But one Union supporter -- a disgruntled engraver from New York City who had failed to win any of the Confederate printing jobs -- became enraged when he discovered that ABNC, and possibly the NBNC as well, continued to execute orders for the Confederates after April 19, despite the Presidential Proclamation making it unlawful to do so. Connecticut-born engraver Waterman Lilly Ormsby possessed immense talent, matched with a fiery temper. His actions in late April 1861 put a severe crimp on the Treasury for many months to come.

Ormsby was no ordinary engraver. He was the inventor of several processes used to make bank notes, and he co-founded the Continental Bank Note Co. in New York in 1863 at the height of the war. In April 1861, though, he was living in New York and owned the New York Note Company, a competitor to the American Bank Note Company and the National Bank Note Company.

In March 1861 when C. G. Memminger appointed G. B. Lamar to negotiate contracts for Confederate registered bonds ("stock") and Treasury notes in New York City, presumably Lamar included Ormsby as owner of the New York Note Company in his dialogue with officials at the ABNC and possibly the NBNC. When Ormsby was awarded none of the Confederate printing business, he must have been infuriated. He was already a hot head, as his biographer wrote that "He displays himself in his writings as a disgruntled eccentric, sensitive about his craftsmanship, and childish about his enmities. He considered himself discriminated against in business."

We do not know how Ormsby discovered that Lamar had placed an order for an extra 1,000 half-sheets of the $50 and $100 Montgomery notes with ABNC after Memminger ordered them on April 11. If an heretofore unknown series of notes was also in production in New York at the time, Ormsby might have discovered that fact as well. It seems reasonable to assume that Ormsby knew about the original orders Lamar placed on behalf of Memminger in March, as there would be few secrets in a tightly knit industry like bank note engraving.

When Ormsby heard that the Confederate Treasury still had unfinished work in New York City after the Presidential Proclamation on April 19, he retaliated from being shut out from any of the business by tipping off U.S. marshals that engravers in New York City were continuing to execute orders for the Confederates even after the Presidential Proclamation. (Ormsby was a colorful character. He is discussed in more detail on page 249.)

Douglas Ball has previously referenced the raid at ABNC and the NBNC on April 25, 1861 in numerous catalog descriptions he wrote of Montgomery notes while at NASCA and R.M. Smythe & Co. But it is not clear if Doug knew that there were actually at least two different raids in New York City after Lincoln's Proclamation on April 19, and the raids were not limited to just the ABNC and the NBNC.

It appears that Memminger heard of the first raid on either April 23 or April 24, 1861. In a telegram dated April 24 to Samuel Smith, principal of the company Samuel Smith & Co. and one of Memminger's two advisors in New Orleans (the other being J. D. Denegre, president of the Citizens Bank of Louisiana), Memminger mentioned a seizure of registers in New York that were ordered in New Orleans and inquired about the status of the coupon bonds also ordered in New Orleans (actual telegram shown on facing page):

> "Newspapers speak of a seizure of registers at New York, which were ordered at New Orleans. How is it with our bonds? We ordered them also in New Orleans. Ascertain if they are really there."

MONTGOMERY, ALA., *April 24, 1861.*

SAMUEL SMITH, Esq.,
     New Orleans.

Newspapers speak of a seizure of registers at New York, which were ordered at New Orleans. How is it with our bonds? We ordered them also in New Orleans. Ascertain if they are really there.

        C. G. MEMMINGER,
             Secretary of the Treasury.

Smith hurriedly telegraphed Memminger the same night that the coupon bonds from ABNC were also being printed in New York City, despite being ordered in New Orleans. Smith's April 24 telegram appears to be Memminger's first recollection that the $500 and $1,000 coupon bonds Memminger had ordered from ABNC in New Orleans were actually being executed in New York, despite being told that fact by Richard Jones back on March 1. Memminger quickly telegraphed Smith the following day that he was surprised to learn that the coupon bonds were being prepared in New York, and he instructed Smith to report which were seized and what Smith intended to do to get them replaced:

> "Surprised to learn by your telegram of last night that our bonds are at the North when they were ordered at New Orleans. Please say which are seized, and if any are safe. Delay is very injurious, and the best thing to be done now is to get others as soon as possible. Have you the forms? Let me know immediately what you propose to do."

Smith must have quickly responded that all the coupon bonds entrusted to the ABNC had been seized, because in a second telegram to Smith from Memminger on the 25th, Memminger ordered Smith to have replacement bonds prepared at once, using lithography if they could be delivered promptly:

> "Have the bonds prepared immediately. Lithograph preferred, if they can be had in time. You do not say whether you have the form of the bond. If you have not the form, let me know and I will send one. Will your subscribers take certificates of stock? We have them."

MONTGOMERY, ALA., *April 25, 1861.*

SAMUEL SMITH, Esq.,
     New Orleans.

Have the bonds prepared immediately. Lithograph preferred, if they can be had in time. You do not say whether you have the form of the bond. If you have not the form, let me know and I will send one. Will your subscribers take certificates of stock? We have them.

        C. G. MEMMINGER,
             Secretary of the Treasury.

Again Smith must have hurriedly telegraphed his contingency plans, for on April 26 Memminger telegraphed Smith his approval of Smith's plans to execute replacement bonds (telegram reproduced below). Presumably Smith immediately instructed Samuel Schmidt, manager of the New Orleans' branch of the ABNC, to prepare plates for the $500 and $1,000 coupon bonds. Luckily, the $50 and $100 coupon bonds had already been completed by John Douglas in New Orleans and were being issued beginning on April 17.

> 'Telegram received about bonds, and approved. Send them as soon as possible. Let me know how much is paid in on loan and where deposited, that the treasurer may be able to check on it."

Ironically, Samuel Smith's apparent telegram to Memminger dated April 25 advising Memminger that the coupon bonds at the ABNC in New York had been seized was false. Even Memminger's telegram dated April 24 mentioned a seizure of registers, not bonds. In reality, the bonds were confiscated the night of April 25, as we will soon see. Thus Smith's answer was incorrect literally only by hours.

It is unclear whether Waterman Ormsby provided the names of specific engravers he knew that continued to print Confederate financial instruments after Lincoln's April 19 Proclamation, or whether the U.S. authorities simply chose to canvass all engravers in New York City. Regardless, we know that the first raid occurred the night of April 21, 1861 at the establishment of Julius Bien. That seizure was reported in *The New York Times* on April 22 as shown at left.

A Check to Treason.—Marshall Murray yesterday seized a vessel just starting from this City for New Orleans with *one thousand barrels of powder* on board. The powder was taken to the Navy-yard, and will be removed this morning to the United States magazine on Ellis' Islnnd.

The Marshal also made a descent upon the lithographic establishment of Julius Brene, No. 188 Broadway, and seized the engraved plate of registry for the *privateering service* of Jeff. Davis' gang of rebels and pirates. The plate was taken into custody, as the proprietor of it will doubtless be if he makes his appearance.

Article from April 22, 1861 Issue of The New York Times.

The fact that U.S. authorities raided the place of business of Julius Bien before raiding either the American Bank Note Company or the National Bank Note Company clearly establishes that the Federal marshals were playing no favorites. Julius Bien (1826-1909) was a giant in the American engraving industry, best known as the creator of the "Bien Edition Prints of the Birds of America" by John James Audubon. These prints were produced in 1858 by John Woodhouse Audubon, son of John James Audubon himself. The younger Audubon recruited the Roe Lockwood Co. in New York to publish the prints and Julius Bien for the lithography. Bien used a novel technique -- chromolithography -- to reduce the costs of production. These images, properly termed "originals," carried the credit line "Chromolithy by J. Bien, New York, 1860."

A year later Bien prepared a "Lithographed Military Map of the U.S. in 1861" just two months after the bombardment of Ft. Sumter. The map was published in the *Atlas to Accompany the Official Records of the Union and Confederate Armies, 1861-65* and was issued by the Government Printing Office in Washington, D.C. in 1891.

Julius Bien must have suffered considerable embarrassment when he discovered that his business had been raided during the dead of night on April 21, 1861. He hastily prepared a letter to the Editor of *The New York Times*, which appeared in the April 23 edition and is reproduced at the top of the facing page. Bien advised that a single lithographic stone with an engraving for Custom House Registers of Confederate States' vessels had been seized. Bien explained that this work had been ordered on March 16, had been abandoned two weeks earlier, and the order for the paper canceled. He maintained that "not a single impression, or even a proof of the engraving, has been furnished."

The following day *The New York Times* editorialized that "we have entirely satisfactory information that no engravings of letters of marquee for the C.S.A. were ever undertaken at his establishment" and concluded that "we have reliable information that Mr. Bien is and has been a thorough Union man."

The seizure of Confederate Custom House registers at Julius Bien's business on April 21, 1861 was probably no more than a minor annoyance to Confederate officials, including Memminger himself. But Memminger recognized that this seizure was probably only the first of more to come. His worst fears were realized just four days later on April 25, 1861, when U.S. marshals raided the establishments of both the American Bank Note Company and the National Bank Note Company. Details of this seizure were first reported in the April 26, 1861 edition of the *New York Tribune*, reproduced earlier on page 119.

Article from April 23, 1861 Issue of The New York Times.

The official records of the Confederate Treasury are surprisingly silent on this hugely important event. The records do include mention of the Bien seizure on April 21, but nothing is mentioned until early May about the April 25 seizure of plates and impressions at the ABNC and the NBNC. It is possible that Memminger's line of communication with Gazaway Bugg Lamar, his agent and advisor in New York, had been completely cut off, as the next communication between the two men was in the form of a short letter delivered to Lamar by Memminger's personal messenger on May 4, 1861.

We know with certainty that G. B. Lamar was suspected of giving aid and comfort to the enemy. Apparently U.S. officials even considered arresting him for treason. In an extraordinary letter dated May 8, 1861 that was written in Savannah, Ga. and copied below, Lamar's son Charles A. L. Lamar wrote Memminger of his father's constant surveillance:

> "My father, Mr. G. B. Lamar now in New York, detained there by the illness of his wife, requests me to write you & ask that you will not address any more letters to him, or to his care, as they will not reach their destination & will tend to add to his embarrassment ~ He writes that he is threatened daily by Mobs ~ that attempts are made to indict him for treason &c (etc) & (an) that any letters from any of our officials may compromise him with the Mobs ~ That he's powerless now to do anything for anyone &'d (and) You will appreciate and understand his motives ~
>
> Very Respectfully, Your Obedient Servant C.A.L. Lamar"

With regular monitoring of his whereabouts and the April 25 seizure of notes and bonds he had ordered, Lamar must have felt that much of his work had been in vain. His personal melancholy reached a new low a few days later on May 1, 1861, when his second wife passed away. After her death, Lamar resolved to return to his beloved South as quickly as possible. In an attempt to elude his potential captors, he took a long and circuitous route back home before finally arriving in Savannah, Ga.

A correct understanding of exactly what was seized by U.S. officials on April 25 is critical to the possibility of discovering a previously unknown print run of Confederate Treasury notes. The April 26 article in the *Tribune* is very precise -- ten plates at the American Bank Note Company and two at the National Bank Note Company, "some of which were completed and others in progress." As Doug Ball pointed out to me years ago, though, there are some inconsistencies in the article itself.

For example, the headline speaks of the seizure of Treasury notes, but the article talks about the confiscation of plates. Yet the article explains that "printing the notes" was claimed to have stopped when the Presidential Proclamation was issued, yet the Federal authorities had proof that they were "engaged in printing the notes as late as last Sunday [April 21]."

So we cannot definitively state that both plates *and* notes were confiscated, although there can be no doubt that plates were seized.

SEIZURE OF PLATES AND TREASURY NOTES OF THE C. S. A.—United States Deputy-Marshals BOAST and HORTON, yesterday seized a large quantity of engraved plates of treasury notes and bonds of the Confederated States of America, some of which were completed, and others in process of manufacture, at the American Bank Note Company and the National Bank Note Company. The plates were of the denomination of $1,000, $500, $100 and $50. The officers of the Bank Note Company stated that they stopped printing the notes, and ceased work on the plates not yet completed, as soon as the President's proclamation was issued; but the United States authories have positive proof that they were engaged in striking off the notes as late as Sunday last.

Article from April 27, 1861 Issue of The New York Times.

I looked for a similar article in *The New York Times* for confirmation of exactly what was seized. In its April 27 edition (one day later than the *New York Tribune* article) as reproduced at left, the *Times* reported virtually the identical details, except it reported the seizure took place on the 26th (the *Tribune* stated the 25th), the *Times* referenced "a large quantity of engraved plates" (the *Tribune* provided precise counts) and the *Times* gave the rank of those conducting the raid as "Deputy Marshals" (the *Tribune* called them "Marshals"). Other than these minor differences, though, both articles are the same.

While the official records make no mention of the event, the additional 1,000 half-sheets of $50 and $100 Montgomery notes Memminger had ordered through Lamar back on April 11 finally arrived in Montgomery prior to May 4, 1861. These notes, bearing serial numbers 608-1607, were signed beginning May 4, 1861, according to Raphael Thian's *Register of the Confederate Debt*, so we can deduce with reasonable confidence that they arrived in Montgomery a day or two, and certainly no more than a week, earlier.

On May 4, 1861, we find the final letter from Memminger to Lamar. Memminger must have known that Lamar was viewed with suspicion by the U.S. authorities -- although he had not yet received the letter from Lamar's son -- and he would not wish to raise the level of distrust any higher. He consequently used a local resident of Montgomery, Mr. Joel White, to hand-deliver the following letter to Lamar:

> "Joel White, Esq.,
> Present.
> DEAR SIR: Herewith I send you an open letter to Mr. Lamar, which please read, and if convenient to you, attend to a request contained.
>
> Respectfully,
> C. G. MEMMINGER

> G.B. Lamar, Esq.
> DEAR SIR: This note will be handed to you by Mr. Joel White, of this city. I have requested him to bring home our Treasury-note plates, if it can be done with safety. We shall need other plates, but it is now necessary to have them made at home. Mr. White will inform you of matters here.
>
> Very truly yours,
> C.G. MEMMINGER"

The preceding letter is bewildering indeed. In it Memminger requested that his messenger, Mr. White, "bring home our Treasury-note plates, if it can be done with safety." By May 4, the date of this hand-delivered letter, surely Memminger was aware that the Montgomery note plates, as well as the bond plates, had been seized on April 25. The local newspaper, the *Montgomery Advertiser*, wrote an article on April 30 "in relation to our lithographic plates being seized in New York," according to a letter dated May 2 from Jefferson Buford, a prominent politician and attorney from Alabama, to L. P. Walker, Secretary of War.

So why did Memminger send his messenger to hand-deliver a letter to Lamar, putting Lamar at even more risk, if Memminger already knew the answer? By May 4 when this letter was dated, Memminger had already received the additional 1,000 half-sheets of $50 and $100 Montgomery notes, and they were being signed. Was the purpose of the letter to determine if plates for a *new* series of notes, not those plates for the Montgomery notes which Memminger knew had been confiscated, been seized as well? In less than two weeks on May 16, Congress would authorize the second issue of $20 million in demand notes. Clearly Memminger was already making plans for these future Treasury notes, and it is highly likely that the engraving process for these notes was already underway. Certainly it was essential that Memminger ascertain exactly what had been seized. Despite the risks, he had no choice but to send his own personal messenger.

Memminger's next letter dated May 7 gives more credence to the theory that a new print run of notes had been printed but seized in New York. Memminger sent this letter to Major George B. Clitherall in Mobile, Ala., along with the final 1,000th half-sheet of $50 and $100 Montgomery notes just received, bearing serial number 1607. In this letter reproduced below, Memminger ordered Major George Clitherall (not Alexander B. Clitherall, the Treasury's Register) to go to New Orleans, meet with Memminger's confidants Samuel Smith and J.D. Denegre, and "make a contract for the printing of five thousand impressions of Treasury notes, corresponding as nearly as possible to the sample herewith furnished you, to be numbered from 1,607, consecutively, letter B." Memminger desired these notes to be delivered "at the earliest possible day, to supply the deficiency caused by the seizure of the plates by the United States authorities."

> "Major Geo. B. Clitherall,
> Mobile, Ala.
>
> SIR: You will please proceed without delay to New Orleans, and, after consulting with Messrs. Samuel Smith and J.D. Denegre, make a contract for the printing of five thousand impressions of Treasury notes, corresponding as nearly as possible to the sample herewith furnished you, to be numbered from 1,607, consecutively, letter B. To this end, you are hereby authorized to execute, on the part of the Confederate States, a contract for the engraving and printing of the said notes, and to take a bond, with surety, from the contractor for the faithful execution of his contract.
>
> It is particularly desired by this Department that these notes be printed and delivered here at the earliest possible day, to supply the deficiency caused by the seizure of the plates by the United States authorities."

Here Memminger provides the clearest evidence yet that an entirely new print run of Treasury notes had been ordered in New York but seized in the raid of April 25. Assuming that Memminger was simply duplicating the order which had been seized, Memminger gives us good clues to know what to look for: 5,000 sheets, with each sheet containing a $50 and $100 denomination. He used the final half-sheet of the Montgomerys numbered 1607 as his model and specified that the new notes were to start with serial number 1608 and bear serial letter B (the Montgomerys bore serial letter A and ended with serial number 1606).

Just a week later, in a letter dated May 14, 1861 from New Orleans, Major Clitherall updated Memminger on his progress by providing him with the following report:

> "SIR: In compliance with your letter of instructions of 7th instant, I arrived at this place [*New Orleans*] on the night of the 10th instant. After diligent inquiry, I became satisfied that Mr. S. Schmidt, No. 12 Royal street, was the only one here by whom the Treasury notes could be satisfactorily executed, and I accordingly entered into a contract with him on yesterday, of which I informed you by telegraph. A memorandum of the contract, signed in duplicate, I have the honor herewith to transmit. I believe it is the best arrangement that could be made in the premises, and if it meets with your approval I shall be fully recompensed for any trouble or expense I may have been at, and make a cheerful tender of my services to the government at any time you may be pleased to command them. With high respect and esteem, I have the honor to be, sir, yours, &c.,
>
> G.B. CLITHERALL
>
> S. Schmidt is an old resident of this city, the managing partner here of the North (sic) American Bank Note Company, having branches in New York, Boston, and elsewhere. This work is to be executed here."

Clitherall advised Memminger that the replacement notes had been contracted with Samuel Schmidt, manager of the American Bank Note Company branch in New Orleans, and a copy of the contract was attached. Recognizing that Memminger had earlier ordered the $500 and $1,000 coupon bonds from Schmidt, only to discover much later that Schmidt had simply forwarded the initial order to New York for execution, where both the plates and any impressions made were seized on April 25, Clitherall was quick to point out that "this work is to be executed here." Today we call these notes, first dated August 27, 1861, the Criswell Type-5 "$100 First Richmond" and the Criswell Type-6 "$50 First Richmond" issues.

The saga of printing the first Treasury notes for the Confederate Treasury is now over. So where is the "smoking gun" to prove the existence of an entirely new print run of Treasury notes not yet found?

First let us review the suggestive statements found in the correspondence trail so far:

I. April 6 Letter from Memminger to Treasurer Elmore. Memminger promised "a larger amount [*of Treasury bills*] can be furnished" after April 17 to familiarize the public with the new currency, yet the original specimens -- a paltry 607 impressions of each denomination of the Montgomery notes -- had already been delivered from which Elmore disbursed a few notes, and the second printing of the extra 1,000 half-sheets may not have even been ordered until April 11. There is simply no way Memminger could have promised more Treasury notes to Elmore from either the first or second printing of the Montgomery notes if they had to be delivered around April 17. Memminger *had* to be planning to deliver additional notes to Elmore from a new print run of Treasury notes not yet found.

II. May 4 letter from Memminger, hand-delivered to G.B. Lamar in New York City. Memminger wrote this letter to Lamar -- recognizing the risk to Lamar -- to request that his messenger "bring home our Treasury note plates." Yet Memminger certainly knew that all Confederate plates, including Treasury notes, bonds and stock, had been confiscated on April 25. Why would he risk capture of his messenger and potential indictment of Lamar unless he urgently needed to know the whereabouts of the plates and impressions of a *new* print run of notes that were ordered after the Montgomerys were requisitioned? It is also possible that Memminger hoped that Lamar had secreted away the plates if not the impressions themselves of such a print run.

III. May 7 letter from Memminger to Major George B. Clitherall. Memminger wrote this letter ordering Clitherall to go to New Orleans and "make a contract for the printing of five thousand impressions of Treasury notes… to supply the deficiency caused by the seizure of the plates by the United States authorities." The specific number of impressions ordered -- 5,000 -- and the urgency demanded certainly suggests that the plates and a large number, perhaps as many as 5,000 impressions, of a new print run of Treasury notes had been confiscated by U.S. marshals in New York on April 25, 1861.

IV. April 26 Newspaper Article in the **New York Tribune.** The April 26 article entitled "Seizure of Treasury Notes of the Southern States" specified that twelve plates were confiscated: ten at the American Bank Note Company and two at the National Bank Note Company, "some of which were completed and others in progress."

The two plates at the National Bank Note Company were certainly the Montgomery Treasury notes. They could have been the tint plate and the face plate, or since the tint plate did not have incriminating text like "Confederate States of America" to identify that it was used to print notes for the Confederates, the two plates might have been the original steel four-subject master plate and a new two-subject copper plate prepared to accommodate the second print run of the $50 and $100 Montgomery notes. Under either scenario though, the two plates at the NBNC are accounted for.

The ten plates at the American Bank Note Company are more difficult to sort out, since the *Tribune* article did not itemize the number of finished plates and incomplete plates. We do know that ABNC had two bond orders in-house: one for four registered bonds ("stock"), with the face of each bond printed in black ink with a prominent red protector and the back containing the transfer certificate printed in red; and a second order for the two highest-denominated coupon bonds forwarded for execution from its New Orleans branch.

$500 Coupon Bond Proof from ABNC-- unique (Courtesy, R. M. Smythe & Co.).

The two coupon bonds were not finished at the time of the seizure and presumably were lost to history until the sale of the ABNC archives in the very early 1990s. In that sale, a single proof of the top half of the $500 coupon bond was discovered (but not the coupons, which apparently had not yet been engraved), as well as a hand-written mock-up of the $1,000 coupon bond with pasted-in vignettes (both of these unique bonds were purchased by Frederick R. Mayer). The top portion of the $500 coupon bond was printed in black ink with a vivid green protector; the fact that the coupons had not yet been engraved and thus were not part of the proof is

consistent with U.S. bonds produced at the same time, according to Gene Hessler.

The color protectors used on the bonds were different from the tint plates used on the Treasury notes. The Montgomery Treasury notes had a tint plate that applied green ink over much of the entire face of the note; while no text identifying it as "Confederate" appeared in the tint plate, its coverage was far more extensive than the use of color in the bonds.

The use of the color protectors on both kinds of bonds was limited to a numeral denoting the denomination of the bond. These color protectors used for the Confederate Treasury bonds were simply "FIFTY", "100", "500", and "1000". These color protectors could certainly be stock items for the engraver. They could just as easily be used on bonds for railroads, steamship companies or foreign governments like the Confederate States of America. We know the various New York engravers re-used the same vignettes, counters, numbers and generic text on different issues; it makes sense that the bonds' color protectors were not created specifically for the Confederate States but rather were re-uses of stock material on hand.

Why is it so important whether these tint plates were generic to the printing industry or specific to a particular customer? The answer lies in the instructions given to the U.S. marshals in New York. Presumably they were ordered to seize "all plates pertaining to the Confederate States of America" or something similar. But when they arrived at ABNC, the face plates for the Confederate work in process might have been in a different location than the protector plates that were constantly used and re-used, since tints were applied the day before the design was added. There would be no reason to seize the generic protector plates.

Whether my hypothesis about the protector plates is right or wrong is easy to prove. We will first assume that the U.S. marshals seized all plates -- face plates and protector plates -- when they arrived at ABNC. We know that the four registered bonds ("stock") were finished and had already been delivered to Montgomery. Assuming the marshals seized the four face plates, the four protector plates and a single plate used to print all four backs, these four registered bonds alone would account for nine of the ten total plates seized. With the sale of the ABNC archives in the 1990s, we also know that the top half of a $500 coupon bond was finished, although the coupon portion was probably incomplete. The top half of this bond, printed in black with a green protector, would have also required two plates. So we have already accounted for at least eleven plates, yet only ten plates were seized.

Further, the *Tribune* article states that some unfinished plates were also seized. The $500 coupon bond was almost certainly in progress, as Gene Hessler believes only one face plate would have been needed for the entire $500 bond -- the top half had already been finished and a proof created, but the coupon portion of the same plate was incomplete -- and it is possible that work on the $1,000 coupon bond had also been started (a hand-written mock-up was found in the ABNC archives).

So, assuming the U. S. marshals seized both face plates and protector plates, including finished plates and unfinished plates, we have just accounted for 11 or 12 plates, yet only ten plates -- finished and unfinished -- were seized. Bottom line, if the U. S. marshals seized all of the plates, both face and protector (tint), they would have seized about a dozen, but they confiscated only ten. Thus the marshals could not have seized all the plates. They must have taken only the face plates, leaving the generic protector plates behind.

If we now assume the U.S. marshals confiscated only the face plates -- those with incriminating text like "Confederate States of America" -- we generate a much lower count. The four registered bonds would require five plates -- four face plates and one back plate. The partially finished $500 coupon bond would require only one face plate, assuming Gene is correct that only one plate was required for both parts of the bond. If we assume that the $1,000 coupon bond had been started but not yet finished, then we have accounted for another unfinished plate. It is also possible that the face plate for the second issue of Treasury notes (those authorized May 16) was underway. So we now count a total of seven plates required to finish the four registered bonds and the two coupon bonds at the ABNC – eight if we add a plate for the second issue.

But the U.S. marshals seized ten plates. So we have two or three plates unaccounted for.

Plenty to engrave and print a formerly unknown print run of Confederate Treasury notes.

My hypothesis -- that U.S. marshals seized the finished face plates and a single back plate of four registered bonds ("stock"), at least one unfinished plate for each of the $500 and $1000 coupon bonds, and two or three finished plates of a heretofore unknown print run of Treasury notes -- has been reviewed by George H. LaBarre, owner of LaBarre Galleries with 3,300 Confederate bonds in inventory, Wendell A. Wolka, antebellum American numismatic researcher, Gene Hessler, noted authority on both currency and bonds, and perhaps most importantly, Gordon O'Malley, print manager of the American Bank Note Company division of ABnote North America, now located in Columbia, Tenn. All agree that this scenario most reasonably represents how ten captured printing plates from the ABNC on April 25, 1861 best aligns with what we know was printed by the ABNC for the Confederate States during March and April, 1861.

V. 1893 Biography of C. G. Memminger by Henry D. Capers. Capers served as Memminger's private secretary and had knowledge of, and contributed to, virtually all of Memminger's decisions during his years as the Secretary of the Treasury. After Memminger died in 1888, five years later in 1893 Capers authored a biography entitled *The Life and Times of C.G. Memminger.* To this day this book serves as a vital reference work to the daily routine at the Confederate Treasury Department. Indeed it was Capers who Memminger appointed to oversee the burning of the fabled $10 Manouvrier, never issued because too many had been stolen while en route from New Orleans to Richmond, Va.

Henry D. Capers, who authored Memminger's biography.

While some critics have ventured that Capers was too loyal to Memminger and overlooked some of Memminger's shortcomings and mistakes, I am unaware of anyone who has questioned Capers' personal integrity or veracity, nor his knowledge of the early days of the Confederate Treasury, and in particular the events that transpired in New York City on April 25, 1861.

Capers discussed the seizure in New York City in his biography of Memminger in two places in Chapter 7. First, on page 317, Capers penned:

> "Acting as our agent, Mr. G.B. Lamar entered into a contract with the American Bank-Note Company for engraving and printing the bonds and treasury notes authorized by act of Congress. The work was handsomely executed on the best of bank-note and bond paper, but, with all the precaution taken by Mr. Lamar, the entire issue fell into the hands of the vigilant servants of the Federal government and was seized as being contraband of war."

Lest some cynic argue that Capers' comment on the previous page was ambiguous as to whether both bonds *and* Treasury notes were seized, Capers cleared up any confusion with a clear and concise statement on page 336 of Chapter 7:

> "The loss of the treasury notes, engraved and printed through the kindness of Mr. G.B. Lamar, by the American Bank-Note Company of New York, necessitated that we should become our own printers."

Surely the statement above is unmistakable and convincing proof that a heretofore unknown print run of Confederate Treasury notes was printed by the ABNC in New York City in April 1861, with both the plates and impressions seized by U. S. authorities on April 25, 1861. Yet some pundits with whom I have already shared my conjecture have already begun to bark that by 1893 too much time had elapsed for Capers to remember such ancient details, or that he was not sufficiently knowledgeable to know the differences between Treasury notes, coupon bonds or registered bonds ("stock").

To state that the private secretary to the Confederate Secretary of the Treasury did not know the difference between Treasury notes and bonds appears preposterous to me and seems a personal affront to a fine gentleman about whom nothing but praise has ever been written. Nevertheless, without more proof, I was forced to be content with my own beliefs about what really happened in New York City on April 25, 1861.

In recent months though, after most of this book had been completed, Crutchfield Williams came across a startling, hand-written letter from Lamar to Memminger -- a letter which will make even the most hard-core skeptic pause for thought.

VI. June 10, 1861 Hand-written Letter from G .B. Lamar to C. G. Memminger. In a remarkable earlier letter dated May 8, 1861, written in Savannah, Ga. by Lamar's son Charles and addressed to Memminger, the younger Lamar asked that Memminger "not address any more letters to [his father]," as "he is threatened daily by mobs" and "that attempts are made to indict him for treason." Memminger respected his wishes. There are no more letters from Memminger to Lamar addressed to New York City in the official records after May 4.

After Lamar's wife died on May 1, 1861, however, Lamar resolved to return to his native Savannah, Ga. as quickly as possible, taking an out-of-the-way route to avoid possible capture. Presumably by the end of May 1861, Lamar had returned, and had already resumed a leading role in the Confederate cause.

On June 10, 1861, Lamar wrote his old friend C. G. Memminger from the safety and security of his own home in Savannah. The hand-written letter had gone unnoticed for years, as it was nothing more than a letter of recommendation asking that Memminger consider a friend of Lamar's to fill a vacant position within the Confederate Government.

But the bombshell is in a post script penned to the bottom of the second page of the letter. The nineteenth-century handwriting is difficult to decipher, so I enlisted the services of Alexia Jones Helsley, archivist for the State of South Carolina for over 25 years and an expert in interpreting eighteenth and nineteenth century handwriting. The actual post script is reproduced at the top of the facing page, with Ms Helsley's translation immediately following:

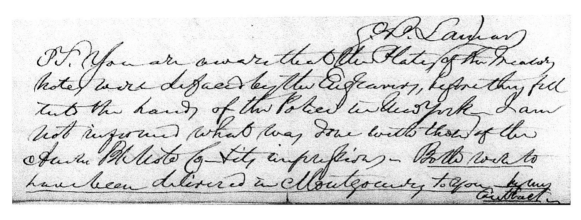

" PS. You are aware that the Plates of the Treasury Notes were defaced by
the Engravers, before they fell into the hands of the Police in New York. I
am not informed what was done with those of the Amer. Bk. Note Co. - &
its impressions. <u>Both were to have been delivered in Montgomery to you by
my Contract</u>. "

This post script was written only six weeks after the seizure in New York on April 25, 1861.
It was written by the individual who served as Memminger's personal agent in New York
and who actually placed the contracts for Treasury notes and bonds on behalf of Memminger. No one better knew the precise details of what the U.S. marshals seized.

Lamar's post script appears clear and unambiguous. He told Memminger he was talking
about "Plates of the Treasury Notes" -- not coupon bonds, not registered bonds. He professed ignorance of what happened with the plates of the Treasury notes at the "Amer. Bk.
Note Co." -- not at the National Bank Note Company. He also was unaware of the disposition of the "impressions" of the Treasury notes printed at the American Bank Note Company -- *confirming that sheets of Treasury notes were actually printed by ABNC.*

Lamar's statements above are compelling evidence that a print run of Treasury notes -- not
known to Confederate collectors today -- was in the process of being printed by the American Bank Note Company on or before April 20, 1861. The impressions and plates were
seized by U. S. marshals on April 25. Based on the replacement order Memminger made
with Major George Clitherall on May 7, presumably there were a total of about 5,000 sheets
being printed at the time of the confiscation, with each sheet containing a $50 and $100 note.

It is reassuring to note that Lamar's first-person account written only 46 days after the actual
seizure coincides exactly with Henry Capers' account 32 years later in his biography of C.
G. Memminger. Apparently this distinguished Southern gentleman suffered neither
memory loss nor ignorance of the difference between Treasury notes and bonds, as his
detractors have charged. His 1893 account aligns precisely with G. B. Lamar's comments
immediately after the incident took place.

I think I have proved my case. The only question remaining is how shall we describe this
new, previously unknown print run of Confederate Treasury notes? We know these notes
were printed after the Montgomery notes, which were all safely delivered despite a close
call for the second printing of the extra $50s and $100s. Conversely, they were printed well
before the so-called "First Richmond" issues -- Criswell Types-5 and 6 -- were even ordered.
I think I shall call them simply the "Really First 'First Richmond'" issues -- and suspend further discussion of this new print run until Volume 2, which will begin with the Criswell
Types-5 and 6.

Chapter 4:

Methodology for the Statistical Analysis of the Montgomery Notes

By Steven A. Feller, Ph.D., Professor of Physics, Coe College, Cedar Rapids, Iowa

This chapter explains how the prices realized for Confederate Montgomery notes at public auction were analyzed to determine each Montgomery note's rate of return and the time required for it to double in value. I wrote the discussion for the layman reader who has little knowledge of advanced mathematics, and I have made a great effort to lay out the story in a non-intimidating way. While elements of arithmetic, algebra and graphing are part of this analysis, the reward for the reader who studies the entire chapter will be an understanding of the analytical approach used in the book.

For each of the four Montgomery notes (Criswell Types -1 through 4), Wayne Hilton provided me with auction dates spanning the years from 1865 to 2010, the note's grade or condition as found in the auction catalog description, the note's serial number if shown and the price realized, including any sales commission. My first step was to plot the raw pricing data against time for each Montgomery note. For example, the plot for the Criswell Type-1, the $1,000 Montgomery, is shown below. To refresh the reader's memory from high school math, the horizontal, or X-scale, shows the "Date" from 1860 to 2020, and the vertical, or Y-scale, shows the "Auction Price" from 0 to $70,000:

Figure 1: Raw auction prices in all grades for Confederate Type-1 $1,000 Montgomery.

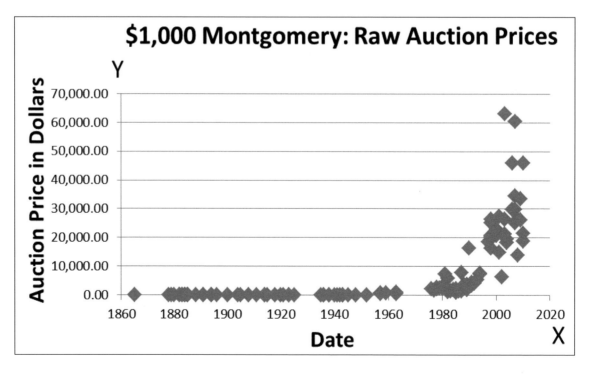

A few observations are immediately evident:

1. There has been a tremendous range in prices realized over the past 150 years – from nearly nothing to over $60,000 for a single note – with the most rapid rise taking place since about 1950.

2. The size limitations of the chart make it very difficult to see individual prices realized, particularly from 1865 until about 1950 when the prices realized seem to hover around zero. Since each increment in the vertical scale of the chart – which is less than an inch – represents $10,000, it is virtually impossible to visualize a low price realized, like $45 for example.

3. It is easy to see that prices increase over time. However, the data points do not line up in a smooth curve, as they would if the data were perfectly correlated. Mathematicians refer to the deviation from the curve as "scatter." This chart shows much scatter, which results from differences in grade, overall economic conditions at the time of the auction, or even something as simple as which collectors happened to show up to bid.

4. From a mathematician's perspective, the graph looks like a depiction of population growth or stock growth. This sort of behavior is known as exponential growth.

Several of the issues leading to "scatter" can be reduced, if not entirely eliminated. Figure 1 does not account for differences in grade, despite common knowledge that higher grades command higher prices. Fortunately we can account for differences in grade and correct for the variations. My basic goal was to transform prices for notes not in "Uncirculated" grade to prices that represent the "Uncirculated" grade by multiplying each note's actual price realized by a constant, but this constant differs depending on the actual grade of the note being corrected. For example, if I were correcting a note whose actual grade was only "Very Good," I would multiply by a relatively high constant to raise it four grades to a theoretical grade of "Uncirculated." Conversely, if the note's actual grade were already "Extremely Fine," I would multiply by a lower constant to raise it only one grade to a theoretical "Uncirculated" grade.

To determine what these constants should be, I used current market values for various grades as found in two different publications: nine editions of Arlie Slabaugh's *Confederate States Paper Money* published from 1958 to 2000, and the five editions of Grover Criswell's *Confederate and Southern State Currency* published from 1957 to 1996. As Wayne noted earlier in the book, both of these publications have long-running multiple editions that have become the standard in establishing current market values for Confederate currency.

While I analyzed current market values for all editions of both Slabaugh's and Criswell's publications, I chose not to show all this voluminous data in this book. Nevertheless, I found it revealing to compare current market values found in the first editions of each publication released in the mid 1950s to the current market values found in the final editions released about 40 years later. For example, the data for the $1,000 Montgomery note found in Slabaugh's first edition in 1958 and his final edition in 2000 look like this:

Edition	Grade					
	Good	**Very Good**	**Fine**	**Very Fine**	**Extremely Fine**	**Uncirculated**
1958	$85	-	-	-	-	$400
2000	$5,000	$10,000	$14,500	$19,000	$25,000	-

Similar data for Criswell look like this:

	Good	**Very Good**	**Fine**	**Very Fine**	**Extremely Fine**	**Uncirculated**
1957	-	-	$300	-	-	$750
1996	-	$10,000	-	-	-	$35,000

I combined Criswell's and Slabaugh's current market prices over time and averaged them to create a constant that I could use to multiply the price realized by a Montgomery note in less than "Uncirculated" grade and thereby generate a theoretical price realized for the note as if it actually graded "Uncirculated." My analysis yielded the following multiplicative constants:

To Represent the Price Realized for an "Uncirculated" Montgomery Note When the Actual Note Graded…	…Then Multiply the Price Realized of the Actual Note By:
Good	4.62
Very Good	2.83
Fine	2.01
Very Fine	1.76
Extremely Fine	1.37

As an example, a Montgomery note that graded "Fine" and realized a price of $8,700 at auction would be corrected to a theoretical "Uncirculated" grade simply by multiplying its actual price realized by the constant for a "Fine" note of 2.01 as follows:

Corrected Price Realized = $8,700 x 2.01 = $17,487.

After correcting the prices realized for the Montgomery notes to account for differences in their grades, the "scatter" observed in Figure 1 was greatly reduced. For example, the plot for the $1,000 Montgomery note, after correcting for differences in grade, is shown in Figure 2 below.

Figure 2: Auction prices corrected for grade using "Uncirculated" as the reference for Confederate Type-1 $1,000 Montgomery.

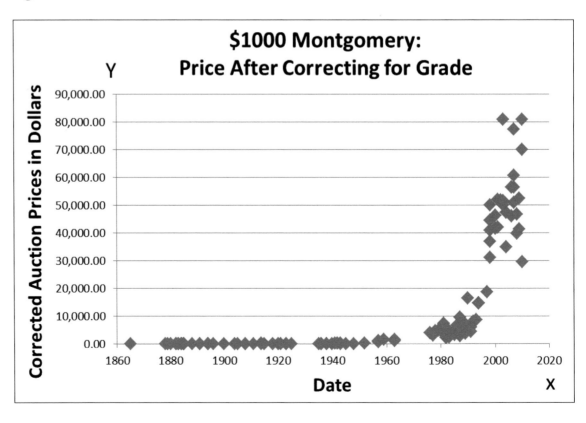

But Figure 2 still does not allow us to visualize prices realized earlier than about 1950. Thus a reasonable next step is to plot the results in a way that allows all prices to be clearly read – even those before 1950. To accomplish this objective, I converted the vertical scale, or "Y-Value", from raw prices realized to the natural logarithm (or "log") of those prices realized. Without going into a major treatise on logarithmic numbers, suffice it to say that they make it easier to graph widely varying numbers on a single chart no taller than the height of a page in this book.

The natural log of a number x is written ln(x). The natural log of a number is the exponent, or "power," to which a special number known as "e" (where "e" is defined by mathematicians to be approximately 2.71828) must be raised to reach any value desired. Most calculators will determine the natural log of any number in a matter of seconds. For example, the ln (100) is about 4.6051702. This numerical expression means that $(2.71828)^{4.6051702} = 100$.

In like fashion we can find the natural log of any number except zero or negative numbers. Zero cannot be used since it is impossible to raise e to any power and end up at zero. Similarly, no negative number will result by raising e to any power. However, these exceptions are not an issue for us, since no Montgomery note has ever sold at public auction for a price of zero or less!

The next graph, like Figure 2, shows the $1,000 Montgomery note corrected for differences in grade. However, unlike Figure 2, Figure 3 (page 144) uses as its vertical or "Y-Value" the natural log of the corrected auction price realized, rather than the actual corrected auction price itself. Our use of the natural log compresses the vertical axis in a special way so that all the prices realized are easily seen. Remarkably, two straight lines emerge. In effect we have compressed the vertical scale from a range of 0.00 to $90,000.00 as shown in Figure 2 to a range of 0.00 to only 12.00 as seen in Figure 3! (To save space I have plotted only the $1,000 Montgomery note. The same relationship exists for the other three Montgomery notes.)

Here is a translation of the vertical scale found in Figure 3 on the following page:

Natural Log of Price Realized	Corrected Price Realized	Natural Log of Price Realized	Corrected Price Realized
0.00	$1.00	7.00	$1,096.63
1.00	$2.72	8.00	$2,980.96
2.00	$7.39	9.00	$8,103.08
3.00	$20.09	10.00	$22,026.47
4.00	$54.60	11.00	$59,874.14
5.00	$148.41	12.00	$162,754.79
6.00	$403.43		

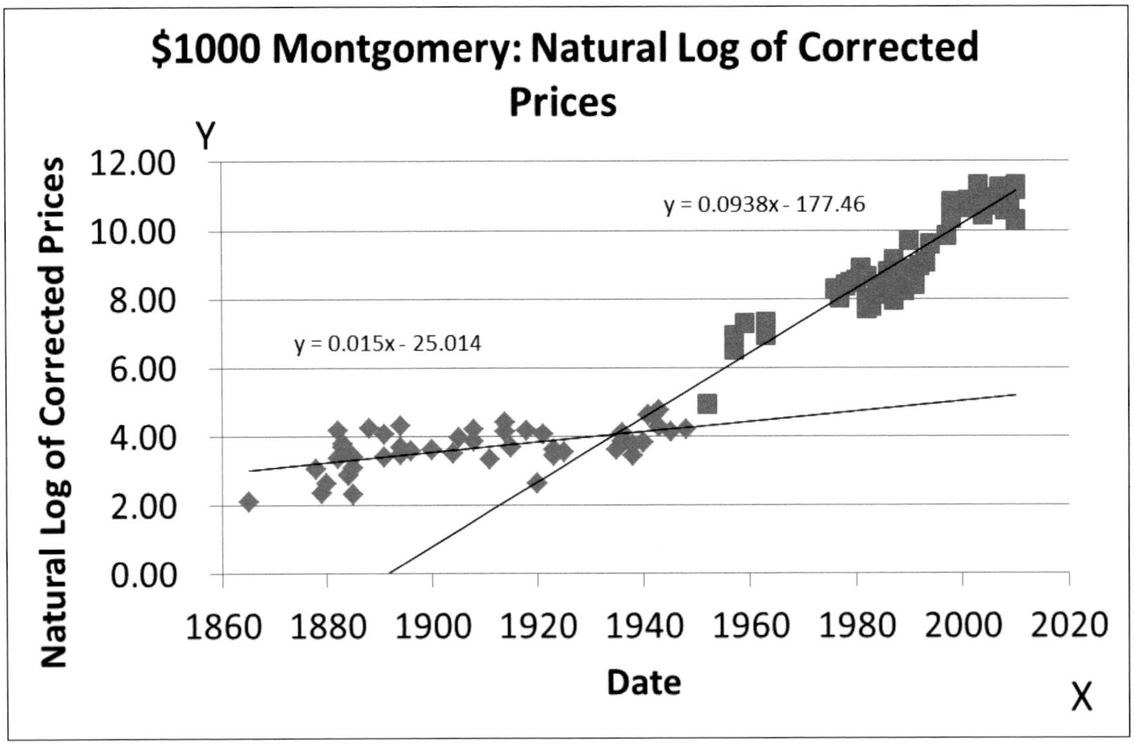

Figure 3: Natural log of corrected auction prices for Confederate Type-1 $1,000 Montgomery.

The two straight lines shown in Figure 3 above represent two regions of differing growth rates: the line through the blue dots shows very slow growth from 1865 to 1950, while the line through the red dots shows growth over six times faster from 1950 to 2010. Said another way, Confederate Montgomery notes took off in price after 1950.

To get the average annual rates of appreciation in each of the two time periods shown above, we use the slopes of the two straight lines. The slope is a measure of how steeply, or rapidly, the prices realized change over time:

1865-1950: slope = 0.0150 (yr^{-1})

1950-2010: slope = 0.0938 (yr^{-1})

The math is about to become more complicated as I show step by step how to come up with annual rates of return and the time required to double in price. The reader may skip these steps and go straight to the solutions shown later if not interested in all the mathematical rigor involved.

The slope in each region is related to price and time by the equation of each straight line:

$\ln(P) = at + \ln(Po)$

where "P" is the price realized at any time, "t"; "a" is the slope of the straight line and "Po" is the initial price when time is zero.

This can be converted directly to a formula for P given t:

$P = Poe^{at}$

Thus if we use two years separated by a single year, t and (t + 1) years, we get:

$P(t) = Poe^{at}$ for the first year and $P(t+1) = Poe^{a(t+1)}$ for the second year.

For ease we choose Po to be $1 at t = 0

Then P at 0 years = P(0) =$1 and

P one year later = P(1) = e^a.

The annual increase will be the difference in these two values: e^a-1.

Thus the annual rate of return is e^a-1 in fractional form and 100(e^a-1) written as a percent.

To conclude the discussion about the annual rate of return, we illustrate the two regions shown in Figure 3 for the $1,000 Montgomery note:

Time Period	Slope, a	Annual Rate of Return (Annual Percent Increase)
1865-1950	*0.0150 (yr^{-1})*	*100(e^a-1) = 1.5%*
1950-2010	*0.0938 (yr^{-1})*	*100(e^a-1) = 9.8%*

Now we turn our attention to the time required to double in price. The **Rule of 72** is often used as an approximate time for prices to double while undergoing exponential growth. The Rule of 72 states that the time required for prices to double, t', is

t' = 72/(annual rate of return as a percent) .

However, as may be a surprise to many readers, the Rule of 72 is only an approximation. Let us calculate the *actual* time for prices to double. Again, we start with:

$P = Poe^{at}$

and now we assign P = 2Po to double the initial price, Po. We then solve for doubling time t' using:

$2Po = P = Poe^{at'}$.

To simplify we divide out the common Po and we have

$2 = e^{at'}$.

Taking the natural log of this equation produces

ln2 = at'

Thus the exact time required for prices to double in value is: t' = ln2/a.

Now we can compare the two methods for calculating the time required for prices to double:

Time Period	Slope, a	Annual Rate of Return (Annual Percent Increase)	Years Needed to Double In Value		% Diff
			Exact	Rule of 72	
1865-1950	*0.0150 (yr^{-1})*	*100(e^a-1) = 1.5%*	*46.2*	*48.0*	*3.9%*
1950-2010	*0.0938 (yr^{-1})*	*100(e^a-1) = 9.8%*	*7.4*	*7.3*	*1.4%*

We see that the actual time required for prices to double in value is somewhat different than results achieved using the Rule of 72; nevertheless, the Rule of 72 is a reasonable approximation.

In all doubling times reported in this book, we used the *exact* doubling times as defined by the equation, t' = ln2/a.

Once I had completed the analysis of prices realized for Confederate Montgomery notes,

Wayne asked that I perform the identical analysis for other asset classes to determine which one enjoyed the highest annual rate of return from 1865 to 2010. Wayne and I both realized that while calculating a precise rate of return for Confederate Montgomery notes is an impressive achievement, it would be even more remarkable if compared to the rate of return of other assets that are popular alternatives for investment. After much thought and discussion with numerous financial advisors, we chose to compare the rate of return of Confederate Montgomery notes to: common stocks like those comprising the S&P 500 Composite Index, precious metals like silver and energy sources like crude oil.

Wayne had great difficulty finding price data for the three alternative investments to Confederate Montgomery notes. He wishes to give immense credit for finding data for the years from 1865 to 1970 to the U.S. Department of Commerce, Bureau of the Census, *Historical Statistics of the United States, Colonial Times to 1970, Bicentennial Edition, Part 1*, published in Washington, D.C. in 1975. Data for years since 1970 were found as follows:

Silver prices, for New York delivery in U.S. dollars per fine ounce (where a fine ounce is a troy ounce of 99.5% purity), for years 1971 through 2009 were found in four annual issues of the *Statistical Abstract of the United States*; namely, the 101st Edition published in 1980, the 110th Edition published in 1990, the 117th Edition published in 1997 and the 129th Edition published in 2010. Wayne gives special thanks to Ian Russell O'Brien, Branch Chief, Statistical Compendia Branch, Bureau of the Census, for providing this updated information. Pricing data for 2010 is published by and courtesy of *Platts Metals Week*.

Domestic crude petroleum prices are measured at the wellhead in U.S. dollars per 42-gallon barrel and include Alaska and Hawaii starting in 1960. Prices for years 1971 through 2009 were found in the same abstracts as noted above for silver. Pricing data for 2010 is preliminary and is provided courtesy of David Gatton, Survey Statistician, U.S. Energy Information Administration.

S&P 500 Composite Index data for years 1971 through 2010 is provided online by Global Financial Data, Inc., Los Angeles, Calif. (*www.globalfinancialdata.com*) and is used with their permission. Wayne gives special thanks to Bryan Taylor, Ph.D., Global Financial Data, Inc. for reviewing his methodology to ensure that the S&P 500 Composite Index data he charted from 1871 through 2010 is a fair reflection of movement within the S&P 500 over an extended time period despite minor changes in the way S&P data has been calculated and reported.[1]

After Wayne obtained the historical price data from the U.S. Department of Commerce for the three investment alternatives to Confederate Montgomery notes, I plotted all three comparative assets on the same logarithmic graph that shows results of the Confederate Montgomery notes. For example, the graph of the S&P 500 Composite Index is shown in Figure 4 on the facing page and is not dissimilar to the graph of the $1,000 Montgomery note shown in Figure 3, with the line through the blue dots in Figure 4 showing slow growth and the line through the red dots showing much faster growth.

I must admit that I was astonished at the final results of our calculations. The final graph for

---

[1] Prior to January 1918, the S&P Composite Index has been converted to the 1941-43 base from the Cowles Commission stock price indices, which are an extension of the S&P indices. The same method of construction was used for both, and, as far as possible the same companies. The formula used for this index is generally defined as a "base-weighted aggregative" expressed in relatives with the average value for the base period (1941-43) equal to 10. From January 1918 through 1970, these indices are based on monthly averages of the S&P stock price indices. From 1971 through 2010, these indices are based on the December 31 close of the S&P stock price indices.

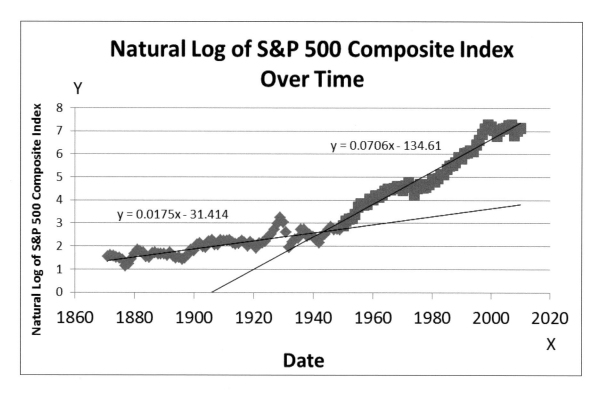

Figure 4:
Natural log
of the S&P 500
Composite Index
over an extended
time frame.

the $1,000 Montgomery, along with plots of the S&P 500 Composite Index, silver and crude oil, is shown on page 177. Similar graphs for the $500, $100 and $50 Montgomery notes — all analyzed using the exact same methodology as the $1,000 Montgomery employed as an example in this chapter — are shown on pages 207, 245 and 283, respectively.

Since this chapter is about the methodology I used in determining a rate of return for Confederate Montgomery notes, I will not address the actual findings here but rather allow Wayne to announce them in the specific chapter for each Montgomery note. I will proclaim, though, that after performing this comprehensive analysis of rates of return for Confederate Montgomery notes and three alternative investments, and being convinced of the findings' validity, I went out and purchased a Criswell Type-4 $50 Montgomery note at the Heritage Auction Galleries sale in Boston, Mass. in August 2010. I put my money where my mouth – and my calculator – are!

Steven A. Feller, Ph.D.

Chapter 5: Summary of Findings

The Confederate $1,000 Montgomery Note:
Its Survival Census and Historical Rate-of-Return

The majestic and stately Confederate $1,000 Montgomery note pictured above (classified as Criswell Type-1, variety 1) is the highest denomination issued by the Confederate Treasury, and indeed the *only* $1,000 denomination released. With only 607 specimens issued, it is tied with the $500 Montgomery as the least emitted note in the entire Confederate series. It is adorned by two native sons of my beloved South Carolina: U.S. Vice President John C. Calhoun on the left and U.S. President Andrew Jackson on the right.

While finding Calhoun, an ardent supporter of the preeminence of states' rights over those of the federal government, on a Confederate note is logical, I find it amusing that Calhoun was paired with Jackson, born in 1767 in South Carolina, the 7th U.S. President, a fervent anti-secessionist and Calhoun's rival. Indeed it was Andrew Jackson, at a dinner on April 13, 1830 attended by both Calhoun and S.C. Senator Robert Hayne, who bellowed, "Our Federal Union: It must be preserved!" in response to a toast from Hayne who proclaimed, "To the Union of the States, and the Sovereignty of the States!"

The Confederate Congress authorized the issuance of $1 million of 3.65% interest-bearing notes on March 9, 1861. As the South had no banknote engravers with state-of-the-art techniques, it made sense to place this order in New York City, the center of banknote activity at that time. Accordingly, Confederate Treasury Secretary Christopher Memminger enlisted the help of Gazaway Bugg Lamar, president of the Bank of the Republic in New York and a Confederate sympathizer, to place and expedite an order for Confederate Treasury Notes.

The Confederate Congress did not specify the denominations to be used on its first Treasury notes; it only required that the denominations be "not less than fifty dollars for any such note." Nothing is found in the written records of the Confederate Treasury to indicate who determined the four denominations to be $1,000, $500, $100 and $50. Apparently that decision was left up to Lamar or officials of the banknote companies.

Lamar contracted with the American Bank Note Company (ABNC) in New York to print registered bonds (called "stock"), in addition to the Treasury notes, the smallest part of the order. The ABNC sub-contracted the Treasury note portion of the order to the National Bank Note Company, also in New York, which printed 607 sheets of notes, with each sheet containing one each of the four denominations. The impressions were delivered to Montgomery, then the Confederate capital, on April 2, 1861, just ten days before hostilities erupted.

Upon delivery, Memminger immediately realized that demand would be stronger for the smaller denominations, so he again contacted Lamar to ask the supplier if it were feasible to furnish an additional 1,000 impressions of each of the $100 and $50 notes. The company prepared a two-subject plate and printed another 1,000 sheets just of the $100 and $50 denominations, which were delivered to Montgomery after the war had begun.

These four denominations of Treasury notes, boldly emblazoned "Montgomery" and the only issue delivered directly to Montgomery, have been known as Montgomerys ever since.

Beautifully engraved and printed on fine banknote paper, the Montgomerys are spectacular works of art. Never intended for general circulation, they bore interest in the nature of bonds and ordinarily would have been held in vaults until redeemed. However, in the chaos of war, some circulated extensively, even to the point of almost being worn out.

Each note bears a written date on the front, mostly between April and June 1861, and collectors are fortunate that Raphael Thian's *Register* shows the date written on each note, arranged by serial number. Many of the notes bear hand-written Issued and Interest Paid endorsements. Each Montgomery bears the signatures of Alexander B. Clitherall as Register and E.C. Elmore as Treasurer (except for a few $500 Montgomerys which will be discussed in Chapter 6).

With only 607 specimens of the $1,000 denomination issued, it should come as no surprise that dealers and collectors alike have attempted for many years to maintain a census of those notes which survived the Civil War. According to an article appearing in the May-June 1994 issue of *Paper Money* written by Brent Hughes, a Confederate scholar, collector and columnist for *Bank Note Reporter*, NASCA-founder Douglas Ball started this census in 1978 and it has been maintained ever since. Contemporaneous records suggest that this 1978 date is correct. As early as May 1977 in Doug's first auction catalog featuring Montgomerys, he made mention of a Montgomery survival census. In June 1980 at the sale of the $1,000 Montgomery with serial number 332, Doug advised that 82 examples of this note were then known.

Over time, other contemporary associates of Ball added to his census, so that by the early 1990s the census was the combined effort of Ball, Hughes, dealers Grover Criswell and Dennis Forgue, collector Arnold Cowan and newcomer Hugh Shull. Sadly, only dealers Forgue and Shull of this group survive, and Hugh, along with other collectors and dealers today, continue to carefully maintain this census of surviving Montgomerys.

Hugh Shull's most recent Montgomery census (with hand annotations), dated October 2011, shows 126 $1,000 Montgomery notes known to survive. Unfortunately, though, in its early days its compilers simply saved the serial numbers, with no regard to the note's whereabouts or its grade. To the extent possible, I have corrected these omissions by updating Hugh's most recent census with a simple parenthetical comment to indicate what is known, if anything, about a specific note.

Those serial numbers followed by a parenthetical (A) appear in Part One of this chapter beginning on page 152. These notes are pedigreed to specific auctions found in Part One and we can be certain of their existence. Similarly, those serial numbers followed by a parenthetical

(B) appear in Part Two of this chapter beginning on page 178. These notes are not pedigreed to any auction, but we know they exist because they are pictured in Part Two as components of an attractive collage. Any serial number new to Shull's most recent census is designated with a green oval.

The current census of the $1,000 Montgomery notes now totals 130 specimens and is shown below, including four new additions to Hugh's latest version. Nearly 70% of these notes (88) are verified to exist in either Part One or Part Two of this chapter immediately following.

Serial Numbers of Surviving $1,000 Montgomery Notes as of January 1, 2012:

12 (A)	87 (B)	231 (A)	322 (A)	441
15 (A)	88 (A)	238	323 (A)	449
29 (A)	89	240 (B)	324 (A)	451
33 (A)	91 (A)	242 (A) NEW	326	453 (A)
34	95 (B)	244 (A)	327 (A)	465 (B)
38 (A)	96	258 (A)	330 (B)	467 (A)
42 (B)	99	261	331 (A)	473 (B)
44 (B)	100	266 (A)	332 (A)	490 (A)
45 (A)	102	267	333 (B)	494 (A)
46 (A)	104 (A)	276	335	503 (A)
48	125 (A)	278 (A)	338	504
52	129 (A) NEW	279	344 (A)	511 (A)
53	133	292 (A)	365 (B)	515 (A)
54 (A)	145 (A)	296 (A)	368 (A)	521 (B)
55 (A)	146 (A)	297 (B)	371 (B)	538
56 (B)	152 (B)	299 (A)	372	555 (A)
57 (B)	162	302 (B)	381 (A)	556
58 (B)	163	304	392 (A)	558
59	166 (A)	306 (A)	397 (A)	563 (B)
61(A)	175 (B)	312 (A)	410	564
65 (A)	176	314 (A)	415 (B)	566 (A)
66	212	315	416 (B) NEW	571 (A)
82 (A)	217 (A)	316	419 (B)	580 (A)
84 (A)	219 NEW	319	420 (A)	593
85 (A)	225	320 (A)	421 (B)	594 (B)
86 (A)	229 (A)	321 (A)	428	595 (A)

Those Montgomerys found in Part One of this chapter beginning on page 152 define the database for the calculation of a rate of return for the $1,000 Montgomery note from 1865 through 2010. As is explained in Chapter 4, rates of return were also obtained for precious metals (namely, silver), energy (specifically, crude oil), and the stock market (that is, the S&P 500 Composite Index) to use for comparative purposes.

The results are perhaps surprising and certainly reassuring for those of us who are passionate about collecting Confederate currency, or at least the Montgomery notes. For nearly a 150-year time span, the $1,000 Montgomery note has increased in value, on average, 6.6% each year, higher than any of the alternative investment opportunities. The highly touted S&P 500 Composite Index placed second, at a rate of return of 4.3% each year (not including the re-investment of any dividends paid by the component stocks of the S&P 500, which would add 1.9% to the total annual return[1]). Crude oil and silver trailed significantly, at annual returns of only 2.4% and 1.6%, respectively.

[1]Used with permission of, and special thanks to, Bryan Taylor, Ph.D., Global Financial Data, Inc., Los Angeles.

These results can easily be seen on the full-page graph shown on page 177. A smaller version of this same graph is shown below:

The $1,000 Montgomery Note Vs. Crude Oil, Silver and the S&P 500: Comparative Price Appreciation Since the End of the Civil War

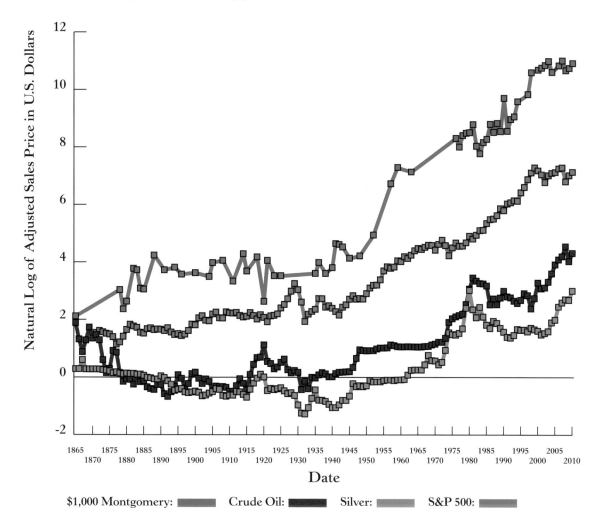

$1,000 Montgomery: ▬ Crude Oil: ▬ Silver: ▬ S&P 500: ▬

The graph above illustrates how little any of the four potential investments grew in value between 1865 and about 1950. Since 1950, though, all four investment options have shown attractive growth, led by the 9.8% enjoyed by the $1,000 Montgomery and followed by the S&P 500 at 7.3%.

Said another way, this analysis suggests that, if these historical rates of return are maintained, a $1,000 Montgomery note purchased January 1, 2011, at a fair market value of $25,000 (as determined in a public auction) would be worth $50,000 on June 1, 2018, about seven and a half years later. On the other hand, an investment of $25,000 on January 1, 2011 in a market basket of common stocks comprising the S&P 500 would not be worth $50,000 until November 1, 2020, nearly 10 years after its purchase.

And I believe that I am safe in assuming that most readers of this book would much prefer to gaze upon a magnificent $1,000 Montgomery note than a stack of musty stock certificates.

Chapter 5: Part One

Quantitative Look at Auction Sales of the Confederate $1,000 Montgomery Note In Chronological Order Since 1865

Auction House	Sale Date	Grade or Condition*	Serial Number	Sales Price
William Elliot Woodward *Boston, Mass.*	19 Dec 1865	VF	-	$4.75

Comments: Consignor of this first-ever Montgomery to appear at public auction is uncertain, although the purchaser was John F. McCoy. Full details, pages 14-16.

John W. Haseltine *Philadelphia, Pa.*	24-25 Apr 1878	UNC	-	$21.00

Comments: Haseltine's own collection of Confederate currency and bonds. Note is hand-dated "May 28." Note described as "uncirculated and clean."

Bangs & Co. *New York, N.Y.*	25 Mar 1879	UNC	-	$10.70

Comments: Consigned by J. E. Barratt, possibly a physician, who died about 1878. Cataloged by C.H. Bechtel. Barratt owned all four Montgomerys, a Confederate cent and the Lovett dies, which sold for $8.00. Note "uncirculated and clean."

Sigismund K. Harzfeld *Philadelphia, Pa.*	9 Apr 1880	cc, VF	12	$8.00

Comments: Consigned by Ferguson Haines, a noted coin collector born in Maine in 1840. Attended Phillips Academy in Andover, Mass. and Dartmouth. Retailed hardware and manufactured textiles. Served as mayor of Biddeford, Me. and was a member of the Maine House of Representatives. Note "has a redeeming cut." Photo (p. 153) courtesy current owner Clint Reynolds, *www.ConfederateTreasury.com*.

*Legend. **cc**: A note with a "cut cancel" has slits usually shaped like a cross but with no paper missing. **poc**: A "punch out cancel" is a series of round holes, from one or two up to six or eight, about the size of a pencil eraser. Depending on the number and size of the holes, some paper is missing. **coc**: A note with a "cut out cancel" has significant paper missing, usually coming in the shape of a pair of triangles or half-moons. **pen c**: A "pen cancel" is an unusual form of cancellation where the word "Cancelled" is written or stamped across the face of the note.

A new war could erupt today over the application of grading standards to Confederate currency. After all, it is the grade that ultimately determines value. Grades in this book are taken from the actual auction catalog description. Certainly grading standards changed over the 150-year duration of these auction results. Abbreviations used, from best to worst, include **CU** - Crisp Uncirculated; **UNC** - Uncirculated; **AU** - About Uncirculated; **XF** - Extremely Fine; **VF** - Very Fine; **F** - Fine; **VG** - Very Good; **G** - Good; **Fr** - Fair and **P** - Poor. A note grading "Crisp Uncirculated" or "Uncirculated" is brand new as if it just came off the printing press. A "Very Fine" note has seen circulation as shown by both vertical and horizontal quarter folds, but the note retains its body or crispness. Conversely, "Good" notes retain no body and have extreme wear, frayed edges or even slight tears, if they do not impinge on the main design.

Auction House	Sale Date	Grade or Condition	Serial Number	Sales Price

Serial number 12: Front and back.

John W. Haseltine
Philadelphia, Pa. 6 Nov 1882 cc, UNC - $29.00

    Comments: Consigned by little-known H. W. Lord. Note described as "cancelled by clean cut, extremely rare and valuable." Sales price not exceeded until 1894.

William Elliot Woodward
Boston, Mass. 28 Dec 1882 cc, Good 125 $14.25

    Comments: Consigned by Paul J. Maas of Laporte, Ind., a major coin collector in the late 1800s. Note described as "somewhat soiled and worn, still in good condition and most desirable, extremely rare; but one has been offered for years."

John W. Haseltine
Philadelphia, Pa. 10 Apr 1883 VF - $25.00

    Comments: Consigned by Harold P. Newlin, a Pennsylvania attorney who "wrote the book" on half dimes and dimes. Note described as "the only $1000 Confederate note that I have ever seen uncancelled."

Edouard Frossard
Brooklyn, N.Y. 12 Dec 1883 VG - $14.00

    Comments: Consigned by William Poillon (1844-1918) of New York City, who owned a clay manufacturing company called Salamander Works. Active in the ANS, serving as secretary, vice president and curator.

John W. Haseltine
Philadelphia, Pa. 28 Aug 1884 cc, poc, VF - $10.00

    Comments: Consignor unknown. Note cancelled by clean cuts and punch marks.

William Elliot Woodward
Boston, Mass. 13 Oct 1884 cc, VF - $10.00

    Comments: Consignor unknown. Note "folded and is cancelled by two clean cuts."

Charles Steigerwalt
Lancaster, Pa. 19-20 Dec 1884 cc, VG - $12.10

    Comments: Consigned by William Starr, about whom little is known. Note described as "cancelled by two clean cuts. Exceedingly rare."

Lyman Haines Low
New York, N.Y. 26 Mar 1885 cc, UNC - $10.25

    Comments: Consignor unknown. Note "uncirculated, cancelled, clean cut."

Auction House	Sale Date	Grade or Condition	Serial Number	Sales Price
Charles Steigerwalt *Lancaster, Pa.*	9-10 Apr 1885	cc, Fine	-	$15.00

Comments: Consigned by the heirs of Henry Barclay, about whom little is known. Note "cancelled by two minute L cuts, scarcely visible. Exceedingly rare."

| Charles Steigerwalt
Lancaster, Pa. | 4-5 Jun 1885 | cc, Fine | - | $11.00 |

Comments: Probably consigned by the heirs of Henry Barclay, although possibly the property of a "Rohrer." Note described as "cancelled by two L cuts, scarcely visible." Virtually the same description as previous note; possibly same note.

| David U. Proskey
New York, N.Y. | 15 Dec 1885 | poc, Fine | - | - |

Comments: Consigned by the celebrated Raphael Prosper Thian, who wrote *Register of the Confederate Debt* (page 41). Note withdrawn prior to sale.

| Edouard Frossard
Brooklyn, N.Y. | 22 Dec 1885 | Fine | - | $15.00 |

Comments: Consigned by Dr. William Lee, professor and author in 1875 of *The Currency of the Confederate States of America* (page 32). Note "fine and very rare."

| S.H. & H. Chapman
Philadelphia, Pa. | 17 Oct 1888 | cc, VG | 125 | $24.50 |

Comments: Second $1000 Montgomery consigned by Ferguson Haines (first on page 152). Note "cancelled through signatures, with the usual straight cuts, the lower limb of which is gone and is cleverly mended with a piece of another note."

| John Walter Scott
New York, N.Y. | 22 Jun 1891 | cc, AU | - | $25.00 |

Comments: Consigned by E. L. Nagel of Terre Haute, Ind., a 19th century collector of coins and medals. Note "cancelled through the signature, the edges have been neatly replaced and are held down by a thin piece of paper pasted on the back."

| George W. Massamore
Baltimore, Md. | 15 Oct 1891 | Fine | - | $29.00 |

Comments: Consigned by little-known William J. Thomsen. Described as "fine."

| Edouard Frossard
Brooklyn, N.Y. | 14 Nov 1893 | cc, XF | - | - |

Comments: Consignor unknown. Note has a "slight invisible cut cancellation, light discoloration at bottom from small piece of paper gummed on back. Perfect."

| John Walter Scott
New York, N.Y. | 26 Jun 1894 | Fine | - | $37.75 |

Comments: Consignor unknown. Note is "whole, uncancelled, in fine condition."

Auction House	Sale Date	Grade or Condition	Serial Number	Sales Price
S.H. & H. Chapman *Philadelphia, Pa.*	3 Dec 1894	cc, VF	-	$22.50

Comments: Consigned by little-known W.H. Spedding. Note "cancelled by cross cuts, no part missing and when laid down the cancellation does not show."

Edouard Frossard *Brooklyn, N.Y.*	19 Dec 1894	XF	-	$23.25

Comments: A third consignment from Ferguson Haines, the noted Maine collector, and probably the best of the three. Note has "small spots, extremely fine."

Charles Steigerwalt *Lancaster, Pa.*	17 Jan 1895	VF	-	-

Comments: Consigned by little-known John Wright. In Steigerwalt's usual terse style, note described simply as a "very fine specimen of a very rare note."

Charles Steigerwalt *Lancaster, Pa.*	25 Jun 1895	XF	-	-

Comments: Consigned by Grant Weaver, about whom little is known. Simply described as an "extremely fine specimen."

Charles Steigerwalt *Lancaster, Pa.*	6 Jan 1896	VF	-	-

Comments: Consigned by little-known Robert Watts. Note a "very fine specimen."

Charles Steigerwalt *Lancaster, Pa.*	16 July 1896	AU	-	$30.25

Comments: Consignor could be "Kerr, Roberts or Sebring"; Steigerwalt does not indicate which one. Note described as "nearly uncirculated, very rare."

S.H. & H. Chapman *Philadelphia, Pa.*	16 Nov 1900	cc, XF	-	$27.50

Comments: Consigned by the eminent Dr. Edward Maris (1832-1900), a Philadelphia Quaker who assembled comprehensive collections of New Jersey cents, autograph letters, Colonial currency and South American coins. Note described as "cancelled by cross clean cuts, no part missing and not noticeable."

Lyman Haines Low *New York, N.Y.*	13 Dec 1904	cc, Poor	320	$3.30

Comments: Uncertain consignor. Worst $1000 Montgomery to appear at auction: "left end burnt off, remainder smoked from the fire at the Richmond evacuation."

Lyman Haines Low *New York, N.Y.*	19 Jan 1905	poc, Fine	-	$26.50

Comments: Consigned by H. G. Brown of Portland, Ore., who bought an 1804 silver dollar from Roland Parvin which he sold to the renowned William F. Dunham.

Auction House	Sale Date	Grade or Condition	Serial Number	Sales Price
Henry Chapman *Philadelphia, Pa.*	19-20 Jun 1908	XF	46	$50.00

Comments: Consigned by Harmon Chambers (1822-1905) of the "Confederate Triumvirate," who founded an insurance brokerage business in Philadelphia (page 51). This note is in the Condition Census Top Ten. Photo below, courtesy current owner Col. Hudson McDonald, Colonel's Coins & Stamps, Spanish Fort, Al.

Serial number 46:
Front and back.

Henry Chapman *Philadelphia, Pa.*	19-20 Jun 1908	cc, Fine	278	$24.00

Comments: Also consigned by Harmon Chambers. Note "has been folded three times and center seam slightly worn. Is also slightly polished." Photo below left, from William Lee's 1875 book, *The Currency of the Confederate States of America.*

Left, serial #278,
right, #392.

Edgar Holmes Adams *New York, N.Y.*	10 Feb 1911	poc, Good	555	$10.00

Comments: Consignor unknown. Note "slightly cancelled round perforations."

Edward Michael *Chicago, Ill.*	9 May 1914	poc, Fine	392	$31.00

Comments: Consigned by Chicagoan Ben Green (p. 52), first Midwestern coin dealer. Note has "3 small cancellation holes." Photo above right, courtesy Christie's.

Samuel Hudson Chapman *Philadelphia, Pa.*	27-29 May 1914	Fine	15	$42.00

Comments: Consigned by William Gable of Altoona, Pa., founder of a large department store and owner of virtually complete U.S. coin series. Note is "stained either end, vertical creases." Photo, top of page 157, courtesy Amanda Sheheen, A&O Currency, LLC, *www.aocurrency.com*

Auction House	Sale Date	Grade or Condition	Serial Number	Sales Price

Serial number 15: Front and back.

Thomas Lindsay Elder
New York, N.Y. — 28 Sep 1915 — cc, Fine — 217 — $20.00

> *Comments:* Consignor unknown. Description reads "handsome, excessively rare."

Lyman Haines Low
New York, N.Y. — 22 May 1918 — Fine — - — $32.50

> *Comments:* Consigned by Henry McCullough, about whom little is known. Note has a "slight tear on base line, well restored. Fine."

B. Max Mehl
Fort Worth, Tex. — 23 Nov 1920 — Poor — - — $1.40

> *Comments:* Consigned by little-known Oscar L. Englestrom. A "Poor" note "from the Richmond fire. Small left portion missing, stained, shows signs of burns."

Thomas Lindsay Elder
New York, N.Y. — 26-27 Aug 1921 — cc, VF — 217 — $33.00

> *Comments:* Consigned by Lewis C. Gehring (1852-1921) of Brooklyn, N. Y., who was born in Rahway, N. J. before moving to Brooklyn. A prominent banker of the Prudential Savings Bank, with other financial interests in feed and milling. Mainly collected gold coins. This note described as "bottom pasted closed."

Stan V. Henkels
Philadelphia, Pa. — 28 Jul 1922 — UNC — - — -

> *Comments:* Consigned by the legendary John C. Browne, perhaps the greatest Confederate collector ever (see page 58). Part of a 90-note "Uncirculated" type set.

B. Max Mehl
Fort Worth, Tex. — 17 Apr 1923 — cc, Fine — - — $18.25

> *Comments:* Consigned by either John Burton, S. H. Huntington or F. L. Bixley, all little-known collectors. Note simply described as "no part of this note is missing."

B. Max Mehl
Fort Worth, Tex. — 17 Apr 1923 — poc, VF — - — $18.00

> *Comments:* Same three possible consignors as the note immediately above. Note tersely described as "cancelled with two small perforations."

Auction House	Sale Date	Grade or Condition	Serial Number	Sales Price
Thomas Lindsay Elder *New York, N.Y.*	9-11 Oct 1924	UNC	46	-

Comments: Consigned by Edward H. Eckfeldt, Jr. of Orange, N.J., a direct descendant of Adam Eckfeldt, the first coiner of the U.S. Mint. Census condition note, described as "the finest known, mounted under glass." Photo of note, p. 156.

Auction House	Sale Date	Grade or Condition	Serial Number	Sales Price
Thomas Lindsay Elder *New York, N.Y.*	9-11 Apr 1925	cc, XF	-	$25.00

Comments: Consignor unknown. Note "cut cancelled and pasted at bottom."

Left, serial #242, right, #392.

Auction House	Sale Date	Grade or Condition	Serial Number	Sales Price
William Hesslein *Boston, Mass.*	22-23 Nov 1929	cc, XF	242	-

Comments: Consigned by H. D. Allen of Boston, whose articles appeared in *The Numismatist* (p. 56). Note "repaired at bottom." Above photo, Slabaugh's 1961 Ed.

Auction House	Sale Date	Grade or Condition	Serial Number	Sales Price
Milfred Henry Bolender *Freeport, Ill.*	15 Oct 1935	VF	45	$21.00

Comments: Consigned by dealer A. M. Smith (1841-1915) of Minneapolis. Note has "a few brown spots and a number of pinholes, but nice." Photo, top of page 162.

Serial number 566: Front and back.

Auction House	Sale Date	Grade or Condition	Serial Number	Sales Price
Milfred Henry Bolender *Freeport, Ill.*	8 Feb 1936	poc, Fine	566	$30.00

Comments: Consigned by A. P. Wylie of Wheaton, Ill., a dealer and collector of U.S. coins and currency. Note "hole cancelled." Above photo from Crutch Williams.

Auction House	Sale Date	Grade or Condition	Serial Number	Sales Price
John Milford Henderson *Columbus, Oh.*	4 Apr 1936	poc, Fine	392	$24.00

Comments: Consigned by Henrie Buck of Delaware, Ohio, ANA member and state president. Note has "three 1/8" cancellation holes." Photo above right, Christie's.

Auction House	Sale Date	Grade or Condition	Serial Number	Sales Price
Milfred Henry Bolender *Freeport, Ill.*	26 Feb 1938	Fine	258	$15.75

Comments: Consignor unknown. Note has "creases and repaired at weak spots."

B. Max Mehl *Fort Worth, Tex.*	22 Mar 1938	cc, XF	15	-

Comments: Consigned by Benjamin H. Collins (1845-1928) of Washington, D.C., a collector, dealer and ANA member. Born in Independence, Mo., he served in the Union Army before finding employment at the U.S. Treasury. Had a coin shop in Washington by 1894. Note sold as part of a set of Montgomerys. Pictured, p. 157.

Stack's *New York, N.Y.*	25 Jun 1938	cc, XF	-	$31.50

Comments: Consignor unknown. Note described as "cancelled, extremely fine."

Serial number 266:
Front and back.

Thomas Lindsay Elder *New York, N.Y.*	12 May 1939	cc, UNC	266	-

Comments: Consignor uncertain. A Census Condition note, described as "neatly cancelled and mended, seems Uncirculated, best offered in years." Photo above.

New Netherlands Coin Co. *New York, N.Y.*	5 Dec 1940	poc, XF	453	$33.00

Comments: Consignor unknown. Note's "punch hole cancellations have been filled." Photo below, courtesy Dale S. Alberstone Family Trust Collection, Los Angeles, Calif.

Serial number 453:
Front and back.

Auction House	Sale Date	Grade or Condition	Serial Number	Sales Price
B. Max Mehl *Fort Worth, Tex.*	3 Jun 1941	XF	15	$76.00

Comments: Consigned by Mehl himself, who bought it from Benjamin Collins (p. 159) and included it within the auction of the celebrated William F. Dunham (1857-1936) of Chicago, former teacher, grocer, pharmacist and stockbroker, who served as chairman of the Board of Governors of the ANA. Photo, top of page 157.

Abe Kosoff *New York, N.Y.*	25 Aug 1942	VF	231	$57.50

Comments: Consignor unknown. Note tersely described as "very fine."

B. Max Mehl *Fort Worth, Tex.*	9 Mar 1943	cc, XF	314	$52.50

Comments: Consigned by Henry E. Elrod of Houston, Tex., ANA member who focused on European coins. Note is cancelled in lower center, skillfully repaired.

Serial number 292: Front and back. (Courtesy, Museum of the Confederacy, Richmond, Va.)

Milfred Henry Bolender *Freeport, Ill.*	10 May 1943	cc, VF	292	$68.00

Comments: Consignor unknown. Note shown above "cancelled as usual, but whole." Given to the Museum of the Confederacy, Richmond, Va. by then-owner and my mentor, Douglas B. Ball, Ph.D.

Serial number 55: Front and back.

Barney Bluestone *Syracuse, N.Y.*	27-28 Apr 1945	Gem UNC	55	$63.00

Comments: Consignor unknown. The finest $1000 Montgomery known. Note pictured above is a "crisp beauty with good margins. Low number 55. A gem of the first water, unsurpassed and a great rarity in this condition. Uncancelled."

Auction House	Sale Date	Grade or Condition	Serial Number	Sales Price
Milfred Henry Bolender *Freeport, Ill.*	2 Oct 1948	Good	166	$24.00

Comments: Consigned by Loring T. Reckard of Chicago, ANA member from 1916 who also collected stamps and coins. Note "good, with some brown stains."

Milfred Henry Bolender *Freeport, Ill.*	23 Feb 1952	cc, F-VF, Repaired	324	$75.00

Comments: Consignor unknown. Note described as having "been torn or cut near bottom for about 3" but no part missing and repaired on back."

Federal Coin Exchange *Cleveland, Oh.*	10-13 Jan 1957	CU	55	$675.00

Comments: The finest $1000 Montgomery was consigned by Charles W. "Suitcase Charlie" Foster of Rushville, N.Y., once ANA librarian and author. Co-founder of Empire State Numismatic Association. Note's description asks, "How many exist today, especially so choice? Crisp Uncirculated." Pictured, bottom of facing page.

D&W Auction Sales *Baltimore, Md.*	26-27 Oct 1957	cc, VF	-	$590.00

Comments: Consignor unknown. Note described as "slight discoloration at signatures. Back clean with six light creases, torn at cut cancel, poor mend."

D&W Auction Sales *Baltimore, Md.*	3 Apr 1959	VF	29	$845.00

Comments: Consignor unknown. Note has "discoloration and is a little soiled."

Federal Brand Enterprises *Cleveland, Oh.*	13-15 Jul 1963	VF	33	$875.00

Comments: Consigned by Grover Criswell, p. 81. Description reads "very fine."

Stack's *New York, N.Y.*	2-5 Oct 1963	cc, F-VF	490	$540.00

Comments: Consigned by George O. Walton of Roanoke, Va., founder of the Mid-Atlantic Numismatic Assoc. Note "has been cut-cancelled and repaired on back."

Serial number 306:
Front and back.

Lester Merkin *New York, N.Y.*	20-21 Aug 1976	cc, VF	306	$2,300.00

Comments: Consignor unknown. Note has six light folds, with one cross-shaped cancellation at bottom, neatly fixed. Photo above, courtesy Neal Auction Co.

Auction House	Sale Date	Grade or Condition	Serial Number	Sales Price
NASCA *Rockville Centre, N.Y.*	27-28 May 1977	cc, Fine+	266	$1,600.00

Comments: Consigned by the Maryland Historical Society. Note "is cancelled with a double cross bank hammer and is backed with glassine tape." Photo, middle p. 159.

Kagin's *Des Moines, Ia.*	29-30 Sep 1978	VF	45	$2,600.00

Comments: Consignor unknown. Note has tiny pin holes in center, four larger pin holes surrounded by rust spots. Photo below, courtesy George B. Tremmel, Raleigh, N.C.

Serial number 45: Front and back.

NASCA *Rockville Centre, N.Y.*	6-7 Dec 1978	cc, Abt. VF	368	$2,310.00

Comments: Consignor unknown. Note "has five vertical folds, two corner folds at left, the paper being soiled at the bottom center." Photo below left, from NASCA catalog.

Left, serial #368, right, #332.

NASCA *Rockville Centre, N.Y.*	30 Apr-1 May 1979	cc, Fine	322	$2,415.00

Comments: Consigned by Dr. Van B. Elliott, coin and currency collector. Note has "double cross bank cancellations in the bottom center to the edge and has been neatly repaired." Photo p. 163, courtesy current owner and former mayor of Asharoken, N.Y., William H. Kelly.

NASCA *Rockville Centre, N.Y.*	6-7 Jun 1980	cc, VF	332	$2,940.00

Comments: Consignor unknown. Note has "four vertical folds in left and right. Double cross bank hammer cancellation. Tight border." Above photo, NASCA.

Auction House	Sale Date	Grade or Condition	Serial Number	Sales Price

Serial number 322: Front and back.

| NASCA | 4-6 Sep 1980 | cc, Abt VF | 229 | $2,520.00 |

Rockville Centre, N.Y.

> *Comments:* Consignor unknown. Note is "quarter folded both ways. Two pin holes in the top, and the bank hammer cancellation at the bottom has been fixed on the back with two paper strips." Photo below, courtesy Neal Auction Co.

Serial number 229: Front and back.

| Grover C. Criswell | 17 Oct 1980 | VF | 420 | - |

Salt Springs, Fla.

> *Comments:* Consigned by little-known Dr. Richard Rich. Simply described as "very fine." Photo below left, courtesy Coin Galleries' 1985 catalog.

| Grover C. Criswell | 17 Oct 1980 | Abt VG, Laminated | 145 | - |

Salt Springs, Fla.

Left, serial #420, right, #145.

> *Comments:* Consigned by little-known Dr. Richard Rich. Low-grade note, described as "laminated." Photo above right from Criswell's 1980 auction catalog.

Auction House	Sale Date	Grade or Condition	Serial Number	Sales Price
Bowers & Ruddy Galleries *Los Angeles, Calif.*	25-26 Mar 1981	VG-F	38	$2,400.00

Comments: From the collection of T. Harrison Garrett (1849-1888) of Baltimore, president of the B&O Railroad, upon de-accession by The Johns Hopkins University. Note has "small pieces missing." Photo below, courtesy R.M. Smythe, New York.

Serial number 38:
Front and back.

NASCA *Rockville Centre, N.Y.*	10-12 Sep 1981	cc, UNC	84	$7,350.00

Comments: Consigned by Stanley Gibbons, London stamp dealer. A census note, "uncirculated, cut cancelled, only five or so are truly uncirculated, all seen by us being cut cancelled." Photo below, courtesy owner Tig Sogoian, *www.CSABig6.com.*

Serial number 84:
Front and back.

NASCA *Rockville Centre, N.Y.*	19-21 Apr 1982	cc, UNC	84	$5,775.00

Comments: Consigned by Grover Criswell, noted dealer (see p.81). Pictured above.

Christie's *New York, N.Y.*	17 Sep 1982	cc, VF	306	$1,760.00

Comments: Consigned by Richard F. Saffin (1894-1982), a partner in the brokerage firm Boland Saffin Gordon & Sauffer. Note is "among the most attractive of the known examples, with the folds visible primarily on the reverse." Photo, page 161.

Christie's *New York, N.Y.*	17 Sep 1982	VF+	45	$1,430.00

Comments: Also from Richard F. Saffin. Note has "many pinholes and is one of few remaining uncancelled. A few larger pinholes showing rust." Photo, top of p. 162.

Auction House	Sale Date	Grade or Condition	Serial Number	Sales Price
Christie's New York, N.Y.	17 Sep 1982	poc, F-VF	467	$1,320.00

Comments: A third $1000 Montgomery from Richard F. Saffin (page 164). Note "punch-out cancelled, with six small holes. Not quite as bright as the last two."

Christie's New York, N.Y.	8 Dec 1982	cc, VF	266	$1,650.00

Comments: Consignor unknown. Note "cut cancelled (repaired)." Photo, page 159.

NASCA Rockville Centre, N.Y.	10-12 Jan 1983	cc, poc, VF	453	$1,365.00

Comments: Part of the massive John C. Browne collection, consigned by Charles J. Affleck (1892-1974) of Winchester, Va., author of *The Obsolete Paper Money of Va.* Note "cut cancelled by bank hammer and holes punched out." Photo, page 159.

Stack's New York, N.Y.	20 Mar 1984	cc, Fine+	344	$1,870.00

Left, serial #344, right, #420.

Comments: From John L. Roper (1902-1983) of Norfolk, Va., a ship builder. Note "quarter folded, a bank hammer cancellation." Photo above left, courtesy Stack's.

Serial number 515: Front and back.

NASCA - Karp New York, N.Y.	28-29 Mar 1985	poc, Good	515	$990.00

Comments: Consigned by little-known Ben O. Anderson. Note has "redrawn date and signatures. Two punch holes." Above photo, courtesy Heritage Auctions.

Coin Galleries New York, N.Y.	10 Apr 1985	VF-XF	420	$2,145.00

Comments: Consignor unknown. Note has "tiny pinholes and edge splits, upper right corner restored. Ink endorsement bleeding to obverse." Photo, above right.

Auction House	Sale Date	Grade or Condition	Serial Number	Sales Price
Coin Galleries *New York, N.Y.*	13 Nov 1985	poc, Fine	420	$2,007.50

Comments: Consignor unknown. Note has "three small cancellation holes and the upper right corner has been filled in and redrawn." Photo right center, p. 165.

NASCA, Div. of Smythe & Co. *New York, N.Y.*	7-10 Mar 1986	poc, Good	515	$1,430.00

Comments: Consignor unknown. Note's "signatures and date traced over. The two punch holes are repaired from the back. Soiling, shaved borders." Photo, p. 165.

Serial number 85: *Front and back.* NASCA, Div. of Smythe & Co. *New York, N.Y.*	6 Mar 1987	cc, F-VF	85	$1,485.00

Comments: Consignor unknown. Note "cut cancelled with a piece out of the lower left hand corner, with tape strips." Above photo, courtesy Crutchfield Williams.

Serial number 244: *Front and back.* Stack's *New York, N.Y.*	9-11 Sep 1987	cc, F-VF	244	$2,530.00

Comments: Consigned by little-known L.S. Ruder. Note has "a neatly repaired cut cancellation at bottom, and a repaired hole." Above photo courtesy R. M. Smythe.

NASCA, Div. of Smythe & Co. *New York, N.Y.*	25-26 Sep 1987	cc, XF+	88	$7,920.00

Comments: Consigned by mentor Douglas B. Ball, Ph.D. (p. 98). Census condition note, whose "left and bottom borders are shaved, the Elmore signature is faint, and there is wrinkling. There is a trace of a fold at left. Ex Philip H. Chase." Photo top of facing page, courtesy R. M. Smythe, New York City.

Auction House	Sale Date	Grade or Condition	Serial Number	Sales Price

Serial number 88:
Front and back.

NASCA, Div. of Smythe & Co.   25-26 Mar 1988   Abt VF   46 $3,630.00
New York, N.Y.

    Comments: Consignor unknown. Census condition note pictured on p. 156. Note "vertically quarter folded, other folds, complete margins." Incorrectly attributed to M. Mehl's 1941 Dunham sale; should have been H. Chapman's 1908 Chambers sale.

Serial number 323:
Front and back.

NASCA, Div. of Smythe & Co.   31 Mar 1989   cc, Abt VF   323 $3,740.00
New York, N.Y.

    Comments: Consignor unknown. Note "hammer cut cancelled at bottom with a glassine hinge there." Above photo, courtesy owner Bill Kelly, Asharoken, N.Y.

Christie's   7 Sep 1989   poc, Fine   392 $1,870.00
New York, N.Y.

    Comments: Consigned by brothers Felix and Henri Weil, founders of Medallic Art Co. Note has "several small hole cancellations backed on reverse." Photo, p. 156.

NASCA, Div. of Smythe & Co.   15-16 Jun 1990   UNC   55 $16,500.00
New York, N.Y.

    Comments: Consigned by Henry Hull, Jacksonville, Fla., a philatelist. Stunning, note is "certainly census condition. The best we have seen anywhere. Probably the best known, a census specimen. Complete borders." Photo, bottom of page 160.

R.M. Smythe & Co.   27 Jun 1991   poc, XF   580 $3,300.00
New York, N.Y.

    Comments: Consignor unknown. Note has "two small holes in the top and four larger ones in signature block, all crudely restored. Some staining." Photo, p. 168.

Auction House	Sale Date	Grade or Condition	Serial Number	Sales Price

Serial number 82: Front and back.

| Christie's New York, N.Y. | 9 Dec 1991 | cc, XF | 82 | $4,400.00 |

Comments: Consignor unknown. Census condition note once part of collector Paul Gibson's famous Confederate currency display. Note "extremely fine, cancelled, well-centered with bright green color." Photo above.

| R.M. Smythe & Co. New York, N.Y. | 23 Nov 1992 | poc, cc, Abt VF | 453 | $4,180.00 |

Comments: Consignor unknown. Note has two small punch holes and four larger ones, all crudely repaired, with a blue Savannah, Ga. stamp on back. Photo, p.159.

Serial number 580: Front and back.

| R.M. Smythe & Co. New York, N.Y. | 22 Nov 1993 | cc, poc, VF-XF | 580 | $5,500.00 |

Comments: Consignor unknown. Has two small and four large holes in signature block. Hit twice with hammer. Above photo courtesy Bill Kelly, Asharoken, N.Y.

| R.M. Smythe & Co. New York, N.Y. | 23 Mar 1994 | Abt VF | 331 | $7,700.00 |

Comments: Possibly owned by John Besante, American Impressionist artist. Note "somewhat aged, trimmed to the border at left and bottom left. Uncancelled." Photo top of page 169, courtesy dealer Hugh Shull, Lexington, S.C.

| R.M. Smythe & Co. New York, N.Y. | 4-5 Nov 1994 | Fine | 322 | $7,260.00 |

Comments: Consignor unknown. Note is "fine or so, some staining." Photo, p. 163.

Auction House	Sale Date	Grade or Condition	Serial Number	Sales Price

Serial number 331:
Front and back.

Signature House
Bridgeport, W.V.
    15 May 1997   cc, UNC   312 $18,700.00

    Comments: Consignor unknown. Note once owned by Grover Criswell. First described as "uncirculated, with no folds and no cancellations," later found to be hammer cut cancelled. A census condition note, no endorsement. Photo below.

Serial number 312:
Front and back.

Stack's
New York, N.Y.
    11-12 Mar 1998   cc, VF   296 $20,900.00

    Comments: From the Joseph C. Mitchelson Collection at the Museum of Connecticut History. Mitchelson (1856-1911) of Tariffville, Conn. was a prominent tobacco dealer. Owned nearly complete collections of colonial coins, private gold issues, fractional and Confederate currency. Note has "some light brown discoloration on the back and around the signatures. A bold black imprint and vivid green overprint with excellent eye appeal." Photo below right, courtesy, Stack's, New York City.

Left, serial #392,
right, #296.

Auction House	Sale Date	Grade or Condition	Serial Number	Sales Price

Serial number 595: *Front and back.*

R.M. Smythe & Co. *New York, N.Y.*	19 Jun 1998	pen c, Fine+	595	$26,400.00

Comments: From Arnold Cowan, Long Beach, Calif. Note trimmed close to borders, endorsed twice on back, pen cancelled on front. Above photo from Marc Helm.

Serial number 494: *Front and back.*

R.M. Smythe & Co. *New York, N.Y.*	19 Jun 1998	cc, poc, VF	494	$25,300.00

Comments: From Arnold Cowan. Note restored. Above photo, Dave Sundstrom.

Serial number 91: *Front and back.*

Withington Auction *Hillsborough, N.H.*	28 Aug 1998	Fine	91	$20,350.00

Comments: Owned by William Mercier. Above photo, Bill Kelly, Asharoken, N.Y.

R.M. Smythe & Co. *New York, N.Y.*	18-19 Sep 1998	cc, F-VF	266	$16,500.00

Comments: From John Sanderson. Has "paper repair pieces, stains." Photo, p. 159.

Auction House	Sale Date	Grade or Condition	Serial Number	Sales Price

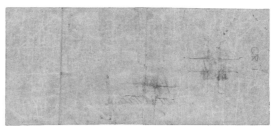

Serial number 299: Front and back.

| Bowers & Merena Galleries *Wolfeboro, N.H.* | 9-12 Aug 2000 | cc, Fine | 299 | $23,000.00 |

Comments: From the Franklin Institute in Philadelphia. Note's "green ink shows light fading. Evidence of moderate wear." Above photo, courtesy Stack's Bowers.

Serial number 321: Front and back.

| Early American History Aucts. *La Jolla, Calif.* | 14 Oct 2000 | cc, Fine | 321 | $20,700.00 |

Comments: Consigned by dealer Hugh Shull. Note's "colors are bright, signatures crisp and bold. Deft restoration work." Above photo, courtesy Dave Nelson.

Serial number 54: Front and back.

| Heritage Auctions *Dallas, Tex.* | 21-22 Sep 2001 | VG | 54 | $14,850.00 |

Comments: Consigned by Dr. Walter B. Jones (1895-1977), State Geologist for Ala. Note restored, particularly on back. Above photo, courtesy Heritage Auctions.

Auction House	Sale Date	Grade or Condition	Serial Number	Sales Price
Lyn Knight Currency Auctions Overland Park, Kan.	30 Nov 2001	cc, Fine+	104	$27,500.00

Comments: Consignor unknown. Note's "circulation appears quite even with excellent color and body. Double hammer cut cancel has been closed." Photo below left, courtesy Lyn Knight Currency Auctions.

Left, serial #104, right, #146.

Butterfields, a Division of eBay San Francisco, Calif.	16 Dec 2002	Poor-Fair	146	$6,462.50

Comments: Consigned by the San Francisco Fine Arts Museum. Note damaged upon removal from album. Skillful repairs. Above photo courtesy Butterfield's.

Serial number 511: Front and back.

Lyn Knight Currency Auctions Overland Park, Kan.	24-27 Apr 2003	cc, F-VF	511	$26,450.00

Comments: Consignor unknown. Past owner Dallas philatelist Gordon Bleuler. Note cut cancelled, deftly repaired. Above photo courtesy Heritage Auctions.

Serial number 61: Front and back.

Auction House	Sale Date	Grade or Condition	Serial Number	Sales Price
R. M. Smythe & Co. *New York, N.Y.*	13-14 Jun 2003	XF-AU	61	$63,250.00

Comments: Consigned by Gene Mintz of San Luis Obispo Co., Calif. (p. 100). Generally considered the second finest of the $1000 Montgomerys. Note "crisp, bright and remarkably vivid. Just the slightest hint of a light vertical fold only visible upon close inspection. Ample margins." Photo, bottom page 172.

R. M. Smythe & Co. *New York, N.Y.*	5-6 Sep 2003	VG-F	38	$21,275.00

Comments: Consigned by Chet Krause, founder of Krause Publications in 1952. The T. Harrison Garrett specimen. Note has moderate repairs. Photo, top of page 164.

Heritage Auctions *Dallas, Tex.*	8-10 Jan 2004	cc, Abt VF	511	$18,400.00

Comments: Consigned by Alabamian Frank T. Kennedy. Note depicted as uncancelled but has been cut cancelled, deftly restored. Not endorsed. Photo, p. 172.

 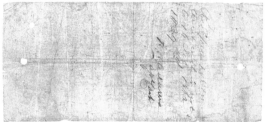

Serial number 397: Front and back.

R. M. Smythe & Co. *New York, N.Y.*	24 July 2004	poc, VG-F	397	$19,550.00

Comments: Consignor unknown. Note has three small punch cancels, pinholes and a fold junction split. Clear margins. Above photo, courtesy R.M. Smythe & Co.

Serial number 86: Front and back.

Heritage Auctions *Dallas, Tex.*	27-28 Apr 2006	cc, F-VF	86	$29,900.00

Comments: Consigned by Ben R. Powel, a noted attorney from Galveston, Tex. Note has a cut cancel repaired with tape. Above photo, courtesy Heritage Auctions.

	Auction House	Sale Date	Grade or Condition	Serial Number	Sales Price

Serial number 327: Heritage Auctions 13-15 Sep 2006 cc, CU 327 $46,000.00
Front and back. Dallas, Tex.

      Comments: Consigned by Troy Wiseman, philanthropist who founded World
      Orphans. Note has repaired cut cancel. Above photo courtesy Heritage Auctions.

Serial number 65: Heritage Auctions 4-6 Jan 2007 Fine 65 $25,300.00
Front and back. Dallas, Tex.

      Comments: Consigned by George P. Hammerly. Note once mounted with stamp
      hinges. A few edge splits. Uncancelled. Above photo courtesy Heritage Auctions.

Serial number 129: R. M. Smythe & Co. 13 Apr 2007 cc, VF 129 $34,500.00
Front and back. New York, N.Y.

      Comments: Consigned by Western Reserve Historical Society in Cleveland. Note
      has seven vertical folds, is neatly cancelled. Above photo courtesy R.M. Smythe.

Auction House	Sale Date	Grade or Condition	Serial Number	Sales Price
R. M. Smythe & Co. *New York, N.Y.*	6 July 2007	cc, XF+	88	$60,375.00

Comments: Consigned by Frederick R. Mayer (1928-2007), a Texas oilman who founded the Exeter Drilling Co., the largest privately owned drilling company in the U.S. (p. 104). A census condition note, previously owned by Philip H. Chase and Douglas B. Ball. Note "is crisp, bright and remarkably vivid. Cancellations done so neatly that they are virtually undetectable from the front." Photo, p. 167.

Auction House	Sale Date	Grade or Condition	Serial Number	Sales Price
R. M. Smythe & Co. *New York, N.Y..*	6 July 2007	cc, F-VF	244	$29,900.00

Comments: Another $1000 Montgomery from Frederick Mayer. Note has been cut cancelled, but the cancellations have been repaired, and a split closed in the left corner. Moderate staining in upper left. Margins clear. Good color. Photo, p. 166.

Serial number 503: Front and back.

Auction House	Sale Date	Grade or Condition	Serial Number	Sales Price
Lyn Knight Currency Auctions *Overland Park, Kan.*	27 June 2008	poc, VF	503	$26,450.00

Comments: Consignor unknown. Note has "two punch cancels near the top and four more in the signatures. Quality is outstanding, totally free of defects. Lovely VF." Note not endorsed. Photo above, courtesy Lyn Knight Currency Auctions.

Auction House	Sale Date	Grade or Condition	Serial Number	Sales Price
Spink Smythe *Dallas, Tex.*	16-17 July 2008	poc, VG	515	$14,015.00

Comments: Consigned by Frederick Forbes Angus of Montreal, Canada, student of Canadian railway history. Note "conserved and the once brilliant green overprint appears a bit washed out. Four small punch holes backed." Photo, bottom p. 165.

Auction House	Sale Date	Grade or Condition	Serial Number	Sales Price
Neal Auction Company *New Orleans, La.*	21-22 Nov 2009	cc, Abt XF	229	$33,460.00

Comments: Consigned by Fisher E. Simmons, Jr., an expert on postal history and steamboats that plied the Mississippi River. Note quarter folded both ways. Bank hammer cancellations at bottom have been fixed with paper strips. Photo, p. 163.

Auction House	Sale Date	Grade or Condition	Serial Number	Sales Price
Neal Auction Company *New Orleans, La.*	21-22 Nov 2009	cc, VF+	306	$26,290.00

Comments: A second $1000 Montgomery from Fisher E. Simmons, Jr. Note has six folds, with one cross-shaped cancellation at bottom, neatly repaired. Photo p. 161.

Auction House	Sale Date	Grade or Condition	Serial Number	Sales Price
Dix Noonan Webb *London, England*	30 Sep 2010	cc, poc, G-VG	571	$18,816.00

Comments: Consignor unknown. Only international auction in database. Note "has cross cancellations and punch holes in signature area, leaving short tear in bottom edge. A few pinholes at left, three creases and light handling, otherwise good to very fine." Photo below, courtesy Dix Noonan Webb, London, England.

Serial number 571: Front and back.

Stack's *New York, N.Y..*	30 Sep 2010	VF 25	15	$46,000.00

Comments: Consigned by the eminent Q. David Bowers, chairman emeritus of Stack's Bowers, prolific numismatic writer and arguably America's premier numismatist of the past fifty years. Note is uncancelled and one of few claiming such a distinction. Stained at either end, with vertical creases. Photo, page 157.

Serial number 381: Front and back.

Neal Auction Company *New Orleans, La.*	20-21 Nov 2010	cc, poc, XF	381	$21,510.00

Comments: Consignor unknown. Note has four 7 mm. cancellation holes, two smaller 4 mm. cancellation holes, partial cancellation punch at top margin, hammer cancelled, slight traces of handling, green stamp on reverse with Savannah, Ga. interest stamp, bright green with crisp paper. Above photo, courtesy Neal Auction Company, New Orleans, La.

The $1,000 Montgomery Note Vs. Crude Oil, Silver and the S&P 500:
Comparative Price Appreciation Since the End of the Civil War

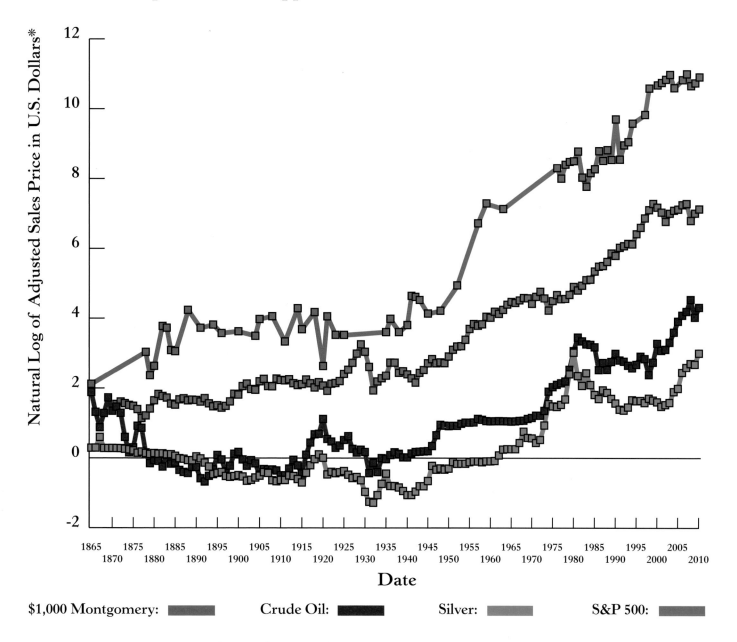

$1,000 Montgomery: ▨   Crude Oil: ▨   Silver: ▨   S&P 500: ▨

Average Annual Rate of Return (Annual Percent Increase)

	From 1865 to 1950	From 1950 Through 2010	Total All Years: 1865 - 2010	Years Needed to Double in Value Since 1950
$1,000 Montgomery Note	1.5%	9.8%	6.6%	7.4
Silver	-1.3%	4.7%	1.6%	15.0
Crude Oil	-0.3%	5.8%	2.4%	12.2
S&P 500 Composite Index	1.8%	7.3%	4.3%	9.8

* The actual average sales price a Confederate Montgomery note, a troy ounce of silver, a barrel of crude oil or a market basket of common stocks comprising the S&P 500 Composite Index fetched during each year. Prices have been adjusted to show as a natural logarithm of the actual sales data to make the graph show differences more clearly. A full explanation of the methodology is provided in Chapter 4, beginning on page 140.

Chapter 5: Part Two

Qualitative Look at the $1,000 Montgomery Note: Its Innate Beauty and Eye Appeal

The Montgomery notes pictured here did not surface at public auction, or at least their serial numbers do not appear in any auction description. Undoubtedly, many did show up in auctions before 1950, when it became commonplace to show serial numbers in descriptions. Pedigreed or not, these notes are as beautiful as those in Part One. Credits on page 299.

The Confederate $500 Montgomery Note:
Its Survival Census and Historical Rate-of-Return

The pastoral Confederate $500 Montgomery note pictured above (classified as Criswell Type-2, varieties 2 and 2-A) is one of only two $500 denominations released by the Confederate Treasury. Like the $1,000 note, only 607 specimens were issued. The central vignette, called "The Crossing," was engraved by James Smille, who Philip Chase called the best miniature pictorial engraver in history. This vignette appeared simultaneously in the North on a $1 note of the North Western Bank of Warren, Penn., and on several other notes still later.

Details about the issuance of the Montgomerys are found earlier and will not be repeated here. I noted that each Montgomery bears the signatures of Alexander B. Clitherall as Register and E.C. Elmore as Treasurer, except for a few $500 Montgomerys with high serial numbers that were signed by Charles T. Jones as Register. Within the survival census, those $500 Montgomerys with numbers 576 or lower have the familiar Clitherall signature as Register. Conversely, those notes numbered 585 or higher have the rare Jones signature as Register, followed by the hand-written date "July 27" next to the signature and *within* the signature block. A sample of Jones' signature and date is shown below. Criswell assigned a different variety number to these notes, Type-2 variety 2-A, although his new number is unwarranted.

Above: Serial number 604 with Jones' signature and 'July 27' date.

According to Doug Ball, who explained, in Smythe's June 1998 auction why Jones signed these notes, when the Confederate capital was relocated to Richmond, Va., Alexander Clitherall chose not to move. Clitherall thus resigned his position as Register, effective July 24, 1861. On that date, those $500 Montgomerys with numbers 577-607 were still unsigned. So Jones, who served as Acting Register when Clitherall was absent, signed these notes on July 27, and someone wrote that date next to his signature. Apparently some doubt surfaced about the legality of Jones' signatures, so the notes were officially dated in the space *above* the signature block "July 23," the day before Clitherall's resignation when Jones would have had the undoubted right to sign for his chief. Doug's explanation, while reasonable, has major errors. According to the records, Clitherall *did* move to Richmond and resigned effective July 22 for health reasons. Thus the significance of the "July 23" and "July 27" dates remains unclear.

The note pictured at the top of the facing page with serial no. 583 is signed and dated differently than all previous Montgomery notes. It carries the Clitherall signature as Register, like all others with numbers below 583, but the "July 27" date has been added within the signature block next to the signature, as is otherwise found only on notes signed by Jones-- yet this "July 27" date is in a different handwriting than all the notes signed by Jones. I have long wondered if this note was executed differently than all lower-numbered notes to signify that this note was the absolute final note that Clitherall signed. I call this $500 Montgomery the "transitional note" to indicate the change from Clitherall signatures to Jones signatures. And with tongue in cheek to illustrate my utter disdain for those, even today, who persist in the mindless proliferation of ultra-minor Confederate varieties, I hereby proclaim this $500 Montgomery note bearing serial number 583 as Criswell Type-2, variety 2-B, possibly unique!

Hugh Shull's Montgomery census dated October 2011 shows 116 $500 Montgomery notes known to survive. I have updated Hugh's census to now include 120 specimens, all shown below. Those serial numbers followed by a parenthetical (A) below are pedigreed to specific auctions found in Part One starting on page 183. Similarly, those serial numbers followed by a parenthetical (B) below, while not pedigreed, are known to exist because we have their photographs in Part Two starting on page 208. Fully 73% of these notes (87) are verified to exist in either Part One or Part Two of this chapter immediately following.

Serial Numbers of Surviving $500 Montgomery Notes as of January 1, 2012:

2 (A) NEW	128 (B)	212 (B)	341	477
4	129 (A)	225 (A)	342 (B) NEW	487 (A) NEW
7 (A)	139 (A)	229	343 (A)	497 (A)
20	141	233	345	498
22 (A)	142 (A)	242 (B)	354 (A)	509 (A)
25 (A)	143	253 (A)	369 (A)	514
41	144 (A)	258 (A)	380 (A)	517 (A)
57 (A)	146	267	388 (A)	520 (A)
59 (A)	147 (B)	269 (B)	402	529 (A)
65 (A)	149	278	406 (A)	536 (A)
66	150 (A)	283 (A)	410	542
68	166 (A)	286 (A)	417 (A)	543 (A)
69 (A)	167 (A)	288 (B)	418 (B)	545 (A)
71 (B)	168	289 (A)	419 (A)	567
72 (B)	169 (A)	290 (B)	422	568
73 (A)	176 (A)	293 (A)	424	569
77	185	297 (A)	425 (B)	576 (A)
85 (A)	191	310 (A)	427 (A)	583 (B)
104 (A)	195	313 (A)	431	585 (A)
107 (A)	196 (A)	322 (A)	433 (A)	593 (B)
120 (A)	198 (A)	331 (A) NEW	434 (A)	594 (A)
123 (A)	201 (A)	332	435 (A)	597 (A)
124 (A)	209 (A)	334 (B)	449 (A)	603 (B)
125 (A)	210 (A)	335 (B)	456 (A)	604 (A)

Those Montgomerys found in Part One of this chapter starting on page 183 define the database for the calculation of a rate of return for the $500 Montgomery note from 1865 through 2010. Rates of return were also obtained for precious metals (i.e., silver), energy (i.e., crude oil), and the stock market (i.e., the S&P 500 Composite Index) to use for comparison.

Results from the $500 Montgomery are virtually identical to those of the $1,000 Montgomery and re-affirm the appropriateness of collecting Confederate Montgomery notes. The $500 Montgomery has increased in value, on average, 6.8% each year since 1865, more than any of the alternative investment opportunities. The much hyped S&P 500 Composite Index placed second, at a rate of return of 4.3% each year (not including the re-investment of any dividends paid, which would add 1.9% to the total annual return[1]). Crude oil and silver trailed sharply.

These results can be seen on the full-page graph on page 207 or on the smaller version below:

The $500 Montgomery Note Vs. Crude Oil, Silver and the S&P 500: Comparative Price Appreciation Since the End of the Civil War

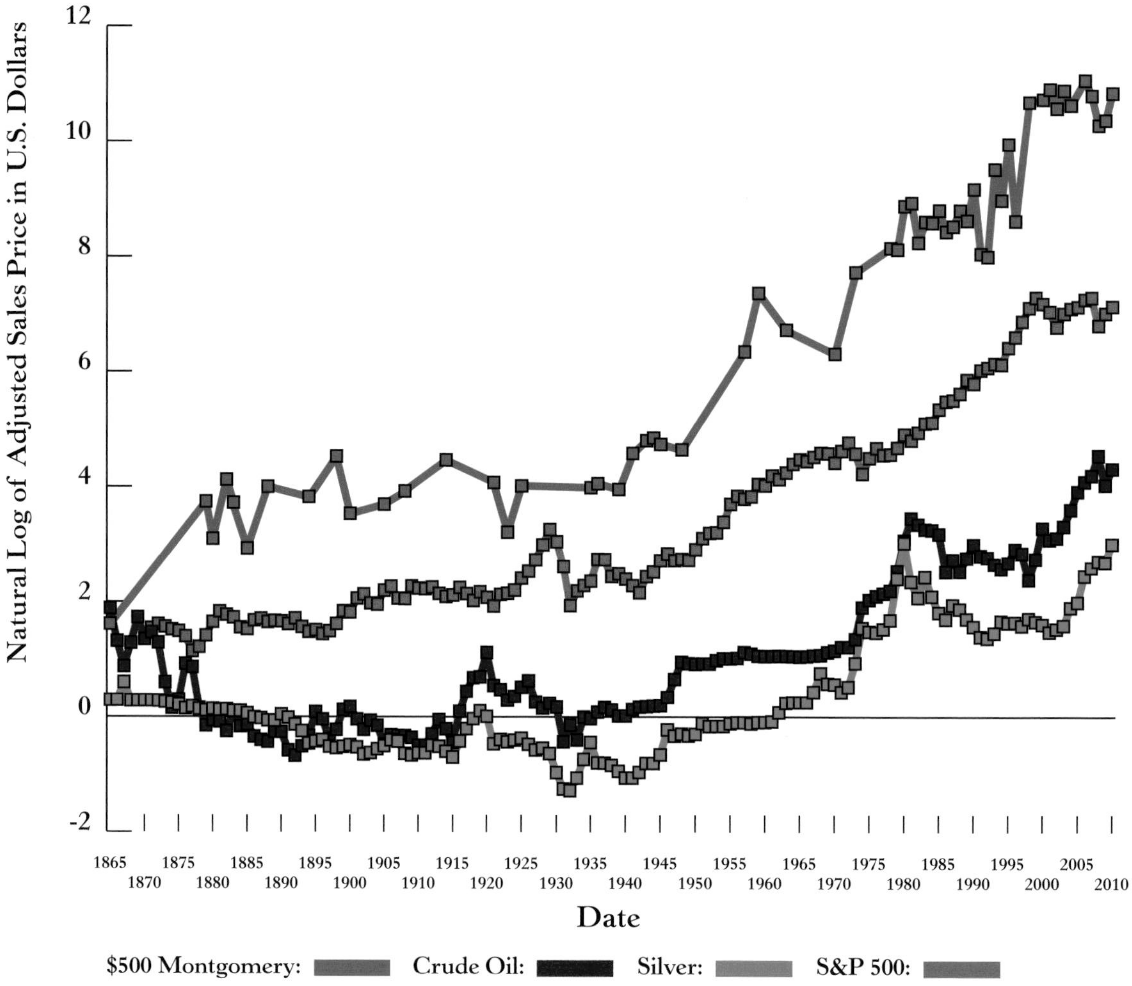

The graph above shows how little any of the four investment choices appreciated between 1865 and 1950. Since 1950, though, all four investment options have shown attractive growth, led by the 9.7% enjoyed by the $500 Montgomery and followed by the S&P 500 at 7.3%.

Said another way, this analysis suggests, that if these historical rates of return are maintained, a $500 Montgomery note purchased January 1, 2011 at a fair market value of $25,000 (as determined in a public auction) would be worth $50,000 on July 1, 2018, about seven and a half years later. On the other hand, an investment of $25,000 on January 1, 2011 in a market basket of common stocks comprising the S&P 500 would not be worth $50,000 until November 1, 2020, nearly 10 years after its purchase.

And frankly, I would rather gaze at a lovely $500 Montgomery note, appreciating both its beauty and its value, than be bored by some clunky silver bullion. Wouldn't you?

[1]Used with permission of, and special thanks to, Bryan Taylor, Ph.D., Global Financial Data, Inc., Los Angeles.

Chapter 6: Part One

Quantitative Look at Auction Sales of the Confederate $500 Montgomery Note In Chronological Order Since 1865

Auction House	Sale Date	Grade or Condition*	Serial Number	Sales Price
William Elliot Woodward *Boston, Mass.*	19 Dec 1865	Fine	-	$2.50

Comments: Consignor unknown. Cannot conclusively establish that this note is a $500 Montgomery, might possibly be the $500 issue of 1864. This note directly follows a $1000 Montgomery in this same auction. Presumably the cataloger would have noted the difference in color if both notes were not Montgomerys, which are green, while the $500 issue of 1864 is pink. Sales price also suggests a Montgomery; the $500 of 1864 sold for only pennies. Note "genuine, fine, scarce."

Bangs & Co. *New York, N.Y.*	25 Mar 1879	poc, Fine	-	$21.00

Comments: Consigned by J. E. Barratt, possibly a physician, who died about 1878. Cataloged by C.H. Bechtel. Barratt owned all four Montgomerys, a Confederate cent and the Lovett dies, which sold for $8.00. Note "cancelled with six small holes. Has been torn and patched, but nothing missing."

Sigismund K. Harzfeld *Philadelphia, Pa.*	9 Apr 1880	Fine	-	$11.00

Comments: Consigned by Ferguson Haines, a noted coin collector born in Maine in 1840. Attended Phillips Academy in Andover, Mass. and Dartmouth. Retailed hardware and manufactured textiles. Served as mayor of Biddeford, Me. and was a member of the Maine House of Representatives. Note "in fine preservation." Note is hand-dated "June 18," indicating a serial number between 232 and 290, according to Raphael Prosper Thian's *Register of the Confederate Debt.*

Legend. ***cc:*** A note with a "cut cancel" has slits usually shaped like a cross but with no paper missing. ***poc:*** A "punch out cancel" is a series of round holes, from one or two up to six or eight, about the size of a pencil eraser. Depending on the number and size of the holes, some paper is missing. ***coc:*** A note with a "cut out cancel" has significant paper missing, usually coming in the shape of a pair of triangles or half-moons. ***pen c:*** A "pen cancel" is an unusual form of cancellation where the word "Cancelled" is written or stamped across the face of the note.

A new war could erupt today over the application of grading standards to Confederate currency. After all, it is the grade that ultimately determines value. Grades in this book are taken from the actual auction catalog description. Certainly grading standards changed over the 150-year duration of these auction results. Abbreviations used, from best to worst, include **CU** - Crisp Uncirculated; **UNC** - Uncirculated; **AU** - About Uncirculated; **XF** - Extremely Fine; **VF** - Very Fine; **F** - Fine; **VG** - Very Good; **G** - Good; **Fr** - Fair and **P** - Poor. A note grading "Crisp Uncirculated" or "Uncirculated" is brand new as if it just came off the printing press. A "Very Fine" note has seen circulation as shown by both vertical and horizontal quarter folds, but the note retains its body or crispness. Conversely, "Good" notes retain no body and have extreme wear, frayed edges or even slight tears, if they do not impinge on the main design.

Auction House	Sale Date	Grade or Condition	Serial Number	Sales Price

Serial number 124:
Front and back.

William Elliot Woodward	28 Dec 1882	VF	124	$35.00
Boston, Mass.				

Comments: Consigned by Paul J. Maas of Laporte, Ind., a major coin collector in the late 1800s. Cataloguer writes "I am unable to quote any price, as I can find no account of its sale." Above photo, courtesy current owner Sidney Scudder, M.D.

John W. Haseltine	10 Apr 1883	VF	-	$23.50
Philadelphia, Pa.				

Comments: Consigned by Harold Newlin, a Pennsylvania attorney who wrote the book on half dimes and dimes. Note "not cancelled. I have seen but one other."

Lyman Haines Low	26 Mar 1885	Ch UNC	-	$11.00
New York, N.Y.				

Comments: Consignor unknown. Note described as "uncirculated, perfect."

David U. Proskey	15 Dec 1885	UNC	-	$20.00
New York, N.Y.				

Comments: From William P. Titcomb, a great early Confederate collector on a par with John Gill and R.P. Thian, into whose auction he consigned this note. Both men had easy access to the "Richmond Hoard." Note "perfect in every respect."

Edouard Frossard	22 Dec 1885	VG	-	$10.50
Brooklyn, N.Y.				

Comments: Consigned by Dr. William Lee, professor and author in 1875 of *The Currency of the Confederate States of America* (page 32). Note "excessively rare."

Serial number 289:
Front and back.

S.H. & H. Chapman	17 Oct 1888	VF	289	$31.00
Philadelphia, Pa.				

Comments: Also consigned by Ferguson Haines (see p. 183). Note "in this state - uncancelled - but three are known." Above photo, courtesy Pink Palace Museum.

Auction House	Sale Date	Grade or Condition	Serial Number	Sales Price
Edouard Frossard *Brooklyn, N.Y.*	14 Nov 1893	poc, UNC	-	-

Comments: Consignor unknown. Note is "punch cancelled, perfect, beautiful."

S.H. & H. Chapman *Philadelphia, Pa.*	3 Dec 1894	VF	-	$34.00

Comments: Consigned by little-known W.H. Spedding. Is "uncancelled, very fine."

Edouard Frossard *Brooklyn, N.Y.*	19 Dec 1894	UNC	-	$35.00

Comments: A third consignment from Ferguson Haines, the noted Maine collector, and certainly the best of the three. Note is "crisp, new, very rare."

Lyman Haines Low *New York, N.Y.*	21 Dec 1898	Good	-	$20.00

Comments: Consigned by James T. Callender, a noted early coin collector, particularly gold coins. Note "complete, in good condition, very rare."

S.H. & H. Chapman *Philadelphia, Pa.*	16 Nov 1900	XF	-	$25.00

Comments: Consigned by the eminent Dr. Edward Maris (1832-1900), a Philadelphia Quaker who assembled comprehensive collections of New Jersey cents, autograph letters, early currency and coins. Note a "beautiful specimen."

Lyman Haines Low *New York, N.Y.*	19 Jan 1905	poc, Fine	-	$20.00

Comments: Consigned by H. G. Brown of Portland, Ore., whose 1804 silver dollar was sold to noted William F. Dunham. Note has three small circular cancellations.

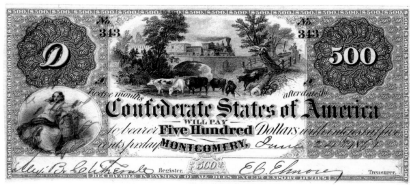

Serial number 343: Front and back.

Henry Chapman *Philadelphia, Pa.*	19-20 Jun 1908	UNC	343	$43.00

Comments: Consigned by Harmon Chambers (1822-1905) of the "Confederate Triumvirate," who founded an insurance brokerage business in Philadelphia (page 51). This note, in the Condition Census, is among the three finest known. Note described as "Uncirculated. Bright, beautiful specimen." Photo above.

Henry Chapman *Philadelphia, Pa.*	19-20 Jun 1908	AU	509	$50.00

Comments: Also consigned by Harmon Chambers. Note "has been folded but does not show on the face. One of the finest specimens known."

	Auction House	Sale Date	Grade or Condition	Serial Number	Sales Price

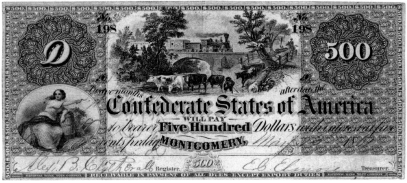

Serial number 198: **Edward Michael**   9 May 1914   VF   198 $50.50
Front and back.   *Chicago, Ill.*

Comments: Consigned by Chicagoan Ben Green (p. 52), first Midwestern coin dealer. Note called "very fine." Above photo, courtesy the late philatelist Gordon Bleuler.

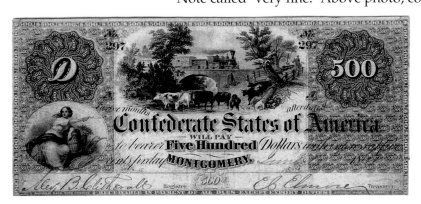

Serial number 297: **Samual Hudson Chapman**   27-29 May 1914   VF   297 $48.00
Front and back.   *Philadelphia, Pa.*

Comments: Consigned by William Gable of Altoona, Pa., founder of a large department store and owner of virtually complete U.S. coin series. Note is "folded but not noticeably damaged." Above photo, courtesy dealer Crutchfield Williams.

Serial number 209: **Thomas Lindsey Elder**   26-27 Aug 1921   UNC   209 $56.00
Front and back.   *New York, N.Y.*

Comments: Consigned by Lewis C. Gehring (1852-1921) of Brooklyn, N. Y., who was born in Rahway, N. J. before moving to Brooklyn. A prominent banker of the Prudential Savings Bank, with interests in feed and milling. This note, in the Condition Census Top Ten, was once owned by John J. Ford. Photo above.

Auction House	Sale Date	Grade or Condition	Serial Number	Sales Price
Stan V. Henkels *Philadelphia, Pa.*	28 July 1922	UNC	-	-

Comments: Consigned by the legendary John C. Browne, perhaps the greatest Confederate collector (see page 58). Part of a 90-note "Uncirculated" type set.

B. Max Mehl *Ft. Worth, Tex.*	17 Apr 1923	VG-F	-	$10.25

Comments: Consignor uncertain. Note is "extremely rare, not cancelled."

Thomas Lindsay Elder *New York, N.Y.*	9-11 Oct 1924	UNC	107	-

Left, serial #107, right, #22.

Comments: Consigned by Edward H. Eckfeldt, Jr. (p. 158). Census condition note, labeled "the finest known." Ex Philip Chase. Photo above left, from Chase's book.

Thomas Lindsay Elder *New York, N.Y.*	9-11 Apr 1925	Fine	-	$26.25

Comments: Consignor unknown. Note "in fine condition and uncancelled."

William Hesslein *Boston, Mass.*	22-23 Nov 1929	AU	-	-

Comments: Consigned by H.D. Allen of Boston, whose articles appeared in *The Numismatist* (page 56). Note "practically uncirculated and beautiful"; probably serial number 331, as Hesslein's September 1929 sale included "a photograph of #331 as a good fill in for the collector who cannot afford to buy an original."

Barney Bluestone *Syracuse, N.Y.*	26 Jan 1935	poc, Fine	22	-

Comments: Consignor unknown. Note "cancelled, strictly fine." Photo, above right.

Serial number 150: Front and back.

Milfred Henry Bolender *Freeport, Ill.*	15 Oct 1935	XF	150	$25.00

Comments: Consigned by dealer A. M. Smith (1841-1915) of Minneapolis. Note, in the Condition Census Top Ten, "has been folded but is choice." Photo above.

	Auction House	Sale Date	Grade or Condition	Serial Number	Sales Price

Serial number 594: *Front and back.*	Benjamin B. DuBose *Ft. Lauderdale, Fla.*	18 Nov 1935	VG-F	594	$35.00

Comments: A little-known auction house operating from Ft. Lauderdale, Fla. and Atlanta, Ga. Dealer Crutchfield Williams discovered this sale and provided the above photo of this rare Criswell variety 2-A with the C.T. Jones signature, one of only a half-dozen or so. Note is uncancelled and not endorsed.

Serial number 543: *Front and back.*	Milfred Henry Bolender *Freeport, Ill.*	8 Feb 1936	poc, Fine	543	$15.00

Comments: Consigned by A. P. Wylie of Wheaton, Ill., a dealer and collector of U.S. coins and currency. Note "hole cancelled." Above photo, Heritage Auctions.

Left, serial #310, right, #406.	John Milford Henderson *Columbus, Oh.*	4 Apr 1936	Fair	310	$20.00

Comments: Consigned by Henri Buck of Delaware, Ohio, ANA member and state president. Note discolored, is missing right bottom corner and a half-inch of left end. Has two short tears. Photo above left, courtesy R.M. Smythe 1992 catalog.

	B. Max Mehl *Ft. Worth, Tex.*	23 Jun 1936	F-VF	-	$26.00

Comments: Consignor uncertain. Note "uncancelled, one of about only six."

Auction House	Sale Date	Grade or Condition	Serial Number	Sales Price
B. Max Mehl *Ft. Worth, Tex.*	22 Mar 1938	AU	406	-

Comments: Consigned by Benjamin H. Collins, detailed on p. 159. Note uncancelled, sold as part of a set of Montgomerys. Photo, bottom right, page 188.

Auction House	Sale Date	Grade or Condition	Serial Number	Sales Price
Thomas Lindsay Elder *New York, N.Y.*	12 May 1939	UNC	209	$52.25

Comments: Consignor uncertain. One of the great $500 Montgomerys, in the Top Ten of the Condition Census, described as "uncirculated, perfection, clean note, a gem." Once owned by John J. Ford, who bought it in 1957. Photo, bottom p. 186.

Auction House	Sale Date	Grade or Condition	Serial Number	Sales Price
Thomas Lindsay Elder *New York, N.Y.*	25 May 1940	VG	-	-

Comments: Consignor uncertain. Note "has several creases."

Auction House	Sale Date	Grade or Condition	Serial Number	Sales Price
B. Max Mehl *Ft. Worth, Tex.*	3 Jun 1941	AU	406	$82.50

Comments: Consigned by Mehl himself, who bought it from Benjamin Collins and included it in the important William Dunham sale (details, p. 160). Note "nearly uncirculated, uncancelled." Photo, bottom right, page 188.

Auction House	Sale Date	Grade or Condition	Serial Number	Sales Price
Milfred Henry Bolender *Freeport, Ill.*	15 Feb 1943	Gem UNC	-	$80.00

Comments: Ostensibly from the collection of the colorful Col. Edward H.R. Green, president of Texas Midland Railroad and son of Hetty Green, the "witch of Wall Street." Serial number unknown. Note an "uncirculated gem, uncancelled."

Auction House	Sale Date	Grade or Condition	Serial Number	Sales Price
B. Max Mehl *Ft. Worth, Tex.*	9 Mar 1943	Fine	166	$77.50

Comments: Consigned by Henry E. Elrod of Houston, Tex., ANA member who focused on European coins. Note "has autographed endorsement on back."

Auction House	Sale Date	Grade or Condition	Serial Number	Sales Price
Milfred Henry Bolender *Freeport, Ill.*	25 Sep 1943	VF	297	$82.50

Comments: Consigned by little-known W.B. Kennedy. Note "uncancelled, very rare." Photo, middle of page 186.

Auction House	Sale Date	Grade or Condition	Serial Number	Sales Price
Barney Bluestone *Syracuse, N.Y.*	27 Jan 1944	VF	-	$72.50

Comments: Consignor unknown. Note is "strictly very fine."

Auction House	Sale Date	Grade or Condition	Serial Number	Sales Price
Barney Bluestone *Syracuse, N.Y.*	27-28 Apr 1945	VF	-	$65.00

Comments: Consignor unknown. Note is "uncancelled and strictly very fine."

Auction House	Sale Date	Grade or Condition	Serial Number	Sales Price
Milfred Henry Bolender *Freeport, Ill.*	20 Mar 1948	VF	497	$60.00

Comments: Consigned by Loring T. Reckard of Chicago, ANA member from 1916 who also collected stamps and coins. Note "very fine." Photo, middle page 192.

Auction House	Sale Date	Grade or Condition	Serial Number	Sales Price
Milfred Henry Bolender *Freeport, Ill.*	2 Oct 1948	Fine	597	$51.00

Comments: Another $500 Montgomery from L. T. Reckard, p. 189. Note very fine.

Federal Coin Exchange *Cleveland, Oh.*	10-13 Jan 1957	poc, Fine	22	$285.00

Comments: Consigned by Charles "Suitcase Charlie" Foster, p. 161. Note is slightly soiled and creased, with six small punch cancels. Photo, middle right, page 187.

Serial number 59: Front and back.

D&W Auction Sales *Baltimore, Md.*	3 Apr 1959	VF	59	$760.00

Comments: Consignor unknown. Note's "signatures somewhat faded. Reverse clean with a few light creases." Above photo, courtesy dealer Hugh Shull.

Federal Brand Enterprises *Cleveland, Oh.*	13-15 Jul 1963	AU	576	$1,125.00

Comments: Consigned by the flamboyant and colorful Grover C. Criswell (see page 81). Note is "practically uncirculated and very rare, especially so choice."

Stack's *New York, N.Y.*	2-5 Oct 1963	Abt. VF	354	$430.00

Comments: Consigned by George O. Walton of Roanoke, Va., founder of the Mid-Atlantic Numismatic Association. Killed while driving to a show in 1962. Note shows "pronounced creases, About Very Fine." Photo, middle right, page 200.

Stack's *New York, N.Y.*	2-5 Oct 1963	VG-F	25	$240.00

Comments: A second $500 Montgomery from George O. Walton. Note is "partially faded and shows improper mounting with cellophane tape many years ago."

Hans M. F. Schulman *New York, N.Y.*	23-25 Mar 1970	poc, Fine	-	$275.00

Comments: Consigned by "Mabbott" or "Rosenbach"; cataloger does not indicate which. Note has "three small punch holes and several ink holes. Badly wrinkled."

New Netherlands Coin Co. *New York, N.Y.*	27 Mar 1973	VF	434	$1,300.00

Comments: Consignor unknown. Note tersely described as having an "endorsed reverse, rare, Very Fine." Photo, top of page 193.

Auction House	Sale Date	Grade or Condition	Serial Number	Sales Price
Kagin's *Des Moines, Ia.*	29-30 Sep 1978	Fine	310	$1,700.00

Comments: Consignor unknown. Note is "Fine, but extensive repairs at left side and lower right corner. Tiny pin holes in center." Photo, lower left, page 188.

NASCA *Rockville Centre, N.Y.*	6-7 Dec 1978	poc, VG	520	$1,312.50

Comments: Consignor unknown. Note "has four punch holes, with a neatly repaired split along a center fold. Soiling." Photo below left, courtesy NASCA.

NASCA *Rockville Centre, N.Y.*	30 Apr - 1 May 1979	poc, Fine+	322	$1,890.00

Left, serial #520, right, #322.

Comments: Consigned by Dr. Van B. Elliott, coin and currency collector. Note is "quarter folded both ways and has six small punch holes, artfully restored. Scattered light staining." Photo above right, courtesy owner Bob Jeter.

NASCA *Rockville Centre, N.Y.*	6-7 Jun 1980	Abt. VF	150	$4,305.00

Comments: Consignor unknown. Note in Condition Census. Uncancelled. Note "clean, vivid and fully margined. Moderate vertical folds." Photo, bottom p. 187.

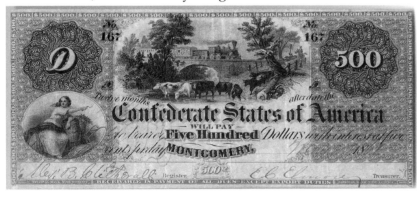 

Serial number 167: Front and back.

Grover C. Criswell *Salt Springs, Fla.*	17 Oct 1980	XF	167	-

Comments: Consigned by little-known Dr. Richard Rich. Note tersely described simply as "Extremely Fine." Above photo, from private Georgia collection.

Grover C. Criswell *Salt Springs, Fla.*	17 Oct 1980	VG+	354	-

Comments: A second $500 Montgomery from Dr. Richard Rich. Note has been restored along some of the fold lines. Good color. Photo, center right, page 200.

	Auction House	Sale Date	Grade or Condition	Serial Number	Sales Price

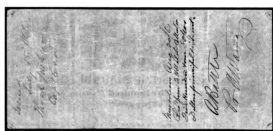

Serial number 123:
Front and back.

Bowers & Ruddy Galleries
Los Angeles, Calif.

25-26 Mar 1981 — VF — 123 — $5,250.00

Comments: From the collection of Harrison Garrett via Johns Hopkins University (full details, p. 164). Note "sharp." Above photo courtesy R.M. Smythe, New York.

Serial number 497:
Front and back.

NASCA
Rockville Centre, N.Y.

10-12 Sep 1981 — Abt. VF — 497 — $6,300.00

Comments: Consigned by Stanley Gibbons, London stamp dealer. Note is "vertically quarter folded. Light back soiling." Above photo, courtesy Joe Bradley.

NASCA
Rockville Centre, N.Y.

10-12 Sep 1981 — poc, VG — 545 — $1,680.00

Comments: Another $500 Montgomery consigned by Stanley Gibbons. Note "punch cancelled, deftly repaired." Photo, below left, from NASCA 1981 catalog.

Left, serial #545,
right, #449.

NASCA
Rockville Centre, N.Y.

19-21 Apr 1982 — AU — 449 — $5,512.50

Comments: Consigned by Grover Criswell, p. 81. Lovely, in the Condition Census Top Ten. Has a "light center fold, with the back endorsement bleeding through. Best $500 Montgomery seen to date." Photo above right, courtesy Tig Sogoian.

Auction House	Sale Date	Grade or Condition	Serial Number	Sales Price

Serial number 434: Front and back.

Christie's
New York, N.Y.
    17 Sep 1982   Fine   434 $1,540.00

> *Comments:* Consigned by Richard F. Saffin, p. 164. Note's "endorsement has bled through to the face. Light finger smudges." Above photo, courtesy Bill Kelly.

Christie's
New York, N.Y.
    8 Dec 1982   Fair   310 $484.00

> *Comments:* Consignor unknown. Note extensively repaired. Photo, bottom p. 188.

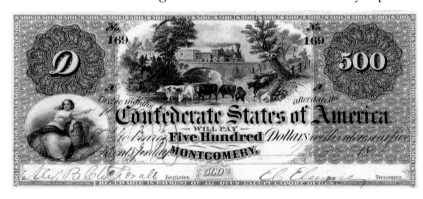 

Serial number 169: Front and back.

NASCA
Rockville Centre, N.Y.
    10-12 Jan 1983   Abt. XF   169 $5,512.50

> *Comments:* Part of the massive John C. Browne collection, consigned by Charles J. Affleck (see page 165). Spectacular note, among the three finest known $500 Montgomery notes. Note has "two light folds, is uncancelled, which is rare, perfectly margined, which is rarer still, and is brightly colored." Photo above.

NASCA
Rockville Centre, N.Y.
    10-12 Jan 1983   cc, poc, Fine   7 $1,050.00

> *Comments:* Also part of the Browne collection consigned by Charles Affleck like above. Note has "four large holes in the signature block, two smaller holes near top and two bank hammer cancellations at center." Photo, top of page 198.

Kagin's
Des Moines, Ia.
    16-20 Aug 1983   VF   104 $2,640.00

> *Comments:* Consignor unknown. Note has "smoothed creases." Photo, page 204.

Auction House	Sale Date	Grade or Condition	Serial Number	Sales Price
NASCA *Rockville Centre, N.Y.*	1-2 Nov 1983	Fair	293	$2,205.00

Comments: Sold to a dealer by Charles Affleck (p. 165) before he died in 1974. Has had extensive restoration. "The worst known $500 Montgomery." Photo, p. 198.

Serial number 435: *Front and back.*	Stack's *New York, N.Y.*	20 Mar 1984 F-VF	435	$2,860.00

Comments: From John L. Roper (1902-1983) of Norfolk, Va., a ship builder. Note is "well folded but with paper crispness." Above photo, courtesy George Tremmel.

 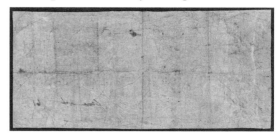

Serial number 419: *Front and back.*	NASCA - Karp *New York, N.Y.*	28-29 Mar 1985 Good	419	$1,595.00

Comments: Consigned by little-known Ben O. Anderson. Note is "stained, repaired splits, shaved borders." Above photo, courtesy Spink Smythe, Dallas, Tx.

Serial number 73: *Front and back.*	NASCA, Div. of Smythe & Co. 7-10 Mar 1986 *New York, N.Y.*	Good	73	$1,100.00

Comments: Consignor unknown. Note horizontally split. Above photo, Bill Kelly.

Auction House	Sale Date	Grade or Condition	Serial Number	Sales Price
NASCA, Div. of Smythe & Co. New York, N.Y.	6 Mar 1987	F-VF	456	$4,070.00

Comments: Consignor unknown. Note "has nine or so folds, is endorsed on the back. Margin complete." Photo, below left, from NASCA 1987 catalog.

Stack's New York, N.Y.	9-11 Sep 1987	poc, cc, VF	253	$1,650.00

Left, serial #456, right, #253.

Comments: Consigned by little-known L.S. Ruder. Note has "cut cancellations and hole cancellations, all repaired with stamp hinges." Photo above right, courtesy The Museum of the Confederacy, Richmond, Va.

Serial number 144: Front and back.

NASCA, Div. of Smythe & Co. New York, N.Y.	25-26 Sep 1987	VF-XF	144	$4,510.00

Comments: Consigned by Douglas Ball (p. 98). Note is "lightly folded, borders are complete, the color vivid." Ex Philip H. Chase. Above photo, courtesy Bill Kelly.

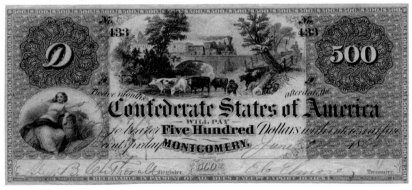 

Serial number 433: Front and back.

NASCA, Div. of Smythe & Co. New York, N.Y.	25-26 Mar 1988	Abt. VF	433	$4,180.00

Comments: Also consigned by Douglas Ball. Note has "six light vertical folds and a trace of a stain." Above photo, courtesy Charles A. Hilton, Graniteville, S.C.

Serial number 176: Front and back.

NASCA, Div. of Smythe & Co. 31 Mar 1989 New York, N.Y.		Fine+	176	$3,520.00

Comments: Consignor unknown. Note is "nicely margined, looks far better than grade would indicate." Above photo, courtesy dealer Hugh Shull, Lexington, S.C.

Left, serial #517, right, #125.

NASCA, Div. of Smythe & Co. 31 Mar 1989 New York, N.Y.		poc, F-VF	517	$2,750.00

Comments: Consignor unknown. Note has "three small and two slightly larger punch holes. Nice margins, good color." Photo above left, from NASCA catalog.

Serial number 85: Front and back.

Christie's New York, N.Y.	7 Sep 1989	VF	85	$3,520.00

Comments: Consigned by brothers Felix and Henri Weil, founders of Medallic Art Co. Note "uncancelled, with bright colors." Above photo courtesy Clint Reynolds.

Christie's New York, N.Y.	7 Sep 1989	G-VG	2	-

Comments: Also consigned by the Weils. This note was part of Lot #322, an album of 193 notes, including both the $50 and $500 Montgomerys. Serial #2 established from the Smythe sale of June 22, 1996, Lot #1384, where Ball references "Serial Number Two."

Auction House	Sale Date	Grade or Condition	Serial Number	Sales Price

Serial number 417:
Front and back.

| NASCA, Div. of Smythe & Co. *New York, N.Y.* | 15-16 Jun 1990 | VF | 417 | $6,050.00 |

Comments: Consignor unknown. Note "looks pristine on its face, is nicely colored, complete margins. Five or so very light folds. Above photo, courtesy Bill Kelly.

Serial number 258:
Front and back.

| R.M. Smythe & Co. *New York, N.Y.* | 27 Jun 1991 | VG-Fine, Repaired | 258 | $1,430.00 |

Comments: Consignor unknown. Note torn in half, deftly restored. Photo above.

| R.M. Smythe & Co. *New York, N.Y.* | 23 Nov 1992 | Abt. VF, Repaired | 310 | $1,870.00 |

Comments: Consignor unknown. Note "deftly restored, moderately heavy foxing, decent margins, six or so folds." Photo lower left, page 188.

Serial number 536:
Front and back.

| R.M. Smythe & Co. *New York, N.Y.* | 18-19 Jun 1993 | Fine+ | 536 | $7,975.00 |

Comments: Consignor unknown. Note has "multiple folds, complete margins."
Above photo, courtesy Dale S. Alberstone Family Trust Collection, Los Angeles, Ca.

	Auction House	Sale Date	Grade or Condition	Serial Number	Sales Price

Serial number 7: Front and back.	R.M. Smythe & Co. *New York, N.Y.*	23 Mar 1994	poc, cc, Abt. VF	7	$5,775.00

Comments: Possibly owned by John Besante, American Impressionist artist. Note "twice cancelled with a bank hammer, with two small punch holes and four larger ones, intact borders." Above photo, courtesy Bill Kelly, Asharoken, N.Y.

R.M. Smythe & Co. *New York, N.Y.*	4-5 Nov 1994	Fine+, Repaired	310	$4,015.00

Comments: Consignor unknown. Note has "extensive restoration work in the left side area, body splits, heavy staining." Photo lower left, page 188.

R.M. Smythe & Co. *New York, N.Y.*	11 Sep 1995	VG	125	$8,250.00

Comments: Once owned by dealer Larry Falater, Allen, Mich. Note cleaned, a bit faded, a trivial closed tear with a back endorsement. Photo right center, p. 196.

R.M. Smythe & Co. *New York, N.Y.*	22 Jun 1996	F-VF, Repaired	293	$3,245.00

Comments: Once owned by Charles J. Affleck, later appearing in NASCA's 1983 Abner Reed sale. Note has been extensively restored on both sides. Color is off, possibly from the chemicals used in restoration. Photo below from R.M. Smythe.

Left, serial #293, right, #57.	Stack's *New York, N.Y.*	11-12 Mar 1998	poc, VF	57	$20,900.00

Comments: From the Museum of Conn. History's Joseph C. Mitchelson Collection. Mitchelson (1856-1911) of Tariffville, Conn. was a major tobacco dealer. Owned nearly complete collections of colonial coins, private gold issues, fractional and Confederate currency. Note "bright and fresh, with a hint of brown discoloration. Six punch cancels, all well centered." Photo above right, from Stack's catalog.

Auction House	Sale Date	Grade or Condition	Serial Number	Sales Price

Serial number 120: Front and back.

| R.M. Smythe & Co. *New York, N.Y.* | 19 Jun 1998 | coc, Abt. XF | 120 | $26,400.00 |

Comments: From Arnold Cowan, a top yachtsman from Long Beach, Cal. Note "has two light folds, good margins, nice color. Was cut cancelled on the bottom edge, deftly restored." Above photo, courtesy current owner Marc Helm.

Serial number 604: Front and back.

| R.M. Smythe & Co. *New York, N.Y.* | 19 Jun 1998 | F-VF | 604 | $37,400.00 |

Comments: Also from Arnold Cowan. Note has "nine or so folds, is uncancelled, with good color and ample margins." The rare Criswell variety 2-A with C.T. Jones' signature, with only a half-dozen or so known to exist. Photo above.

| R.M. Smythe & Co. *New York, N.Y.* | 19 Jun 1998 | Fine+ | 210 | $25,300.00 |

Comments: Yet another from Arnold Cowan. Note has "complete borders, good color, crisp paper." Photo below left, courtesy conservationist Paul Thevenet.

| R.M. Smythe & Co. *New York, N.Y.* | 18-19 Sep 1998 | F-VF | 434 | $28,600.00 |

Left, serial #210, right, #434.

Comments: From John Sanderson. Note stained in lower right corner, back endorsed, ink bleed through. Photo above right, courtesy Bill Kelly (see front and back, p. 193).

	Auction House	Sale Date	Grade or Condition	Serial Number	Sales Price

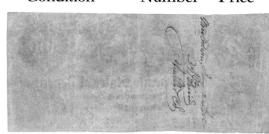

Serial number 196: Front and back.

| | Bowers & Merena Galleries Wolfeboro, N.H. | 9-12 Aug 2000 | Fine | 196 | $23,000.00 |

Comments: From the Franklin Institute in Philadelphia. Note slightly aged with numerous creases, complete margins, bright color. Above photo courtesy Stack's.

| | M&M America, Ltd. Washington, D.C. | 3 Aug 2001 | Fine | 65 | - |

Comments: Consignor unknown. Extensive restoration. Photo, top of page 201.

Left, serial #69, right, #354.

| | Lyn Knight Currency Auc. Overland Park, Kan. | 17-18 Aug 2001 | VF | 69 | $28,644.00 |

Comments: Consignor unknown. Major repairs. Photo above courtesy Lyn Knight.

Serial number 201: Front and back.

| | Heritage Auctions Dallas, Tex. | 21-22 Sep 2001 | VF-XF | 201 | $38,500.00 |

Comments: Consigned by Dr. Walter B. Jones (1895-1977), State Geologist for Ala. Note has vivid color, minimal wear, original. Above photo from W. McNair Tornow.

| | Lyn Knight Currency Auc. Overland Park, Kan. | 30 Nov 2001 | Fine+ | 354 | - |

Comments: Consignor unknown. Repairs. Photo above right courtesy Lyn Knight.

Auction House	Sale Date	Grade or Condition	Serial Number	Sales Price
Heritage Auctions *Dallas, Tex.*	10-12 Jan 2002	VF-XF	201	$25,300.00

Comments: Consignor unknown. Vivid color, minimal wear. Photo, bottom p. 200.

Serial number 65:
Front and back.

Lyn Knight Currency Auc. *Overland Park, Kan.*	24-27 Apr 2003	F-VF	65	$16,100.00

Comments: Consignor unknown. Extensive, though professional, restoration. Clear signatures. Above photo, courtesy Amanda Sheheen, A&O Currency, LLC.

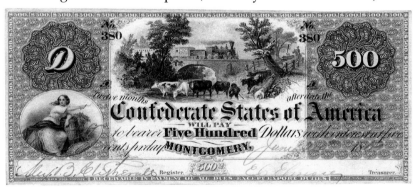

Serial number 380:
Front and back.

R.M. Smythe & Co. *New York, N.Y.*	13-14 Jun 2003	VF-XF	380	$63,250.00

Comments: Consigned by Gene Mintz (p. 100). Striking note in the Condition Census Top Ten. Note is "a choice example," with excellent color and ample margins. Appears Uncirculated. Neither cancelled nor endorsed. Photo above.

Serial number 225:
Front and back.

R.M. Smythe & Co. *New York, N.Y.*	5-6 Sep 2003	VG, Repaired	225	$18,400.00

Comments: Consigned by Chet Krause, founder of Krause Publications in 1952. Note pressed and professionally repaired. Above photo, courtesy R.M. Smythe.

	Auction House	Sale Date	Grade or Condition	Serial Number	Sales Price

Serial number 283: Front and back. Heritage Auctions, Dallas, Tex. — 8-10 Jan 2004 — VF — 283 — $22,200.00

Comments: Consigned by Alabamian Frank T. Kennedy. Note enhanced by minor repairs, outstanding eye appeal. Above photo, courtesy Heritage Auctions.

Left, serial #529, right, #543. Lyn Knight Currency Auc., Overland Park, Kan. — 10-13 Jun 2004 — VF — 529 — $20,700.00

Comments: Consignor unknown. Note "shows no signs of redemption and if cancelled I have not been able to see it." Photo above left, courtesy Lyn Knight.

Serial number 313: Front and back. R.M. Smythe & Co., New York, N.Y. — 24 July 2004 — Fine — 313 — $29,325.00

Comments: Consignor unknown. Note has "four clear margins and nice color. Strictly original in every way." Above photo, courtesy R.M. Smythe, New York.

Heritage Auctions, Dallas, Tex. — 27-28 Apr 2006 — poc, Fine — 543 — $37,375.00

Comments: Consigned by Ben R. Powel, a noted attorney. Has "punch cancels and possibly a pinhole. Sound edges." Photo, middle page 188.

Auction House	Sale Date	Grade or Condition	Serial Number	Sales Price

Serial number 142: Front and back.

R.M. Smythe & Co. *New York, N.Y.*	12 July 2006	Fine	142	$30,475.00

Comments: Consignor unknown. Has "four heavy vertical folds. Endorsement on back bleeds to front. Corners rounded." Above photo, courtesy R.M. Smythe.

Heritage Auctions *Dallas, Tex.*	13-15 Sep 2006	poc, Fine	543	$28,750.00

Comments: Consigned by Troy Wiseman, philanthropist who founded World Orphans. Note has three small circular punch cancels. Photo, middle page 188.

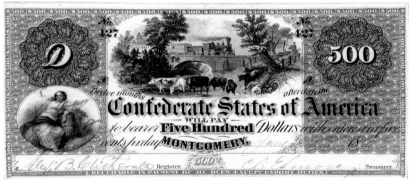

Serial number 427: Front and back.

Heritage Auctions *Dallas, Tex.*	4-6 Jan 2007	Ch AU	427	$57,500.00

Comments: Consigned by William A. Bond, a Texan who was an avid hunter and collector of Civil war relics. Simply stunning note, among the Top Three of the Condition Census. "Brilliant color, hint of a center fold, solid edges." Photo above.

Serial number 388: Front and back.

Heritage Auctions *Dallas, Tex.*	4-6 Jan 2007	VG-F	388	$21,850.00

Comments: Consigned by George P. Hammerly. Has "a few edge splits and tears repaired with stamp hinges." Above photo, courtesy Heritage Auctions.

	Auction House	Sale Date	Grade or Condition	Serial Number	Sales Price

Serial number 585: Front and back.

| | R.M. Smythe & Co. New York, N.Y. | 13 Apr 2007 | VF | 585 | $31,050.00 |

Comments: Consigned by the Western Reserve Historical Society, Cleveland. Rare variety 2-A with C.T. Jones' signature. Above photo, courtesy R.M. Smythe.

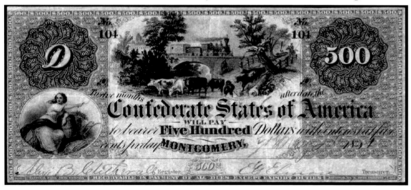 

Serial number 104: Front and back.

| | R.M. Smythe & Co. New York, N.Y. | 6 July 2007 | VF | 104 | $27,600.00 |

Comments: Consigned by Frederick R. Mayer, p. 104. Note "has a few pinholes, trimmed close on left, vivid green color." Above photo, courtesy R.M. Smythe.

| | R.M. Smythe & Co. New York, N.Y. | 6 July 2007 | VF | 123 | $26,450.00 |

Comments: Also from Frederick Mayer. Note has "a few pinholes, trivial rust stains, trace of bleed through." The Garrett specimen. Photo, top of page 192.

 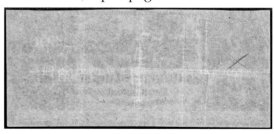

Serial number 286: Front and back.

| | Lyn Knight Currency Auc. Overland Park, Kan. | 27 Jun 2008 | VF+ | 286 | $31,050.00 |

Comments: Consignor unknown. Note has dynamic colors and a bold presentation, with even centering. Above photo, courtesy Donald Kagin, Ph.D.

Auction House	Sale Date	Grade or Condition	Serial Number	Sales Price

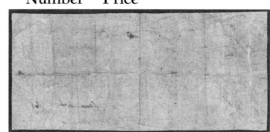

Serial number 419:
Front and back.

| Spink Smythe | 16-17 July 2008 | VG-F, | 419 | $9,875.00 |
| Dallas, Tex. | | Repaired | | |

Comments: Consigned by Frederick Forbes Angus of Montreal, Canada, student of Canadian railway history. Note has "professional restorations, predominantly along the vertical center fold." Above photo, courtesy Spink Smythe, Dallas, Tex.

Serial number 369:
Front and back.

| Spink Smythe | 26-27 Jun 2009 | poc, Abt. Fine | 369 | $17,350.00 |
| Dallas, Tex. | | | | |

Comments: Consignor unknown. Note "has vivid green tints and decent signatures. Strictly original, with two small punch holes." Above photo, courtesy Spink Smythe, Dallas, Tex.

Serial number 129:
Front and back.

| Neal Auction Company | 21-22 Nov 2009 | Ch XF | 129 | $25,095.00 |
| New Orleans, La. | | | | |

Comments: Consigned by Fisher E. Simmons, Jr., an expert on postal history and steamboats that plied the Mississippi River. Note "has excellent color and crisp paper, traces of vertical folds on reverse, nice borders, an ink stain, endorsed in red ink on reverse." Above photo, courtesy Neal Auction Co., New Orleans, La.

Auction House	Sale Date	Grade or Condition	Serial Number	Sales Price
Heritage Auctions Dallas, Tex.	28-30 Apr 2010	Ch VF	286	$34,500.00

Comments: Consignor unknown. Note has "nice color, bright paper, strong signatures and not a trace of restoration. Was once hinged, a very common practice among early collectors." Once owned by Donald Kagin, who showed me this beautiful note at Long Beach some years ago. Photo, bottom page 204.

Serial number 139: Front and back.	Stack's New York, N.Y.	30 Sep 2010	VF	139	$43,125.00

Comments: Consigned by the eminent Q. David Bowers, chairman emeritus of Stack's Bowers, prolific numismatic writer and arguably America's premier numismatist of the past fifty years. Note has "the look of a new note at first glance. Except for being a bit tight at the far left, the margining is quite superior. A historic piece in excellent condition." Above photo, courtesy Stack's, New York.

Serial number 487: Front and back.	Neal Auction Company New Orleans, La.	20-21 Nov 2010	cc, poc, AU	487	$25,095.00

Comments: Consignor unknown. Note has "four 7 mm. punch cancellations at bottom, two smaller 4 mm. cancellations at top, hammer cancelled, green Savannah, Ga. interest stamp on reverse. Above photo, courtesy Neal Auction Company, New Orleans, La.

The $500 Montgomery Note Vs. Crude Oil, Silver and the S&P 500: Comparative Price Appreciation Since the End of the Civil War

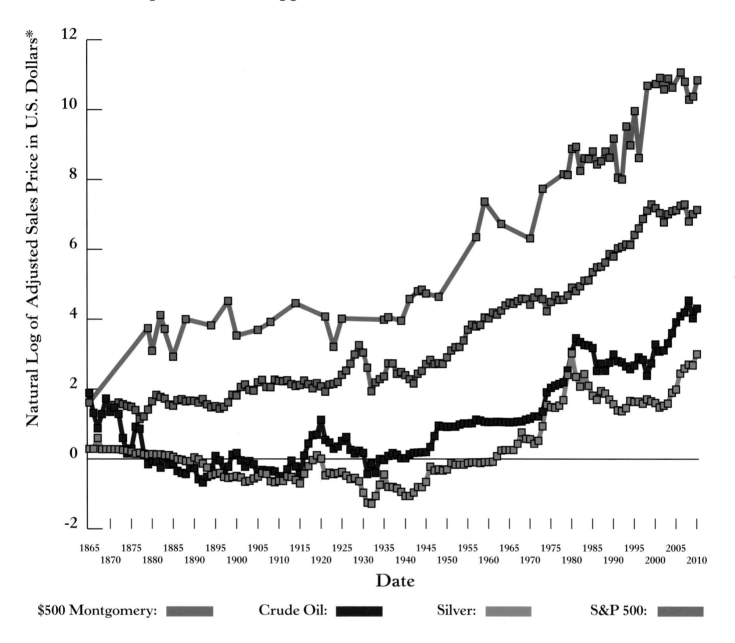

$500 Montgomery:　　Crude Oil:　　Silver:　　S&P 500:

Average Annual Rate of Return (Annual Percent Increase)

	From 1865 to 1950	From 1950 Through 2010	Total All Years: 1865 - 2010	Years Needed to Double in Value Since 1950
$500 Montgomery Note	2.0%	9.7%	6.8%	7.5
Silver	-1.3%	4.7%	1.6%	15.0
Crude Oil	-0.3%	5.8%	2.4%	12.2
S&P 500 Composite Index	1.8%	7.3%	4.3%	9.8

* The actual average sales price a Confederate Montgomery note, a troy ounce of silver, a barrel of crude oil or a market basket of common stocks comprising the S&P 500 Composite Index fetched during each year. Prices have been adjusted to show as a natural logarithm of the actual sales data to make the graph show differences more clearly. A full explanation of the methodology is provided in Chapter 4, beginning on page 140.

Chapter 6: Part Two

Qualitative Look at the $500 Montgomery Note: Its Innate Beauty and Eye Appeal

The serial numbers of the Montgomery notes pictured on this spread do not appear in public auction records, although they may well have been auctioned at some point. It only became common practice to show serial numbers in auction catalogs from 1950 forward. Although undocumented, these notes are as visually appealing as those in Part One. Credits on page 300.

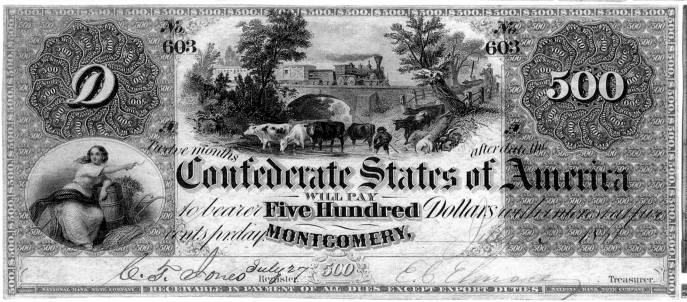

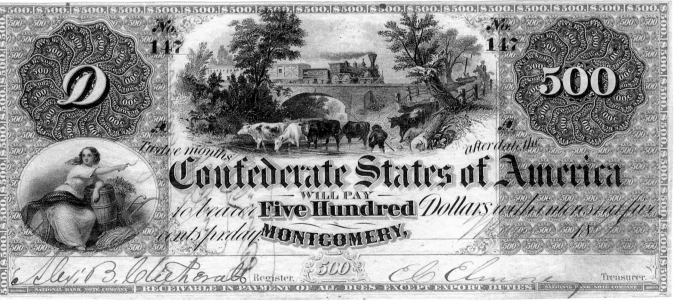

Chapter 7: Summary of Findings

The Confederate $100 Montgomery Note:
Its Survival Census and Historical Rate-of-Return

The impressive and striking Confederate $100 Montgomery note pictured above (classified as Criswell Type-3, variety 3) is the second of the Montgomery series to be adorned with a locomotive and illustrates the vital role transportation played in the Southern economy. Like the $50 note, a total of 1,606 specimens were issued during two different print runs. According to Arlie Slabaugh's *Confederate States Paper Money*, this same vignette was found both on a $3 note of the American Bank, Baltimore, Md., and a $5 note of the Commercial Bank, Memphis, Tenn., concurrent with its use on the Montgomery note above. Its frequent confusion with the locomotive vignette appearing on the Confederate $100 First Richmond note (Criswell Type-5, variety 5) is surprising, since the locomotive on the two notes is moving in different directions.

Details about the issuance of the Montgomery notes are found on pages 148-149 and will not be repeated here. It was noted earlier that the National Bank Note Company of New York originally printed 607 sheets of Treasury notes, with each sheet containing one each of the denominations of $1,000, $500, $100 and $50. The first 607 sheets were delivered to Montgomery, Ala., then the Confederate capital, on April 2, 1861, just before war erupted.

Upon delivery, Treasury Secretary Memminger immediately realized that demand would be stronger for the smaller denominations, so he contacted his New York agent to ask the supplier to furnish an additional 1,000 impressions of each of the $100 and $50 notes. The company prepared a new plate and printed another 1,000 two-subject sheets just of the $100 and $50 values, which were delivered to Montgomery about May 3, 1861 -- well after war erupted.

Of the 1,000 additional impressions of the $100 and $50 denominations printed by the National Bank Note Company, 999 of them were issued, bearing serial numbers 608-1606, according to Raphael Thian's *Register*. Many researchers have wondered what happened to the 1,000th sheet. The mystery has been solved in a letter dated May 7, 1861 from Secretary Memminger to Major George B. Clitherall in Mobile, Ala., shown at the top of the next page:

"Sir: You will please proceed without delay to New Orleans, and after consulting with Messrs. Samuel Smith and J.D. Denegre, make a contract for the printing of five thousand impressions of Treasury notes, *corresponding as nearly as possible to the sample herewith furnished you* [Author's italics], to be numbered from 1,607, consecutively, letter B."

Thus the 1,000th and final sheet of the second printing of the $100 and $50 Montgomerys bearing serial number 1607 was used as a model for the $100 and $50 First Richmond issues printed in New Orleans by the Southern Bank Note Company, a fact that explains the great similarity in appearance between the Montgomery and First Richmond issues.

With a miniscule 607 specimens of the $1,000 and $500 Montgomerys issued (all of the first printing) and a still-tiny 1,606 impressions of the $100 and $50 Montgomerys released (607 of the first printing and 999 more of the second), I noted in Chapter 5 (see page 149) how dealers and collectors alike have tried for many years to maintain a census of those Montgomerys which survived the Civil War. This effort was started by my mentor and friend Douglas B. Ball in the mid 1970s and has been maintained and updated by passionate collectors and current dealers ever since, most notably dealer Hugh Shull of Lexington, S.C.

The survival census for the $100 Montgomerys has been updated and is shown on the next page. But Doug Ball raised a perplexing question about the survival rates of the $100 and $50 Montgomery notes years ago -- and the question is still baffling years later. Doug noted that the survival rate of the first printing of the $100 and $50 Montgomery notes was far lower than the survival rates of their second printing. In fact, it is remarkable that far fewer $100 and $50 Montgomerys of the first printing survived the Civil War than either of the $1,000 or $500 Montgomerys. The chart below illustrates the dramatic difference:

Comparison of Montgomery Note Survival Rates by First and Second Printings:

	$1,000	$500	$100	$50
Number Issued from 1st Printing:	607	607	607	607
Number Surviving from 1st Printing:	130	120	37	51
Percentage Surviving from 1st Printing:	21.4%	19.8%	6.1%	8.4%
Number Issued from 2nd Printing:	-0-	-0-	999	999
Number Surviving from 2nd Printing:	-	-	147	125
Percentage Surviving from 2nd Printing:	-	-	14.7%	12.5%

The chart above shows that about 20% of both the $1,000 and $500 Montgomerys survived the Civil War. But significantly fewer -- less than 10% -- of the $100 and $50 Montgomerys of the first printing survived, despite all four notes being delivered and issued at the same time. Even the second printing of the $100 and $50 Montgomery notes has lower survival rates than the only printing of the $1,000 and $500 -- about 12-15% compared to about 20%.

These differences are real -- mathematicians would call them "statistically significant" -- yet no one knows why. I suspect that the lower denominated $100 and $50 Montgomerys saw far more circulation than the $1,000 or $500 Montgomerys, both of which would be viewed as oddities even today. Part of the explanation might be that the more extensive circulation seen by the $100 and $50 led them to break down and wear out more quickly than the higher denominations -- but even that explanation fails to reconcile the large differences in survival rates between the first and second printings of the $100 and $50 Montgomery notes.

Hugh Shull's most recent Montgomery census dated October 2011 (with hand annotations) shows 178 $100 Montgomery notes known to survive. I have updated Hugh's census to now include 184 specimens, all shown below. Those serial numbers followed by a parenthetical (A) below are pedigreed to specific auctions found in Part One starting on page 214. Similarly, those serial numbers followed by a parenthetical (B) below, while not pedigreed, are known to exist because we have their photographs in Part Two starting on page 246. Any serial number new to Shull's latest census is designated with a green oval. Fully 65% of these serial numbers (119) are verified to exist in either Part One or Part Two of this chapter.

Serial Numbers of Surviving $100 Montgomery Notes as of January 1, 2012:

6 (A)	662 (A)	913 (A)	1139	1337 (A)
12 (B)	666 (A)	916 (A)	1140 (A)	1338 (A)
21 (A)	685	917	1141 (B)	1342 (A)
34 (A)	708	918 (A)	1142 (A)	1343
44	716	943	1143 (A)	1344 (B)
49 (B)	729	948 (A)	1144	1346 (A)
72	776	985	1146 (B)	1350 (A)
110	779	987 (A)	1147 (A)	1367 (A)
124 (A)	792	1001 (A)	1148 (B)	1376 (A)
140 (A)	811 (B) NEW	1004	1149 (A)	1378 (A)
167 (B)	813 (A)	1006 (A)	1150 (A)	1379
209 (B)	814 (B)	1010 (B)	1168 (B)	1380 (B)
215 (A)	815 (A)	1014 (A)	1189	1381
242 (B)	820	1015	1200	1382 (A)
264	822 (B)	1016	1201	1390 (A)
269 (B)	830	1018 (A)	1202	1397 (A)
284	831 (A)	1019 (A)	1203	1402 (A)
297 (B)	832 (A)	1020 (A)	1216 (A)	1419 (B)
298	833 (B)	1021 (A)	1227 (B)	1429 (B)
306 (B) NEW	834	1023	1228 (A)	1441 (A)
314 (A)	838	1025 (A)	1229	1452 (A)
319 (B)	851	1026 (A)	1235	1461 (A)
386 (A)	858 (A)	1043	1236 (A)	1471 (A)
397	859	1049	1237 (B)	1474
400	861	1066	1240	1478 (B)
408 (A)	862 (A)	1067 (A)	1249 (B)	1488
491	863	1074 (B) NEW	1262 (B)	1492 (A)
508 (B)	864 (A)	1076	1264 (A)	1497 (A)
512 (B)	884 (B)	1081 (A)	1266	1508 (B)
530	885 (B)	1088 (A)	1278	1537 (B)
532	886 (B)	1091 (B)	1279 (A)	1539 (A)
536	887 (A)	1095 (A)	1285 (A)	1547
539 (A)	888	1096 (B)	1286	1550 (A)
553 B)	889 (A)	1098	1287	1557
567 (A)	890 (B)	1102 (A)	1294 (A)	1602
569 (B)	892 (A) NEW	1117	1300	1604 (A) NEW
602	906 (A)	1137 (A) NEW	1329 (A)	

Those Montgomerys found in Part One of this chapter starting on page 214 define the database for the calculation of a rate of return for the $100 Montgomery note from 1865 through 2010. Rates of return were also obtained for precious metals (i.e., silver), energy (i.e., crude oil), and the stock market (i.e., the S&P 500 Composite Index) to use for comparison.

Results from the $100 Montgomery wallop those from the $1,000 and $500 Montgomerys and add an exclamation point to the rightness of collecting Confederate Montgomery notes. The $100

Montgomery has increased in value, on average, 7.4% each year since 1865, more than any of the alternative investment opportunities. The ballyhooed S&P 500 Composite Index placed second, at a rate of return of 4.3% each year (not including the re-investment of any dividends paid, which would add 1.9% to the total annual return[1]). Crude oil and silver trailed sharply.

These results can be seen on the full-page graph on page 245 or on the smaller version below:

The $100 Montgomery Note Vs. Crude Oil, Silver and the S&P 500:
Comparative Price Appreciation Since the End of the Civil War

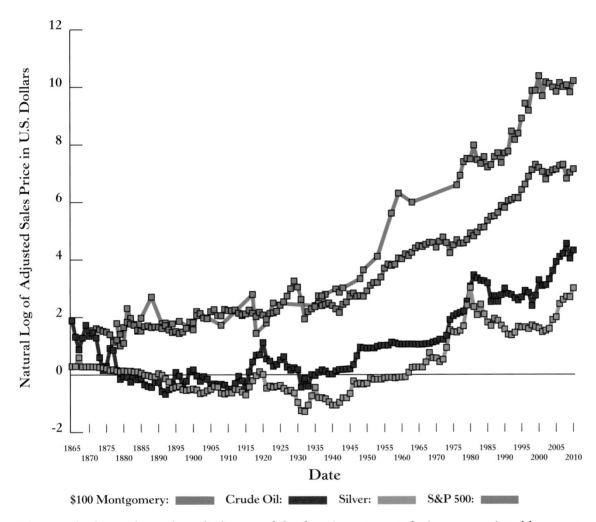

The graph above shows how little any of the four investment choices appreciated between 1865 and 1950. Since 1950, though, all four investment options have shown attractive growth, led by the flashy 11.0% enjoyed by the $100 Montgomery, followed by the S&P 500 at 7.3%.

Said another way, this analysis suggests that, if these historical rates of return are maintained, a $100 Montgomery note purchased January 1, 2011 at a fair market value of $25,000 (as determined in a public auction) would be worth $50,000 on August 1, 2017, about six and a half years later. On the other hand, an investment of $25,000 on January 1, 2011 in a market basket of common stocks comprising the S&P 500 would not be worth $50,000 until November 1, 2020, nearly 10 years after its purchase.

And I know that a stunning and lovely $100 Montgomery note is easier on my eyes than a rusty, albeit valuable, barrel filled with sticky, viscous, sour, foul-smelling, brown crude oil.

[1]Used with permission of, and special thanks to, Bryan Taylor, Ph.D., Global Financial Data, Inc., Los Angeles.

Chapter 7: Part One

Quantitative Look at Auction Sales of the Confederate $100 Montgomery Note In Chronological Order Since 1865

Auction House	Sale Date	Grade or Condition*	Serial Number	Sales Price
John W. Haseltine *Philadelphia, Pa.*	24-25 Apr 1878	UNC	-	$6.50

Comments: It is surprising that the first $100 Montgomery note was sold at public auction over 12 years after the first $1000 and $500 Montgomerys, both far rarer. This note is from Haseltine's own collection of Confederate currency and bonds. It is hand-dated "May 22," indicating a serial number between 1239 and 1450, according to R. P. Thian's *Register* (p. 41). Note is "Uncirculated and clean, rare."

Bangs & Co. *New York, N.Y.*	16 Nov 1978	UNC	-	$5.50

Comments: Consignor unknown. Note is also hand-dated "May 22," indicating a serial number between 1239 and 1450. Note is "Uncirculated and clean."

Bangs & Co. *New York, N.Y.*	25 Mar 1879	UNC	-	$2.75

Comments: Consigned by J. E. Barratt, possibly a physician, who died about 1878. Cataloged by C.H. Bechtel. Barratt owned all four Montgomerys, a Confederate cent and the Lovett dies, which sold for $8.00. Hand-dated "May 16," indicating a serial number between 985 and 1237. Note is "Uncirculated, beautiful, clean."

John W. Haseltine *Philadelphia, Pa.*	10 Feb 1880	poc, Fine	-	$1.50

Comments: Consignor unknown. Hand-dated "May 16," indicating a serial number between 985 and 1237. Note is "Fine, cancelled by small punch holes."

*Legend. **cc**:* A note with a "cut cancel" has slits usually shaped like a cross but with no paper missing.
poc: A "punch out cancel" is a series of round holes, from one or two up to six or eight, about the size of a pencil eraser. Depending on the number and size of the holes, some paper is missing.
coc: A note with a "cut out cancel" has significant paper missing, usually coming in the shape of a pair of triangles or half-moons.
pen c: A "pen cancel" is an unusual form of cancellation where the word "Cancelled" is written or stamped across the face of the note.

A new war could erupt today over the application of grading standards to Confederate currency. After all, it is the grade that ultimately determines value. Grades in this book are taken from the actual auction catalog description. Certainly grading standards changed over the 150-year duration of these auction results. Abbreviations used, from best to worst, include **CU** - Crisp Uncirculated; **UNC** - Uncirculated; **AU** - About Uncirculated; **XF** - Extremely Fine; **VF** - Very Fine; **F** - Fine; **VG** - Very Good; **G** - Good; **Fr** - Fair and **P** - Poor. A note grading "Crisp Uncirculated" or "Uncirculated" is brand new as if it just came off the printing press. A "Very Fine" note has seen circulation as shown by both vertical and horizontal quarter folds, but the note retains its body or crispness. Conversely, "Good" notes retain no body and have extreme wear, frayed edges or even slight tears, if they do not impinge on the main design.

Auction House	Sale Date	Grade or Condition	Serial Number	Sales Price
John W. Haseltine *Philadelphia, Pa.*	16 Jun 1881	poc, Fine	-	$5.00

Comments: Consigned by Henry Ahlbornges, a German immigrant born in 1835 who came to America in 1855 and was living in Boston in 1860. In 1875 he published a list of coins he wished to buy, and he owned an elusive 1804 silver dollar. Note is "Fine, cancelled by small punch holes, very rare."

John Walter Scott *New York, N.Y.*	20 Mar 1882	Fine	-	$4.25

Comments: Consigned by little-known William P. Brown. Note is "very rare."

William Elliot Woodward *Boston, Mass.*	28 Dec 1882	UNC	-	$6.00

Comments: Consigned by Paul J. Maas of Laporte, Ind., a major coin collector in the late 1800s. Note described as "Uncirculated and clean."

John W. Haseltine *Philadelphia, Pa.*	10 Apr 1883	cc, UNC	-	$7.50

Comments: Consigned by Harold P. Newlin, a Pennsylvania attorney who "wrote the book" titled *The Early Half Dimes of the United States* on half dimes and dimes. Note described as "clean, cancelled by smooth cut. Excessively rare."

John W. Haseltine *Philadelphia, Pa.*	15-16 Nov 1883	UNC	-	$4.50

Comments: Consigned by little-known Bernard Schramm. Note is "Uncirculated, new and clean. Uncancelled. Very rare in this condition."

John W. Haseltine *Philadelphia, Pa.*	12-13 Mar 1884	UNC	-	$4.35

Comments: Consignor unknown. Note tersely described as "Uncirculated. Rare."

William Elliot Woodward *Boston, Mass.*	13 Oct 1884	UNC	-	$5.50

Comments: Consignor unknown. Note simply described as "Uncirculated and uncancelled, extremely rare."

Henry G. Sampson *New York, N.Y.*	12-13 Feb 1885	UNC	892	$4.50

Comments: Consignor unknown. Note simply described as "Uncirculated. Very rare. Series A."

Lyman Haines Low *New York, N.Y.*	26 Mar 1885	VF	-	$4.05

Comments: Consignor unknown. Note is "Very Fine, clean, rare."

Lyman Haines Low *New York, N.Y.*	26 Mar 1885	Fine	-	$2.00

Comments: Consignor unknown. Note is "a duplicate of last. Fine, a trifle soiled."

Auction House	Sale Date	Grade or Condition	Serial Number	Sales Price
David U. Proskey *New York, N.Y.*	15 Dec 1885	poc, Good	-	$5.25

Comments: From a "Betts," presumably Benjamin (1822-1908), a founder of the ANS who consigned this note to the celebrated auction of R. P. Thian's collection (page 41). Betts sold his coins at auction between 1871 and 1907. Note is "punched."

Edouard Frossard *Brooklyn, N.Y.*	22 Dec 1885	VF	-	$3.50

Comments: Consigned by Dr. William Lee, professor and author in 1875 of *The Currency of the Confederate States of America* (page 32). Note "Very Fine, clean."

S.H. & H. Chapman *Philadelphia, Pa.*	17 Oct 1888	pen c, cc, VF	1338	$8.50

Comments: Consigned by Ferguson Haines, a noted coin collector born in Maine in 1840. Attended Phillips Academy in Andover, Mass. and Dartmouth. Retailed hardware and manufactured textiles. Served as mayor of Biddeford, Me. and was a member of the Maine House of Representatives. Note is "cancelled in two places with straight cuts (nothing gone). Lightly stamped across face, 'Cancelled.' Back also endorsed. Very Fine. Letter A."

John Walter Scott *New York, N.Y.*	22 Jun 1891	AU	-	$5.00

Comments: Consigned by E. L. Nagel of Terre Haute, Ind., a 19th century collector of coins and medals. Note is "practically uncirculated. Very rare."

Edouard Frossard *Brooklyn, N.Y.*	9 Jun 1892	UNC	-	$4.50

Comments: Consigned by Hiram E. Deats (1870-1963) of Flemington, N. J., foreman of the grand jury that indicted Bruno Hauptman for kidnapping the Lindbergh baby. Deats was a charter member and the senior member at the time of his death of both the ANA and the American Philatelic Society. Note described as "crisp, new, rare."

John Walter Scott *New York, N.Y.*	29 Jun 1892	Fine	-	$4.10

Comments: Consignor unknown. Note simply described as "Fine, rare."

Edouard Frossard *Brooklyn, N.Y.*	14 Nov 1893	VF	-	-

Comments: Consignor unknown. Note part of a set of all four Montgomerys which sold for $87.50. Described as "Very Fine and rare."

Edouard Frossard *Brooklyn, N.Y.*	19 Dec 1894	UNC	-	$5.90

Comments: Three consecutive lots consigned by Ferguson Haines, who consigned a lesser note to a Chapman Brothers' auction in 1888 (see above). Note is "crisp, new, rare."

Edouard Frossard *Brooklyn, N.Y.*	19 Dec 1894	UNC	-	$5.90

Comments: The second lot from Ferguson Haines. Note is "crisp, new, rare."

Auction House	Sale Date	Grade or Condition	Serial Number	Sales Price
Edouard Frossard *Brooklyn, N.Y.*	19 Dec 1894	UNC	-	-

Comments: The third lot from Ferguson Haines. Note is "crisp, new, rare."

Charles Steigerwalt *Lancaster, Pa.*	17 Jan 1895	UNC	-	-

Comments: Consigned by little-known John Wright. Note simply and tersely described as "Uncirculated."

Charles Steigerwalt *Lancaster, Pa.*	25 Jun 1895	UNC	-	-

Comments: Consigned by little-known Grant Weaver. Note simply and tersely described as "Uncirculated."

Charles Steigerwalt *Lancaster, Pa.*	6 Jan 1896	Fine	-	-

Comments: Consigned by little-known Robert Watts. Note simply described as "Fine, rare."

John Walter Scott *New York, N.Y.*	20 Jan 1896	VF	-	-

Comments: Consignor unknown. Lot consisted of a Thian album containing 59 notes, including both the $100 and $50 Montgomerys. Entire lot sold for $17.50.

Charles Steigerwalt *Lancaster, Pa.*	24 Mar 1896	AU	-	$7.00

Comments: Consigned by little-known John Wilson. Note simply described as "Nearly uncirculated. Rare."

Charles Steigerwalt *Lancaster, Pa.*	16 July 1896	UNC	-	$5.00

Comments: Consignor uncertain. Note simply described as "Uncirculated."

Charles Steigerwalt *Lancaster, Pa.*	25 Apr 1899	AU	-	-

Comments: Consignor unknown. Note described as "Almost uncirculated."

Charles Steigerwalt *Lancaster, Pa.*	25 Apr 1899	F-VF	-	-

Comments: Consignor unknown. Note called "a duplicate. Would be Very Fine but somewhat stained."

S.H. & H. Chapman *Philadelphia, Pa.*	16 Nov 1900	CU	-	$4.80

Comments: Consigned by the eminent Dr. Edward Maris (1832-1900), a Philadelphia Quaker who assembled comprehensive collections of New Jersey cents, autograph letters, Colonial currency and South American coins. Original classifier of the 1794 cent varieties. Owned original charter granted to William Penn for the Commonwealth of Pennsylvania. Note described as "Uncirculated, crisp, in beautiful condition. Rare."

Auction House	Sale Date	Grade or Condition	Serial Number	Sales Price
Lyman Haines Low *New York, N.Y.*	18 Jun 1901	Fine	-	$4.50

Comments: Most likely consigned by R.O. Montambault, a Canadian from Quebec who joined the ANA in 1920. Note described simply as "Fine, rare."

Charles Steigerwalt *Lancaster, Pa.*	9 Jan 1906	Fine	-	-

Comments: Consignor unknown. Note described as "Fine, but slightly stained."

Thomas Lindsay Elder *New York, N.Y.*	26-27 Feb 1908	UNC	-	$5.00

Comments: Most likely consigned by J. N. T. Levick (about 1828-1908) of New York City, one of the earliest American numismatists who served with distinction during the Civil War. Active in the ANS, in 1866 he proposed a monthly journal that continues to be published to this day. Note tersely described as "rare."

Henry Chapman *Philadelphia, Pa.*	19-20 Jun 1908	UNC	1147	$5.75

Comments: Consigned by Harmon Chambers (1822-1905) of the "Confederate Triumvirate," who founded an insurance brokerage business in Philadelphia (page 51). Note is "Uncirculated, brilliant and bright. Rare." Photo below left.

Left, serial #1147, right, #1140.

Charles Steigerwalt *Lancaster, Pa.*	24 Feb 1909	Fine	-	-

Comments: Consigned by little-known Adam Eberly. Note in "Fine condition except for stains."

Ben G. Green *Chicago, Ill.*	28 Mar 1913	XF	-	$6.20

Comments: Consigned by little-known Charles Morris VI. Note is hand-dated "May 22," indicating a serial number between 1239 and 1450, according to R. P. Thian's *Register*. Note has "three pin holes. Rare."

Edward Michael *Chicago, Ill.*	9 May 1914	UNC	1140	$8.25

Comments: Consigned by the estate of Ben Green of Chicago (p. 52), generally considered the first Midwestern coin dealer. Note simply described as "New, very rare." Photo above right, courtesy R. M. Smythe 1992 catalog.

Auction House	Sale Date	Grade or Condition	Serial Number	Sales Price
Samuel Hudson Chapman *Philadelphia, Pa.*	27-29 May 1914	VG	-	$2.75

Comments: Consigned by William Gable of Altoona, Pa., founder of a very large department store and owner of virtually complete U.S. coin series. Note has "a small piece out of the lower border."

U.S. Coin Company *New York, N.Y.*	29 Jun 1914	UNC	-	$7.50

Comments: Consignor unknown. Note is hand-dated "May 22," indicating a serial number between 1239 and 1450. Note "extremely rare, endorsed on reverse."

Lyman Haines Low *New York, N.Y.*	22 Jun 1917	Very Fair	-	$2.50

Comments: Consignor unknown. An amusing grade -- not of "Fair" -- but of "Very Fair." Note tersely described as "rare."

Thomas Lindsay Elder *New York, N.Y.*	9-11 May 1918	poc, Abt Fine	1137	$2.10

Comments: Consigned by Benjamin P. Wright (1857-1922), president of the ANA from 1901-1904. From Hamlin, N.Y., Wright graduated from the University of Michigan Medical School in 1885 and practiced in Upstate New York. Assembled the largest collection of American store cards ever. Note simply described as "rare."

Thomas Lindsay Elder *New York, N.Y.*	23-26 Feb 1921	CU	1025	$5.50

Comments: Consigned by the estate of M. K. McMullin, who collected American and foreign gold coins. Elder described note as "Very rare, the finest I have seen."

Serial number 1378: Front and back.

Thomas Lindsay Elder *New York, N.Y.*	26-27 Aug 1921	UNC	1378	$6.00

Comments: Consigned by Lewis C. Gehring (1852-1921) of Brooklyn, N. Y., who was born in Rahway, N. J. before moving to Brooklyn. A prominent banker of the Prudential Savings Bank, with interests in feed and milling. Collected gold coins. Note described as "very rare." Above photo, courtesy R.M. Smythe & Co., N.Y.C.

Stan V. Henkels *Philadelphia, Pa.*	28 July 1922	UNC	-	-

Comments: Consigned by the legendary John C. Browne, perhaps the greatest Confederate collector (see page 58). Part of a 90-note "Uncirculated" type set.

Auction House	Sale Date	Grade or Condition	Serial Number	Sales Price
B. Max Mehl *Fort Worth, Tex.*	17 Apr 1923	XF-AU	-	$8.80

Comments: Consignor uncertain. Note is "nearly uncirculated. Very rare."

Serial number 314:
Front and back.

Thomas Lindsay Elder *New York, N.Y.*	9-11 Oct 1924	AU	314	-

Comments: Consigned by Edward H. Eckfeldt, Jr. of Orange, N.J., a direct descendant of Adam Eckfeldt, the first coiner of the U.S. Mint. Note described as "Very rare, mounted under celluloid." Above photo, courtesy Col. Hudson McDonald, Colonel's Coins & Stamps, Spanish Fort, Alabama.

William Hesslein *Boston, Mass.*	20-21 Sep 1929	VF	-	-

Comments: Consigned by H. D. Allen of Boston, whose articles on Confederate currency appeared in *The Numismatist* from 1917-1919 (p. 56). Note is "very rare."

William Hesslein *Boston, Mass.*	22-23 Nov 1929	XF	-	-

Comments: Another consignment from H. D. Allen. Note is "very rare."

Milfred Henry Bolender *Freeport, Ill.*	15 Oct 1935	VF	-	$6.25

Comments: Consigned by dealer Andrew Mason Smith (1841-1915) of Minneapolis, whose coin collection totaled over 15,000 pieces and included the unique 1884 proof set struck in copper. Note described as "extremely rare."

Left, serial #1143,
right, #1236.

Milfred Henry Bolender *Freeport, Ill.*	8 Feb 1936	UNC	1143	$11.00

Comments: Consigned by A. P. Wylie of Wheaton, Ill., a dealer and collector of U.S. coins and currency. Note "very rare." Photo above left, from NASCA catalog.

Auction House	Sale Date	Grade or Condition	Serial Number	Sales Price
John Milford Henderson *Columbus, Oh.*	4 Apr 1936	pen c, UNC	1140	$13.00

> *Comments:* Consigned by Henrie Buck of Delaware, Ohio, ANA member and state president. Note "cancelled by pen." Photo, right center, page 218.

| Stack's
New York, N.Y. | 3-4 Dec 1937 | UNC | - | $11.00 |

> *Comments:* Consignor unknown. Note simply described as "very rare."

Serial number 386:
Front and back.

| Milfred Henry Bolender
Freeport, Ill. | 26 Feb 1938 | VF | 386 | $9.25 |

> *Comments:* Consignor unknown. Note has "slight creases" and was donated by Doug Ball. Above photo, courtesy Museum of the Confederacy, Richmond, Va.

| B. Max Mehl
Ft. Worth, Tex. | 22 Mar 1938 | UNC | 1236 | - |

> *Comments:* Consigned by Benjamin H. Collins (1845-1928) of Washington, D.C., a collector, ANA member and dealer with a coin shop in Washington. Born in Missouri, he served in the Union Army before finding employment at the U.S. Treasury. Note sold as part of a set of Montgomerys. Photo bottom right, p. 220.

| Thomas Lindsay Elder
New York, N.Y. | 12 May 1939 | UNC | - | - |

> *Comments:* Consignor uncertain. Note described as "very rare."

| Stack's
New York, N.Y. | 27-28 May 1941 | VF | - | $10.50 |

> *Comments:* Consignor uncertain. Note hand-dated "May 23," indicating a serial number between 1451 and 1545. Note is "above average, not cancelled."

| B. Max Mehl
Ft. Worth, Tex. | 3 Jun 1941 | UNC | 1236 | $21.00 |

> *Comments:* Consigned by Mehl himself, who bought it from Benjamin Collins (see above) and included it within the auction of the celebrated William F. Dunham (1857-1936) of Chicago, former grocer, teacher and stockbroker who served as chairman of the Board of Governors of the ANA. Note "Uncirculated. Just as perfect as the day issued. Endorsed in red ink." Photo, bottom right, page 220.

Auction House	Sale Date	Grade or Condition	Serial Number	Sales Price
Milfred Henry Bolender *Freeport, Ill.*	2 Dec 1942	Ch UNC	-	$17.50

Comments: Consigned by little-known Harry L. Smith. Note described as "Choice Uncirculated. This one worth $25. Seldom obtainable."

Milfred Henry Bolender *Freeport, Ill.*	15 Feb 1943	Ch UNC	-	$17.50

Comments: Consigned by little-known John M. Vinton. Note's description reads, "Lists at $15 when Fine, this one worth $25. One sold in my Dec. 2 sale at $17.50."

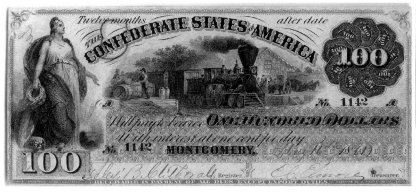

Serial number 1142: *Front and back.*	B. Max Mehl *Ft. Worth, Tex.*	9 Mar 1943	UNC	1142	$18.75

Comments: Consigned by Henry E. Elrod of Houston, Tex., active ANA member who focused on European coins and also consigned U.S. coins to this sale, including four-dollar and fifty-dollar gold pieces. Note is "Uncirculated. Endorsement on back." Above photo, courtesy a private Georgia collection.

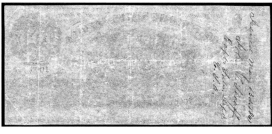

Serial number 1006: *Front and back.*	Milfred Henry Bolender *Freeport, Ill.*	25 Sep 1943	XF	1006	$19.00

Comments: Consigned by little-known W. B. Kennedy. Note described as "Extremely Fine. Uncancelled. Very rare." Above photo, courtesy R. M. Smythe & Company, New York City.

Barney Bluestone *Syracuse, N.Y.*	27-28 Apr 1945	CU	-	$16.50

Comments: Consignor unknown. Note described as "Uncancelled, uncirculated, crisp. Lists at $15 in only Fine."

Auction House	Sale Date	Grade or Condition	Serial Number	Sales Price

Serial number 567:
Front and back.

Milfred Henry Bolender	2 Oct 1948	VF	567	$16.00

Freeport, Ill.

> *Comments:* Consigned by Loring T. Reckard of Chicago, ANA member from 1916 who also collected stamps and coins. Note "Very Fine, looks much better than its grade." Note once owned by Dallas philatelist Gordon Bleuler. Photo above.

Milfred Henry Bolender	16 Apr 1949	Fine	-	$19.00

Freeport, Ill.

> *Comments:* Consignor uncertain. Note simply described as "Fine. Rare."

New Netherlands Coin Co.	26 Sep 1953	UNC	916	$61.00

New York, N.Y.

> *Comments:* Consigned by Hillyer Ryder (about 1851-1928) of New York, author of *The Colonial Coins of Vermont* and *The Copper Coins of Massacusetts*. Member of the ANA and New York Numismatic Club. Collection sold to Wayte Raymond in 1945, who sold much of the coinage at a public auction in November 1945, with remnants sold by New Netherlands. Note described as "Strictly uncirculated."

Federal Coin Exchange	10-13 Jan 1957	XF	1020	$200.00

Cleveland, Oh.

> *Comments:* Consigned by Charles W. "Suitcase Charlie" Foster of Rushville, N.Y., once ANA librarian and curator. Authored *Historical Arrangement of United States Commemorative Coins*. Co-founder of Empire State Numismatic Association. Note described as "Crisp and clean looking. Few light creases. Extremely Fine." Photo below left, from Federal Coin Exchange catalog.

James, Inc.	29 Mar 1957	CU	1492	-

Louisville, Ky.

Left, serial #1020,
right, #1067.

> *Comments:* Consignor unknown. Note described as "Crisp Uncirculated. Few negligible pin holes. Should fetch a record price." Photo, bottom of page 242.

Auction House	Sale Date	Grade or Condition	Serial Number	Sales Price
D&W Auction Sales *Baltimore, Md.*	3 Apr 1959	VF-XF	1081	$297.50

Comments: Consignor unknown. Note has an "almost perfect obverse, reverse has light creases."

Federal Brand Enterprises *Cleveland, Oh.*	13-15 Jul 1963	AU	-	$425.00

Comments: Consigned by the larger-than-life Grover Criswell, whose career is summarized on page 81. Note is "virtually uncirculated."

Stack's *New York, N.Y.*	2-5 Oct 1963	F-VF	1402	$200.00

Comments: Consigned by George O. Walton (about 1907-1962) of Roanoke, Va. and later Charlotte, N.C. Founder of the Mid-Atlantic Numismatic Association. Killed in head-on auto crash en route to coin show. Owned a genuine 1913 Liberty Head Nickel. Collection was strong on U.S. gold and Pioneer and Territorial gold. Note "Fine to Very Fine. About average for this denomination."

Lester Merkin *New York, N.Y.*	20-21 Aug 1976	UNC	1067	$725.00

Comments: Labeled the Brussels Collection and cataloged by Douglas Ball. Note has "glue mount stains on corners. Endorsement May 25, 1861 at Lynchburg, Va. Rare, choice." Photo below left, courtesy Amanda Sheheen, A&O Currency, LLC.

Left, serial #1067, right, #1441.

NASCA *Rockville Centre, N.Y.*	27-28 May 1977	VF	386	$575.00

Comments: Consigned by the Maryland Historical Society. Note "is crisp, bright and vivid, but has been quarter folded vertically, the center being pronounced. There are nine pin holes in the left center and the remnants of a stamp hinge on the left reverse." Photo, page 221.

Kagin's *Des Moines, Ia.*	29-30 Sep 1978	VF	1441	$850.00

Comments: Consignor unknown. Note has "nice margins." Photo above right.

NASCA *Rockville Centre, N.Y.*	6-7 Dec 1978	VG-F	1088	$761.25

Comments: Labeled The Sands Point Collection. Note's "left border has been lightly trimmed and there are half a dozen pinholes in the left vignette. Has an endorsement on the reverse." Photo, bottom right, page 225.

Auction House	Sale Date	Grade or Condition	Serial Number	Sales Price
NASCA *Rockville Centre, N.Y.*	30 Apr - 1 May 1979	pen c, cc, VF-XF	1337	$1,050.00

Comments: Consigned by Dr. Van B. Elliott, coin and currency collector. Note has "vertical center folds at right and two slash cancellations about a quarter of the way in. Margins complete except at the right bottom corner which is trimmed. Far better than average." Photo below left, courtesy dealer Crutchfield Williams.

Kagin's *Des Moines, Ia.*	13-14 Jul 1979	CU	832	$2,100.00

Left, serial #1337, right, #1279.

Comments: Consignor unknown. Note described only as "endorsed." Photo below, courtesy current owner Tig Sigoian, *www.CSABig6.com*

Serial number 832: Front and back.

NASCA *Rockville Centre, N.Y.*	6-7 Jun 1980	XF	1279	$1,365.00

Comments: Consignor unknown. Note has "three vertical folds and is crisp and bright with a slightly shaved right border." Photo above right, from NASCA.

NASCA *Rockville Centre, N.Y.*	4-6 Sep 1980	AU	831	$1,575.00

Left, serial #831, right, #1088.

Comments: Sale labeled as "New York Collection." Note is "a bright, fully margined choice note, with just a corner fold and top edge crease and soiling taking it out of the Uncirculated class." Photo above left, from NASCA catalog.

	Auction House	Sale Date	Grade or Condition	Serial Number	Sales Price

Serial number 1346: Grover C. Criswell   17 Oct 1980   XF   1346   -
Front and back.   *Salt Springs, Fla.*

Comments: Consigned by little-known Dr. Richard Rich. Note quarter folded both ways, with ink stains and narrow margins. Above photo from Crutch Williams.

Serial number 1550: Grover C. Criswell   17 Oct 1980   coc, XF   1550   -
Front and back.   *Salt Springs, Fla.*

Comments: Also consigned by little-known Dr. Richard Rich. Note has "four cut-out cancels professionally repaired. Beautiful appearance." Above photo, courtesy Dale S. Alberstone Family Trust Collection, Los Angeles, California.

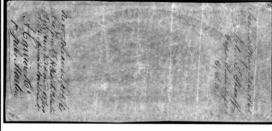

Serial number 987: Bowers & Ruddy Galleries   25-26 Mar 1981   VF   987 $1,800.00
Front and back.   *Los Angeles, Calif.*

Comments: From the collection of T. Harrison Garrett (1849-1888) of Baltimore, president of the B&O Railroad, upon de-accession by The Johns Hopkins Univ. His coin collection was considered second only to the Parmalee collection. This note endorsed on reverse "May 23, 1861." Above photo, courtesy R. M. Smythe.

Auction House	Sale Date	Grade or Condition	Serial Number	Sales Price

Serial number 1397: Front and back.

| NASCA | 10-12 Sep 1981 | VF-XF | 1397 | $1,785.00 |

Rockville Centre, N.Y.

Comments: Consigned by Stanley Gibbons, London stamp dealer. Note is "bright, fully margined, with three light vertical folds, four corner folds. Four paper clip rust stains on face and back." Above photo, courtesy Bill Kelly, Asharoken, N.Y.

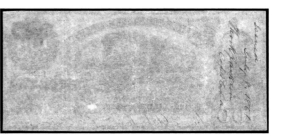

Serial number 1228: Front and back.

| NASCA | 19-21 Apr 1982 | VF | 1228 | $1,365.00 |

Rockville Centre, N.Y.

Comments: Consigned by Grover Criswell, noted dealer (see p.81). Note "quarter folded both ways with glue remnants at the top edge on the back. Red ink endorsement. Margins complete." Above photo, courtesy R. M. Smythe & Co.

| NASCA | 19-21 Apr 1982 | Abt. VF | 862 | $971.25 |

Rockville Centre, N.Y.

Comments: A second consignment from Grover Criswell. Note "quarter folded on the back both ways with other petty folding." Photo below left from NASCA.

| NASCA | 19-21 Apr 1982 | pen c, VG-F | 6 | $446.25 |

Rockville Centre, N.Y.

Left, serial #862, right, #6.

Comments: Yet a third consignment from Grover Criswell. Note is "badly stained. Stamp cancelled on face and back. The staining is serious, the bottom border shaved." Photo above right from the NASCA 1982 catalog.

Auction House	Sale Date	Grade or Condition	Serial Number	Sales Price
Christie's *New York, N.Y.*	17 Sep 1982	UNC	1067	$1,980.00

Comments: Consigned by Richard F. Saffin (1894-1982), a partner in the brokerage firm Boland Saffin Gordon & Sauffer. Note is "uncancelled. Fully bright and crisp, and among the finest known to exist in all grades." Photo, left center, page 224.

Christie's *New York, N.Y.*	17 Sep 1982	F-VF	1441	$935.00

Comments: Also from Richard F. Saffin. Note has "a few folds that are a bit heavy, but there are no pinholes or other problems." Photo, right center, page 224.

Christie's *New York, N.Y.*	17 Sep 1982	VG-F	1001	$825.00

Comments: Another from Richard F. Saffin. Note well-circulated, but no stains or damage. Appears nicer on the face than the back. Photo below left, from NASCA.

Left, serial #1001, right, #1382.

Christie's *New York, N.Y.*	8 Dec 1982	Fine	386	$880.00

Comments: Consignor unknown. Note has "traces of hinge glue, numerous pin holes, three vertical creases. Back endorsement has bled through." Photo, p. 221.

NASCA *Rockville Centre, N.Y.*	10-12 Jan 1983	AU	1140	$1,155.00

Comments: Part of the massive John C. Browne collection, consigned by Charles J. Affleck (1892-1974) of Winchester, Va., author of *Obsolete Paper Money of Va.* Note has a light crease, a stain and a back endorsement. Photo, right center, p. 218.

Serial number 864: Front and back.

NASCA *Rockville Centre, N.Y.*	10-12 Jan 1983	Abt. VF	864	$892.50

Comments: Also from Browne via Affleck. Note has "a horizontal fold and six vertical folds. Good color." Above photo, courtesy George Tremmel, Raleigh, N.C.

Auction House	Sale Date	Grade or Condition	Serial Number	Sales Price
NASCA Rockville Centre, N.Y.	10-12 Jan 1983	Abt. VF	1382	$813.75

Comments: Also from Browne via Affleck. Note has "six light folds, pin holes, ink stains. Good color, tight margins." Photo, right center, p. 228, from NASCA.

Serial number 1461: Front and back.

NASCA Rockville Centre, N.Y.	10-12 Jan 1983	VG-F	1461	$708.75

Comments: Also from Browne via Affleck. Note is "stained, well margined, pin holed, with back endorsement." Above photo courtesy Bill Kelly, Asharoken, N.Y.

Kagin's Des Moines, Ia.	16-20 Aug 1983	Abt. XF	1378	$990.00

Comments: Consignor unknown. Note has only minor problems. Smoothed vertical and horizontal creases, couple pinholes. Photo, p. 219, from R.M. Smythe.

NASCA Rockville Centre, N.Y.	1-2 Nov 1983	Fine	1026	$761.25

Comments: Contained within the Abner Reed Catalog, but probably consigned by John Ford. Reed (1771-1866) was a bank note engraver, whose proof notes were acquired by F.C.C. Boyd and later John Ford. This note has "corner and other stains. Borders are complete." Photo, below left, from NASCA catalog.

NASCA Rockville Centre, N.Y.	1-2 Nov 1983	VG+	1088	$735.00

Left, serial #1026, right, #1088.

Comments: Also from Abner Reed. Note has "complete edges, is endorsed on the back and good even wear." Photo above right, from NASCA 1985 catalog.

NASCA Rockville Centre, N.Y.	1-2 Nov 1983	cc, VG	215	$735.00

Comments: Another from Abner Reed. Note has a "trimmed top border, with a massive long tear and a knife cut cancel, both deftly repaired." Photo, page 231.

Auction House	Sale Date	Grade or Condition	Serial Number	Sales Price
Stack's *New York, N.Y.*	20 Mar 1984	VF	1150	$1,100.00

Comments: From John L. Roper (1902-1983) of Norfolk, Va., a ship builder. Note has "two vertical folds, a horizontal one, with two pinholes in the center. Two corner borders are shaved, with a back endorsement." Photo, top of page 239.

Auction House	Sale Date	Grade or Condition	Serial Number	Sales Price
NASCA-Karp *New York, N.Y.*	28-29 Mar 1985	Fine	1285	$770.00

Comments: Consigned by little-known Ben O. Anderson. Note has "top border lightly shaved, one pinhole, issued on back by A. J. Guirot, June 6, 1861." Photo, below left, courtesy NASCA 1985 catalog.

Left, serial #1285, right, #124.

Auction House	Sale Date	Grade or Condition	Serial Number	Sales Price
NASCA, Div. of Smythe & Co. *New York, N.Y.*	28-31 Oct 1985	F-VF	124	$825.00

Comments: Sale is labeled "The Clinton Collection," although no details are provided about who or what Clinton is. Note "is choice from the first printing. Margins are complete, if close, and there are eleven distinct folds visible from the back." Photo, above right, courtesy NASCA 1985 catalog.

Auction House	Sale Date	Grade or Condition	Serial Number	Sales Price
NASCA, Div. of Smythe & Co. *New York, N.Y.*	28-31 Oct 1985	Fine	1088	$825.00

Comments: A second consignment from "The Clinton Collection." Note is "issued on back by Thos. K. Jackson. There are four pinholes at the left, and the left border is shaved." Photo, bottom right, page 229.

Serial number 1550: Front and back.

Auction House	Sale Date	Grade or Condition	Serial Number	Sales Price
NASCA, Div. of Smythe & Co. *New York, N.Y.*	28-31 Oct 1985	F-VF, Repaired	1550	$605.00

Comments: Yet a third consignment from "The Clinton Collection." Note is "crisp, bright, vivid, a few light folds. A spade-shaped piece has been deftly restored in the top edge." Above photo, courtesy Dale S. Alberstone Family Trust Collection.

Auction House	Sale Date	Grade or Condition	Serial Number	Sales Price

NASCA, Div. of Smythe & Co. New York, N.Y.	28-31 Oct 1985	cc, VG, Repaired	215	$550.00

Left, serial #215, right, #1001.

Comments: Final consignment from "The Clinton Collection." Note part of the "scarce first printing. Much face wear, top border badly trimmed, slash cancelled with deftly restored body holes." Photo above left, from NASCA 1985 catalog.

NASCA, Div. of Smythe & Co. New York, N.Y.	7-10 Mar 1986	pen c, Fine	1461	-

Comments: Consignor unknown. Note is "soiled with a cluster of pinholes at left, lightly pen cancelled across face. Endorsed on the back." Photo, top of page 229.

NASCA, Div. of Smythe & Co. New York, N.Y.	7-10 Mar 1986	Fine+	1001	$935.00

Comments: Consignor unknown. Note has "light soiling; endorsements on back for issue date at top and redemption date on bottom." Photo, above right.

NASCA, Div. of Smythe & Co. New York, N.Y.	20-21 Jun 1986	pen c, Fine	1461	$726.00

Comments: Presumably consigned from the archives of the Penn Central Railroad. Note is "soiled with a cluster of pinholes at left, lightly pen cancelled across face. Endorsed on the back." Photo, top of page 229.

Stack's New York, N.Y.	9-11 Sep 1987	AU	1149	$1,540.00

Comments: Consigned by little-known L.S. Ruder. Note has "just one vertical fold, uncancelled. Bright paper and ink." Photo below left, from Slabaugh's 10th Ed.

NASCA, Div. of Smythe & Co. New York, N.Y.	25-26 Sep 1987	Abt. VF	386	$1,430.00

Left, serial #1149, right, #386.

Comments: Consigned by my mentor Douglas B. Ball (p. 98). Note is "quarter folded vertically, a face stain, hinges on back, peppered with pinholes. Part of the rare first printing." Photo of front only, above right; color photo both sides, p. 221.

	Auction House	Sale Date	Grade or Condition	Serial Number	Sales Price

Serial number 913:
Front and back.

| | NASCA, Div. of Smythe & Co. New York, N.Y. | 25-26 Sep 1987 | UNC | 913 | $1,925.00 |

Comments: Also from Doug Ball's Richmond Sale in 1987. A superb note, generally considered the finest in the Condition Census Top Ten. Note is "crisp, bright, vivid, the borders are complete." Ex Philip H. Chase. Ex Doug Ball. Ex Paul Gibson, who displayed it in his spectacular Type Set Collection. Photo above.

| | NASCA, Div. of Smythe & Co. New York, N.Y. | 25-26 Mar 1988 | Fine | 314 | $1,210.00 |

Comments: Consignor unknown. Note has "good even wear with fold stains and a back endorsement." Photo, top of page 220.

| | NASCA, Div. of Smythe & Co. New York, N.Y. | 31 Mar 1989 | XF | 1143 | $1,265.00 |

Comments: Consignor unknown. Note has "a fold off center to the right. Looks Uncirculated. Crisp, bright, with nearly complete borders." Photo lower left p.220.

| | Christie's New York, N.Y. | 7 Sep 1989 | AU | 1019 | $1,320.00 |

Comments: Consigned by brothers Felix and Henri Weil, founders of Medallic Art Co. Note is "bright, uncancelled, several very light folds." Photo, top of page 235.

Serial number 815:
Front and back.

| | NASCA, Div. of Smythe & Co. New York, N.Y. | 15-16 Jun 1990 | UNC | 815 | $2,420.00 |

Comments: Consignor was presumably Henry Hull of Jacksonville, Fla., who consigned the finest-known $1,000 Montgomery to this same auction. A magnificent note, usually considered the second finest in the Condition Census Top Ten, second only to No. 913 above. Described as "a superb note with just the hint of a shaved left border. Interesting back issue endorsement." Photo above.

Auction House	Sale Date	Grade or Condition	Serial Number	Sales Price

Serial number 1014: Front and back.

| NASCA, Div. of Smythe & Co. *New York, N.Y.* | 15-16 Jun 1990 | AU | 1014 | $2,035.00 |

Comments: Probably a second consignment from philatelist Henry Hull (see p. 232). Another spectacular note, also in the Condition Census Top Ten. Note "About Uncirculated. Clean, tightly but completely margined, a barely detectable center fold. Back issue endorsement." Photo above.

| R.M. Smythe & Co. *New York, N.Y.* | 27 Jun 1991 | poc, Fine | 1102 | $1,210.00 |

Comments: Consignor unknown. Has "light staining, four punch holes only seen when held up to light. Endorsed on back." Photo below left, from R. M. Smythe.

Left, serial #1102, right, #1497.

| R.M. Smythe & Co. *New York, N.Y.* | 22 Nov 1991 | Abt VF | 1346 | $1,540.00 |

Comments: Consignor unknown. Note is "quarter folded both ways, ink stains, narrow margins, a back ink endorsement." Photo, top of page 226.

| R.M. Smythe & Co. *New York, N.Y.* | 23 Nov 1992 | VF-XF | 1140 | $3,300.00 |

Comments: Consignor unknown. Note is "quarter folded, light edge folds, two back mounting hinges and a trivial foxing spot." Photo, right center, page 218.

| R.M. Smythe & Co. *New York, N.Y.* | 18-19 Jun 1993 | Fine | 1461 | - |

Comments: Consignor unknown. Note is "somewhat weak in appearance, barely complete borders, much endorsed on the back." Photo, top of page 229.

| R.M. Smythe & Co. *New York, N.Y.* | 18-19 Jun 1993 | F-VF, Repaired | 1497 | $962.50 |

Comments: Consignor unknown. Note has seen much repair. "Cut in half right of center and rejoined with a glue stain." Photo above right, courtesy R. M. Smythe.

Auction House	Sale Date	Grade or Condition	Serial Number	Sales Price
R.M. Smythe & Co. *New York, N.Y.*	18-19 Jun 1993	Fair	408	$715.00

Comments: Consignor unknown. Note is "Fair, split in half, scotch taped at corners and center, missing edge pieces, but essentially complete. Mounted on paper. A filler for the impecunious." Photo below left, courtesy R. M. Smythe.

Left, serial #408, right, #887.

R.M. Smythe & Co. *New York, N.Y.*	22 Nov 1993	Abt VF	1441	$3,850.00

Comments: Consignor unknown. Note has "seven or so folds. Margins and color are good, but there is ink bleed-through from back." Photo, below right.

R.M. Smythe & Co. *New York, N.Y.*	23 Mar 1994	VG-F	887	$1,980.00

Comments: Possibly owned by John Besante, American Impressionist artist. Note has "paper aging and soiling. The borders are intact, two back endorsements and a small center split." Photo above right, courtesy, R. M. Smythe catalog.

R.M. Smythe & Co. *New York, N.Y.*	14 Mar 1995	Fine+	1471	$4,290.00

Comments: Consignor unknown. Note has "complete borders, somewhat dark, a dismounting remnant at the left." Photo below left, courtesy R. M. Smythe.

Left, serial #1471, right, #1441.

R.M. Smythe & Co. *New York, N.Y.*	11 Sep 1995	XF	1492	$8,525.00

Comments: Consignor unknown. Note has "a faint double center fold, light lower left corner handling and hinge remnants along the top. The borders are full and quite square, color in vivid. Ex Abner Kreisberg." Photo, bottom of page 242.

R.M. Smythe & Co. *New York, N.Y.*	11 Sep 1995	Good	539	$1,210.00

Comments: Consignor unknown. Note has "edge chinks, slits, faded color. Still one of the few available examples of the first issue."

Auction House	Sale Date	Grade or Condition	Serial Number	Sales Price

Serial number 1019: Front and back.

R.M. Smythe & Co. *New York, N.Y.*	22 Jun 1996	VF	1019	$7,700.00

Comments: Consignor unknown. Note "looks almost new on the face, but back has a center fold and multiple light edge folds." Above photo from R. M. Smythe.

Currency Auctions of America *Forest Hills, N.Y.*	2-3 May 1997	poc, G-VG	34	$2,585.00

Comments: Consignor unknown. Note has "four punch-out cancels, a bit of ink erosion and some margin nicks. Good color." Photo below left, courtesy CAA.

Stack's *New York, N.Y.*	11-12 Mar 1998	VF	662	$9,900.00

Left, serial #34, right, #662.

Comments: From the Museum of Conn. History's Joseph C. Mitchelson Collection. Mitchelson (1856-1911) was a prominent tobacco dealer (see p. 169). Note has "a bold imprint, with some faded purple spots." Photo above right, from Jim Glass.

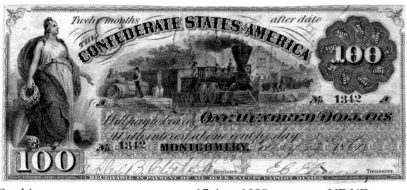

Serial number 1342: Front and back.

Stack's *New York, N.Y.*	15 Apr 1998	VF-XF	1342	$13,420.00

Comments: By far the finest Montgomery in the Mitchelson Collection above, and pushing for inclusion in the Condition Census Top Ten. Note is "attractive, bright green color and acceptable margins. Destined for a fine collection." Photo above.

Auction House	Sale Date	Grade or Condition	Serial Number	Sales Price
R.M. Smythe & Co. New York, N.Y.	19 Jun 1998	Ch UNC	1067	$19,800.00

Comments: From Arnold Cowan, avid yachtsman from Long Beach. Condition-Census quality. Note is "crisp, bright and vivid with good margins, a hint at left of ink bleed-through from back endorsement." Photo, bottom right, page 223.

Serial number 889: Front and back.

R.M. Smythe & Co. New York, N.Y.	19 Jun 1998	Abt XF	889	$15,400.00

Comments: Arnold Cowan's second $100 Montgomery, also of remarkable Condition-Census quality. Note is "crisp, bright, vivid, with close although complete margins. A center fold and handling signs at both sides." Photo above.

Serial number 858: Front and back.

R.M. Smythe & Co. New York, N.Y.	18-19 Sep 1998	Fine+	858	$12,100.00

Comments: Consigned by John L. Sanderson of Westchester Co., N.Y., a securities dealer. Note has complete borders, good color. Above photo, courtesy Bill Kelly.

Serial number 21: Front and back.

R.M. Smythe & Co. New York, N.Y.	19 Jun 1999	pen c, poc, Fine	21	$7,700.00

Comments: Consignor unknown. Looks better than its "Fine" grade. Small, neat punch cancels, with a pen cancel on face. Above photo, courtesy W. McNair Tornow.

Auction House	Sale Date	Grade or Condition	Serial Number	Sales Price
Lyn Knight Currency Auctions *Overland Park, Kan.*	20-24 Oct 1999	VF-XF	1006	$15,400.00

Comments: Consignor unknown. Note is "beautiful, with bold colors, excellent centering, problem-free and good signatures. Does great justice to the engraving. Endorsed on the back with date May 23, 1861." Photo, bottom of page 222.

R.M. Smythe & Co. *New York, N.Y.*	16 Jun 2000	VF-XF	1397	$14,850.00

Comments: Consigned by Samuel E. Roakes, Jr., author of articles appearing in *Paper Money* and owner of Kennesaw Coins and Currency. Note has "three vertical folds and four light corner folds. Borders complete. Some bleed-through from the back endorsement of June 19, 1861." Photo, top of page 227.

Bowers & Merena Galleries *Wolfeboro, N.H.*	9-12 Aug 2000	VF	1018	$25,300.00

Comments: From the Franklin Institute in Philadelphia. Note is "bright, very pleasing, essentially problem-free aside from a few scattered pinholes near the center. Borders mostly even. A high degree of aesthetic appeal in terms of quality as well as design." Photo below left, courtesy Bowers & Merena Galleries.

Lyn Knight Currency Auctions *Overland Park, Kan.*	11-12 Aug 2000	coc, cc, VF	666	-

Left, serial #1018, right, #1367.

Comments: Consignor unknown. Note has "two 'V' cancellations at the top and two cross cut cancels that are virtually invisible. Is evenly circulated and well centered. Also has interesting notations on the back." Photo below, courtesy Heritage Auctions, Dallas, Texas. (www.ha.com)

Serial number 666: Front and back.

Lyn Knight Currency Auctions *Overland Park, Kan.*	17-18 Aug 2001	VF+	1367	$14,740.00

Comments: Consigned by little-known Sam Feldman. Note simply described as a "problem-free, well-centered beauty." Photo above right, courtesy Lyn Knight.

Auction House	Sale Date	Grade or Condition	Serial Number	Sales Price

Serial number 1095: Front and back.

| Heritage Auctions Dallas, Tex. | 21-22 Sep 2001 | poc, Fine | 1095 | $5,500.00 |

Comments: Consigned by Dr. Walter B. Jones (1895-1977), State Geologist for Ala. Has "excellent color, five punch cancels." Above photo from Heritage Auctions.

| Centennial Auctions North Conway, N.H. | 24 Sep 2002 | Fine | 1294 | $12,937.50 |

Comments: Consignor unknown. Note is neither "punch, cut or pen cancelled. Bears June 7, 1861 back endorsement." Photo below, courtesy Heritage Auctions.

Serial number 1294: Front and back.

| Heritage Auctions Dallas, Tex. | 9-11 Jan 2003 | Fine+ | 1294 | $13,972.50 |

Comments: From the Gen. Felix Zollicoffer Camp Collection of Overton Co., Tenn. Note is "fully original, completely unmolested, with no repairs or problems of any kind. Moderately circulated." Above photo, courtesy Heritage Auctions.

Serial number 1329: Front and back.

| Lyn Knight Currency Auctions Overland Park, Kan. | 24-27 Apr 2003 | VG-F | 1329 | $9,200.00 |

Comments: Consignor unknown. Superbly restored. Above photo from Lyn Knight.

Auction House	Sale Date	Grade or Condition	Serial Number	Sales Price

Serial number 1150: Front and back.

Auction House	Sale Date	Grade or Condition	Serial Number	Sales Price
R.M. Smythe & Co. *New York, N.Y.*	13-14 Jun 2003	VF-XF	1150	$18,400.00

Comments: Consigned by Gene Mintz of San Luis Obispo Co., Calif. (p. 100). Note is "crisp, bright and vivid. Close margins at left and lower right. Small pinhole." Above photo, courtesy R. M. Smythe & Co., New York.

| R.M. Smythe & Co. *New York, N.Y.* | 5-6 Sep 2003 | VF-XF | 1006 | $13,800.00 |

Comments: Consigned by Chet Krause, founder of Krause Publications. Note "appears Almost Uncirculated. Light folds barely visible." Photo, bottom p. 222.

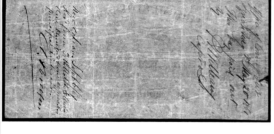

Serial number 906: Front and back.

| Heritage Auctions *Dallas, Tex.* | 8-10 Jan 2004 | F-VF | 906 | $11,500.00 |

Comments: Consigned by Alabamian Frank T. Kennedy. Note has a few minor pinholes, a couple of small ink smears. Above photo, courtesy Heritage Auctions.

Serial number 1350: Front and back.

| Heritage Auctions *Dallas, Tex.* | 21-23 Sep 2005 | F-VF | 1350 | $4,887.50 |

Comments: Consignor unknown. Note almost impossible to grade. Several defects, including two paper pulls, a corner tip off. Above photo from Crutch Williams.

*Serial number 918:
Front and back.*

Heritage Auctions Dallas, Tex.	21-23 Sep 2005	CU	918	$37,375.00

Comments: Consigned by Paul Angenend, an attorney in Austin, Texas focusing on transportation law. Certainly in the Top Ten of the Condition Census, this note is described as "by far the finest we have ever handled. Nicely margined, brilliantly colored, utterly original, and not a hint of a defect except the merest trace of a center bend." Above photo, courtesy Heritage Auctions, Dallas, Tex.

*Serial number 813:
Front and back.*

Heritage Auctions Dallas, Tex.	27-28 Apr 2006	Ch CU	813	$24,725.00

Comments: Consigned by Ben R. Powel, a noted attorney from Galveston, Tex. This fully original note "was able to avoid circulation, yet later was mounted with half-moon mounts in each corner." Above photo, courtesy Heritage Auctions.

*Serial number 1452:
Front and back.*

Heritage Auctions Dallas, Tex.	27-28 Apr 2006	VF+	1452	$21,850.00

Comments: Also from Ben R. Powel. "A perfect high-end circulated specimen with great color and eye appeal. No defects." Above photo, Heritage Auctions.

Auction House	Sale Date	Grade or Condition	Serial Number	Sales Price

Serial number 1390: Front and back.

| R.M. Smythe & Co. *New York, N.Y.* | 12 July 2006 | Fine | 1390 | $10,350.00 |

Comments: Consignor unknown. Note is "pleasant, with some bleed-through from the back endorsements." Above photo, courtesy R.M. Smythe & Company.

Serial number 1021: Front and back.

| Heritage Auctions *Dallas, Tex.* | 13-15 Sep 2006 | VF-XF | 1021 | $14,950.00 |

Comments: Consigned by Troy Wiseman, philanthropist who founded World Orphans. Note "has natural paper surfaces and dark green ink. Edges and colors are wholesome." Above photo, courtesy Heritage Auctions, Dallas, Texas.

| Heritage Auctions *Dallas, Tex.* | 4-6 Jan 2007 | Ch CU | 813 | $28,7500.00 |

Comments: Consigned by George P. Hammerly. Note "is one of the nicest we have seen. Brilliant colors, original surfaces, back endorsement." Photo, middle p. 240.

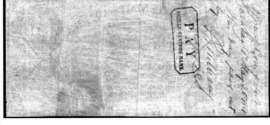

Serial number 948: Front and back.

| Heritage Auctions *Dallas, Tex.* | 4-6 Jan 2007 | poc, cc, F-VF | 948 | $7,187.50 |

Comments: Also from George Hammerly. Note's "cut and punch cancels have been neatly repaired, are hard to see." Above photo, courtesy Heritage Auctions.

Auction House	Sale Date	Grade or Condition	Serial Number	Sales Price

Serial number 1216: Front and back.

R.M. Smythe & Co. New York, N.Y.	13 Apr 2007	AU	1216	$26,450.00

Comments: Consigned by Western Reserve Historical Society in Cleveland. Note has "great color, with a small ink spot just above 'Montgomery.' Very light traces of mounting. Clear margins all around." Above photo, courtesy R.M. Smythe.

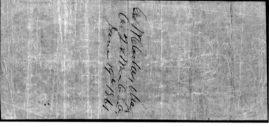

Serial number 1539: Front and back.

R.M. Smythe & Co. New York, N.Y.	5-6 July 2007	F-VF	1539	$10,925.00

Comments: Consignor unknown. Note has "beautiful deep green overprint and frame, two pinholes with light rust spots." Above photo, courtesy R. M. Smythe.

Serial number 1492: Front and back.

R.M. Smythe & Co. New York, N.Y.	5-6 July 2007	XF	1492	$25,300.00

Comments: The first of five consecutive consignments from Frederick R. Mayer (1928-2007), a Texas oilman who founded the Exeter Drilling Co., the largest privately owned drilling company in the U.S. (p. 104). Note has "a faint double center fold. Light corner handling, some hinge remnants on the back. Few pinholes near center. Ex Abner Kriesberg." Above photo, courtesy R. M. Smythe.

Auction House	Sale Date	Grade or Condition	Serial Number	Sales Price
R.M. Smythe & Co. New York, N.Y.	6 July 2007	XF	1378	$19,550.00

Comments: Frederick R. Mayer's second consignment. Note has "two pinholes, very light mounting traces, minor bleed, excellent color." Photo, bottom page 219.

Auction House	Sale Date	Grade or Condition	Serial Number	Sales Price
R.M. Smythe & Co. New York, N.Y.	6 July 2007	VF-XF	1228	$19,550.00

Comments: Frederick R. Mayer's third consignment. Note has "adequate margins, rich color, excellent paper quality, traces of hinge mounts." Photo, middle p. 227.

Auction House	Sale Date	Grade or Condition	Serial Number	Sales Price
R.M. Smythe & Co. New York, N.Y.	6 July 2007	VF-XF	1019	$16,100.00

Comments: Frederick R. Mayer's fourth consignment. Note has "some scattered pinholes and bleed-through. Color and margins excellent." Photo, top of p. 235.

Auction House	Sale Date	Grade or Condition	Serial Number	Sales Price
R.M. Smythe & Co. New York, N.Y.	6 July 2007	VF	987	$9,775.00

Comments: Frederick R. Mayer's fifth consignment. Note has "light stains in the corners. Color tint is vivid green. Ex T. Harrison Garrett." Photo, bottom p. 226.

Serial number 140: Front and back.

Auction House	Sale Date	Grade or Condition	Serial Number	Sales Price
Lyn Knight Currency Auctions Overland Park, Kan.	27 Jun 2008	VF	140	$16,100.00

Comments: Consignor unknown. Note has "exquisite color. Centering is quite nice, framing the note well. A problem-free note." Above photo, courtesy Lyn Knight.

Serial number 1264: Front and back.

Auction House	Sale Date	Grade or Condition	Serial Number	Sales Price
Spink Smythe Dallas, Tex.	16-17 July 2008	Fine	1264	$12,750.00

Comments: Consigned by Frederick Forbes Angus of Montreal, Canadian railway historian. Note is "professionally restored." Above photo, courtesy Spink Smythe.

Auction House	Sale Date	Grade or Condition	Serial Number	Sales Price
Heritage Auctions *Dallas, Tex.*	8-11 Jan 2009	F-VF	1539	-

Comments: Consignor unknown. Note has a couple of trivial ink-burn holes from the back endorsement. Has original surfaces, sound edges. Photo, middle p. 242.

Spink Smythe *Dallas, Tex.*	26-27 Jun 2009	AU	1492	$20,800.00

Comments: Consignor unknown. Note has "a few scattered pinholes at center, not readily visible. Clear margins all around. Great color." Photo, bottom page 242.

Serial number 1376: **Front and back.**	Neal Auction Company *New Orleans, La.*	21-22 Nov 2009	CU	1376	$15,535.00

Comments: Consigned by Fisher E. Simmons, Jr., an expert on postal history and steamboats that plied the Mississippi River. Note has "good margins, back ink endorsement has some bleed-through." Above photo, courtesy Neal Auction Co.

Stack's *New York, N.Y.*	30 Sept 2010	AU	918	$29,900.00

Comments: Consigned by Q. David Bowers, chairman emeritus of Stack's Bowers, prolific numismatic writer and one of America's premier numismatists ever. Census-condition note is "a high-grade example, essentially as made, with bold color." Ex William Philpott/Sexton/R.F. Schermerhorn. Photo, top of page 240.

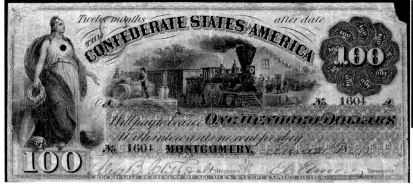
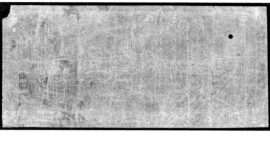

Serial number 1604: **Front and back.**	Neal Auction Company *New Orleans, La.*	20-21 Nov 2010	poc, VG	1604	$7,320.00

Comments: Consignor unknown. Note has "one small 2 mm. punch cancellation, top right corner missing, bottom right corner reattached, some scattered stains mostly on the back." Above photo, courtesy Neal Auction Co., New Orleans, La.

The $100 Montgomery Note Vs. Crude Oil, Silver and the S&P 500: Comparative Price Appreciation Since the End of the Civil War

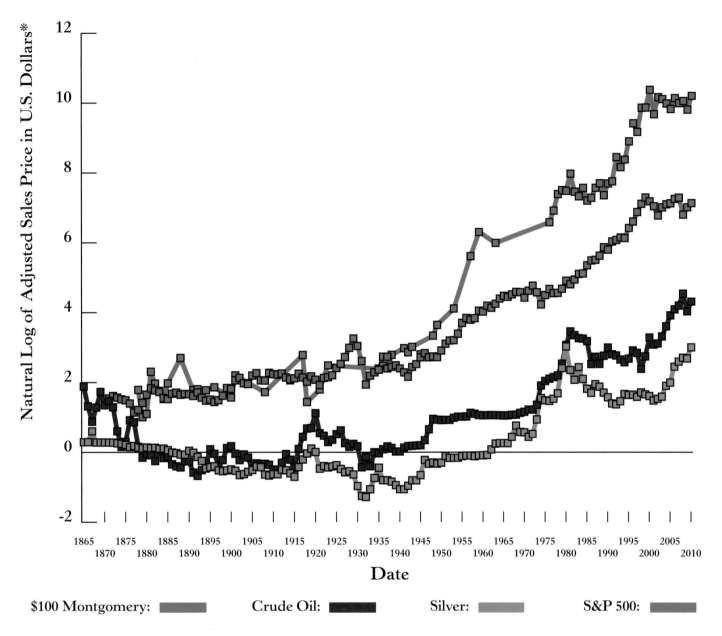

$100 Montgomery: Crude Oil: Silver: S&P 500:

Average Annual Rate of Return (Annual Percent Increase)

	From 1865 to 1950	From 1950 Through 2010	Total All Years: 1865 - 2010	Years Needed to Double in Value Since 1950
$100 Montgomery Note	1.8%	11.0%	7.4%	6.6
Silver	-1.3%	4.7%	1.6%	15.0
Crude Oil	-0.3%	5.8%	2.4%	12.2
S&P 500 Composite Index	1.8%	7.3%	4.3%	9.8

* The actual average sales price a Confederate Montgomery note, a troy ounce of silver, a barrel of crude oil or a market basket of common stocks comprising the S&P 500 Composite Index fetched during each year. Prices have been adjusted to show as a natural logarithm of the actual sales data to make the graph show differences more clearly. A full explanation of the methodology is provided in Chapter 4, beginning on page 140.

Chapter 7: Part Two

Qualitative Look at the $100 Montgomery Note: Its Innate Beauty and Eye Appeal

The Montgomery notes pictured here may have been auctioned before 1950, when it became commonplace to list serial numbers in auction descriptions – or perhaps they were never auctioned at all. In any case, there is no auction trail of their numbers, but that fact does not dim their beauty. They elicit as much enjoyment as those in Part One. Credits on page 301.

247

Chapter 8: Summary of Findings

The Confederate $50 Montgomery Note:
Its Survival Census and Historical Rate-of-Return

The beautiful, agrarian Confederate $50 Montgomery note pictured above (classified as Criswell Type-4, variety 4) is the smallest denomination of the four notes comprising the Montgomery series. Like the $100 Montgomery described in Chapter 7, a total of 1,606 specimens were issued -- 607 from the first printing and 999 more from a second printing that came perilously close to being confiscated by Federal officials in New York City.

The central vignette titled "Slaves Hoeing Cotton" is certainly the most appropriate of the four Montgomery vignettes for use by a fledging nation located in the southern part of North America. The "Slaves Hoeing Cotton" vignette was also used on the Confederate Type-41 issue and on other Southern bank notes, but, not surprisingly, given what would have been a polarizing image, I am not aware of its use on any note issued by the North. As such, the $50 Montgomery is the most uniquely Confederate of all the Montgomery issues; all the vignettes used on the other Montgomerys were being used on Northern notes at about the same time they appeared on the Montgomerys.

Details about the issuance of the Montgomery notes are found on pages 148-149 and will not be repeated here. It was noted earlier that the National Bank Note Company of New York (NBNC) originally printed 607 sheets of Treasury notes, with each sheet containing one each of the denominations of $1,000, $500, $100 and $50. The first 607 sheets were delivered to Montgomery, Ala., then the Confederate capital, on April 2, 1861, just before war erupted.

Upon delivery, Treasury Secretary Memminger immediately realized that demand would be stronger for the smaller denominations, so he contacted his New York agent, Gazaway Bugg Lamar, president of the Bank of the Republic, to ask the supplier to furnish an additional 1,000 impressions of each of the $100 and $50 notes. The company prepared a new two-subject plate and printed another 1,000 two-subject sheets just of the $100 and $50 denominations.

But the political climate had changed after the first printing of 607 sheets was delivered on April 2, 1861. Bombardment of Fort Sumter by Confederate forces had begun on April 12, and President Abraham Lincoln responded with two proclamations on April 15 and April 19 that ordered a blockade of Southern ports and a call-up of 75,000 Union militia. A state of war now existed between the two sides; the act of providing Treasury notes to the Rebel government could be considered aiding and abetting the enemy, a treasonable offense.

But an offense is a crime only when the transgression is discovered. How is it, then, that the second printing came so dangerously near confiscation by Federal officials in New York? The answer lies in a brilliant but unhappy New York engraver named Waterman L. Ormsby, who was briefly mentioned on page 128.

Waterman Lilly Ormsby was a Connecticut-born engraver of immense talent. He invented several processes used in the manufacture of bank notes, and he co-founded the Continental Bank Note Company in New York in 1863 while the war was raging.

Ormsby is an interesting character. *The Dictionary of American Biography* relates that he was born in 1809 and was soon apprenticed to an engraving establishment. At age 20 he enrolled at the National Academy of Design in New York, and in his early career he worked in Rochester, Albany and Lancaster, Mass., where he was employed by the firm of Carter, Andrews and Co. Finally, he settled in New York City and became owner of the New York Note Company, a competitor to the American Bank Note Company (ABNC) and the NBNC.

When Secretary Memminger appointed Gazaway Bugg Lamar as his agent in New York to contract for Confederate registered bonds (called "stock"), and Treasury notes, presumably Lamar held discussions with Ormsby at the New York Note Company, as well as with officials at the ABNC, which was ultimately awarded the contract (and which in turn sub-contracted the Treasury note portion of the order to the NBNC).

Ormsby must have been enraged that he received none of the Confederate printing business. He was already a hot head, as his biographer wrote that "He displays himself in his writings as a disgruntled eccentric, sensitive about his craftsmanship, and childish about his enmities. He considered himself discriminated against in business."

We do not know how Ormsby discovered that Lamar had ordered a second printing of the $100 and $50 denominations, but in a tightly knit industry like bank note engraving, it is reasonable to assume that there are few secrets, and Ormsby was presumably already aware that the Confederate Treasury had earlier placed an order for stocks, bonds and Treasury notes.

When Ormsby heard that the Confederate Treasury ordered more notes, he retaliated from being shut out from any of the business by tipping off the Union government that the NBNC was printing more Confederate currency. According to the *New York Tribune*, Federal marshals raided both the ABNC and NBNC on April 25, 1861 -- well after Lincoln's proclamations of April 15 and April 19 making actions such as printing Rebel stocks, bonds and Treasury notes a treasonable offense. The marshals succeeded in confiscating plates from both establishments, but the 1,000 two-subject sheets of $100 and $50 Montgomery notes had already been shipped. They finally arrived in Montgomery by May 4, as officials began issuing them on that date, according to Raphael P. Thian's *Register of the Confederate Debt*.

And who was the enterprising young newspaper reporter who scooped the front-page story for the *New York Tribune*? None other than Waterman Lilly Orsmby, Jr. -- son of the engraver Waterman Lilly Ormsby who tipped off the authorities in the first place.

Happily all the Montgomery notes ultimately arrived safely, so we can still amuse ourselves by updating the census of those notes that survived the war. Hugh Shull's most recent Montgomery census dated October 2011 (with hand annotations) shows 168 $50 Montgomery notes known to survive. I have updated Hugh's census to now include 176 specimens, all shown below. Those serial numbers followed by a parenthetical (A) below are pedigreed to specific auctions found in Part One starting on page 252. Similarly, those serial numbers followed by a parenthetical (B) below, while not pedigreed, are known to exist because we have their photographs in Part Two starting on page 284. Any serial number new to Shull's latest census is designated with a green oval. Fully 60% of these serial numbers (105) are verified to exist in either Part One or Part Two of this chapter.

Serial Numbers of Surviving $50 Montgomery Notes as of January 1, 2012:

7	373 (A)	847	968 (B)	1259 (B)
63 (A)	388	860 (B)	970	1266 (A)
88	393	862 (A)	983	1273
93	394 (A)	868	992 (A)	1283 (B)
94 (A)	398 (A) NEW	870	993	1294 (B)
113	403 (B) NEW	871 (B)	995 (B)	1304
121	407	873 (B)	997	1307 (A)
148 (A)	411 (A)	876 (A)	1004 NEW	1309
163 (B)	415 (B) NEW	881	1005 (A)	1311
177 (A)	424 (A)	882	1026	1315 (A)
179 (A)	431 (B)	888 (B)	1039 (A)	1319 (A) NEW
188 (A)	434 (B)	889 (A)	1067	1321
202	447 (A)	890 (B)	1079	1333
213 (B)	448	894 (B)	1083 (A)	1334
228	458 (A)	895	1084 (A)	1335 (A)
242 (A)	617	898 (B) NEW	1085 (A)	1350
243	676	901 (A)	1094	1365 (B)
247 (B)	678	902 (B)	1095 (A)	1367 (A)
248 (A)	685 (A)	914 (A) NEW	1126	1372 (B)
249 (A)	696 (B)	915 (A)	1128 (B)	1397
251 (A)	715 (A)	916 (A)	1130 (A)	1399 (A)
256	730	920 (A)	1136 (A)	1432
265 (A)	735 (A)	921 (B)	1137 (A) NEW	1439 (A)
271	814	922 (A)	1139 (A)	1441 (A)
275 (B)	816	923 (A)	1140 (A)	1465 (A)
276 (B)	817 (A)	924	1142	1473 (B)
287	818 (A)	925 (A)	1147 (A)	1481 (A)
288 (B)	819 (A)	929 (A)	1173 (A)	1546
310	820 (A)	936 (A)	1191	1561
311	826	943	1194 (B)	1574 (A)
315	834 (B)	945	1207 (A)	1576
327 (A)	840 (B)	949 (A)	1208	1578
330 (A)	842	955 (A)	1209	
342	843	961	1211	
349 (B)	845 (A)	965	1234	
358 (A)	846	967 (B)	1241	

Those Montgomerys found in Part One of this chapter starting on page 252 define the database for the calculation of a rate of return for the $50 Montgomery note from 1865 through 2010. Rates of return were also obtained for precious metals (i.e., silver), energy (i.e., crude oil), and the stock market (i.e., the S&P 500 Composite Index) to use for comparison.

Results from the $50 Montgomery mimic the remarkable returns achieved by the $100 note and provide solid affirmation of the suitability of collecting Confederate Montgomery notes. The $50 Montgomery has increased in value, on average, 7.3% each year since 1865, more than any of the alternative investment options. The much hyped S&P 500 Composite Index placed second, at a rate of return of 4.3% each year (not including the re-investment of any dividends paid, which would add 1.9% to the total annual return[1]). Crude oil and silver trailed sharply.

These results can be seen on the full-page graph on page 283 or on the smaller version below:

The $50 Montgomery Note Vs. Crude Oil, Silver and the S&P 500:
Comparative Price Appreciation Since the End of the Civil War

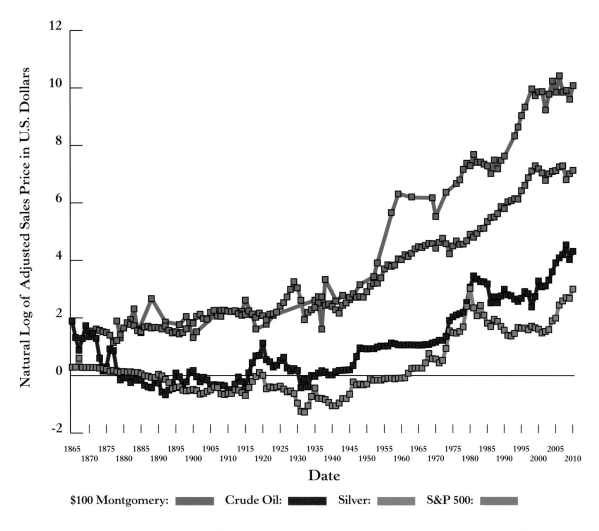

The graph above shows how little any of the four investment choices appreciated from 1865 to 1950. Since 1950, though, all four investment alternatives have shown attractive growth, led by the gaudy 11.0% enjoyed by the $50 Montgomery, followed by the S&P 500 at 7.3%.

In other words, this analysis suggests that, if these historical rates of return are maintained, a $50 Montgomery note purchased January 1, 2011 at a fair market value of $25,000 (as determined in a public auction) would be worth $50,000 on September 1, 2017, about six years eight months later. On the other hand, an investment of $25,000 on January 1, 2011 in a market basket of common stocks comprising the S&P 500 would not be worth $50,000 until November 1, 2020, nearly 10 years after its purchase.

And neither shiny bars of silver, stacks of shares of stocks comprising the S&P 500 nor tankers of sticky crude oil can hold a match to the intrinsic beauty of a $50 Montgomery note.

[1]Used with permission of, and special thanks to, Bryan Taylor, Ph.D., Global Financial Data, Inc., Los Angeles.

Chapter 8: Part One

Quantitative Look at Auction Sales of the Confederate $50 Montgomery Note In Chronological Order Since 1865

Auction House	Sale Date	Grade or Condition*	Serial Number	Sales Price
John W. Haseltine *Philadelphia, Pa.*	24-25 Apr 1878	UNC	-	$5.50

Comments: Like the $100 Montgomery, it is surprising that the first $50 was sold at public auction over 12 years after the first $1000 and $500 Montgomerys, both far rarer. This note is from Haseltine's own collection of Confederate currency and bonds. It is hand-dated "May 3," indicating a serial number between 266 and 465, according to R. P. Thian's *Register* (p. 41). Note is "Uncirculated, clean, rare."

Bangs & Co. *New York, N.Y.*	16 Nov 1878	pen c, Poor	-	$1.00

Comments: From Dr. William Lee, professor and author in 1875 of *The Currency of the Confederate States of America* (page 32). Lee consigned most of his collection to Frossard in 1885. Note dated May 3 and is "Poor, torn, and stamped Cancelled."

Bangs & Co. *New York, N.Y.*	25 Mar 1879	UNC	-	$3.70

Comments: Consigned by J. E. Barratt, possibly a physician, who died about 1878. Cataloged by C.H. Bechtel. Barratt owned all four Montgomerys, a Confederate cent and the Lovett dies, which sold for $8.00. Hand-dated "May 14," indicating a serial number between 810 and 959. Note is "Uncirculated, beautiful, clean."

John Walter Scott *New York, N.Y.*	20 Mar 1882	Fine	-	$4.60

Comments: Consigned by little-known William P. Brown. Note "Very rare."

*Legend. **cc**:* A note with a "cut cancel" has slits usually shaped like a cross but with no paper missing.
***poc**:* A "punch out cancel" is a series of round holes, from one or two up to six or eight, about the size of a pencil eraser. Depending on the number and size of the holes, some paper is missing.
***coc**:* A note with a "cut out cancel" has significant paper missing, usually coming in the shape of a pair of triangles or half-moons.
***pen c**:* A "pen cancel" is an unusual form of cancellation where the word "Cancelled" is written or stamped across the face of the note.

A new war could erupt today over the application of grading standards to Confederate currency. After all, it is the grade that ultimately determines value. Grades in this book are taken from the actual auction catalog description. Certainly grading standards changed over the 150-year duration of these auction results. Abbreviations used, from best to worst, include **CU** - Crisp Uncirculated; **UNC** - Uncirculated; **AU** - About Uncirculated; **XF** - Extremely Fine; **VF** - Very Fine; **F** - Fine; **VG** - Very Good; **G** - Good; **Fr** - Fair and **P** - Poor. A note grading "Crisp Uncirculated" or "Uncirculated" is brand new as if it just came off the printing press. A "Very Fine" note has seen circulation as shown by both vertical and horizontal quarter folds, but the note retains its body or crispness. Conversely, "Good" notes retain no body and have extreme wear, frayed edges or even slight tears, if they do not impinge on the main design.

Auction House	Sale Date	Grade or Condition	Serial Number	Sales Price
William Elliot Woodward *Boston, Mass.*	28 Dec 1882	VF	-	$3.00

Comments: Consigned by Paul J. Maas of Laporte, Ind., a major coin collector in the late 1800s whose focus went from U.S. coins, medals and store cards to foreign coins only. Note dated May 16 and described as "Very fine and rare."

John W. Haseltine *Philadelphia, Pa.*	10 Apr 1883	cc, VF	-	$9.00

Comments: Consigned by Harold P. Newlin, a Pennsylvania attorney who "wrote the book" titled *The Early Half Dimes of the United States* on half dimes and dimes. Note described as "Very fine. Clean, cancelled by smooth cut. Excessively rare."

John W. Haseltine *Philadelphia, Pa.*	15-16 Nov 1883	Fine	-	$3.25

Comments: Consigned by little-known Bernard Schramm. Note is "Very rare."

John W. Haseltine *Philadelphia, Pa.*	12-13 Mar 1884	UNC	-	$4.25

Comments: Consignor unknown. Note tersely described as "Uncirculated. Rare."

John W. Haseltine *Philadelphia, Pa.*	28 Aug 1884	UNC	-	$3.00

Comments: Consignor unknown. Note simply described as "Uncirculated. Rare."

William Elliot Woodward *Boston, Mass.*	13 Oct 1884	VF	-	$4.00

Comments: Consignor unknown. Note simply described as "Clean, uncancelled and extremely rare."

Charles Steigerwalt *Lancaster, Pa.*	19-20 Dec 1884	Fine	-	$5.10

Comments: Consigned by little-known William Starr. Note is "Fine, very rare."

Left, serial #922, right, #819.

Henry G. Sampson *New York, N.Y.*	12-13 Feb 1885	UNC	922	$3.63

Comments: Consignor unknown. Note is "Uncirculated. Rare." Photo above left, courtesy Amanda Sheheen, A&O Currency, LLC, *www.aocurrency.com.*

Lyman Haines Low *New York, N.Y.*	26 Mar 1885	VF	-	$3.50

Comments: Consignor unknown. Note simply described as "Very Fine and clean."

Auction House	Sale Date	Grade or Condition	Serial Number	Sales Price
Charles Steigerwalt *Lancaster, Pa.*	11 Apr 1885	Fine	-	$2.25

Comments: Possibly consigned by Robert Herr or a Barclay; Steigerwalt does not suggest which one. Note described as "Fine, very rare."

Charles Steigerwalt *Lancaster, Pa.*	4-5 Jun 1885	AU	-	$3.00

Comments: Consigned by either "Barclay" or "Rohrer"; Steigerwalt does not indicate which one. Note is "Almost uncirculated. Very rare."

George W. Massamore *Baltimore, Md.*	21 Nov 1885	VF	-	$2.50

Comments: Consignor unknown, although the first auction of a $50 Montgomery by George W. Massamore, who wrote *Descriptive and Chronological Catalogue of Confederate Currency* in 1889. Note simply described as "Very Fine. Series A."

David U. Proskey *New York, N.Y.*	15 Dec 1885	poc, Fine	-	$3.50

Comments: From a "Betts," presumably Benjamin (1822-1908), a founder of the ANS who consigned this note to the celebrated auction of R. P. Thian's collection (p. 41). Betts sold his coins at auction between 1871 and 1907. Note is "punched."

Edouard Frossard *Brooklyn, N.Y.*	22 Dec 1885	Fine	-	$1.50

Comments: Consigned by Dr. William Lee, professor and author in 1875 of *The Currency of the Confederate States of America* (page 32). Lee earlier consigned a very poor specimen of a $50 Montgomery to a Bangs & Co. sale in 1878. Note "Fine."

Serial number 251: Front and back.

S.H. & H. Chapman *Philadelphia, Pa.*	17 Oct 1888	VF	251	$8.25

Comments: Consigned by Ferguson Haines, a noted coin collector born in Maine in 1840. Attended Phillips Academy in Andover, Mass. and Dartmouth. Retailed hardware and manufactured textiles. Served as mayor of Biddeford, Me. and was a member of the Maine House of Representatives. Note is "Uncancelled. Very Fine. Very rare." Above photo, courtesy current owner Marvin Ashmore.

George W. Massamore *Baltimore, Md.*	15 Oct 1891	UNC	-	-

Comments: Consigned by little-known William Thomsen. Note "crisp, very rare."

Auction House	Sale Date	Grade or Condition	Serial Number	Sales Price
Edouard Frossard *Brooklyn, N.Y.*	9 Jun 1892	UNC	-	$4.50

Comments: Consigned by Hiram E. Deats (1870-1963) of Flemington, N. J., foreman of the grand jury that indicted Bruno Hauptman for kidnapping the Lindbergh baby. Deats was a charter member and the senior member at the time of his death of both the ANA and the American Philatelic Society. Note described as "crisp, new, rare."

John Walter Scott *New York, N.Y.*	29 Jun 1892	Fine	-	$4.50

Comments: Consignor unknown. Note simply described as "Fine, rare."

John Walter Scott *New York, N.Y.*	26-27 Jun 1893	Fine	-	-

Comments: Consigned by little-known J.E. Herman. Note part of a 57-note lot.

Edouard Frossard *Brooklyn, N.Y.*	14 Nov 1893	UNC	-	-

Comments: Consignor unknown. Note part of a set of all four Montgomerys which sold for $87.50. Described as "Crisp, new, very rare."

Charles Steigerwalt *Lancaster, Pa.*	28 Jun 1894	poc, XF	-	$2.50

Comments: Consigned by little-known Charles Luckenbach. Note is "Extra fine, cancelled by six minute holes. Rare."

Edouard Frossard *Brooklyn, N.Y.*	19 Dec 1894	UNC	-	$4.30

Comments: Four consecutive lots consigned by Ferguson Haines, the noted coin collector and politician from Maine who was both a retailer and manufacturer and who consigned a lesser note to a Chapman Brothers' auction in 1888 (see facing page). This first note is "crisp, new, rare."

Edouard Frossard *Brooklyn, N.Y.*	19 Dec 1894	UNC	-	$5.00

Comments: The second lot from Ferguson Haines. Note is "crisp, new, rare."

Edouard Frossard *Brooklyn, N.Y.*	19 Dec 1894	XF	-	$4.30

Comments: The third lot from Ferguson Haines. Note is "Extremely fine, rare."

Edouard Frossard *Brooklyn, N.Y.*	19 Dec 1894	XF	-	$4.30

Comments: The fourth lot from Ferguson Haines. Note is "Extremely fine, rare."

Charles Steigerwalt *Lancaster, Pa.*	17 Jan 1895	poc, XF	-	-

Comments: Consigned by little-known John Wright. Note described as "Extra Fine, cancelled by six minute holes."

Auction House	Sale Date	Grade or Condition	Serial Number	Sales Price
Charles Steigerwalt *Lancaster, Pa.*	25 Jun 1895	poc, XF	-	-

Comments: Consigned by little-known Grant Weaver. Note described as "Extra Fine, cancelled by six small holes."

Charles Steigerwalt *Lancaster, Pa.*	6 Jan 1896	poc, AU	-	-

Comments: Consigned by little-known Robert Watts. Note described as "Nearly Uncirculated. Cancelled by six small punch holes."

John Walter Scott *New York, N.Y.*	20 Jan 1896	VF	-	-

Comments: Consignor unknown. Lot consisted of a Thian album containing 59 notes, including both the $100 and $50 Montgomerys. Entire lot sold for $17.50.

Charles Steigerwalt *Lancaster, Pa.*	24 Mar 1896	AU	-	$4.60

Comments: Consigned by little-known John Wilson. Note "About uncirculated."

Charles Steigerwalt *Lancaster, Pa.*	24 Mar 1896	poc, VF	-	$4.00

Comments: Also from John Wilson. Note is "cancelled by six punch holes."

Charles Steigerwalt *Lancaster, Pa.*	16 July 1896	AU	-	$4.40

Comments: Consignor uncertain. Note "practically uncirculated. Scarcely less."

Lyman Haines Low *New York, N.Y.*	21 Dec 1898	VG	-	$2.75

Comments: Consigned by James T. Callender, a noted early coin collector, particularly gold coins. Note "Very Good, rare."

Charles Steigerwalt *Lancaster, Pa.*	25 Apr 1899	AU	-	-

Comments: Consignor unknown. Note is "Practically uncirculated."

Charles Steigerwalt *Lancaster, Pa.*	25 Apr 1899	poc, XF	-	-

Comments: Consignor unknown. Note called a "duplicate. Extremely fine but cancelled with two holes, 1/8 in. and four smaller holes."

S.H. & H. Chapman *Philadelphia, Pa.*	16 Nov 1900	CU	-	$4.50

Comments: Consigned by the eminent Dr. Edward Maris (1832-1900), a Philadelphia Quaker who assembled comprehensive collections of New Jersey cents, autograph letters, Colonial currency and South American coins. Original classifier of the 1794 cent varieties. Owned original charter granted to William Penn for the Commonwealth of Pennsylvania. Note described as "Crisp, uncirculated note in beautiful condition. Rare."

Auction House	Sale Date	Grade or Condition	Serial Number	Sales Price
S.H. & H. Chapman *Philadelphia, Pa.*	16 Nov 1900	pen c, cc, VF	-	$1.75

Comments: Second consignment from Edward Maris. Note is "stamped 'Cancelled' across the face and cross cut, nothing removed. Very fine."

| Lyman Haines Low
New York, N.Y. | 18 Jun 1901 | AU | - | $3.85 |

Comments: Most likely consigned by R.O. Montambault, a Canadian from Quebec who joined the ANA in 1920. Note described as "few pinholes in center and one perpendicular crease, otherwise about perfect. Rare."

| Charles Steigerwalt
Lancaster, Pa. | 9 Jan 1906 | poc, VF | - | - |

Comments: Consignor unknown. Note "has six cancel holes. Very fine."

| Thomas Lindsay Elder
New York, N.Y. | 26-27 Feb 1908 | Fine | - | $5.00 |

Comments: Most likely consigned by J. N. T. Levick (about 1828-1908) of New York City, one of the earliest American numismatists who served with distinction during the Civil War. Active in the ANS, in 1866 he proposed a monthly journal that continues to be published to this day. Note "rare."

| Henry Chapman
Philadelphia, Pa. | 19-20 Jun 1908 | XF | 845 | $6.25 |

Comments: Consigned by Harmon Chambers (1822-1905) of the "Confederate Triumvirate," who founded an insurance brokerage business in Philadelphia (page 51). Note is hand-dated May 14 and is "Extremely Fine. Rare."

| Charles Steigerwalt
Lancaster, Pa. | 24 Feb 1909 | poc, Fine | - | - |

Comments: Consigned by little-known Adam Eberly. Note is "Fine except six small cancel holes."

| Ben G. Green
Chicago, Ill. | 28 Mar 1913 | XF | - | $6.20 |

Comments: Consigned by little-known Charles Morris VI. Note is hand-dated "May 16," indicating a serial number between 960 and 1253, according to R. P. Thian's *Register*. Note has "two pin holes. Rare."

| Edward Michael
Chicago, Ill. | 9 May 1914 | VG | 251 | $5.25 |

Comments: Consigned by the estate of Ben Green of Chicago (p. 52), generally considered the first Midwestern coin dealer. Note simply described as "Very Good. Small tear. Rare." Photo, page 254.

| Samuel Hudson Chapman
Philadelphia, Pa. | 27-29 May 1914 | poc, VF | - | $3.00 |

Comments: Consigned by William Gable of Altoona, Pa., founder of a very large department store and owner of virtually complete U.S. coin series. Note is "cancelled, small holes."

Auction House	Sale Date	Grade or Condition	Serial Number	Sales Price
U.S. Coin Company *New York, N.Y.*	29 Jun 1914	XF	-	$7.50

Comments: The unknown owner consigned this lot to the United States Coin Company, founded in 1912 by Wayte Raymond, one of America's greatest numismatists of all time. Note is hand-dated "May 21," indicating a serial number between 1257 and 1259. Note "very rare, endorsed on reverse."

U.S. Coin Company *New York, N.Y.*	5 Jun 1917	XF	-	$6.00

Comments: Consigned by either H. H. Butler or F.Y. Parker -- Raymond does not indicate which one. Note is hand-dated "May 14," indicating a serial number between 810 and 959. Note is "clean, crisp, very rare." Purchased by A.P. Wylie of Wheaton, Ill., who apparently sold this note at a Bolender auction in 1936.

Lyman Haines Low *New York, N.Y.*	22 May 1918	cc, Fine	-	$2.50

Comments: Consigned by little-known Henry McCullough. Note described as "Fine, cancelled, note complete. Rare."

B. Max Mehl *Ft. Worth, Tex.*	17 Apr 1923	AU	-	$6.80

Comments: Consignor uncertain. Note described as "Practically uncirculated."

Serial number 94: Front and back.

Thomas Lindsay Elder *New York, N.Y.*	28 Sep 1915	cc, Fine	94	$6.50

Comments: Consignor unknown. This note represented Elder's first sale of a $50 Montgomery. Note "cancelled by a slit. Guirot signature on reverse." Above photo, courtesy of the late great philatelist Gordon Bleuler of Dallas, Texas.

Wayte Raymond *New York, N.Y.*	4 Dec 1918	VF	-	-

Comments: The unknown owner consigned this lot to Wayte Raymond, whose U.S. Coin Company had dissolved just before this sale. Note "Very Fine."

Thomas Lindsay Elder *New York, N.Y.*	23-26 Feb 1921	poc, Good	1137	$1.10

Comments: Consigned by the estate of M. K. McMullin, who collected American and foreign gold coins. Elder described note as "Extremely rare."

Auction House	Sale Date	Grade or Condition	Serial Number	Sales Price

Serial number 1084: Front and back.

Thomas Lindsay Elder *New York, N.Y.*	26-27 Aug 1921	UNC	1084	$6.25

Comments: Consigned by Lewis C. Gehring (1852-1921) of Brooklyn, N. Y., who was born in Rahway, N. J. before moving to Brooklyn. A prominent banker of the Prudential Savings Bank, with interests in feed and milling. Collected gold coins. Note described as "very rare." Above photo, courtesy owner William H. Kelly.

Stan V. Henkels *Philadelphia, Pa.*	28 July 1922	UNC	-	-

Comments: Consigned by the legendary John C. Browne, perhaps the greatest Confederate collector (see page 58). Part of a 90-note "Uncirculated" type set.

Thomas Lindsay Elder *New York, N.Y.*	9-11 Oct 1924	AU	914	-

Comments: Consigned by Edward H. Eckfeldt, Jr. of Orange, N.J., a direct descendant of Adam Eckfeldt, the first coiner of the U.S. Mint. Note described as "Very rare gem, mounted under celluloid."

William Hesslein *Boston, Mass.*	20-21 Sep 1929	VF	-	-

Comments: Consigned by H. D. Allen of Boston, whose articles on Confederate currency appeared in *The Numismatist* from 1917-1919 (p. 56). Note is "rare."

William Hesslein *Boston, Mass.*	22-23 Nov 1929	cc, VF	-	-

Comments: Another consignment from H. D. Allen of Boston (see above). Note is "cut cancelled in two places and restored. Very rare."

Milfred Henry Bolender *Freeport, Ill.*	15 Oct 1935	XF	-	$10.00

Comments: Consigned by dealer Andrew Mason Smith (1841-1915), of Minneapolis, whose coin collection totaled over 15,000 pieces and included the unique 1884 proof set struck in copper. Note hand-dated "May 16," indicating a serial number between 960 and 1253. Note described as "very rare."

Milfred Henry Bolender *Freeport, Ill.*	8 Feb 1936	XF	920	$10.00

Comments: Consigned by A. P. Wylie of Wheaton, Ill., a dealer and collector of U.S. coins and currency. This note appears to be the same note Wylie bought at a U.S. Coin Co. sale in 1914 (see p. 258). Note dated "May 14," called "very rare."

Auction House	Sale Date	Grade or Condition	Serial Number	Sales Price
John Milford Henderson *Columbus, Oh.*	4 Apr 1936	VG	-	$3.60

Comments: Consigned by Henrie E. Buck of Delaware, Ohio, first ANA vice president in 1908. Note described as "Very Good. One mend at top."

Stack's *New York, N.Y.*	3-4 Dec 1937	UNC	-	$5.00

Comments: Consignor unknown. Note simply described as "very rare."

B. Max Mehl *Ft. Worth, Tex.*	22 Mar 1938	UNC	819	-

Comments: Consigned by Benjamin H. Collins (1845-1928) of Washington, D.C., a collector, ANA member and dealer with a coin shop in Washington. Born in Missouri, he served in the Union Army before finding employment at the U.S. Treasury. Note is part of a set of Montgomerys which sold for $170. Photo bottom right, page 253, from Max Mehl catalog.

Barney Bluestone *Syracuse, N.Y.*	7-8 Oct 1938	XF	-	$20.50

Comments: Consignor unknown. Note simply described as "very rare."

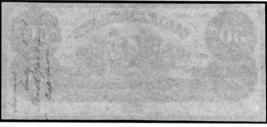

Serial number 876:
Front and back.

Thomas Lindsay Elder *New York, N.Y.*	12 May 1939	UNC	876	-

Comments: Consignor uncertain. Note impressively described as "A gem." Above photo, courtesy Heritage Auctions, Dallas, Texas, *www.ha.com*

B. Max Mehl *Ft. Worth, Tex.*	3 Jun 1941	UNC	819	$13.25

Comments: Consigned by Mehl himself, who bought it from Benjamin Collins (see above) and included it within the auction of the celebrated William F. Dunham (1857-1936) of Chicago, former grocer, teacher and stockbroker who served as chairman of the Board of Governors of the ANA. Note "Perfect. As fine as exists. Endorsed on back as usual." Photo, bottom right, page 253.

B. Max Mehl *Ft. Worth, Tex.*	9 Mar 1943	UNC	447	$13.50

Comments: Consigned by Henry E. Elrod of Houston, Tex., active ANA member who focused on European coins and also consigned U.S. coins to this sale, including four-dollar and fifty-dollar gold pieces. Note "endorsed on back."

Auction House	Sale Date	Grade or Condition	Serial Number	Sales Price

Serial number 394: Front and back.

| Milfred Henry Bolender *Freeport, Ill.* | 23 Jun 1943 | Fair | 394 | $3.25 |

Comments: Consigned by little-known "Patterson" or "Hand." Note described as "Very Fair. Rare." Above photo, courtesy William H. Kelly, Asharoken, N.Y.

| Barney Bluestone *Syracuse, N.Y.* | 27-28 Apr 1945 | CU | - | $14.00 |

Comments: Consignor unknown. Note described as "Uncancelled. Crisp. Uncirculated. Lists $12.50 in Fine, should realize more."

Serial number 685: Front and back.

| Milfred Henry Bolender *Freeport, Ill.* | 20 Mar 1948 | XF | 685 | $16.00 |

Comments: Consigned by Loring T. Reckard of Chicago, ANA member from 1916 who also collected stamps and coins. Note "Extra Fine and choice." Photo above.

Serial number 373: Front and back.

| Milfred Henry Bolender *Freeport, Ill.* | 2 Oct 1948 | Fine | 373 | $12.50 |

Comments: Also consigned by Loring T. Reckard (see above). Note described as "Fine. Rare. Catalogs for $12.50. One Extra Fine sold at $16 in my last sale." Above photo, courtesy Heritage Auctions, Dallas, Texas, *www.ha.com*

Auction House	Sale Date	Grade or Condition	Serial Number	Sales Price
Milfred Henry Bolender _Freeport, Ill._	23 Feb 1952	Ch UNC	876	$31.00

Comments: Consignor is uncertain; probably owned by Bolender himself. Note described as "Uncirculated, choice and never folded. Worth $25." Photo, p. 260.

| New Netherlands Coin Co. _New York, N.Y._ | 26 Sep 1953 | AU | 1095 | $42.00 |

Comments: Consigned by Hillyer Ryder (about 1851-1928) of New York, author of _The Colonial Coins of Vermont_ and _The Copper Coins of Massacusetts._ Member of the ANA and New York Numismatic Club. Collection sold to Wayte Raymond in 1945, who sold much of the coinage at a public auction in November 1945, with remnants sold by New Netherlands. Note "About uncirculated. A few pinholes."

Serial number 1136: Front and back.

| Federal Coin Exchange _Cleveland, Oh._ | 10-13 Jan 1957 | XF | 1136 | $210.00 |

Comments: Consigned by Charles W. "Suitcase Charlie" Foster of Rushville, N.Y., once ANA librarian and curator. Authored _Historical Arrangement of United States Commemorative Coins._ Co-founder of Empire State Numismatic Association. Note tersely described as "Worth $50." Above photo, courtesy owner Tig Sogoian.

Serial number 188: Front and back.

| James, Inc. _Louisville, Ky._ | 29 Mar 1957 | Abt XF | 188 | - |

Comments: Consignor unknown. Note described as "Small ink-acid tear near flourish. Otherwise About Extremely Fine and Crisp. Brought $210 in January." Above photo, courtesy Heritage Auctions, Dallas, Texas, _www.ha.com._

| D&W Auction Sales _Baltimore, Md._ | 3 Apr 1959 | VF-XF | 901 | $297.50 |

Comments: Consignor unknown. Has "almost perfect obverse, creases on reverse."

Auction House	Sale Date	Grade or Condition	Serial Number	Sales Price
Federal Brand Enterprises *Cleveland, Oh.*	13-15 Jul 1963	XF	-	$375.00

Comments: Consigned by the larger-than-life Grover Criswell (see page 81). Note is hand-dated "May 16," indicating a serial number between 960 and 1253, according to R. P. Thian's *Register*. Note "is clean and extremely fine."

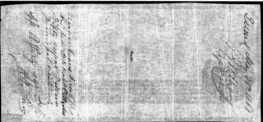

Serial number 1147:
Front and back.

Stack's *New York, N.Y.*	2-5 Oct 1963	VF	1147	$270.00

Comments: Consigned by George O. Walton (about 1907-1962) of Roanoke, Va. and later Charlotte, N.C. Founder of the Mid-Atlantic Numismatic Association. Killed in head-on auto crash en route to coin show. Owned a genuine 1913 Liberty Head Nickel. Collection strong on U.S. gold and Pioneer/Territorial gold. Note "Very Fine, average condition." Above photo, courtesy Heritage Auctions.

Serial number 916:
Front and back.

Lester Merkin *New York, N.Y.*	28-29 Mar 1969	pen c, poc, VG	916	$170.00

Comments: Consignor unknown. Note has "small cancellation holes at either end." Above photo, courtesy William H. Kelly, Asharoken, N.Y.

Hans M. F. Schulman *New York, N.Y.*	23-25 Mar 1970	Fine	-	$125.00

Comments: Consigned by either "Mabbott" or "Rosenbach," neither known to most numismatists. Note is a "Nice Fine. Badly wrinkled."

New Netherlands Coin Co. *New York, N.Y.*	27 Mar 1973	XF	1266	$425.00

Comments: Consignor unknown. Note "endorsed on reverse. Extra fine, two hinges, rare." Photo, bottom page 267.

	Auction House	Sale Date	Grade or Condition	Serial Number	Sales Price

Serial number 1130:
Front and back.

Lester Merkin
New York, N.Y.
20-21 Aug 1976 — XF — 1130 — $575.00

Comments: Labeled the Brussels Collection and cataloged by Douglas Ball. Note is "a seemingly uncirculated note with two light center, vertical folds and mounting stains." Above photo, courtesy a private Georgia collection.

Serial number 1315:
Front and back.

NASCA
Rockville Centre, N.Y.
27-28 May 1977 — Fine+ — 1315 — $475.00

Comments: Consigned by the Maryland Historical Society. Note has "a large oval seal on reverse in black on the left end reading 'Hohenthal & Reichman' with 'OK' in center. Note is well folded, bright and vivid with some crispness and no cancellation marks." Above photo, courtesy Amanda Sheheen, A&O Currency.

Serial number 63:
Front and back.

Kagin's
Des Moines, Ia.
29-30 Sep 1978 — cc, Fine — 63 — $625.00

Comments: Consignor unknown. Note has "closed cut cancels at left and right sides." Note once owned by Douglas Ball and donated to The Museum of the Confederacy, Richmond, Va., which provided the above photo.

Auction House	Sale Date	Grade or Condition	Serial Number	Sales Price
NASCA *Rockville Centre, N.Y.*	6-7 Dec 1978	F-VF	920	$745.50

Comments: Labeled The Sands Point Collection. Note "has nine vertical folds and one horizontal fold with four center pinholes. Paper is clean, crisp, wrinkled at center, the top border being slightly shaved. A better than average specimen."

NASCA *Rockville Centre, N.Y.*	30 Apr - 1 May 1979	F-VF	1136	$892.50

Comments: Consigned by Dr. Van B. Elliott, coin and currency collector. Although "note has folds suitable to the grade of Fine, its vivid printing, clean paper and the presence of only one small spot in the top border, combined with its good margins, justifies a better grade. Lovely." Photo, middle page 262.

NASCA *Rockville Centre, N.Y.*	6-7 Jun 1980	XF+	922	$1,575.00

Comments: Consignor unknown. Note has "a long corner fold at bottom left, two folded corner tips and multiple pinholes in the center. Remnants of a back mounting hinge. Issue endorsement in red ink." Photo, bottom left, page 253.

Serial number 1335: Front and back.

NASCA *Rockville Centre, N.Y.*	4-6 Sep 1980	Fine	1335	$945.00

Comments: Consignor unknown. Note has "typical wear for the grade, more than a hint of crispness, moderate paper aging and seven or so pinholes. Margins are complete and better than average." Above photo, courtesy R. M. Smythe & Co.

NASCA *Rockville Centre, N.Y.*	4-6 Sep 1980	poc, VG	1039	$341.25

Left, serial #1039, right, #179.

Comments: Consignor unknown. Note is "impaired, with six punch holes, splits and pieces missing from the left edge and on the lower left corner. Still a collectible example of this rare type." Photo above left, from NASCA catalog.

Auction House	Sale Date	Grade or Condition	Serial Number	Sales Price
Grover C. Criswell *Salt Springs, Fla.*	17 Oct 1980	UNC	876	-

Comments: Consigned by little-known Dr. Richard Rich. Note certainly merits consideration for inclusion in the Condition Census Top Ten. Paper bright, colors vivid, signatures clear and note well margined all around. Photo, page 260.

| Grover C. Criswell *Salt Springs, Fla.* | 17 Oct 1980 | Abt VG, Repaired | 179 | - |

Comments: Also consigned by little-known Dr. Richard Rich. Note is extensively repaired, lower left quarter being replaced. Photo, bottom right, page 265.

Left, serial #411, right, #248.

| Bowers & Ruddy Galleries *Los Angeles, Calif.* | 25-26 Mar 1981 | pen c, cc, F-VF | 411 | $1,200.00 |

Comments: From the collection of T. Harrison Garrett (1849-1888) of Baltimore, president of the B&O Railroad, upon de-accession by The Johns Hopkins Univ. His coin collection was considered second only to the Parmalee collection. This note "slit cancelled, hardly noticeable." Photo above left, courtesy Gordon Bleuler.

Serial number 818: Front and back.

| NASCA *Rockville Centre, N.Y.* | 10-12 Sep 1981 | UNC | 818 | $2,205.00 |

Comments: Consigned by Stanley Gibbons, London stamp dealer. Simply exceptional note, in the Condition Census Top Ten and a leading contender for the finest $50 Montgomery known. Graded by the conservative Ball as "Uncirculated. A lovely note trimmed close at bottom left with light mounting stains on the back. Six pinholes in the center." Ex William H. Kelly. Photo above.

| NASCA *Rockville Centre, N.Y.* | 19-21 Apr 1982 | F-VF | 248 | $1,470.00 |

Comments: Consigned by Grover Criswell, noted dealer (see page 81). Note has "about ten vertical folds and a center horizontal fold. Margins are complete and note is endorsed on the back." Photo above right, from NASCA 1982 catalog.

Auction House	Sale Date	Grade or Condition	Serial Number	Sales Price

NASCA
Rockville Centre, N.Y.
19-21 Apr 1982 · pen c, Fine · 358 · $630.00

Left, serial #358, right, #63.

Comments: A second consignment from Grover Criswell. Note has "cancellation stamps on the face and back." Photo above left, from NASCA 1982 catalog.

Serial number 1130: Front and back.

Christie's
New York, N.Y.
17 Sep 1982 · VF-XF · 1130 · $1,155.00

Comments: Consigned by Richard F. Saffin (1894-1982), a partner in the brokerage firm Boland Saffin Gordon & Sauffer. Note has "half dozen vertical folds that are all light, and there are no pinholes, smudges, stains, nicks to keep it from looking Uncirculated. A beautiful note." Above photo from a private Georgia collection.

Serial number 1266: Front and back.

Christie's
New York, N.Y.
17 Sep 1982 · VF · 1266 · $935.00

Comments: Also from Richard F. Saffin. Note is "uncancelled. Nearly as nice as the last, but a couple of the folds are a bit heavier." Above photo from Bill Kelly.

Christie's
New York, N.Y.
17 Sep 1982 · pen c, cc, F-VF · 63 · $605.00

Comments: Another from Richard F. Saffin. Note "cut and stamp cancelled. Well circulated, but bright, clean, undamaged. Face stamp light." Photo, bottom p. 264.

Auction House	Sale Date	Grade or Condition	Serial Number	Sales Price
Christie's *New York, N.Y.*	8 Dec 1982	VF	330	$1,210.00

Comments: Consignor unknown. Note uncancelled. Vertical folds not noticeable.

Christie's *New York, N.Y.*	8 Dec 1982	Fine	1315	$605.00

Comments: Consignor unknown. Note uncancelled. Portion of endorsement bleeds through to face. Numerous folds, moderately limp. Photo, middle p. 264.

Christie's *New York, N.Y.*	8 Dec 1982	pen c, poc, VG	916	$660.00

Comments: Consignor unknown. Pen and punch cancelled. Photo, middle p. 263.

Serial number 1399: *Front and back.*	NASCA *Rockville Centre, N.Y.*	10-12 Jan 1983	VG-F	1399	$656.25

Comments: Part of the massive John C. Browne collection, consigned by Charles J. Affleck (1892-1974) of Winchester, Va., author of *Obsolete Paper Money of Va*. Note "uncancelled. Traces of crispness, water stains." Above photo from Spink Smythe.

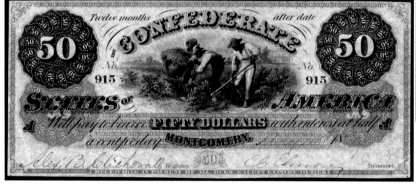 

Serial number 915: *Front and back.*	Kagin's *Des Moines, Ia.*	16-20 Aug 1983	cc, XF	915	$990.00

Comments: Consignor unknown. Note "near perfect except for slight toning and corner crease." Above photo, courtesy R. M. Smythe & Company, New York.

NASCA *Rockville Centre, N.Y.*	1-2 Nov 1983	Fair	179	$367.50

Comments: Listed in the Abner Reed Catalog, but probably consigned by John Ford. Reed (1771-1866) was a bank note engraver; his proof notes were obtained by F.C.C. Boyd and later Ford. Problem with this note "is that the lower left quadrant has been restored in toto. Looks passable." Photo, bottom right, p. 265.

Auction House	Sale Date	Grade or Condition	Serial Number	Sales Price

Serial number 929: Front and back.

Stack's
New York, N.Y.
20 Mar 1984 — F-VF — 929 — $825.00

Comments: From John L. Roper (1902-1983) of Norfolk, Va., a ship builder. Note has "a dozen or so folds, but the paper is still crisp, the top border shaved. Endorsed on the back in red ink." Above photo, courtesy Heritage Auctions.

NASCA - Karp
New York, N.Y.
28-29 Mar 1985 — poc, Good — 1173 — $357.50

Comments: Consigned by little-known Ben O. Anderson. Note has "six filled punch holes, shaved borders. Faded back endorsements. Good." Photo below left, from NASCA 1985 catalog.

NASCA - Karp
New York, N.Y.
28-29 Mar 1985 — Fair — 148 — $231.00

Left, serial #1173, right, #148.

Comments: Another consignment from Ben O. Anderson. Note is "Fair, with re-traced signatures. Two pieces gone from the bottom left corner and right bottom edge. Faded back issue endorsement." Photo above right, from NASCA catalog.

NASCA, Div. of Smythe & Co.
New York, N.Y.
28-31 Oct 1985 — pen c, poc, Fine+ — 916 — $935.00

Comments: Sale is labeled "The Clinton Collection," although no details are provided about who or what Clinton is; it might refer to the village of Clinton, Conn. Note is "pen cancelled on face with two small punch holes at the side. Two endorsements on the back. The left border is shaved." Photo, middle of page 263.

NASCA, Div. of Smythe & Co.
New York, N.Y.
28-31 Oct 1985 — Fine — 1399 — $880.00

Comments: A second consignment from "The Clinton Collection." Note is described as "Fine, with some paper crispness. There is soiling. Assistant Treasurer Guirot has endorsed note on the back. There is also water staining." Photo, middle of page 268.

Auction House	Sale Date	Grade or Condition	Serial Number	Sales Price
NASCA, Div. of Smythe & Co. *New York, N.Y.*	28-31 Oct 1985	hoc, VG	1139	$495.00

Comments: Yet a third consignment from "The Clinton Collection." Note is "Very Good, holed, restored. Paper soft and soiled, hole left of center restored in such a way as to resemble a stain of some kind." Photo below, from NASCA catalog.

Left, serial #1139, right, #820.

| NASCA, Div. of Smythe & Co.
New York, N.Y. | 7-10 Mar 1986 | poc, G-VG | 1173 | $330.00 |

Comments: Consignor unknown. Note is "heavily but evenly worn, four filled punch holes, faded signatures, uneven borders." Photo middle left, page 269.

| Stack's
New York, N.Y. | 9-11 Sep 1987 | Ch XF | 820 | $1,265.00 |

Comments: Consigned by little-known L.S. Ruder. Note is "another bright, crisp, uncancelled note, with decent margins. There are a half dozen pinholes hidden in central vignette. A premium example." Photo above right, from Stack's catalog.

| NASCA, Div. of Smythe & Co.
New York, N.Y. | 25-26 Sep 1987 | cc, Fine+ | 63 | $1,182.50 |

Comments: Consigned by Douglas B. Ball (page 98). Note has "even wear, the top border shaved, endorsed on the back. Ex Lot 403 of our Maryland sale May 27-28, 1977, with the lot card." Photo, bottom of page 264.

| NASCA, Div. of Smythe & Co.
New York, N.Y. | 25-26 Sep 1987 | Abt XF | 955 | $1,320.00 |

Comments: Also from Doug Ball's Richmond Sale in 1987. Note has "three light folds, the left border is shaved." Photo below left, from NASCA catalog.

Left, serial #955, right, #1319.

| NASCA, Div. of Smythe & Co.
New York, N.Y. | 25-26 Mar 1988 | cc, coc,
F-VF | 1439 | $770.00 |

Comments: Consignor unknown. Note has "15 or so folds, two hammer cancels and two cut out areas at the top deftly restored. A few pinholes and stains." Endorsed on back. Photo, top of p. 271, courtesy Dale Alberstone Family Trust Collection.

Auction House	Sale Date	Grade or Condition	Serial Number	Sales Price

Serial number 1439: Front and back.

NASCA, Div. of Smythe & Co.   31 Mar 1989   Abt VF   242 $1,072.50
New York, N.Y.

Comments: Consignor unknown. Note is "About Very Fine, has seven light creases, good margins. A note with good eye appeal. No. 242 of the first printing of 607 pieces, of which only 84 were uncancelled in 1865." Photo below, courtesy The Honorable William H. Kelly, Asharoken, New York.

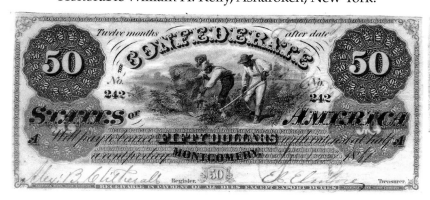

Serial number 242: Front and back.

Christie's   7 Sep 1989   VF   1441 $1,045.00
New York, N.Y.

Comments: Consigned by brothers Felix and Henri Weil, founders of Medallic Art Company in New York City in 1910 when they purchased the assets of the Deitsch Brothers. This note is "Very Fine, uncancelled, well centered and sound." Photo below, courtesy R. M. Smythe & Company, New York, N. Y.

Serial number 1441: Front and back.

Christie's   7 Sep 1989   G-VG   -   -
New York, N.Y.

Comments: Also consigned by the Weil Brothers (see above). This note was part of an album with 193 notes, including both the $500 and $50 Montgomerys.

Auction House	Sale Date	Grade or Condition	Serial Number	Sales Price
NASCA, Div. of Smythe & Co. _New York, N.Y._	15-16 Jun 1990	UNC	818	$2,310.00

Comments: Consignor was presumably Henry Hull of Jacksonville, Fla., who consigned the finest-known $1,000 Montgomery to this same auction. A magnificent note, usually considered a contender for the finest known in the Condition Census Top Ten. Ball described the note as "Uncirculated, but we must note small pinholes at the center." Photo, bottom of page 266.

Serial number 923: Front and back.

Auction House	Sale Date	Grade or Condition	Serial Number	Sales Price
NASCA, Div. of Smythe & Co. _New York, N.Y._	15-16 Jun 1990	AU	923	$1,870.00

Comments: Probably a second consignment from philatelist Henry Hull (see above). Another spectacular note, also contending for inclusion in the Condition Census Top Ten. Note has "a folded corner tip, other handling traces and a red ink endorsement on the back. Bright." Above photo, courtesy William H. Kelly.

Serial number 177: Front and back.

Auction House	Sale Date	Grade or Condition	Serial Number	Sales Price
R. M. Smythe & Co. _New York, N.Y._	18-19 Jun 1993	F-VF	177	$1,815.00

Comments: Consignor unknown. Note "looks better on the face, with seven or so hard folds. Margins are good. There is a back endorsement." Photo above.

Auction House	Sale Date	Grade or Condition	Serial Number	Sales Price
R. M. Smythe & Co. _New York, N.Y._	18-19 Jun 1993	Fine	1319	$3,300.00

Comments: Consignor unknown. Note is "Fine, somewhat aged, endorsed by A. J. Guirot in New Orleans. Complete borders." Photo, bottom right, page 270.

Auction House	Sale Date	Grade or Condition	Serial Number	Sales Price
Coin Galleries _New York, N.Y._	14 Jul 1993	cc, VG	394	$1,045.00

Comments: Consignor unknown. Note's "right edge has a small piece out, and is tape repaired on the back. Cut cancels are neatly reinforced." Photo, top of p. 261.

Auction House	Sale Date	Grade or Condition	Serial Number	Sales Price
R. M. Smythe & Co. New York, N.Y.	22 Nov 1993	Fine+	1315	$3,410.00

Comments: Consignor unknown. Note has "good margins, soiling on left and right edges. Stamp at back bottom." Ex Douglas B. Ball. Photo, middle page 264.

Auction House	Sale Date	Grade or Condition	Serial Number	Sales Price
R. M. Smythe & Co. New York, N.Y.	23 Mar 1994	Fine	1481	$3,080.00

Comments: Possibly owned by John Besante, American Impressionist artist. Note has "intact borders, back endorsement, staining." Photo below left, from Smythe.

Left, serial #1481, right, #949.

Auction House	Sale Date	Grade or Condition	Serial Number	Sales Price
R. M. Smythe & Co. New York, N.Y.	11 Sep 1995	Abt VF	188	$5,225.00

Comments: Consignor unknown. Note is "quarter folded both ways, other folds, minor ink erosion, still crisp and vivid." Ex Abe Kreisberg. Photo, bottom p. 262.

Auction House	Sale Date	Grade or Condition	Serial Number	Sales Price
R. M. Smythe & Co. New York, N.Y.	22 Jun 1996	F-VF	1441	$6,600.00

Comments: Consignor unknown. Note is "a bit tight at top, light foxing, decent borders. A pleasing representative of this esteemed note." Photo, bottom p. 271.

Auction House	Sale Date	Grade or Condition	Serial Number	Sales Price
R. M. Smythe & Co. New York, N.Y.	19 Jun 1998	Ch UNC	922	$22,000.00

Comments: From Arnold Cowan, avid yachtsman from Long Beach, Cal. Stunning note at the top of the Condition Census. Perhaps the only $50 Montgomery note Ball graded as "Choice Uncirculated." Note is "crisp, bright, vivid, nicely margined for this series. Virtually unimprovable." Photo, bottom left, page 253.

Serial number 925: Front and back.

Auction House	Sale Date	Grade or Condition	Serial Number	Sales Price
R. M. Smythe & Co. New York, N.Y.	19 Jun 1998	Abt VF	925	$13,200.00

Comments: Arnold Cowan's second $50 Montgomery, also pushing for inclusion in the Condition Census. Note is crisp, bright, vivid, with complete borders. Endorsed on the back in red ink. Eight or so very light folds." Photo above.

Auction House	Sale Date	Grade or Condition	Serial Number	Sales Price
R. M. Smythe & Co. *New York, N.Y.*	18-19 Sep 1998	Abt VF	1130	$14,300.00

Comments: Consigned by John L. Sanderson of Westchester Co., N.Y., a securities dealer. Note has "roughly ten light vertical folds, but the face is bright, the borders complete, some ink bleed-through at lower left." Photo, middle page 267.

Auction House	Sale Date	Grade or Condition	Serial Number	Sales Price
R. M. Smythe & Co. *New York, N.Y.*	19 Jun 1999	pen c, cc, F-VF	411	$7,975.00

Comments: Consignor unknown. Note is slit canceled, perhaps with a pen knife, face is stamped 'Cancelled.'" Ex T. Harrison Garrett. Photo, top left, page 266.

Serial number 862: Front and back.

Auction House	Sale Date	Grade or Condition	Serial Number	Sales Price
R. M. Smythe & Co. *New York, N.Y.*	17-18 Sep 1999	Abt VF	862	$10,725.00

Comments: Consignor unknown. Spectacular note, vying for inclusion in the Condition Census Top Ten. Note has "complete borders, good color. Endorsed on the back. About half a dozen folds, not visible on the face." Photo above.

Serial number 715: Front and back.

Auction House	Sale Date	Grade or Condition	Serial Number	Sales Price
R. M. Smythe & Co. *New York, N.Y.*	16 Jun 2000	poc, VG-F	715	$7,150.00

Comments: Consigned by Samuel E. Roakes, Jr., author of articles appearing in *Paper Money* and owner of "Kennesaw Coins and Currency." Note has four punch holes, light aging, two edge chinks into border. Above photo, courtesy Bill Kelly.

Auction House	Sale Date	Grade or Condition	Serial Number	Sales Price
Bowers & Merena Galleries *Wolfeboro, N.H.*	9-12 Aug 2000	Ch VF	949	$12,650.00

Comments: From the Franklin Institute in Philadelphia. Note has "just a few light creases, though a small mounting tab remains affixed to the back edge. A few areas of discoloration and pinholes at the center. Margins somewhat uneven. Retains most of its crispness." Photo top right, p. 273, courtesy Bowers & Merena.

Auction House	Sale Date	Grade or Condition	Serial Number	Sales Price
Early American History Auctions *La Jolla, Calif.*	14 Oct 2000	pen c, poc, VF	916	$10,450.00

Comments: Consigned by dealer Hugh Shull of Lexington, S.C. Note is "bright and attractive, but with numerous folds and wrinkles. However, there is plenty of crispness left. Two small punch holes appear on opposite sides of the note, near the ends. Manuscript hand-cancellation runs vertically across the face of the note. Back is also endorsed." Photo, middle page 263.

Auction House	Sale Date	Grade or Condition	Serial Number	Sales Price
R. M. Smythe & Co. *New York, N.Y.*	2 Mar 2001	Abt VF	735	$10,450.00

Comments: Consignor unknown. Note is "About Very Fine, quarter folded both ways with other folds. Very nicely margined, scotch tape has been deftly removed from both side edges." Photo below left, courtesy eBay.

Auction House	Sale Date	Grade or Condition	Serial Number	Sales Price
Lyn Knight Currency Auctions *Overland Park, Kan.*	17-18 Aug 2001	AU	1005	$13,200.00

Left, serial #735, right, #1005.

Comments: Consigned by little-known Sam Feldman. Note "has central fold and a half dozen trivial pinholes. Otherwise it looks Uncirculated. I thought about calling it XF-AU, but it is just too pretty." Photo above right, courtesy Lyn Knight.

Auction House	Sale Date	Grade or Condition	Serial Number	Sales Price
Heritage Auctions *Dallas, Tex.*	21-22 Sep 2001	F-VF	373	$13,475.00

Comments: Consigned by Dr. Walter B. Jones (1895-1977), State Geologist for Ala. Note is "Fine-Very Fine, absolutely problem-free with nary a trace of restoration or 'improvement' of any kind." Photo, bottom page 261.

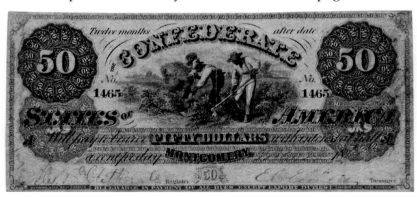 

Serial number 1465: Front and back.

Auction House	Sale Date	Grade or Condition	Serial Number	Sales Price
Lyn Knight Currency Auctions *Overland Park, Kan.*	13-15 Jun 2002	Fine+	1465	$11,500.00

Comments: Consignor unknown. Note is "a perfect problem-free $50 Montgomery that is evenly circulated and beautiful for the grade. Signatures on face are clear and back is endorsed." Above photo, courtesy Amanda Sheheen, A&O Currency.

Auction House	Sale Date	Grade or Condition	Serial Number	Sales Price
R. M. Smythe & Co. New York, N.Y.	29 July 2002	coc, Fine	936	$2,750.00

Comments: Consignor unknown. Note described as "Fine, cut-out cancels, a tear at the center bottom. Top right corner nipped. Serial number is unlisted in Criswell." Photo below, courtesy Heritage Auctions, Dallas, Texas, *www.ha.com*

Serial number 936: Front and back.

Heritage Auctions Dallas, Tex.	9-11 Jan 2003	coc, VF	936	$9,200.00

Comments: Amusingly, this note is the same as consigned immediately above to a Smythe auction just six months earlier. Now it comes from the General Felix K. Zollicoffer Camp Collection of Overton County, Tenn., a multi-generational family collection, many notes of which have not been on the market for decades. Note has "at least four cut-out cancellations, but the missing pieces have been expertly replaced and the design redrawn. A corner repair." Photo above.

R. M. Smythe & Co. New York, N.Y.	13-14 Jun 2003	VF	929	$11,212.50

Comments: Consigned by Gene Mintz of San Luis Obispo Co., Calif. (p. 100). Note is "quarter folded both ways. Top and right margins are trimmed close, but the color is bright, and this lovely note retains much of its crispness. Tiny pinholes in the corners, hardly visible and not distracting." Photo, top of page 269.

Serial number 1140: Front and back.

R. M. Smythe & Co. New York, N.Y.	5-6 Sep 2003	F-VF	1140	$9,487.50

Comments: Consigned by Chet Krause, born in Iola, Wis. and founder of Krause Publications. Elected to ANA Hall of Fame in 1977 and to its board in 2007. Note is "vivid green, with deep blue serial numbers. Fine-Very Fine, trimmed just into the bottom border." Above photo, courtesy R. M. Smythe & Co., New York.

Auction House	Sale Date	Grade or Condition	Serial Number	Sales Price

R. M. Smythe & Co.   2 Dec 2003   F-VF   249 $9,200.00
New York, N.Y.

Left, serial #249, right, #1207.

Comments: Consignor unknown. Note described as "Fine-Very Fine, minor fold junction holes, ink stains, ample margins. Endorsed on the back by A. J. Guirot, May 13, 1861. In our September 2003 auction a $50 Montgomery graded 'F-VF' realized $9,487.50; the current example has better margins, but is not quite as bright." Photo above left, courtesy R. M. Smythe & Company, New York.

Serial number 1574: Front and back.

Heritage Auctions   8-10 Jan 2004   VF   1574 $15,600.00
Dallas, Tex.

Comments: Consigned by Alabamian Frank T. Kennedy. Note has "perfect colors and bold signatures and is perfectly original and problem-free save for moderate wear, several pinholes and a bold endorsement on the back that is partially visible from the face." Above photo, courtesy Heritage Auctions, Dallas, Texas.

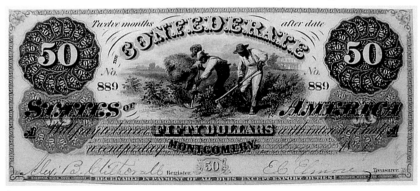 

Serial number 889: Front and back.

Briggs Auction   3 Dec 2004   VF-XF   889 $18,150.00
Garnet Valley, Pa.

Comments: Consignor unknown. Note has several creases and a hard fold in the lower left. Back endorsement in red ink. Above photo from Amanda Sheheen.

Auction House	Sale Date	Grade or Condition	Serial Number	Sales Price

Serial number 265:
Front and back.

Heritage Auctions
Dallas, Tex.

| | 13-15 Jan 2005 | Abt Fine | 265 | $9,487.50 |

Comments: Consignor unknown. Note is "completely original with no signs of repairs or restoration, solid paper." Above photo, courtesy Heritage Auctions.

Serial number 1307:
Front and back.

Heritage Auctions
Dallas, Tex.

| | 5-7 Jan 2006 | VG | 1307 | $10,062.50 |

Comments: Consignor unknown. Note has edge furling, nicks and tears. Good color. Very unusual back endorsement. Above photo, courtesy Heritage Auctions.

Heritage Auctions
Dallas, Tex.

| | 27-28 Apr 2006 | Ch AU | 876 | $34,500.00 |

Comments: Consigned by Ben R. Powel, attorney from Galveston, Tex. Note looks UNC, is "bright, colors vivid, signatures clear and well margined." Photo, p. 260.

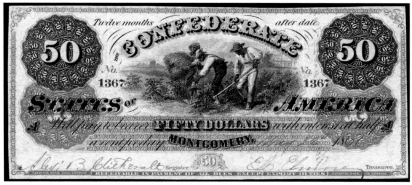

Serial number 1367:
Front and back.

Heritage Auctions
Dallas, Tex.

| | 27-28 Apr 2006 | XF | 1367 | $23,000.00 |

Comments: Also from Ben R. Powel. Lovely note has "light handling, nice green ink and wholesome edges. Endorsed on back." Above photo, from Heritage Auctions.

Auction House	Sale Date	Grade or Condition	Serial Number	Sales Price

Serial number 817: Front and back.

Lyn Knight Currency Auctions   16-18 Jun 2006   Ch AU   817   -
Overland Park, Kan.

> *Comments:* Consignor unknown. Note is "so nice it must rate right up with the finest ever seen. Graded 'Choice About New 58' by PMG because of a tiny corner-tip fold. I just cannot imagine that makes it 'AU.' New addition to the Montgomery census." Above photo, courtesy Heritage Auctions, Dallas, Texas.

Heritage Auctions   13-15 Sep 2006   F-VF   188 $18,400.00
Dallas, Tex.

> *Comments:* Consigned by Troy Wiseman, philanthropist who founded World Orphans. Note has "nice color, sound edges and original paper surfaces. The even wear includes a penned issuance date." Photo, bottom page 262.

Serial number 1083: Front and back.

Heritage Auctions   4-6 Jan 2007   VF-XF   1083 $16,675.00
Dallas, Tex.

> *Comments:* Consigned by William A. Bond, a Texan who was an avid hunter and collector of Civil war relics, including this note which probably resided in his collection since the early 1960s. Bond also consigned one of the three finest known $500 Montgomerys to this auction. This note has "great color and overall appearance and should grade higher; however, it has some restorative work on the right edge. Boldly endorsed on back." Above photo, courtesy Heritage Auctions.

Heritage Auctions   4-6 Jan 2007   F-VF   1147 $12,075.00
Dallas, Tex.

> *Comments:* Consigned by little-known George P. Hammerly. Note is "a very attractive Fine-Very Fine $50 Montgomery with nice color and original paper surfaces. There is a small tape repair in the lower right-hand corner. Overall even wear includes a penned issuance date of May 31, 1861." Photo, top of page 263.

Auction House	Sale Date	Grade or Condition	Serial Number	Sales Price

Serial number 992: Front and back.

R. M. Smythe & Co. New York, N.Y.	13 Apr 2007	XF-AU	992	$23,000.00

Comments: Consigned by Western Reserve Historical Society in Cleveland. Note is "vivid green, strictly original color, on crisp translucent white paper. Moderate vertical centerfold, minor mounting traces." Above photo, courtesy R. M. Smythe.

R. M. Smythe & Co. New York, N.Y.	6 July 2007	cc, VF-XF	915	$16,100.00

Comments: The first of four consecutive consignments from Frederick R. Mayer (1928-2007), a Texas oilman who founded the Exeter Drilling Co., the largest privately-owned drilling company in the U.S. (see page 104). Note is "Ex Kagin's 1983 auction where it was described as 'XF. Near perfect except for slight toning and corner crease. Slit cancelled.' The slit cancellation is virtually undetectable, and without the provenance it may have gone unnoticed." Photo, bottom p. 268.

R. M. Smythe & Co. New York, N.Y.	6 July 2007	F-VF	1335	$9,200.00

Comments: Mayer's second consignment. Note has "a few pinholes, clear margins, light bleed-through from endorsement, a trace of toning." Photo, middle p. 265.

R. M. Smythe & Co. New York, N.Y.	6 July 2007	Fine+	1441	$10,925.00

Comments: Mayer's third consignment. Note has "clear but narrow margins, hint of age toning." Ex Christie's Sept 1989. Ex Smythe Jun 1996. Photo, bottom p. 271.

Serial number 327: Front and back.

R. M. Smythe & Co. New York, N.Y.	6 July 2007	pen c, cc, Fine+	327	$9,775.00

Comments: Mayer's fourth consignment. Note is "spindle cancelled, no pieces missing. Large stamp cancellation across the face." Above photo from Smythe.

Auction House	Sale Date	Grade or Condition	Serial Number	Sales Price
Heritage Auctions *Dallas, Tex.*	10-12 Jan 2008	UNC	817	$25,300.00

Comments: Consignor unknown. "Few Montgomery issues show the beautifully textured, bright white paper exhibited by this $50. The mint green overprint is as deep as the day it was printed, as are the blue serial numbers and black ink devices. Two minor tip folds, both outside the design, account for the grade: 'New 62' by PCGS. Previously, the finest example of this issue to pass through our auctions was a PCGS 'About New 58.'" Photo, top of page 279.

Serial number 458:
Front and back.

Lyn Knight Currency Auctions *Overland Park, Kan.*	27 June 2008	VF	458	$13,352.65

Comments: Consignor unknown. Note is "problem-free with exceptional centering and incredible pizzazz for the grade. Excellent signatures and no flaws. Signed on the back from redemption." Above photo, courtesy Lyn Knight.

Spink Smythe *Dallas, Tex.*	16-17 July 2008	F-VF	1399	$9,875.00

Comments: Consigned by Frederick Forbes Angus of Montreal, Canada, noted author and historian on railway and tramway history, as well as all things Victorian. Note is "nice looking that might even slab higher than our grade of Fine-Very Fine." Photo, middle of page 268.

Heritage Auctions *Dallas, Tex.*	8-11 Jan 2009	UNC	817	$25,300.00

Comments: Consignor unknown. This note offered by Heritage a year earlier at the top of this page. Description is identical to that shown above, except the new comment that the Condition Census includes notes ranging from Uncirculated down to Abt Uncirculated -- this note being a true Uncirculated. Photo top p. 279.

Spink Smythe *Dallas, Tex.*	26-27 Jun 2009	poc, Fine+	1207	$8,150.00

Comments: Consignor unknown. Note described as a "nice looking note with six small punch holes." Photo top right, page 277, courtesy the late Gordon Bleuler.

Spink Smythe *Dallas, Tex.*	27-28 Aug 2009	Fine	1399	$9,875.00

Comments: Consignor unknown. Note has "some staining; however, this is still a very nice looking note. Issuing signature of A. J. Guirot is noticed on back. This nicely circulated example is completely whole." Photo, middle of page 268.

Auction House	Sale Date	Grade or Condition	Serial Number	Sales Price

Left, serial #424, right, #398.

Auction House	Sale Date	Grade or Condition	Serial Number	Sales Price
Neal Auction Company *New Orleans, La.*	21-22 Nov 2009	VF	424	$8,365.00

Comments: Consigned by Fisher E. Simmons, Jr., an expert on postal history and steamboats that plied the Mississippi River. Note has six folds, crisp paper, three nice margins and bright color. Photo above left, courtesy Neal Auction Company.

Heritage Auctions *Dallas, Tex.*	28-30 Apr 2010	VF 30	929	$17,825.00

Comments: Consignor unknown. Note "has nice color with overall even wear. Has a June 30, 1861 issuance endorsement penned in red ink by Capt. Thos. K. Jackson. Graded 'Very Fine 30' by PMG." Photo, top of page 269.

Spink Smythe *Dallas, Tex.*	14-15 May 2010	Fine	1465	-

Comments: Consignor unknown. Note has "great color with even circulation. Issuing signature of Ferdinand Malloy on June 14, 1861 is noticed on the back at top, with a Mayer Bros. endorsement at the bottom." Photo, bottom page 275.

Heritage Auctions *Dallas, Tex.*	11-13 Aug 2010	pen c, cc, Fine 12	398	$6,325.00

Comments: Consignor unknown. Cataloger writes, "We do not recall seeing a cancellation on the face of a Montgomery note. PMG indicates repairs, which include closed cancellations and strengthening." Photo above right from Heritage.

Serial number 1085: Front and back.

Stack's *New York, N.Y.*	30 Sep 2010	VF 30	1085	$19,550.00

Comments: Consigned by Q. David Bowers, chairman emeritus of Stack's Bowers, prolific numismatic writer and one of America's premier numismatists ever. Note is graded 'Very Fine 30' by PMG. Issued on the back on June 25, 1861. This note "likely falls in the middle grade range. Bold color and well margined for the type." Above photo, courtesy Stack's, New York, N.Y.

The $50 Montgomery Note Vs. Crude Oil, Silver and the S&P 500:
Comparative Price Appreciation Since the End of the Civil War

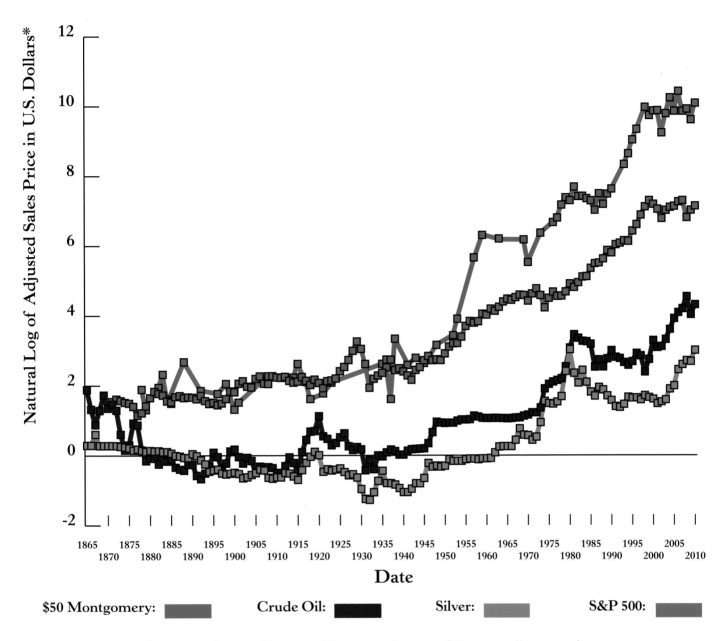

$50 Montgomery: Crude Oil: Silver: S&P 500:

Average Annual Rate of Return (Annual Percent Increase)

	From 1865 to 1950	From 1950 Through 2010	Total All Years: 1865 - 2010	Years Needed to Double in Value Since 1950
$50 Montgomery Note	1.7%	11.0%	7.3%	6.7
Silver	-1.3%	4.7%	1.6%	15.0
Crude Oil	-0.3%	5.8%	2.4%	12.2
S&P 500 Composite Index	1.8%	7.3%	4.3%	9.8

* The actual average sales price a Confederate Montgomery note, a troy ounce of silver, a barrel of crude oil or a market basket of common stocks comprising the S&P 500 Composite Index fetched during each year. Prices have been adjusted to show as a natural logarithm of the actual sales data to make the graph show differences more clearly. A full explanation of the methodology is provided in Chapter 4, beginning on page 140.

Chapter 8: Part Two

Qualitative Look at the $50 Montgomery Note: Its Innate Beauty and Eye Appeal

Serial numbers in auction records are a relatively recent practice, dating back only to 1950. The Montgomery notes pictured here have no public auction records, although some or all may have been auctioned pre-1950. Despite the mystery surrounding their ownership over the years, their beauty is as compelling as the fully pedigreed notes pictured in Part One. Credits on page 302.

Credits and Bibliography

By Wendell A. Wolka

**Photos of Non-Pedigreed $1,000 Montgomery Notes on Pages 178-179
Used Courtesy Of:**

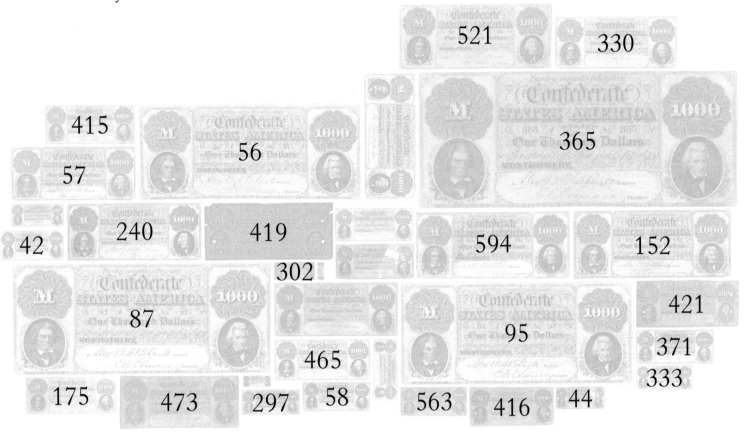

No. 42. Albert Pick, *Standard Catalog of World Paper Money*, 1994, 7th Edition, Krause Publications.

No. 44. W. Crutchfield Williams, II, Quinlan, Tex.

No. 56. J. Wayne Hilton, Graniteville, S.C.

No. 57. William H. Kelly, Asharoken, N.Y.

No. 58. Greg Ton, Oxford, Miss.

No. 87. J. Wayne Hilton, Graniteville, S.C.

No. 95. J. Wayne Hilton, Graniteville, S.C.

No. 152. J. Wayne Hilton, Graniteville, S.C.

No. 175. Pink Palace Museum, Memphis, Tenn.

No. 240. Abraham Lincoln Library and Museum, Harrogate, Tenn.

No. 297. W. Crutchfield Williams, II, Quinlan, Tex.

No. 302. Claud E. Fuller, *Confederate Currency and Stamps*, 1949, Tennessee Division of United Daughters of the Confederacy.

No. 330. A Private Georgia Collection.

No. 333. James F. Morgan, *Graybacks and Gold: Confederate Monetary Policy*, 1985, The Perdido Bay Press.

No. 365. Charles A. Hilton, Graniteville, S.C.

No. 371. William H. Kelly, Asharoken, N.Y.

No. 415. Douglas B. Ball, Slide Presentation, 1985, American Numismatic Society.

No. 416. Joe Bradley, Colorado Springs, Co.

No. 419. Greg Ton, Oxford, Miss.

No. 421. Buz Sundstrom, Burtonsville, Md.

No. 465. W. Crutchfield Williams, II, Quinlan, Tex.

No. 473. William H. Kelly, Asharoken, N.Y.

No. 521. W. McNair Tornow, McNair Collection, Beech Mountain, N.C.

No. 563. Bob Jeter, Byromville, Ga.

No. 594. William H. Kelly, Asharoken, N.Y.

Photos of Non-Pedigreed $500 Montgomery Notes on Pages 208-209
Used Courtesy Of:

No. 71.   William H. Kelly, Asharoken, N.Y.

No. 72.   W. Crutchfield Williams, II, Quinlan, Tex.

No. 128. Amanda Sheheen, A&O Currency, Camden, S.C.

No. 147. J. Wayne Hilton, Graniteville, S.C.

No. 212. W. Crutchfield Williams, II, Quinlan, Tex.

No. 242. William H. Kelly, Asharoken, N.Y.

No. 269. William H. Kelly, Asharoken, N.Y.

No. 288. Arlie R. Slabaugh, *Confederate States Paper Money*, 10th Edition, 2000, Krause Publications.

No. 290. W. Crutchfield Williams, II, Quinlan, Tex.

No. 334. William Lee, *The Currency of the Confederate States of America*, 1875.

No. 335. Raphael P. Thian, 1875 Album of Confederate Notes.

No. 342. Douglas B. Ball, Slide Presentation, 1985, American Numismatic Society.

No. 418. Hudson McDonald, Spanish Fort, Al.

No. 425. Albert Pick, *Standard Catalog of World Paper Money*, 1994, 7th Edition, Krause Publications.

No. 583. J. Wayne Hilton, Graniteville, S.C.

No. 593. Grover C. Criswell, *Comprehensive Catalog of Confederate Paper Money*, 1996, BNR Press.

No. 603. J. Wayne Hilton, Graniteville, S.C.

Photos of Non-Pedigreed $100 Montgomery Notes on Pages 246-247
Used Courtesy Of:

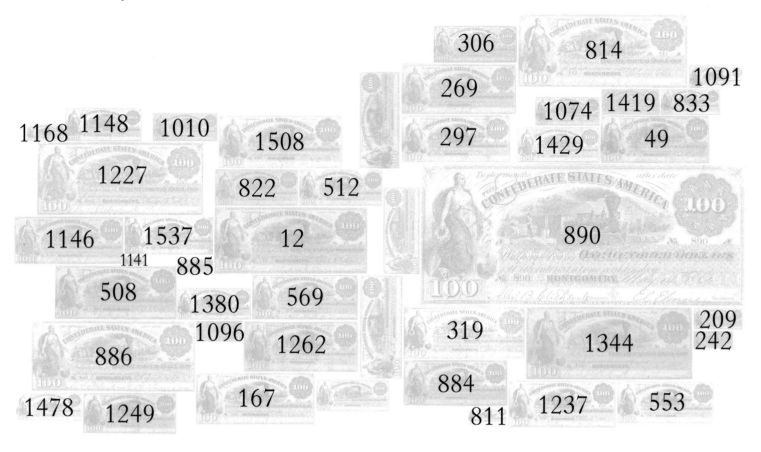

No. 12. Clint Reynolds, *The Confederate Treasury*, Tennessee Ridge, Tenn.

No. 49. Joe Bradley, Colorado Springs, Co.

No. 167. Greg Ton, Oxford, Miss.

No. 209. David F. Schnorr, Lomita, Calif.

No. 242. Bob Jeter, Byromville, Ga.

No. 269. William H. Kelly, Asharoken, N.Y.

No. 297. William H. Kelly, Asharoken, N.Y.

No. 306. W. Crutchfield Williams, II, Quinlan, Tex.

No. 319. Raphael P. Thian, 1875 Album of Confederate Notes.

No. 508. Heritage Auctions, Dallas, Tex. (www.ha.com)

No. 512. Hugh Shull, Lexington, S.C.

No. 553. William H. Kelly, Asharoken, N.Y.

No. 569. Dave Nelson, Jacksonville, Fla.

No. 811. Douglas B. Ball, Slide Presentation, 1985, American Numismatic Society.

No. 814. J. Wayne Hilton, Graniteville, S.C.

No. 822. J. Wayne Hilton, Graniteville, S.C.

No. 833. W. Crutchfield Williams, II, Quinlan, Tex.

No. 884. John N. Rowe, III, Dallas, Tex.

No. 885. J. Wayne Hilton, Graniteville, S.C.

No. 886. J. Wayne Hilton, Graniteville, S.C.

No. 890. J. Wayne Hilton, Graniteville, S.C.

No. 1010. Hugh Shull, Lexington, S.C.

No. 1074. Matthew Botkin, Tulsa, Ok.

No. 1091. Pink Palace Museum, Memphis, Tenn.

No. 1096. Hugh Shull, Lexington, S.C.

No. 1141. W. Crutchfield Williams, II, Quinlan, Tex.

No. 1146. Greg Ton, Oxford, Miss.

No. 1148. Marvin D. Ashmore, Sour Lake, Tex.

No. 1168. Don C. Kelly, Oxford, Ohio.

No. 1227. J. Wayne Hilton, Graniteville, S.C.

No. 1237. William H. Kelly, Asharoken, N.Y.

No. 1249. Phillip Lamb, Montreat, N.C.

No. 1262. W. Crutchfield Williams, II, Quinlan, Tex.

No. 1344. Charles A. Hilton, Graniteville, S.C.

No. 1380. Amanda Sheheen, A&O Currency, Camden, S.C.

No. 1419. Jhon E. Cybuski, Highland Village, Tex.

No. 1429. Paul Thevenet, Nazareth, Pa.

No. 1478. Grover & Clarence Criswell, *Confederate and Southern State Currency*, Volume 1, 1957, Criswell's Publications, Inc.

No. 1508. William H. Kelly, Asharoken, N.Y.

No. 1537. Claud E. Fuller, *Confederate Currency and Stamps*, 1949, Tennessee Division of United Daughters of the Confederacy.

Photos of Non-Pedigreed $50 Montgomery Notes on Pages 284-285
Used Courtesy Of:

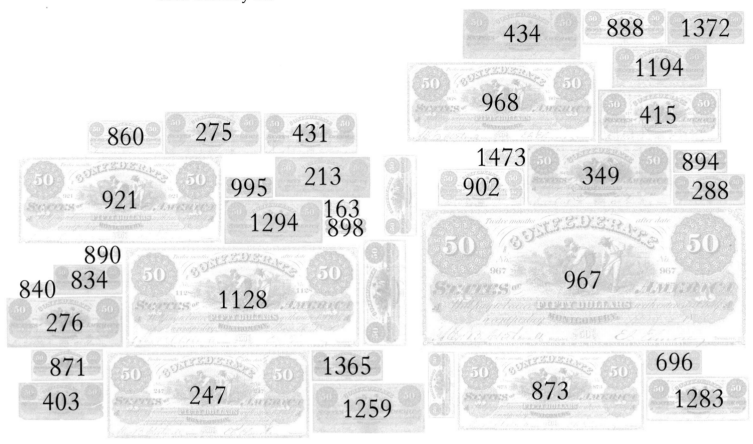

Selected Bibliography

Author J. Wayne Hilton included many of his sources for information within the text itself to mitigate the need for a comprehensive *Bibliography*. For example, auction catalogs are not included here but are referenced within the text. Sources not referenced include:

Adams, John W. — *United States Numismatic Literature*, Volumes I and II, George Frederick Kolbe Publications, Mission Viejo and Crestline, Calif., 1982 and 1990, respectively.

Allen, H.D. – "The Paper Money of the Confederate States – With Historical Data," *The Numismatist*, series running from June, 1917 to February, 1919.

American Council of Learned Societies — *Dictionary of American Biography*, Volume 14, C. Scribner's Sons, 1934.

Ball, Douglas B., Ph.D. -*Comprehensive Catalog and History of Confederate Bonds*, BNR Press, Port Clinton, Ohio, 1998.

Ball, Douglas B., Ph.D. – *Financial Failure and Confederate Defeat*, University of Illinois Press, Urbana, Ill., 1991.

Barker, Charles, D. – "Barker's Description and Price List of Genuine Confederate Treasury Notes," Privately Published, Atlanta, Ga., ca. 1894.

Bechtel, C.H. – *Album for Confederate Currency with Descriptive Index*, Privately Published, New York City, N.Y., 1877.

Bowers, Q. David — *The Treasure Ship S.S. Brother Jonathan*, Bowers & Merena Galleries, Inc., Wolfeboro, N.H., 1990.

Bradbeer, William West – *Confederate and Southern State Currency*, Mount Vernon, N.Y., 1915; ensuing reprints: R. Green, Chicago, Ill., 1945 and Aubrey Bebee, Omaha, Neb., 1956.

Capers, Henry D. – *Life and Times of C.G. Memminger*, Everett Waddey Co., Richmond, Va., 1893.

Chaplin, Charles – "The Chemicograph Backs," *American Journal of Numismatics*, Volume 12, no. 1 and Volume 13, no. 2, July, 1877 and October, 1878.

Chase, Philip H. – "Basic Classification and Listing, Confederate States of America Paper Money, 1861-1865," Privately Published, Bala Cynwyd, Pa., 1936.

Chase, Philip H. – "Price List Supplement, Confederate States of America Paper Money, 1861-1865," Privately Published, Philadelphia, Pa., 1941.

Chase, Philip H. – *Confederate Treasury Notes: The Paper Money of the Confederate States of America*, Privately Published, Philadelphia, Pa., 1947.

Coughlin, Thomas Lamar – *Those Southern Lamars – The Stories of Five Illustrious Lamars*, Privately Published, 2000.

Criswell, Grover C. – *Comprehensive Catalog of Confederate Paper Money*, BNR Press, Port Clinton, Ohio, 1996.

Criswell, Grover C. – *Confederate and Southern State(s) Currency*, various editions and publishers, 1957-1992.

Criswell, Grover C. – *Confederate and Southern States Bonds*, Criswell's and Criswell's Publications, Fort McCoy, Fla., first and second editions, 1961, 1979-80.

Cuhaj, George S., Editor — *Confederate States Paper Money*, 11th edition, Krause Publications, Inc., Iola, Wis., 2008.

Dietz, August – *The Postal Service of the Confederate States of America*, Press of the Dietz Printing Company, Richmond, Va., 1929.

Douglas, B.M. and Hughes, B.H. — *Catalogue of Confederate and Southern States Currency*, Douglas and Hughes, Washington, D.C., 1955.

Emmet, Thomas Addis – "Table of Confederate Currency," *American Journal of Numismatics*, Volume 2, Nos. 1,3, and 4, May, July, and August, 1867.

Fuller, Claud E. – *Confederate Currency and Stamps*, Parthenon Press under auspices of The Tennessee Division, United Daughters of the Confederacy, Nashville, Tenn., 1949.

Gengerke, Martin — *American Numismatic Auctions*, 8th Edition, Self-Published, Woodside, N.Y., 1990 and now available on line (most recent update 2009).

Haseltine, John W. – "Descriptive Catalog of Confederate Notes and Bonds for Sale by John Haseltine," Privately Published, Philadelphia, Pa., 1876.

Kerksis, Sydney C. and Ford, John J., Jr. — *The Confederate States of America: Its Currency, Bonds and Fiscal Paper*, Unpublished Manuscript, 1954.

Kohler, Rud – "Price and Check List of Confederate Notes, Confederate States Currency, etc.", Privately Published, New York City, N.Y., ca. 1924.

Lee, William, M.D. – *The Currency of the Confederate States of America*, Privately Published, Washington, D.C., 1875.

Marsh, Richard C. – The Military Trial of Gazaway Bugg Lamar, "The Georgia Historical Quarterly" - Quarterly Journal of The Georgia Historical Society, Volume 85, No. 4, pp. 555-591, Savannah, Ga., 2001.

Massamore, George W. – *Descriptive and Chronological Catalogue of Confederate Currency*, Privately Published, Baltimore, Md., 1889.

Mathis, Robert Neil – Gazaway Bugg Lamar: A Southern Businessman and Confidant in New York City, "New York History" – Quarterly Journal of the New York State Historical Association, Volume LVI/3, pp. 298-313, Cooperstown, N.Y., July, 1975.

National Archives Microfilm Publications - 1966, Microcopy No.499, Title: Letters Received by the Confederate Secretary of the Treasury 1861-1865, Roll 31, L-Leig; Treasury Department Collection of Confederate Records, Group 365, Lamar, Charles A., Son of G. B. Lamar - 60 and Lamar, Gazaway B., Georgia banker - 30. Microcopy privately digitized 2009 by Crutchfield Williams, Hugh Shull, Randy Shipley and Wayne Hilton.

Shull, Hugh — *A Guide Book of Southern States Currency*, Whitman Publishing, LLC, Atlanta, Ga., 2007.

Slabaugh, Arlie R. – *Confederate States Paper Money*, ten editions, various publishers, 1958-2000.

Smith, Pete — *American Numismatic Biographies*, Gold Leaf Press, Rocky River, Ohio, 1992 and now available on line (most recent update 2010).

Thian, Raphael P. – *Confederate Note Album for a Complete Collection (with Descriptive Letter Press)*, Privately Published, Washington, D.C., 1876.

Thian, Raphael P. – *The Currency of the Confederate States, Arranged by Issues, Denominations and Series*, Privately Published, Washington, D.C., 1885.

Thian, Raphael P. – The Currency of the Confederate States of America, Its Issues, Types and Series; With Descriptive Letter Press, (Unpublished Manuscript), Washington, D.C., ca. 1890.

Thian, Raphael P. – *Register of Issues of Confederate States Treasury Notes Together with Tabular Exhibits of the Debt, Funded and Unfunded of the Confederate States of America 1861-1865*, Privately Published, Washington, D.C., 1880.

Thian, Raphael P. – *Register of the Confederate Debt*, Quarterman Publications, Boston, Mass., 1972 (Reprint of 1880 work).

Thian, Raphael P. - Compilation of Correspondence relating to the Treasury Department of the Confederate States of America, published by War Department, Washington DC. (1) "Of" the Treasury 1861-1865, Appendix Part IV, 1879; and, (2) "With" the Treasury 1861-1862, Appendix Part V, 1880. National Archives microfilm publication T1025 (two rolls) War Department Record Group 109, 1966. Privately digitized 2008 by Crutchfield Williams, Hugh Shull, Randy Shipley and Wayne Hilton.

Todd, Richard Cecil – *Confederate Finance*, The University of Georgia Press, Athens, Ga., 1954.

Tremmel, George B. – *A Guide Book of Counterfeit Confederate Currency – History, Rarity, and Values*, Whitman Publishing LLC, Atlanta, Ga., 2007.

Werlich, Robert — *United States, Canadian and Confederate Paper Money*, Self-Published, Washington, D.C., 1965